THE HOUSE WHERE GOD LIVES

THE HOUSE WHERE GOD LIVES

Renewing the Doctrine of the Church for Today

Gary D. Badcock

WILLIAM B. EERDMANS PUBLISHING COMPANY

GRAND RAPIDS, MICHIGAN / CAMBRIDGE, U.K.

Published 2009 by
Wm. B. Eerdmans Publishing Co.
2140 Oak Industrial Drive N.E., Grand Rapids, Michigan 49505 /
P.O. Box 163, Cambridge CB3 9PU U.K.

Printed in the United States of America

14 13 12 11 10 09   7 6 5 4 3 2 1

Library of Congress Cataloging-in-Publication Data

Badcock, Gary D.
The house where God lives: renewing the doctrine of the church for today /
Gary D. Badcock.
p.   cm.
Includes bibliographical references.
ISBN 978-0-8028-4582-5 (pbk.: alk. paper)
1. Church.   I. Title.

BV600.3.B33   2009
262′.7 — dc22

2009015431

www.eerdmans.com

*to Walter and Irene MacPherson
and Joe and Carole Burton*

*who first taught me that there is
something of interest in the church*

2 TIMOTHY 3:14-15

Contents

Preface

Prefaces are often written after much of the rest of a book has been written, and they usually offer some kind of explanation of what follows. This preface is certainly no exception.

This book began to take shape in response to an idea that I came across some years ago in a volume of addresses given in a mission to Oxford University students in 1986 by John V. Taylor. Taylor, who had the distinction of serving as a missionary, an Anglican bishop, and a theologian of some note, was moved to preach openly to his would-be converts that "for most of the time the church, whichever branch you look at, is humiliatingly disappointing and a major obstacle to belief in God."[1] At its worst, the church can be sterile, self-serving, backward-looking, and intellectually shallow. Whereas the best advice to the faithful might seem to be to run from it so as to find life, and turn from death by following Christ as best we can, Taylor maintains that in the Christian faith we cannot do without the church. Despite its failings, it is, in the final analysis, "all we have got" (p. 77).

As might be expected, Taylor encouraged his young audience to bring their idealism to the church in order to transform it. His public frankness was refreshing — such honesty on the part of a churchman is astonishingly rare — and his goal of infusing the church with new energy was and is a laudable one. But the response he offered was still only partial. For surely the

1. John V. Taylor, *A Matter of Life and Death* (London: SCM Press, 1986), p. 76. Hereafter, page references to this and other volumes will be cited parenthetically in the text wherever possible.

church is not simply "all we have got." The church is also what we have been given, or better still, what has been entrusted to us. The church in this sense belongs to the structure of Christian faith itself. "I believe in the holy catholic church," we confess in the Apostles' Creed, the great baptismal creed of the West. To believe in something that all too often seems an *impediment* to faith requires us, by existential as well as logical necessity, to be able to see beyond appearances and discern something of deeper significance than what can literally be seen. In other words, for the church to be something we believe in requires that there be more to the church than meets the eye. It must be possible, in principle, to transcend the fussiness and tediousness of so much of what passes for ecclesiology.

Unfortunately, developments in ecclesiology that lead one to a transcendence of what can be so disappointing are rather rare. John Milbank, in a memorable *mot juste* (about which there will no doubt be numerous howls of protest) has recently spoken of the steady degeneration of current liberal thought about the church in North America into a "gnosis of campdom."[2] Milbank rightly asks what can possibly be said to be theologically interesting or significant in any of this, observing wryly that the real problem for the church establishment is less how to deal with the vexed question of homosexuality and more how to deal honestly with the sexual differentiation of male and female. It is the widespread confusion about the latter in church and world alike, he suggests, that has generated the current confusion. In all cases, the real question is how to escape the narrow perspectivalism and assertive subjectivism that dominates so much ecclesiological discourse, and to find instead some place to stand that is theologically grounded and theologically informed.

However, the "gnosis of campdom" is only a symptom of the problem rather than the problem itself, for there are multitudes of parallel "*gnôseis*" being offered, each of which is represented by its own camp of followers: liberationists, certain kinds of feminists surely, and devotees of praxis in goodly numbers are among them. There are also the evangelicals, for a good many of whom private religious experience is everything, and the church is some kind of suburban association for those initiated into the mystery of personal conversion, which the church "experience" is intended to promote. Among the many misguided versions of the doctrine of the church out there, this

---

2. John Milbank, "The Gospel of Affinity," in Carl E. Braaten and Robert W. Jenson, eds., *The Strange New World of the Gospel* (Grand Rapids: Eerdmans, 2002), p. 17.

one is arguably as bad as any. As we shall see, the church is more — much more — than this.

At the heart of Milbank's complaint, and a good deal of what else ails us in contemporary ecclesiology, is the fact that the culture in which the church of the Western world lives today is dominated by ideas deriving from political, social, and economic liberalism. The individualistic values of democratic citizenship in the modern liberal state are so much what Western Christians "really" believe that the distinctive thoughts of the church as "creature of the Word of God" are seldom heard. As Milbank hints, this is nowhere more obvious than in what is called "mainline" North American Protestantism, where the churches are effectively content to serve as the civil religion of the state. Theological attachment to "inclusiveness" is an excellent case in point, for inclusion as a dominant social ideal is the holy grail of the political liberalism that surrounds us, rather than, as tends to be claimed, the substance of the Christian gospel itself.[3] Furthermore, if the fundamental individualism that these churches work at, defend, and proclaim — in the "pastoral care movement," for instance — is one with what is worked at, defended, and proclaimed in the liberal state, what is there to tell them apart? In both cases, the flourishing individual of the modern West stands front and center. In what sense can it honestly be said of the membership of these churches that their true "citizenship" is in heaven rather than on the earth (Phil. 3:20)?[4]

At this point, a certain clearing of the throat and regathering of thought becomes necessary. Theology is really about God — about God not only first of all, but indeed last of all as well. Therefore, theology is also about learning not to "use" God for one purpose or another, no matter how right it might seem to do so, or how naturally attuned to the concerns of the gospel the purpose in view ("justice" is a particular favorite) might appear to be.[5] The question theology must always ask is whether we are talking about God *for God's own sake*, instead of for the sake of some cause or other that we want God to serve, or for the reinforcement of personal or social gain. Only when

3. John Gray, "Inclusion: A Radical Critique," in Peter Askonas and Angus Stewart, eds., *Social Inclusion* (New York: St. Martin's, 2000), pp. 19-36.

4. Unless otherwise indicated, all Scripture quotations are from the *New Revised Standard Version*, copyright © 1989, Division of Christian Education of the National Council of the Churches of Christ in the United States of America.

5. The biblically literate might notice that these two propositions correspond to the first two of the Ten Commandments.

we have answered that question appropriately can we really claim to be theologians. On such terms, I shall argue in what follows, the flourishing individual of modern liberalism is more or less an irrelevance to the task of theology, which has its own ways of defining and defending the goodness and dignity of the human creature. Where this is not made clear — as in much of the church today — we can be sure that something has gone seriously wrong.

Therefore, the goal of this book is to see beyond the church itself to the ground of the church's life, or, to put the same thing more plainly, to pose the question of what it is that makes ecclesiology theologically interesting. Like Taylor's young audience, I once thought the answer to this was, "Not a great deal." I now know different. The roots of the church reach deep into the mystery of God, and it is in nurturing the life of the church as it springs up in the world from these roots that the fundamental task of ecclesiology consists. A French word, much used in modern Roman Catholic theology, sums up the approach to be taken: *ressourcement,* the return to roots, is what can be expected in the argument that follows.[6] Without this return, in this age as in all ages, the church must wither and die.

I owe a debt of thanks to Kevin J. Vanhoozer for the invitation he extended to me long ago to write this volume, and to my wife and family for their longsuffering patience while I struggled with it. As with all books, its author is very much aware that it is an unfinished project. But in this instance the book is all the more unfinished because of a family tragedy that interrupted its completion, sapping my energy and attention. No doubt I have left much unsaid, and much is poorly said; moreover, there was much that at the best of times I hardly knew how to say. Such as it is, I dedicate this book with gratitude to former pastors who taught me the Christian faith and whose witness, which happily was always to those roots from which the church lives, continues by God's mercy to sustain me in it.

<hr />

6. An accessible introduction to this word is provided in Fergus Kerr, "French Theology: Yves Congar and Henri de Lubac," in David F. Ford, ed., *The Modern Theologians,* 2nd ed. (Oxford: Blackwell, 1997), pp. 105-17.

CHAPTER 1

Theology and Ecclesiology

Framing the Ecclesiological Question

In a recent book, *Church, World and the Christian Life*, Nicholas Healy has argued that ecclesiology at its best is quite simply a theology that helps the church to live more faithfully.[1] To achieve this, he argues, requires that a doctrine of the church pay close attention to the setting in which the church actually lives so that it can speak critically about the shape that the church's life assumes in it from the standpoint of the gospel story. Therefore, ecclesiology is best when it is both "practical" and "prophetic," or in Healy's all-in-one phrase, "practical-prophetic." In keeping with these claims, Healy also constructs a case against what he calls "blueprint ecclesiology" (pp. 25-27). The "blueprint" approach in Healy's usage is the attempt to argue the converse: that the doctrine of the church can be comprehensively handled via theoretical constructs divorced from practice and the vagaries of life, as if theory alone could provide an account of the true nature of things.

One of the examples of the blueprint approach that Healy cites is the idea that the church is in its deepest essence a communion. Here the claim would be that believers have communion with God through Jesus Christ by virtue of the gift of the Holy Spirit, and with one another by virtue of their common bond in Christ and their common experience of the Spirit. These are powerful and striking ideas that are deeply rooted in Scripture, creed,

---

1. Nicholas M. Healy, *Church, World and the Christian Life* (Cambridge, UK: Cambridge University Press, 2000).

1

and liturgy. However, the problem from Healy's point of view lies in the persistent temptation in all such accounts of the church to downgrade the importance of everyday reality and to highlight instead the theoretical construct. Thus the church is still said to be a communion, even though its actual life is always marred by division or unfaithfulness to its Lord; hence, in the end, theory wins out in the struggle with reality, while division and faithlessness can all too easily persist. The ideal essence of the church found in the blueprint is, in Healy's view, interpreted as if it were something that subsists on its own and is only secondarily to be realized in the church's concrete life.

According to Healy, blueprint ecclesiologies have dominated the landscape of treatments of the church for more than a century. This has ostensibly been a time of astounding ecclesiological development, from the ferment in Roman Catholicism that culminated in the Second Vatican Council (1962-1965), to the rise of ecumenism in the early decades of the twentieth century to its fruition after World War II, and not least to the demographic transformation of Christianity from a religion of predominantly northern peoples to a religion predominantly of the global south. Nevertheless, Healy suggests, Christian thought about the church has been defective throughout this period. In particular, it has persistently failed to reckon with the profound ambiguities that result from taking the empirical character of the church's life in the world with due seriousness. Instead, ecclesiologies have tended to be ideological constructs that develop an understanding of the church from theological first principles rather than from the exigencies of everyday ecclesiastical life. Citing the Anglican theologian Stephen Sykes, he concludes that to understand the church "as if it has a definable essence, a single principle in terms of which one could systematically map the whole, is inevitably to distort it" (Healy, p. 35).[2] In short, it is time for theology to move on — time, we might say, for systematic theologies of the church (such as the one I will attempt to construct) to be put in their place.

The alternative posited by Healy is so far a straightforward one:

> The concrete church, living in and for the world, performs its tasks of witness and discipleship within particular, ever shifting contexts, and its performance is shaped by them. Critical theological analysis of those contexts, and the present shape and activity of the church within

2. Stephen Sykes, *The Identity of Christianity* (Philadelphia: Fortress Press, 1984).

them, should therefore be one of the central tasks of ecclesiology. (p. 39)

No doubt it should be a central task, though whether the whole of the argument that leads to this conclusion in the present instance can be sustained is, I shall argue, highly questionable.

Though one would hardly know it from Healy's account, the preference for a practical theology over a systematic (and particularly a dogmatic) treatment of the *doctrine* of the church has in fact been commonplace in much theological thought for quite a long time. Books in ecclesiology today belong, mostly as a matter of course, to the genre of practical or applied theology. The preference for this approach is nowhere more clear than among the clergy, which is perhaps understandable, given the many practical roles they must play.[3] What is commended, and what is called for, is the simple, seemingly obvious point that how Christian faith is lived in the context of the life of a given church is more important than any doctrine of the church. And that implies that it is not what we say or think that matters, but what we actually do and are in our concrete identities in particular times and places.

If, for example, we say that the church is holy, and we believe that this is theological truth secured for us by revelation — and thus known with certainty by divine authority — we may well be tempted to ignore the claims of those inside or outside the church who draw painful attention to its sinfulness. For example, what about those who have been tortured and killed in the name of the Christian faith, including their faith in the church? Are their cries to be ignored in the present, much as they were in the past? What about the church's long marginalization of women? In more recent history, what about the relative silence of the European churches in the 1930s and 1940s — Protestant, Catholic, and Orthodox — concerning the evils of fascism? And what about the similar taste for it that so disfigured South American Christianity in the decades that followed? Or, closer to our time again, what about the allegations concerning the ecclesiastical tolerance of pedophilia in the

---

3. One might well observe in passing, however, that the multitude of practical roles thrust on the clergy is powerfully reinforced by the theoretical emphasis on and preference for praxis over all else in contemporary theology. The trouble with this is not only theoretical but also practical and pastoral, for the moralizing demand for ever-greater commitments to one or the other pattern of praxis has become a crushing weight on the clergy, and ministry, accordingly, an intolerable burden. In ministry, as in much else in the church, a word of grace in the current situation is badly needed.

ranks of the clergy? Such sins (the list of which could readily be multiplied) seem to make the claim to holiness sound very hollow indeed, and they profoundly reinforce the line of argument that Healy develops. Therefore, attention to empirical reality should serve as a check against the tendency to resolve all ecclesiological questions into one or the other theological abstraction.

However, Healy's contention that the theological "blueprint" necessarily serves as an impediment to genuine understanding and change should be more difficult to accept. For example, one of the approaches he criticizes is that of Karl Rahner, who famously, in volume 6 of his monumental *Theological Investigations*, introduced the idea of "anonymous Christianity" into twentieth-century Roman Catholic ecclesiology. Anonymous Christians, who in Rahner's view would seemingly constitute the bulk of the human race, while not identifying themselves with the (Catholic) church or with the Christian faith, are nonetheless beneficiaries of Christian revelation and are to that extent fellow members of the people of God.[4] Rahner developed his theory for a number of reasons, not the least of which was to offer an alternative to the fortresslike mentality of the Roman Catholic ecclesiology of the late nineteenth and early twentieth centuries. In doing so, he created a space for the coexistence of three key theological principles: first, that some kind of faith is necessary for salvation; second, that there is no salvation outside the church; and third, the idea of the universal salvific will of God (p. 134). We can see that, in order to secure the third, Rahner developed an extremely generous interpretation of the first — and with it, the second — of these principles.

Drawing on and developing the traditional theme that God is to be found at the heart of human existence, Rahner argued that an unfathomable gift of grace, or of God's "self-communication," is implicit in the depth of every human being. To the extent that individuals respond to this self-communication in their knowing and loving, reaching up toward the call of the infinite truth and goodness of God in their finite responses to the true and the good along the way of ordinary human life, they can be said to respond to God in a kind of implicit faith. To this extent, such individuals must be said to be implicitly members of the people of God, and hence implicitly members of the church, or "anonymous Christians." What is explic-

4. Karl Rahner, "Anonymous Christians," in Rahner, *Theological Investigations*, trans. K. H. and B. Kruger, 20 vols. (London: Darton, Longman and Todd, 1969), 6: 390-98.

itly recognized in the visible church about the grace of God's self-communication is thus also a prior truth that pertains to the human race as a whole. The implication is that the great difference between the anonymous Christian and the plain, ordinary variety is simply that, for the former, the primordial offer of God's own self in the gift of grace remains unthematic and unrecognized, whereas, for the latter, it has become something conscious and explicit. Therefore, the visible church expresses something that is implicit about humanity in general, a more universal truth for which the existence of the church itself serves as an explicit sign, or "sacrament."

Healy's basic criticism of Rahner's ecclesiological concept (as of the blueprint approach to ecclesiology generally) is that it favors the universal and the abstract over the concrete and particular. Hence, in Rahner's theology the actual identity of the existing Buddhist is submerged in a tide of abstraction, suffocating all claims that the Buddhist might make in order to differentiate herself from the "people of God" so defined. This favoring of the universal over the particular is precisely the kind of thing that Healy wishes us to reject. An important strand of the argument he makes is that Rahner's ecclesiological agenda conflicts sharply with the postmodern conviction that all human awareness is mediated by particular cultures, traditions, and languages, and that there simply is no access to anything "higher" than such particularity in human consciousness. To think at all is to use a specific language, a time-bound and culturally defined system of physical signs. Therefore, even to think theologically is not to probe the heavens so as to pronounce on the order of things *sub specie aeternitatis,* but to participate in the ongoing life of a particular human community, the values of which are embedded in the language it uses to regulate a common life.

Healy's argument is familiar. Rather like the Platonic "forms," which critics from the time of Aristotle have seen to be fine in theory but irrelevant in practice, the trouble with highly theoretical approaches to the church is that they require us to make what is, in the final analysis, an implausible leap from the ideal to the real. Since it is also impossible to recognize in the real the full shape of the ideal, we tend to be downgrade the real to something of lesser importance. The net result is that, in Rahner's theology, as in all "blueprint" ecclesiology generally, we are left to struggle with a divided mentality: though living in the real, we believe in the ideal — and never the twain shall meet.

We must admit the force of this criticism. Yet one of the curious features of Healy's account is the fact that, in his very effort to give adequate attention to the concrete situations in which the church exists, he ignores the massive achievement of Rahner in helping to alter the actual historical situation in which the Roman Catholic Church existed in the first half of the twentieth century — and in facilitating the reforms of Vatican II. One might well say that, in a sense, without Rahner's theoretical constructions (along with those of his theological peers at the time), there would have been precious little scope for a Healy to argue the case he does in Roman Catholic ecclesiology today. Therefore, we need to more carefully scrutinize the argument that the theoretical accounts of the church represented by "blueprint" ecclesiology are by definition wrong-headed and impractical.

In fact, the achievement of Rahner would appear to suggest something very foreign to the spirit and substance of the postmodern argument: that is, that highly theoretical accounts of the being of the church have had, and can thus presumably still have, a massive impact on the concrete reality of the church. Therefore, what one *thinks* would appear to make a great deal of difference to what one *does,* how one *acts,* what one concretely *is.* Perhaps, in this light, we might even dare to suggest that all ecclesiology, including the approach that ostensibly places praxis at the center, is necessarily an expression of theological theory. After all, isn't there something profoundly counterintuitive about the case made? If praxis were the real source and goal, then presumably the point would lie in the doing rather than in the writing of books or the formulation of arguments.

It is also presumably true that such a praxis-based approach would be capable of generating more profound ecclesiological change than a "blueprint" ecclesiology such as Rahner's could ever do. Yet it is difficult to envision an ecclesiology such as Healy's inspiring great changes in the life of the church. Movements for change presuppose a motivating vision, and a vision is never a matter of praxis so much as it is a matter of ideas or, perhaps more simply, of one great idea that is capable of inspiring a praxis.

I could readily cite alternative examples of the practical effect of theoretical approaches to the doctrine of the church; but, for the sake of argument, I shall refer to only one: the doctrine of the church in Karl Barth's theology. Barth, it must be said, would have regarded the attempt to ground an ecclesiology in any sense at all in postmodern theory as a fundamentally mistaken, antitheological strategy, because the doctrine of the church is in Barth's hands something rooted solidly in revelation, and ultimately in God — and that in the strictest possible sense — rather than in the human context. Barth famously regarded even the quest for a "point of contact" between revelation and world, a point that might allow for the significance of the church to be interpreted afresh in every age, as illegitimate in principle. Yet his theological "blueprint" mapped out a framework that proved to be an invaluable resource for Christians in contexts as varied as Europe and North America prior to and during World War II, in Eastern Europe during the Cold War years, in South Africa during the apartheid era, and in South Korea at the end of the twentieth century. The World Council of Churches, in the early decades of its work, also drew extensively on Barth's approach, as did Roman Catholic theology in the era of Vatican II (e.g., Hans Urs von Balthasar and Hans Küng). In retrospect, it may well be that it was precisely because Barth's theology was *not* a "practical-prophetic" construct — so that his ecclesiology was not principally an attempt to engage with a particular situation but rather with the great claims of the Christian gospel as they must be heard not only in our time but in all times — that his theological system could be so pregnant with meaning in such diverse practical situations.

Nevertheless, it is possible to travel with Healy, and with the whole contemporary movement that seeks to set the praxis of the church front and center in ecclesiology, at least to this extent: that an ecclesiology that cannot show its relevance to the actual life of the church is of questionable value. For example, an approach to the doctrine that cannot unite people because it amounts to a recipe for theological dissension, or one that clearly impedes the apostolic mission of the church to proclaim the gospel, will be a theology that one should rightly ignore as a useless abstraction. Of course, there are many such useless abstractions in Christian theology, and not all of them are theoretical "blueprints," for a good many come from those who push some version of praxis in the faces of the faithful.

In the pages that follow, we will need to bear in mind this reprimand of the theologians and of the task of theology as done today, so that we do not fall from our *own* ideal. But this is not the same as saying that the development of a full-blooded theological account of the being of the church, constructed from the wells of the gospel and integrated with the organic structures of Christian theology, is necessarily vanity. Nor is it the same as concurring with the view that such an account of the doctrine of the church can have no practical relevance.

The Problem and Promise of Ecclesiology

Much of the detail of ecclesiology, like much of the life of the church itself, is a tedious business. It is not always a subject that is intrinsically able to inspire the mind or to enliven the soul. Yet the truth is that the doctrine of the church, for all its painfulness, also occupies a unique place in the structure of theology. Much of what we proclaim in the Christian faith is either hidden from sight or related to events in the remote past or in the anticipated future. What concerns us in Christian theology can be elusive, that is, available only to faith rather than sight. Faith is, of course, explicitly defined in Hebrews 11:1 as "the assurance of things hoped for, the conviction of things not seen"; on this rests the burden of the work of theology, which is massively preoccupied, both historically and even today, with what we might call the "unseen world." "No one has ever seen God," John 1:18 reminds us, and it is only in the light of such frank confession that we can speak at all about God.[5]

However, the church is not like this. "We believe in one holy, catholic, and apostolic church," we confess in the great ecumenical creed, but here at least, something of what we say we believe in *can* be seen in space and time as an ordinary human institution. Though we may draw Augustinian distinctions between the visible and the invisible church, mainstream Christian theology is committed to the view that the one holy, catholic, and apostolic church is, in the final analysis, what we can actually see. There is in ecclesiology no final escape into otherworldliness. What we confess can be discussed sociologically or anthropologically as well as theologically, as statistics about the "one, holy, catholic, and apostolic church" are compiled and its human history examined.

The church that we say we believe in is also a "place" we can attend physically on Sundays and, if we are observant, on other days of the week as well. We can become its adherents, members, or leaders in some official capacity, so that we have regular voting rights, temporal obligations, and even earned

---

5. In this study, I will use the conventional male pronouns to refer to God, but want to insist from the outset that such theological language is merely conventional. The names "Father" and "Son," however, since they come to us in revelation, are far less so. I was tempted to speak in terms of "the Father . . . she," but this would seem absurd. Better simply to insist that the image should be taken "imagelessly," that is, under the qualification that God is "beyond speech," however carefully or correctly constructed.

salaries within it. The church is something to which we tend to contribute money in limited quantities, but occasionally in grand gestures of financial largesse. Even if such capital is not something that could be easily "realized" on the open market, the truth is that the financial assets and property holdings of the churches collectively are enormous. If taken as a whole — on an objective basis, on a worldwide scale, and across the denominations — they would dwarf the assets of multinational corporations.

Yet it is also within this church, or, more specifically, within some small part of it, that we come to hear the Word of God, the message of the saving acts of God in human history, and the promise of our own salvation. Within the church we are baptized with water and fed in the Eucharist. In it we learn how to live by word and example, and through varieties of ecclesiastical discipline others help to ensure that we "walk the talk." Through it all, within the church we come to faith and we learn Christian discipleship. Understood in this way, there would surely be no Christian theology apart from the church, or none to speak of, for apart from the church there would not be the faith and common life to sustain it.

Furthermore, in the life of the church, visible and human though it is, a good deal of the more hidden content of the faith is portrayed in the world for all to see. In short, the structures, life, and witness of the church image what is otherwise invisible. In its care for the outcast, the church images the love of God; in its power structures it reflects the authority of God — at least as the church conceives it; and conversely, in the sins that exist in the life of the church, it too often makes plain its distortions of the God it claims to serve.

The existence of the church, its faith, its worship, and its witness, constitute in this sense a kind of theater within which all else in theology is given a role and finds a place. The church, as such, is a central point of contact between people, the world, and the gospel of God, or a market where the point of it all is "cashed out." Or, to use more powerful and more precise language, the church can be understood as a "sacrament" of encounter with God, for it is a visible token of the possibility of such an encounter, and a concrete means — perhaps even *the* means — of realizing this possibility. Like a sacrament, it is a physical "element"; yet, also like a sacrament, its meaning lies beyond its worldly character in what it symbolizes and realizes in ways that are more than material.

However, this is the source alternatively of the sense of promise and disappointment alike in the ordinary experience of churchgoers. We all know that there is a vast difference between a "good" church and a "dead" one. A good church will have the life- and light-giving flame of the Spirit burning bright within it in word, worship, and example. It will be one in which we can readily find a home, one to which we can bring our friends without embarrassment and to which we can comfortably entrust our children. Such a church will also challenge and teach us humility and service in a way that draws us from death to life, by drawing us into unity with the crucified and risen one, Jesus Christ. This is why it is so important for us to make every effort to get the church right, rather than to put up with stagnation, institutionalism, or faithlessness.

The tendency of the church as an institution to fossilize in its traditions and its bureaucracy, and in so doing to lose contact with the source of its life, is an understandable one and perhaps even something that results from a necessary dynamic. No human society can exist for long, nor can it pass on a tradition from one generation to the next without an institutional framework that sustains it. Whether it be in times of stress and uncertainty or in times of plenty, when complacency becomes its posture, it is natural that these "media" should themselves tend to be confused with the "message," since the loss of them seems to threaten what they have been so carefully constructed to conserve and pass on.

Of course, the truth is that such media are at best provisional; indeed, if we are speaking theologically, they can only be provisional because the church lives under an eschatological qualification. "Thy kingdom come," it prays, thereby signaling that the kingdom has not come yet, and thus that the life of the church as it presently exists cannot be identified as the final goal. Therefore, the church is something anticipatory, or provisional. This provisional character of the church, even at the level of its doctrine, is also a necessary byproduct of the fact that it is located in space and time and made up of human beings. Though forgiven and called to holiness, its members remain sinful; hence the pettiness, pride, and prejudice of its members are woven into the fabric of the church's existence.

Historically, the church has found it difficult to deal with its failures and limitations. The assumption that it is holy, since it has been established by God and thus everything in it has divine sanction, is largely responsible for this. Much of the church has actually gone so far as to insist that, in the long run and due to the faithfulness and presence of God, the church is formally incapable of failure, that it is "indefectible." This idea, in its extreme forms, leads to appalling forms of clerical authoritarianism. Hans Küng, in one of several books that led to his being disciplined by a church hierarchy that was acting — as he saw it — in precisely this way, argues that the idea of indefectibility can be defended insofar as one can make allowances for human error, sin, and finitude. Yes, God graciously holds us in his truth, but this does not mean that God inspires each word and action infallibly.[6] Fortunately, the idea of indefectibility has also been offset historically by the presence in the church of men and women who have recognized its failings and work within it for change, people whose work has been the cause of reform. Often they have been unheard, but sometimes, whether by historical accident or by divine providence, their voices and actions have been heeded, and the church has moved on to new things, whether through sheer moral repentance or through administrative change or the acceptance of some new insight into the meaning of the gospel.

What is theologically significant in the history of the Christian church is, I suggest, largely the history of these renewal movements, which attempt to work like the yeast in dough to affect and alter the whole: asceticism, monasticism, the Gregorian reforms of the eleventh century, the mendicant movement of the high Middle Ages, the conciliar movement in the era of the divided papacy, the work of the "Brethren of the Common Life" in the late medieval period, the Protestant Reformation, Pietism, Methodism, liberal Protestantism in its original flourishing, the work of the missionary societies and of the antislavery societies, the modern ecumenical movement, and the Second Vatican Council have all been renewal or reform movements that have decisively shaped the history of the Christian churches. Each movement has also brought about profound shifts in the tone and texture of the theological understanding of the church.

Reform is in this sense a profoundly universal ecclesiological concern, and not merely a preoccupation of Protestants. Indeed, the principle that is commonly supposed to be a distinctive teaching of the Reformation, *"ecclesia semper reformanda,"* can with far greater plausibility be regarded as common ground among all the Christian confessions. It is certainly true that the Roman Catholic Church has been more actively engaged in "reformation" during the past century than have any of the Protestant churches, and that it has a much longer history of such attempts at reform than do any of those Protestant churches. The desire for reform can arise from a growing

---

6. Hans Küng, *The Church — Maintained in Truth?* trans. E. Quinn (New York: Seabury Press, 1980).

desire for renewal of the spiritual life, or through a rediscovery of the "strange new world of the Bible," or through some new awareness of the missionary task of the church, or through some political or practical crisis, or simply as a result of the work of a great leader or theologian. Concerning this, Hans Urs von Balthasar draws attention to the particular importance of the great mystics and visionaries, arguing that renewal can never result from a mere "program":

> [T]he great movements and reforms of the Church, in the present and the future, will not be initiated by . . . panels and boards but by saints, the ever-unique and solitary ones who, struck by God's lightning, ignite a blaze all around them. This process is totally different from skillful organization.[7]

The task of doing ecclesiology, Healy suggests, is tied to the needs of the church in particular times and contexts, and it is specifically connected with the goal of helping the church to live more faithfully. But what is this goal if not reform and renewal? For to say that the church needs to live more faithfully assumes that it is not living as faithfully as it should be living, that it has fallen away from its first love for God in some way, and that it needs to recover that love afresh, that it needs to see its life and work with new eyes. If so, the task of an ecclesiology is a noble one, even if we have to say, with von Balthasar, that it is "God's lightning" alone that must kindle the flame of love and illuminate the way.

A great many factors suggest that some such renewal of ecclesiological vision is needed in our time. One of the most important is that there has come about a fundamental change in the cultural, social, and political contexts in which the church is located. Today the Christian church exists in settings that are very different from those that prevailed in the era of the Constantinian settlement, or in the Reformation of early modern Europe, or even a century and a half ago, when the foundations of liberal Protestantism were firmly established. In fact, the situation has changed more radically than most of us realize. Globalization, for example, has transformed the cultural setting of the churches to the extent that today, for the first time since the early centuries of its existence, an awareness of religious pluralism is everywhere a regular feature of the church's life.

7. Hans Urs von Balthasar, *The Office of Peter and the Structure of the Church*, trans. Andrée Emery (San Francisco: Ignatius Press, 1986), p. 42.

Closely related to that is the fact that, on the worldwide scale, Christianity is no longer a "Western" religion. There are today about as many Christians in Africa as there are in Europe, almost as many Christians in Latin America as there are in the whole of Europe and North America combined, and as many in Asia as there are in North America. It's true that the numerical decline in membership of the churches in Europe and North America has been dramatic; but it has been accompanied by a tremendous increase in the number of Christians in Africa and Asia. Although most Western Christians perceive this only dimly right now, in another fifty years it will likely be obvious to everyone how the balance of the Christian world has shifted.

In the new global situation of the Christian church, some of the usual expectations of church leaders and theologians need to be turned on their heads.

> [W]here Christianity is spreading most rapidly, it is distinguished by a multiplication of small locally led congregations, as in Latin America, the Philippines, and China, a weakening of central control, as in many parts of Africa, and a preference for loose federations of churches, as in China and Zaïre, rather than interconfessional schemes of church union. The overall picture is one of vitality advancing hand in hand with diversity.[8]

This is clearly the polar opposite of mainstream ecclesiastical developments in most of the Western world, where a continuing desire for bureaucratic centralization is unmistakable. However, the full implication of the demographic shifts in contemporary Christianity is that the church of the future will increasingly become predominantly non-Western in thought, structure, ethics, and worship. The situation today is similar to what happened nineteen centuries ago, when the primitive church became non-Jewish and predominantly Greco-Roman in its thinking and practice. On a worldwide scale, the days of conformity to Western confessional and organizational models are already past, though it would appear that a good many Western church leaders have yet to grasp the fact.

One particular factor that arises in this connection is the polarization of "liberal" and "conservative" factions in all but the smallest and narrowest of

---

8. John Taylor, "The Future of Christianity," in John McManners, ed., *The Oxford Illustrated History of Christianity* (Oxford and New York: Oxford University Press, 1990), p. 659.

the churches in the Western and non-Western worlds. A good example was the recent election of Cardinal Joseph Ratzinger to the office of pope. Ratzinger, now Pope Benedict XVI, was well known as the champion of Roman Catholic theological conservatism, and on these grounds there was much hand-wringing in parts of Europe and North America over his election; by contrast, his election was broadly welcomed among African and Asian Catholics as a sign that some of the more stridently left-wing voices in the Western church had not prevailed and that a much more clearly conservative theological ethos had been secured in Rome. Such tensions are of real concern, and in some cases they threaten to break a number of the major ecclesiastical bodies in the world apart.

The Roman Catholic Church is certainly under no such threat at present, but other church bodies certainly are. For example, the Presbyterian Church U.S.A. is strained to the breaking point today, and similar things can be said of other "mainline" Protestant churches in America. Unquestionably, the best example is the Anglican Communion, because of its uniquely global situation and its theological character as having both a "Protestant and Catholic" tradition. In particular, one thinks of the hostile debates concerning biblical authority, ethics, sexuality, and ministry that erupted violently at the 1998 and 2008 Lambeth Conferences and are likely to reverberate for many years to come, both within the Anglican Communion and beyond.

All of this cries out for a renewal of ecclesiological vision. Our theology has to somehow be generous enough to embrace those who disagree — even fundamentally — on points of doctrine, interpretations of Scripture, theologies of the Christian life, patterns of organization, and questions of ethics. There must be limits, but they must be reasonable and modest. After all, the liberal and conservative theological worlds are both filled with good and devout people, and much that is of genuine theological value can be found on both sides, as can much that is theologically and religiously ill-formed. Unfortunately, however, the left and right "wings" of the churches can each be insufferably intolerant — anticonservative bigotry being just as much alive and well on the left as are the characteristic forms of right-wing religious narrowness — and much work needs to be done. There is no doubt that the main task for the church in face of the stresses of the present time is to return to its heart, to leave aside its obsession with matters of political influence, and to form or reform itself as a proper place of prayer, mission, and renewal. But this is a massive task: its inception would require nothing less than "God's lightning," and its realization would involve nothing less than the renewal of the church as a whole, since so much of what people call sacred would need to fall by the wayside.

Must the Church "Change or Die"?

I can illustrate the depth of the problem that we face in realizing any such goal by referring to the work of John Shelby Spong, the retired bishop of Newark in the Episcopal Church of the United States. Spong is not a professional theologian, but he is an important character in "mainline" North American church life; and he is easily the most visible American representative of a wider movement in recent theology that is best described as "nonobjective theism." The basic claim of this movement, as it is developed in one of Spong's representative publications, *Why Christianity Must Change or Die,* is that God does not "exist" at all as a "being" transcendent to humanity.[9] Rather, the whole "God" question is to be understood as a fundamental dimension of *human* existence itself, or, more specifically, as a function of the *depth* dimension in human self-consciousness. For Spong, this idea is the golden thread that can lead through the labyrinth of the postmodern situation of the contemporary church and show the way beyond the present religious confusion of the Western world.

In other words, Spong's basic claim is that God is not to be found "above" us, but rather "in" us, in our own psychological depths as animals who have evolved in such a way as to be capable of apprehending moral and religious meaning. Adapting an argument that was classically formulated by Ludwig Feuerbach early in the nineteenth century, reformulated by Sigmund Freud early in the twentieth century, and taken over in great measure by Spong's own theological teacher, Paul Tillich, the argument is that the "theistic" God of classical religious thought is dead, but that the same psychodynamic impulses that led humans in evolutionary history to *create* such a God are still as alive and well as ever in the human psyche. For the Christian church, caught as it is between its ancient sources and the postmodern context in which it struggles in the West today, it is imperative to find another "God language." Only thus will it be possible to create the sphere of religious meaning anew for the third Christian millennium, that is,

9. John Shelby Spong, *Why Christianity Must Change or Die* (San Francisco: Harper, 1998).

to carve out a meaningful place for Christianity today and in the future (Spong, p. 55).

Spong's theology at this point vividly illustrates how highly theoretical positions have, in fact, obvious practical implications, and we will need to trace these. His basic contention is that the more adequate "God language" sought can best be identified simply as what calls forth and sustains life in the *person*. God has always been identified as the giver of life, whether in the pagan fertility cults of antiquity or in the monotheistic biblical account of God as the Creator of heaven and earth. For Spong, neither of these ancient alternatives is actually available to us today, because we belong to a scientific age and to a humanity come of age. Nonetheless, the question of what calls forth and sustains life in the human being and in the human community is still of vital importance. What summons it forth in humans, Spong argues, is ultimately the mysterious and infinite power of love. It is love that calls all things into being, and there is in the depths of the human self a "call to love" that is at the same time a "call to being." For Spong, this is what we really mean by the word "God," and, given our coming of age, it is this sense that we must learn to give, explicitly and with open eyes, to our "God language" if that language is to survive at all. Spong puts the case bluntly: "The artifacts of the faith of the past must be understood in a new way if they are to accompany us [into the future], and those that cannot be understood differently will have to be laid aside" (p. 70).

Spong has developed his portrait of Jesus in the light of these assumptions, and I must mention it briefly. Given what we have seen, the view he develops is predictable: Jesus is, for him, "a whole human being who lived fully, who loved wastefully, and who had the courage to be himself under every set of circumstances." Therefore, Jesus appears in Spong's theology as a representation and demonstration of the *human* meaning of "God," understood as "the source of life, the source of love, and the ground of being" (pp. 128-29). In support of this thesis, Spong provides an overview of the consensus of the more radical strands of modern biblical scholarship on the historical Jesus: he maintains that we, as heirs of the modern era, cannot but unquestioningly accept this "scientific" treatment of Jesus as a purely human figure — time-bound, earthly, and so forth. All else in biblical scholarship is dross. However, this does not entail an absence of religious significance according to Spong's terms. He puts it this way: "The divine is simply the depth dimension of the human," while transcendence "symbolizes the endless depths of life" (p. 130).

Both the biblical writers and the later formulators of the creeds of the church were limited by their cultural perspectives, and so they interpreted Jesus' significance in terms of the literalist theistic religious assumptions of their day. The extraordinary indifference to the subtlety of ancient thought implicit in this sweeping claim in Spong's theology need not detain us, though it does deserve to be noted. However, Spong's point is that we no longer inhabit the intellectual world of the ancients any more than we can walk down the street of first-century Antioch or fifth-century Chalcedon. From the standpoint of a contemporary faith that recognizes at last that what we mean by "God" is found at the heart of human life, in the depth of the human psyche, it is still possible to speak of Jesus' divinity, but in the thoroughly reinterpreted sense that he was a man profoundly in touch with these deepest sources of human life, the *human* sources that humans have throughout history named "God."

Therefore, to be a disciple of this Jesus today does not require assent to a series of theistic statements concerning a being "who supposedly invaded our world and who lived among us for a time in the person of Jesus." For Spong, this would be a dishonest and irresponsible answer to the question of discipleship on our part. But an alternative is available. "It only requires me to be empowered by him to imitate the presence of God in him by living fully, by loving wastefully, and by having the courage to be all that God created me to be" (p. 132). "Empowered by him," as Spong puts it here, can only mean "inspired by his example," or perhaps "inspired by his example as lived out in the Christian community."

The example of Jesus in welcoming the outcast, in extending table fellowship to the "tax collectors and sinners," he takes to be of special importance. Spong is an American liberal individualist, and it is principally on this basis that he goes on to sketch the moral shape of discipleship, saying: "I cannot serve this nontheistic God or this revelatory Christ except by seeking to build a world in which all barriers to full humanity for every person have been removed" (p. 133). It is thus consistent with the deepest foundations of Christian faith, he argues, that the church through history should gradually have learned, or that it should gradually have been compelled by the impetus of Jesus, to choose what draws us toward fullness of life and to move beyond those barriers that keep us and all individuals from it.

Consequently, the removal of prejudice is the major moral theme in Spong's theological vision (pp. 129-30). In Spong's history of the church, the events and movements that matter are not, say, the conversion of Constantine or of the Germanic tribes; not the establishment of classical orthodoxy or the evolution of the papacy; indeed, not even the Reformation, with its oft-cited affirmation of subjective freedom. Rather, what matters in the Christian church's history is the fact that, in its beginnings, gentiles were welcomed alongside Jews; that in the context of its more recent history, slavery at last was ended; that in our contemporary life spans, women have achieved ecclesiastical office; that divorced people have been offered a second chance, at least in some of the churches; and that gay and lesbian people are increasingly being accepted for who they are in the name of Christ within the churches. In short, prejudices have fallen one by one in the inclusive community that gathers around Jesus.

For Bishop Spong, the task of the church is not to indoctrinate people in a series of biblical or creedal theological truths (though, paradoxically, his ideas described above certainly do function as "truths" to be tacitly and even explicitly taught); nor is it to relate people as finite sinners through the sacraments to a God who lives in unutterable transcendence. Rather, the church's task is to teach them and to provide opportunities for them to discover that what he calls the "Holy God" is already and always to be found as the "Ground of their Being" in their *own personhood* (p. 66).

Obviously, Spong's theology is essentially a humanism, and — at least to initiates — its affinity with other theological systems, such as those of the nineteenth-century humanist radicals Ludwig Feuerbach and David Friedrich Strauss, are immediately apparent. What requires less specialist knowledge to grasp is that this is hardly the kind of view that could ever serve as the basis for the coexistence of the liberal and conservative wings of the churches. Indeed, the whole point of Spong's argument is precisely the opposite: to declare the fundamental rightness of the faction he represents and to attempt to resist what he sees as the irrational and reactionary conservatism that refuses to make peace with what he assumes to be rationality and modernity.

It is imperative that we take this challenge to traditional Christian faith and ecclesiastical self-understanding seriously, for the radical voices of leaders such as John Shelby Spong resonate remarkably deeply in the churches. The great ecclesiastical mistake today, according to Spong, is to seek to preserve the last vestiges of the theological literalism that asserts a make-believe world as the true one and practices social discrimination in the name of an inhuman God. All this must die. There can be no doubt that Spong is a man with a mission, and in this matter he has many influential followers. Owing especially to the influence of feminist and other liberationist voices, to a powerful ethic of social inclusion, and to a corresponding view of what discipleship means in terms of political and moral commitments, the position Spong represents has been widely embraced, implicitly and explicitly, by pastors and activists in mainline North American Christianity over the past three decades. Therefore, Spong's significance is that he speaks a standard vocabulary with special clarity; it is not original by any stretch of the imagination, but it is, in a variety of incipient forms, extremely common.

"Inclusiveness" and the Doctrine of the Church

The theology of John Shelby Spong forces on us a question that is almost never raised in contemporary Western ecclesiology, since the very posing of the question requires us, in a manner of speaking, to step outside our cultural skins. Nevertheless, it strikes at the heart of what the doctrine of the church is about. Spong articulates the issue nicely when he speaks of the "Christpower" at work in the community of believers, and of this power as the impetus to ensure that "all barriers to full humanity for every person have been removed." However, Spong is by no means unique in insisting on the broad principle of the dignity of the individual as a matter of ultimate theological principle. Spong expresses this principle in the form of "inclusivism," the virtue of which is apparently self-evident. In point of fact, in his commitment to the equality of persons Spong shares much with his fellow Americans on the opposite side of the political and social divide in contemporary America. For the American right, the focus on the dignity of the individual is harnessed to a different set of social and political goals: not inclusion but religious and personal freedom. Indeed, during the Cold War, American evangelicalism gave expression to this commitment as readily and regularly as Protestant liberals did to the value of inclusion. But the idea of the individual is the basic principle of both. This situation is by no means unique to the United States. Three decades ago a British writer expressed the point with particular clarity:

> The present relationship between Christianity and the ideals of Western liberalism is an extremely close one. . . . [T]he Churches have come to regard Human Rights as something like fundamental Christianity.[10]

---

10. Edward Norman, *Christianity and the World Order* (Oxford: Oxford University Press, 1972), p. 29.

Can the church really content itself with this view? Or, to put the question differently, why should the church exist at all according to this view?

In the case of evangelicalism, of course, the commitment to the free religious individual who must "choose" Christ and so be saved answers the question asked. The church exists insofar as there are individuals who make this decision; conversely, such individuals come together as a congregation so that their decision can be confirmed and sustained, and for the sake of those others who still must make a similar "choice" for Christ. As we will see, we are a long way here from having an adequate ecclesiology. Recently, however, a number of writers have begun to criticize a more dangerous side of evangelical self-understanding (and liberal Western religious self-understanding generally).[11] This is particularly true in the United States, where evangelicalism is particularly influential. By accepting the idea that the proper sphere of religion is the private world of conscience ("choice") rather than the public world of political life, American evangelicals have been decisively shaped by modernity's curbing of religion, according to which religion can have no place in public life precisely because it is particular, perspectival, and nonobjective. The universal standpoint belongs to the state alone. The fact that much of American evangelicalism has been content to support the global *pax Americana* — and in fact to serve as some of its most willing foot soldiers — is evidence of the extent to which it has been shaped by the dominant political liberalism.

Evangelicals may not recognize it — and Spong may not either — but on the opposite side of the ecclesiastical divide, a similar shaping of the church by Western liberalism is equally obvious. A particular view of the nature of the individual is involved here, and it has simply been assumed to be normative in theological thought and practice. But it requires identification and critical scrutiny. In the case of Spong's theology, which represents this tendency in one of its purest forms, the function of the church is to draw out from individuals a *presupposed* principle that is latent in their own humanity. In the strict sense, Spong's vision says that we need nothing more or other than ourselves in order to be complete, fulfilled human beings, that we need to resist the idea that it is only by placing ourselves in a right relationship to an objective moral or theological order that we humans can be rec-

---

11. John Milbank, *Theology and Social Theory*, 2nd ed. (Oxford: Blackwell, 2005); Stanley Hauerwas, *After Christendom* (Nashville: Abingdon, 1991); Oliver O'Donovan, *The Desire of the Nations* (Cambridge, UK: Cambridge University Press, 1996).

onciled to our true identity. Instead, the peculiar dignity of the person is immediate and precisely his or her own, and thus it does not derive from anything that lies outside or beyond the self, or anything to which a person must stand in a right relationship.

But does the innermost mystery of the person merit such "theological" reverence? To be sure, some elements of the church, including contemporary hymnody, attempt to elicit such a response:

> We are the young, our lives are a mystery,
> we are the old who yearn for your face;
> we have been sung throughout all of history,
> called to be light to the whole human race.

> Gather us in, the lost and forsaken,
> gather us in, the blind and the lame;
> call to us now, and we shall awaken,
> we shall arise at the sound of our name.
>
> (Marty Haugen, "Here in this Place")

Such words echo remarkably deeply in the souls of those brought up on the assumption that the world works by exclusion, by the favoring of the values and thoughts of the powerful at the expense of the values and thoughts of the weak. The marginalized are also human and thus must have a place at the table of God in the counterculture of the community of Jesus. Such is the sentiment and the theology of the songs of our time, and many do celebrate the vision they offer.

Alternatively, it must inevitably dawn on others that there must be better ways of demonstrating this unambiguous affirmation of individual humanity than through religious faith. This is especially true because the medium of oppression is, of course, tradition, and religion is closely bound up with tradition. Varieties of technological advancement and political or social activism must be preferable options. After all, overt secularism must be the work of sages wiser even than the prophets, preachers, and religious teachers of old, who, in their many and varied — but always upward — appeals to the heavens, were evidently so badly mistaken about the point of religious faith. The point is the individual who exists here and now. Given this assumption, the old religious practices appear to be hollow shells.

One is reminded here of Alisdair MacIntyre's seminal study in moral philosophy, *After Virtue*, and of the book's thesis that, without a clear sense of the purpose of human life, the moral virtues oriented toward it inevitably disintegrate, though a fragmentary form of moral discourse may survive.[12] It must surely be thus with the church — its worship, its values, its order, and its claims. Once the point of its life has been abandoned, its prayer, ministry, and proclamation (which in a sense constitute the forms of its existence) no longer have any coherent purpose. Having lost their anchor in God and in the revelation of God, they appear as a kind of flotsam drifting on the wide ocean of human experience, and they become expressions not of the worship and service of God, but of the experience, worship, and service of humanity itself.

In this view, the church can no longer be a means by which the individual can attain a relationship to an objective spiritual order. Since no such order exists, neither the individual nor the church is to be defined in relationship to it. However, the implications of this are truly enormous. Rather than bringing to people a world of promise and judgment entirely from outside themselves, by way of "representing God" in some way, what is left for the church to be is at best a kind of grand encounter group in which the gifts of each unique individual are to be affirmed and shared with others, but in which the value of each individual is recognized as immediate above all. The church's usual understanding of Christ as a continuing presence in the life of the community is thus transformed to that of a cipher for the breaking down of the walls that prevent the full disclosure of each person to himself and to others (Spong's "Christpower"). The cipher of Christ *facilitates*, but the risen Lord Jesus Christ himself does not and cannot *mediate*, the fullness desired.

The basic theme here is a pervasive one, well adapted to a world that is convinced of the case made by postcolonialist, feminist, and postmodern sources against the power claims implicit and explicit in the structures, truth claims, and value judgments of the church in earlier ages. For this basic theme would declare that these claims and judgments merely excluded all who threatened the social order that the dominant group favored and imposed. Thus the desire to develop a more inclusive polity in the church, measured by such standards, can only be a welcome initiative, and it would be unworthy of any of us to resist it. The theological position advanced also

---

12. Alasdair MacIntyre, *After Virtue* (Notre Dame, IN: University of Notre Dame Press, 1981).

meshes neatly with the recent "rights revolution" of the Western world. In other words, allied as it is with the dominant ideals of contemporary political liberalism, the new ecclesiology seems unassailable.

The *claim* of this basic theme is that an inclusive theology represents and advocates for the weak; the *reality*, however, is rather more subtle. For example, the law of all the Western liberal democracies is now firmly on the side of the inclusiveness agenda. Furthermore, within political liberalism it is the individual and her rights alone that matter; everything is understood in this light. The function of the state and of law, rightly conceived, is thus to allow the individual to flourish in her own freedom. And if this is the good as the Christian religion also defines it, then clearly the function of the church can only be to align itself with the forces of political liberalism. To this extent, however, the inclusive ecclesiology of our time is allied, not first and foremost with the voice of the marginalized, but rather with the dominant political movement of our time, a movement so dominant that it can coherently be seen as the single most powerful contemporary political voice on earth.

This may or may not be a good thing. Power is not evil in itself, so there is no necessary contradiction: the exercise of genuine "goodness" through power must by definition be good. Therefore, the question concerns whether this is "good" power or "bad," or — as may be likely — some mixture of the two. But it is clear and striking that an immense power is at work here all the same. This explains why Spong's theology, for those who believe that the true dignity and freedom of humanity lies in obedience to God, or only in an objective moral order to which humans must submit, represents such a repressive polemic. The fact is that inclusiveness itself must, by its own innermost logic, deconstruct all alternative claims: paradoxically, it must exclude them and attempt to destroy them as something alien.

If this were not such a serious matter, it would be an amusing spectacle. For example, Spong genuinely appears not to grasp how violent his position is toward those with whom he disagrees in the church — which is, of course, the great majority. The destructiveness of his inclusivity is precisely what must immediately strike the ordinary Catholic, Orthodox, or evangelical believer whose theology Spong alternately damns and ridicules. We should not lose sight of this internal contradiction in the inclusiveness project as we proceed, and it certainly merits much more careful reflection than it generally gets. The paradox is that the assertion of freedom is, for those outside the circle of both "includers and included," impossible to distinguish from a kind of tyranny. I will return to this idea in the final chapter.

The Church as the House Where God Lives

Suppose, then, that we were to conceive of the church in very different terms, not as an assembly of individuals who are in themselves the focal point of religious interest, but as something that mediates religious meaning from a very different direction and must orient itself with respect to this fundamental fact. What would then follow? Rather than emerging from the sheer given-ness of our being human, it would be true that faith, worship, and service in the context of the church come "from above," to use the familiar theological phrase. In this view, which naturally would solidly represent the vast majority of "great tradition" Christianity, the church is called by God from the world and given by God to the world in order to speak a word of judgment and of promise, so that the world can, in its turn, come to God and in so doing find salvation and orient its life aright.

The implication of this would be that the individual, rather than being complete in and of himself, would find fulfillment only in the context of an objective order given by God in creation, providence, and salvation. Along with the church, this objective order would include such institutions as the family and the state, apart from which it is, in the first case, impossible to be human at all — or indeed to exist — and in the second case, scarcely possible. Morality, truth, and so forth would also belong here, for we live in relationship to those values as well. According to such a view, the notion that all one needs to do in order to find the fullness of life that God intends is to draw freely from one's "inner well" seems more than a little absurd; and the theology that seeks to accommodate the doctrine of the church to it amounts to an absurdity of massive proportions.

It is strangely necessary, given the pervasive present theological confusion, to put this as clearly as possible so as to avoid misunderstanding. There would be a series of "middle ways" between the two extremes, of course, some of them ad hoc and unintentional no doubt, but some also more reflective. As an example, St. Augustine, who inherited and developed a massive ecclesiology along the lines of the second option, also managed to maintain that God is in all things, and that the human mind by nature exists in relationship to the eternal Word and wisdom of God (the relationship being one of "illumination"), so that turning inward becomes *one* of the principal means by which we can discern the reality of God, whose truth shines in upon the mind. But this is not the same as to suggest that God is identical with the depth dimension, or that the idea of metaphysical transcendence can be dispensed with, or that human wholeness can be found apart from the will of God.

In summary, in order for us to develop an adequate ecclesiology, we must begin not with the human creature, but with God. Furthermore, it is of decisive importance to recognize that the mystery of God is not something merely identical with human existence: the worship and service of God is thus not reducible to the sentimental, humanistic moralism that permeates so much of contemporary Western Christianity. And the doctrine of the church — "one, holy, catholic, and apostolic" — can never be made to be merely an expression of what is at best an atheological and at worst an antitheological social theory.

I must confess that the biblical claims and creedal confessions surrounding the church are some of the hardest points in all of Christian theology. "I believe in the church," I say along with everyone else; but, like others, I often find myself obliged *not* to believe in much of what I see in it. I am certainly not alone: the theologians' discomfort with creedal confessions regarding ecclesiology is well documented in the history of their glosses on the idea. Since "every creature is vain," as no less a theological figure than Albert the Great once argued, it is strictly inappropriate to confess belief in the church in the same sense as one confesses belief in God. What we are really doing in the creedal confession, therefore, is acknowledging belief in the Holy Spirit who is communicated to the church.[13] By implication, saying that we believe in the church, that "vain" creature, is saying that we believe in it only insofar as the Spirit is given to it.

The title of this book draws attention to the fact that the doctrine of the church is rooted in God's gracious outreach to the world. To speak of the church as the house where God lives is indeed to grasp it as a product of the incarnation of God in Jesus Christ, and of God's continuing activity in "indwelling" the creature in the specific and special ways that are denoted when we talk about the gift of the Holy Spirit. Therefore, everything we say about the church needs to be developed from a theocentric standpoint. And since the theocentric standpoint proclaimed in the Christian gospel has a Trinitarian form and content, we must take our stand at the outset with the doctrine of the Trinity, asking how it structures an understanding of the church, not as sociological phenomenon or as liberative

---

13. Cited in Yves Congar, *I Believe in the Holy Spirit*, trans. David Smith, 3 vols. (London: Geoffrey Chapman, 1983), 2: 5-7.

project, but as a core *doctrine* of the faith. What we must try to see is how the doctrine of the church belongs in the strictest possible sense to the gospel itself, so that it is not an addendum to its central claim, but part of its central claim. To return to the great creeds once more, the doctrine of the "one, holy, catholic, and apostolic church" is something we *confess*.

In the Epistle to the Ephesians, we read of the "mystery" of God's will "to bring all things in heaven and on earth together under one head, even Christ" (Eph. 1:9-10). Though this has yet to be realized in its fullness, still this mystery of God's purpose is being realized in anticipatory and partial ways in the life of the church in this world. Putting it another way, we might say that Christ's person and work is such that it creates a space for others, so that Christ himself is not without those whom he calls to believe and follow. Long ago, according to Ephesians, God purposed to bring all things into unity with himself. To Abraham he gave the promise of blessing to all nations, and through the prophets he made himself known as the God of all the earth. God is now realizing this in the creation of a people that includes Jews and gentiles in one body, who together have one head in the one Lord Jesus Christ. Thus is the church part of the mystery: derivatively but decisively, it shares in the story of salvation. And if so, then the proper task of the doctrine of the church must be to attempt to understand the church in its theological dimensions. To grasp the doctrine of the church aright is to begin from God: in the context of the biblical witness, this entails, in the first place, the question of God's relationship to a people. Fortunately, here is where we find something ecclesiological to believe in.

CHAPTER 2

The God of the Church

Ekklêsia and "People of God"

In the common Greek spoken in much of the Mediterranean basin in the New Testament era, *ekklêsia* was an ordinary word without distinctively religious connotation. Its meaning in secular Greek is best captured by the English word "assembly." The Greek noun derives from the verb *kalein* ("to call"): accordingly, in secular Greek, an *ekklêsia* was the convened assembly of the citizens of a city, which in the ancient Greek city-states had once been responsible for legislative and judicial matters.[1] In the Roman empire, of course, such political and legal functions were ultimately under the jurisdiction of the imperial authorities, so that the role of the Hellenic *ekklêsia* had been greatly diminished. Nevertheless, the word continued to be used for the gatherings of citizens with respect to matters of public concern. This usage is even to be found in the New Testament: in Acts 19:32, a gathering of the citizens of Ephesus who meet to *reject* the missionary work of Paul and his associates is spoken of as an *ekklêsia*.

However, precedent for a more distinctive, sacred use of the word was available to New Testament writers from a different source: Jewish Greek. In the Septuagint, the standard Greek translation of Hebrew Scripture used both by first-century Hellenistic Jews and by the early church, the word *ekklêsia* had translated the Hebrew word *qâhâl* (e.g., Deut. 23:2ff.). *Qâhâl* is especially prominent in the biblical narrative of the Exodus, where it refers to the "as-

---

1. Geoffrey Preston, *Faces of the Church* (Grand Rapids: Eerdmans, 1997), p. 5.

27

sembly" of the people of God.[2] It is significant that another Greek word that was also used to translate this Hebrew original in Jewish Greek, *synagôgê*, was not destined to be taken up by the Christians. "Synagogue," of course, already had an established religious usage in the Judaism of the time, even in the Aramaic-speaking Judaean context. If for no other reason than simply that of the legal status of Judaism as a licit religion in the Roman world, the word "synagogue" was not "available" to the followers of Jesus. The Jewish usage of "synagogue" for *qâhâl* would survive into Judaism's rabbinic period, down to our day; Christians, by contrast, chose to use the word *ekklêsia*.

The origin and significance of this usage is much disputed. It is often noted that in the Greek New Testament the word *ekklêsia* is found on the lips of Jesus himself only twice; both of these instances appear in the Gospel of Matthew (16:18; 18:17). The first is the famous text in which Simon Peter confesses Jesus to be "the Christ, the Son of the living God," to which Jesus replies: "I tell you, you are Peter [*Petros*], and on this rock [*petra*] I will build my church [*ekklêsia*], and the gates of Hades will not prevail against it." Longstanding theological debates about whether or not the "rock" in question is to be understood as a literal person (Peter, followed by his institutional successors, upon whose ministry the church will rest) have made this a difficult text to interpret.

The second instance in which Jesus uses the word *ekklêsia*, however, at least shows that such an institutional emphasis, which could in principle include a concern for a recognized central leadership centered around the figure of Peter, is perfectly conceivable as a theme of the Gospel of Matthew. For in Matthew 18:17, the *ekklêsia* of Jesus has clearly taken on the characteristics of the synagogue, and thus of a public religious institution, complete with processes for legal arbitration. The context of the text is the problem of dispute in the community of believers, which is clearly seen not only as a liturgical body, but also as a legal body with authority to discipline and exclude: "If [your brother] sins against you, go and point out the fault when the two of you are alone" (18:15); if that avenue is unsuccessful, there is then authorization to call in witnesses (18:16); and if that does not lead to a resolution, "tell it to the church; and if the offender refuses to listen even to the church, let such a one be to you as a Gentile and a tax collector" (18:17).

2. K. L. Schmidt, *"Ekklêsia,"* in Gerhard Kittel et al., eds., *Theological Dictionary of the New Testament,* trans. Geoffrey W. Bromiley, 10 vols. (Grand Rapids: Eerdmans, 1964-1976), 3: 519-522.

Many historical-critical scholars dispute that the sayings can genuinely be dominical, arguing that such usage is a later projection onto the teaching of Jesus by the early Christian community that produced the Gospel of Matthew. However, all such judgments are speculative, and certainly not all of them are as politically or as religiously neutral (by the assumed canons of the historical-critical method) as they claim to be. Admittedly, it is striking that the other Gospels do not report similar usages by Jesus; to that extent, the evidence of concern on Jesus' part for institutional order seems specifically Matthean, and hence is most likely shaped by the context within which the Gospel of Matthew was written down.

However, the argument advanced "proves" nothing in itself. Though Jesus himself, whose mother tongue was Aramaic, would probably not have used the Greek word *ekklêsia* in conversation with his disciples, the truth is that the underlying idea of the *qâhâl* that underlies the word is so pervasive in Judaism that it is simply inconceivable that Jesus, either as a Jew or as a Jewish religious teacher, would have had no thoughts on the subject. Furthermore, the widespread adoption of the idea of the *ekklêsia* by his followers must have occurred at a very early stage of the tradition, for it is used by Paul in the earliest documents of the New Testament in a way that evidently draws on an already established vocabulary. It is thus an imposition on the text to assume that any and all talk of an *ekklêsia* must by definition be later than Jesus himself, or to suppose that the extent to which it was destined to be taken up as normative in subsequent centuries necessarily represents a distortion — rather than a development — of his own teaching.

What ultimately underlies the use of the word is the simple fact that in the New Testament the faith of the church is paradoxically understood to be religiously continuous with the faith of biblical Judaism. Accordingly, despite institutional Judaism's rejection of Jesus, those who hold the new faith in Jesus as the Christ, the members of the church, are understood to stand in continuity with the Jews. Many of them — for example, almost certainly all the writers of the New Testament — were themselves ethnic Jews, of course, but almost from the beginning there were a great many others who were not Jewish, but rather gentiles drawn from the far-flung corners of the wider world, who came to believe in Jesus as the Jewish messiah and the savior of the world. On the basis of their faith, they were also acknowledged to worship and serve the one true God, who was explicitly identified in the Christian movement as the God of the Jews.

Underlying the New Testament word *ekklêsia* (or "church"), then, is a more ancient and foundational conception: the idea of the "people of God," which stands accordingly among the central themes of New Testament theology. Christianity has historically been a religion of "the nations," for the church in all ages has been a product of the missionary expansion of the apostolic period and of subsequent centuries, which radiated out from the person and work of Jesus of Nazareth, and which generated the various writings of the New Testament themselves. Yet the roots of the New Testament theology of the church are to be found in Hebrew Scripture. As we shall see, those roots reach deep into one particular theme of Hebrew Scripture: the theme of election.

Election and the People of God

In the great foundational text of Judaism, an ancient man of faith, Abram, together with his descendants through his wife, Sarai, are chosen and called into a specific covenantal relationship with God that separates them from all others as God's own.[3] In Genesis 12:1-3, the paradigmatic story of calling in the Bible, God summons Abram: "Go from your country and your kindred and your father's house to the land that I will show you. I will make of you a great nation . . . and in you all the families of the earth shall be blessed." Abram, the man of faith, went as the Lord told him. Years later, though as yet childless, he receives the promise that his own child will be his heir (Gen. 15:4). He is told of the fate of his descendants as slaves for a time in an alien land and of their ultimate deliverance (Gen. 15: 13-14). God then makes a covenant with him, the terms of which have proven fateful even down to our own day: "To your descendants I give this land, from the river of Egypt to the great river, the river Euphrates, the land of the Kenites . . . the Amorites . . . and the Jebusites" (Gen. 15:18-21). Thus Abram is assured of a great nation as his posterity, and of the land that they will inhabit, in the divine covenant. Later he receives the covenantal sign of circumcision (Gen. 17:9-14), together with a new name, Abraham (17:5), signifying his many descendants. With this name, he is also given a son, Isaac, through whom the divine covenant would be established (17:15-22).

3. Cf. Daniel J. Harrington, *God's People in Christ* (Philadelphia: Fortress Press, 1980), pp. 1-16; Michael Maeder, *Church as People* (Collegeville, MN: St. John's University Press, 1968), pp. 3-31.

One of the great "confessions of faith" of the Old Testament sums up this basic reference in the story of the Jews, together with its outworking in the narratives of the Bible. The substance of faith itself consists in an acknowledgment of the call of Abram, of the acts of God in the salvation of his descendants from their bondage in Egypt, and of the land of promise as the gift of God:

> A wandering Aramean was my ancestor; he went down into Egypt and lived there as an alien, few in number, and there he became a great nation, mighty and populous. When the Egyptians treated us harshly and afflicted us, by imposing hard labor on us, we cried to the LORD, the God of our ancestors; the LORD heard our voice and saw our affliction, our toil, and our oppression. The LORD brought us out of Egypt with a mighty hand and an outstretched arm, with a terrifying display of power, and with signs and wonders; and he brought us into this place and gave us this land. . . . (Deut. 26:5-9)

It is important to observe that the story of this covenant of God with the Jews is the story of God's covenant of *grace*. The priority of God's gracious initiative in the story of election and salvation is clear in all of biblical Judaism. This point is stated with great exactness in another of the great texts of Old Testament, Deuteronomy 7:6-9:

> For you are a people holy to the LORD your God; the LORD your God has chosen you out of all the peoples on earth to be his people, his treasured possession. It was not because you were more numerous than any other people. . . . It was because the LORD loved you and kept the oath that he swore to your ancestors, that the LORD has brought you out with a mighty hand, and redeemed you from the house of slavery, from the hand of Pharaoh . . . Know therefore that the LORD your God is God, the faithful God who maintains covenant loyalty with those who love him and keep his commandments, to a thousand generations. . . .

Gracious election and salvation is the major theme here; loving God and keeping his commandments follows from it.

The Jewish consciousness of election has been an extraordinarily important factor in world history, as from it stems not only the strong sense of identity that has (astonishingly) preserved Judaism as a faith and the Jewish people historically, but also, derivatively, the "daughter" religions of Christianity and Islam, both of which draw heavily — though in very different ways and to strikingly different effect — on the heritage of Judaism. The tension created within Judaism by the nascent Christian movement of the first century — on the one hand, by the Christians' faith in Jesus as Israel's Messiah, and on the other, by the gentile mission of the earliest Christians — is also a factor of immense importance for a proper understanding of the early Christian movement.

There can be no doubt that New Testament writers do take the view that the church is indeed the people of God, a people, moreover, who stand in continuity with the people of God of the Hebrew Scripture. This idea appears in a number of places, including the well-known text of 1 Peter 2:9-10:

> [Y]ou are a chosen race, a royal priesthood, a holy nation, God's own people, in order that you may proclaim the mighty acts of him who called you out of darkness into his marvelous light. Once you were not a people, but now you are God's people; once you had not received mercy, but now you have received mercy.

This is perhaps the most unambiguous statement of the theme in the New Testament. Drawing on at least three separate texts (Exod. 19:6; Isa. 43:20-21; also, more freely, Hos. 1:6, 9-10; 2:1, 27), the author of 1 Peter here takes the titles, privileges, and missionary responsibility of Israel and applies them to the church. What the final relationship between the church and Israel is in the theology of 1 Peter is rather unclear: the idea that the church has straightforwardly "supplanted" Israel in the theology of the Epistle is almost certainly to be rejected in favor of the idea that the exact relationship is simply undefined,[4] though obviously the traditional Jewish self-understanding has been abandoned as partial and inadequate in the face of what has happened in the coming of Jesus.[5] However, the language of "chosen race, royal

---

4. J. N. D. Kelly, *A Commentary on the Epistles of Peter and of Jude* (London: Adam and Charles Black, 1969), p. 96.

5. Paul J. Achtemeier, *1 Peter* (Minneapolis: Fortress Press, 1996), p. 167. Achtemeier lists the following scholarly views of the relationship between the church and Israel in the epistle — continuation, fulfillment, reenactment, and replacement — but himself contends merely that the author is "steeped in [Old Testament] language and the traditions of Israel," that he is aware of the relationship between the church and Israel, but that beyond that, we are unable to define the relationship more precisely (p. 167).

priesthood, holy nation, and God's own people" is clearly charged with significance. To cite one small example, the word for "people" *(laos)* is used in the Septuagint only of Israel, as distinguished from the gentiles.[6]

Other direct references in the New Testament to the church as God's people are found at Titus 2:14 (which directly cites Deut. 7:6); 2 Corinthians 6:16; Hebrews 8:10; Revelation 21:3; and, perhaps most important, Romans 9:25-26. All of these passages either directly quote or allude to crucial texts from the Old Testament concerning this theme, so that biblical statements concerning Israel now come, in the hands of the New Testament writers, to refer to the church of Jew and gentile.

There are in addition a large number of more oblique references in the New Testament to our theme. To do justice to it, we would need to take account of the whole thrust of the Acts of the Apostles, for example, which takes up the tension between the Jews as the people of God, on the one side, and the gentile mission of the earliest church, on the other, as one of its basic questions. In the narrative of Acts, it is God himself, through the risen Christ (Acts 22:21) and the outpoured Holy Spirit (Acts 10:34-48), who signals that the eschatological gathering of the gentiles has begun — much to the astonishment of the earliest Jewish Christians. Other pivotal texts are found in the Pauline Epistles, for example, in Galatians 3:29 and Romans 4:16, where gentile Christians are spoken of as *Abraham's* descendants. Here Paul takes up the theme of universality in the foundational narratives of Judaism, in which Abraham is spoken of as the father of many nations, not just of one (Gen. 17:4, a text of which relatively little could be made within the Judaism of Paul's time). An equally surprising text is Galatians 6:15-16, which refers to the "new creation" of the church, rather than to the Jews, as "the Israel of God." Philippians 3:3 also develops this last idea, according to which (gentile) Christians are spoken of as the "circumcision." This is, of course, a metaphorical use of the word, for in the theology of Philippians the people of God are those who do not rely on the physical sign of literal circumcision, but who instead worship by the Spirit and put no confidence in the flesh. The Epistle to the Ephesians also contains an important discussion of how

---

6. Leonard Goppelt, *A Commentary on 1 Peter*, ed. Ferdinand Hahn, trans. John E. Alsup (Grand Rapids: Eerdmans, 1993), p. 148. In the same vein, "nation" in the singular is used in biblical Greek of Israel, and in 1 Peter of the church, whereas "the nations" in the plural refers to the gentiles. Thus a specific vocabulary in Jewish Greek, drawing mainly from the Septuagint, is here used of the church (pp. 148-49).

Jew and gentile are made one in Christ, being reconciled in the one body through the cross, so that the gentiles are made fellow citizens with the saints of the Old Testament (Eph. 2:11-21). This idea, with its theme of the breaking down of ancient barriers, is paralleled by another familiar text, Galatians 3:28: "There is no longer Jew or Greek . . . slave or free . . . male or female; for all of you are one in Christ Jesus."

Together, such sources constitute an impressive body of evidence for the importance of the people-of-God theme in New Testament ecclesiology. However, the *locus classicus* for this subject is undoubtedly Romans 9–11, which discusses the relationship between the physical descendants of Abraham and the church of the gentile mission at length. For Paul, and evidently for his Roman readers, this was among the most important questions raised by the new faith in Jesus. As we shall see, the answer to the question, for Paul, is to be discerned by appealing to the ancient scriptures of Judaism itself.

As elsewhere in the Pauline corpus, the relationship between the Jews and the members of the church in Romans 9–11 is close but not unambiguous. As we have seen, members of the gentile church are said (in Rom. 4) to be numbered among Abraham's descendants, since Abraham, the man of faith, is by virtue of God's promise "the father of us all" (Rom. 4:16). Paul then takes up this same theme in a more polemical way in Romans 9:8, where he flatly states that not all of Abraham's descendants are God's people: "It is not the children of the flesh who are the children of God, but the children of the promise are counted as descendants." It could be argued from this last text that, for Paul, the Jews have been separated from God's people. This is, after all, something that is apparently taught elsewhere in the New Testament, having even come from the lips of Jesus, who speaks of the expulsion of the children of the kingdom (Matt. 8:11f.; Luke 13:28), and who prophesies that the vineyard would be given to another people (Luke 20:15-18). Yet in the Epistle to the Romans, Paul can also affirm the abiding significance of the election of Abraham and of his physical descendants. For Paul, "to [the Jews] belong the adoption, the glory, the covenants, the giving of the law, the worship, and the promises" (Rom. 9:4). Indeed, in one of the great contradictions to all subsequent anti-Jewish sentiment on the part of Christians, Paul can go so far as to claim that "all Israel will be saved" (Rom. 11:26), since "the gifts and the calling of God are irrevocable" (v. 29).

These statements are notoriously difficult to interpret. Romans as a whole is a highly rhetorical document, and the rhetorical character of the Epistle is nowhere more clear than in chapters 9–11. A good example is found in the classic statement of predestinarian thought in Romans 9:19-24, which, precisely because of its literary flavor, has proved to be an intractable problem in the history of Christian theology. What if, Paul asks his hearers, God has dealt with some as special objects of affection destined for glory, and with others as objects destined for wrath? Scripture says, after all, that God himself hardened Pharaoh's heart (Rom. 9:17-18)! But whether or not we are to draw fixed conclusions concerning predestination from Paul's rhetorical interrogative ("What if . . . ?") is a matter of considerable unclarity, in the face of which it is undoubtedly wisest to err on the side of caution.

The question of the relationship between the gentile church and the Jewish people has come to new prominence in recent decades, partly because of a rise of interest in interreligious dialogue, but above all because of the Holocaust of the Jews under Nazism and the increasing recognition among Christians of the sin of anti-Semitism. The years following World War II have brought with them a tremendous effort by both Jews and Christians to reassess the question of Christian-Jewish relations. For example, a notable rise of interest in Jesus among Jewish scholars has been discernible in recent decades, while an even more intense interest in the Jewish matrix within which Jesus himself and the earliest Christianity existed is perhaps the single most important feature of the work of Christian biblical scholars during this same period.

A representative treatment is found in the work of the New Testament scholar Markus Barth, who (following his father, Karl Barth) has argued that Romans 9–11 constitutes the definitive canonical ban against all anti-Jewish theology on the part of Christians. The point of the argument in Romans, he maintains, is that it is only because God is faithful to *Israel* that the gentiles, too, can be saved. Their status as "descendants of Abraham" has not come about because they have *superseded* the Jews; on the contrary, it is only because they have been *grafted into* the ancient covenantal people of God.[7] Thus, the Christian "people of God" have not replaced the Jews; rather, the "wild olive shoot" of the gentiles has been made to share the life of the "rich root of the [Jewish] olive tree" (Rom. 11:17). Though it has often been used as

---

7. Markus Barth, *The People of God* (Sheffield: JSOT Press, 1983), pp. 28-29. See also the useful overview of Bruce D. Marshall, "Christ and the cultures: the Jewish people and Christian theology," in Colin Gunton, ed., *The Cambridge Companion to Christian Doctrine* (Cambridge, UK: Cambridge University Press, 1997), pp. 81-100.

such (particularly in homiletical expositions of Rom. 3), Romans as a whole provides no warrant for downgrading the theological status or religious dignity of the Jews or, indeed, of Judaism.

For Markus Barth, Paul's argument in Romans 9–11 hinges on two principles: the first is the faithfulness of God, which is utterly steadfast; the second is that the ways in which this divine faithfulness is expressed are beyond human telling, for, as Paul sees things, it apparently issues in the mystery of the "hardening" of Israel, which takes place so that both gentile and Jew may ultimately be saved (11:25ff.). Furthermore, Paul seems to see the rejection of Christ by the Jewish people as an instance of the tragic suffering of the Jews throughout history, a suffering that has occurred precisely for the sake of God's name. Thus the text is misunderstood when it is allied to a supersessionist view of the Christian faith's relationship to Judaism. Paul's point in Romans is the reverse: the gentiles are brought into the number of the children of Abraham and made to share in the spiritual blessings of the Jews (Rom. 15:27).

Thus the people of God remains intact, though the family is immeasurably enlarged to include those who are foretold in Hebrew Scripture to be destined to receive the blessings of the covenant people. In the church, Abraham has indeed become one in whom all the families of the earth are blessed, and the father of many nations (Gen. 12:3; 17:4). Or, to quote Paul again, "In the very place where it was said to them, 'You are not my people,' there they shall be called children of the living God" (Rom. 9:26, citing the prophet Hosea). Such a reading of Romans not only has the advantage of excluding all anti-Jewish sentiment from Christian theology, but also the advantage of making it clear why the very gospel preached by Paul, the "apostle to the Gentiles" (Rom. 15:16), is acknowledged from the outset to be intended in the strictest possible sense "for the Jew first," and then for the gentile (Rom. 1:16).

The "People of God" and Egalitarian Liberalism

Much rests, therefore, on the classic claim of Christianity to the title "the people of God": for example, matters as important as the church's use of the Old Testament, its general relationship to Judaism, the nature of the church itself, and its claims regarding God in particular. However, there is a major strand within contemporary Christian thought that tends to construe the concept of the people of God very differently. It involves the assumption that

that concept instead is the grounds for an ecclesiastical ethos of mutual acceptance, equality, and toleration — in other words, the standard doctrine of justice and love that characterizes theological liberalism.

The idea can be found in unusual places. A representative statement of this basic misunderstanding is found in an influential book by the conservative Roman Catholic theologian (now Cardinal) Avery Dulles, *Models of the Church.* This work, which has been among the most widely read studies in ecclesiology in the English language during recent decades, puts the point as follows:

> For many purposes the analogues of Body of Christ and People of God are virtually equivalent. Both of them are more democratic in tendency than . . . hierarchical models [of the church]. They emphasize the immediate relationship of all believers to the Holy Spirit, who directs the whole Church. Both focus attention likewise on the mutual service of the members toward one another and on the subordination of the particular good of any one group to that of the whole Body or People.[8]

It is easy to see that the ideas expressed here, however amenable to the dominant cultural assumptions of an American Catholic such as Dulles, are nonetheless extraordinarily detached from the biblical concept of the people of God.

The ultimate source of the problem in Dulles's argument stems from the fact that the people-of-God idea came to new prominence in Roman Catholic ecclesiology in the twentieth century through the Second Vatican Council, which made the concept one of the leading themes of its doctrine of the church. In the development of the council's theology, the people-of-God concept does indeed secure just those values of which Dulles speaks. The goal was to find some way to move on from the old hierarchical ecclesiology represented by the Councils of Trent and Vatican I. Also discernible in the theology of the church of the Second Vatican Council is a desire to bypass the theology of the "mystical body" found in Pius XII's encyclical *Mystici Corporis,* which again, it was felt, contained too much emphasis on the institutional ecclesiastical hierarchy. In the debates that took place at the time, these older themes had threatened to dominate the ecclesiology of Vatican II. The problem was resolved by the insertion of a chapter entitled *De*

8. Avery Dulles, *Models of the Church* (London: The Catholic Book Club, 1976), p. 49.

Populo Dei before the chapter on the hierarchy and bishops in the structure of the key document of Vatican II, the Dogmatic Constitution on the Church, *Lumen Gentium*.[9] The main thrust of *De Populo Dei* was to affirm what all members of the church possess in common, to emphasize what is held in common over what is given only to some. Hence it placed emphasis on the whole "people of God," and indeed on the idea of the common priesthood of all Christians, which qualifies the presentation in the remainder of the constitution of what still seems, to an outside observer, to be an extraordinarily centralized and "top-down" model of ecclesiological authority.

Given this context, the thinking behind Dulles's claims was perhaps entirely understandable, as was the thinking of the council that informed Dulles's approach. Nevertheless, assuming that we agree that the proper content of the people-of-God concept should be regulated by the biblical witness, it must be said that it still represents rather poor theology, whether that theology be the work of an individual theologian or the outcome of a council. The truth of the matter is that the New Testament's talk about the church as the people of God does not strictly have to do with any egalitarian or democratic ideal (though these may indeed be desirable); nor can it honestly be said to relate in any meaningful sense to the problem of clericalism. Rather, it has to do specifically with the relationship of the church to the people of Israel, and ultimately to the God of the Jews, who is also the God and Father of Jesus Christ. The point of the language, as we have seen, is to affirm that the God who called Abraham and his descendants to be his people, and the God who now calls the nations to faith and obedience, is one and the same. The gracious freedom of election in God's choice of this people is, in the final analysis, what is at stake from beginning to end in the biblical concept of the people of God.

The Doctrine of God and the Problem of Election

The problem of the doctrine of God and its relationship to the doctrine of the church is among the most pressing issues in contemporary ecclesiology. Indeed, despite current preferences for practical themes in treatments of the church, the great ecclesiological questions have always been closely connected to the theological question. Oddly enough, one person who clearly

9. Maeder, *Church as People*, pp. 32-36.

perceives this is John Shelby Spong, whose central ecclesiological contentions flow from a revised and modernized understanding of God, which necessarily leads to massive shifts in ecclesiastical self-understanding.[10] Since God, in Spong's thought, has essentially become a depth-psychological means to the realization of the kind of authentic selfhood exemplified in Christ, the ideal church must accordingly become an open, caring, and inclusive community in which such self-realization can take place. It follows that we must relinquish all ideas of the church as a divine institution in order to make way for the realization of this human potentiality.

For Spong, then, what people think of God has a huge bearing on what they think of the church, as indeed what they think of human life generally. In Spong's own case, the crucial experience was that of living through the civil rights struggles of the 1960s in the American South. The fact that racism and religious belief went together in those circumstances clearly left its mark: one's God can be alienating or liberating, and so Spong saw his fundamental task as making faith in God a liberating influence in church and world alike. The questions concerning the nature of God and the nature of the church are themes that have to be handled together. If nothing else, theologies such as Spong's show how deep the problem of the doctrine of God runs in approaches to the church.

We have already seen from our survey of the biblical idea of the people of God that the problem of the electing God, and of the God who elects precisely because he is sovereign, gracious, and loving, is one of the foundational themes on which the doctrine of the church as the people of God must draw. As a function of this same problem, it again poses the problem of the *Christian* doctrine of God as also the God of the Jews — the God of Israel who is, according to the Christian tradition, one and the same as "the God and Father of our Lord Jesus Christ." For these reasons, tackling this doctrine is no small task. Only a theology that effectively descends into outright Gnostic individualism can avoid it.[11] Issues of great theological importance, and in some cases of considerable controversy, are thus at stake.

10. Spong's position itself follows in a tradition of radical thought on this question, a tradition that notably includes certain of the popular writings of John Robinson. The crucial text is John A. T. Robinson, *Honest to God* (London: SCM Press, 1963), but it was followed by works such as Robinson's *The New Reformation?* (London: SCM Press, 1965).

11. Such theologies are, of course, a contemporary commonplace. A useful treatment is that of Philip J. Lee, *Against the Protestant Gnostics* (New York and Oxford: Oxford University Press, 1987).

Among the key texts mentioned in the previous section's biblical survey was 1 Peter 2:9-10:

> [Y]ou are a chosen race, a royal priesthood, a holy nation, God's own people. . . . Once you were not a people, but now you are God's people; once you had not received mercy, but now you have received mercy.

The phrase "chosen race" *(genos eklekton)*, here transferred from Israel to the church, is a striking one. Its roots in the overall theology of the New Testament, and in the theology of the people of God in particular, are clear and emphatic. However, in 1 Peter the theme is absolutely central, so much so that 1 Peter 1:1–2:10 has been said to provide the fullest treatment of the election of the church in the whole of the New Testament.[12]

The theme of the election of the church in 1 Peter is announced right at the beginning, in the Epistle's salutation, which reads simply: "Peter, an apostle of Jesus Christ, to the elect. . . ."[13] The idea culminates in 1 Peter 2:10. In between, the moral obligations that flow from the character of the God who elects and from the means by which the divine election is realized in time through the work of Christ are drawn out (1:13ff.). It is also significant that the theme of election is used twice in connection with Christology in 1 Peter, directly at 2:4, where Jesus himself is the "elect" *(eklekton)* cornerstone, and indirectly at 1:20, where he is spoken of in cognate terms as the one "foreknown" by God before the creation of the world. Such ideas are pregnant with theological implication, for what thus comes into focus is a connection between Christ as himself elect and the church that is elect in Christ.

Though Latin theology, following in the tradition of Augustine, is historically the principal "site" for the development of the doctrine of election in the Christian tradition, the truth is that this connection was only very partially and imperfectly drawn out during the course of the doctrine of election's development in mainstream Latin theology, which, on the whole, proceeded along a very different course. The most consistent advocates of the doctrine in the Latin theological tradition, particularly as mediated through later adaptations of Augustinian theology, tend to emphasize the idea that the proper function of the doctrine of election is to exclude human freedom

---

12. Achtemeier, *1 Peter,* p. 81.
13. My translation of 1 Peter 1:1; the NRSV is woefully inadequate on this verse.

from the event of salvation, and thus to secure the priority of grace over all human effort. In a wide-ranging survey of the doctrine of election in historical perspective, for example, a modern heir of the Augustinian tradition, the Reformed theologian G. K. Berkouwer, maintains that the singular theological error repelled by the doctrine of election is quite simply any and all "synergism" of human freedom and divine grace. For Berkouwer, nothing less than the central thrust of the Christian gospel turns on the success or failure of this defensive posture.[14] Nor is such a position on the nature of the problem unique to representatives of strict Calvinism. On the contrary, polemics from different theological traditions against the overtly predestinarian approaches to salvation of classical Calvinism tend to defend just such a "synergy" of human and divine will in the process of salvation, and to interpret the doctrine of election accordingly.[15] What they lose sight of in doing so is the idea that election in the biblical sources is concerned with another question in the strict sense: the choice of fellowship with a people *by God*.

As I have already noted, the fountainhead of the Western doctrine of election, and the source of much of the problem with it, is St. Augustine, whose theology exerted an immense influence over centuries of subsequent Latin theology. Augustine's ecclesiology is subtle and massively developed, and doing it justice requires treating it at some length.

To begin with, one can discern in Augustine's approach to the theology of the church during his early years as a Christian thinker the basic conviction that only a certain universality in the social, intellectual, and geographical location of the catholic church can secure its authority. As heirs of the missionary project of the church of the fourth century to Christianize the Roman empire, most of the Christians of Augustine's generation shared this conviction. The attitude was echoed by Augustine's contemporary St. Vincent of Lerins, for example, who in an influential statement that came to be known as the "Vincentian Canon," spoke of the catholic tradition as "what has been believed everywhere, always, and by all." In short, catholicism is holistic or it is nothing.

Consecrated as a North African bishop at the end of the fourth century (395), Augustine had learned early in his ecclesiastical career to face the chal-

---

14. G. K. Berkouwer, *Divine Election,* trans. Hugo Bekker (Grand Rapids: Eerdmans, 1960), pp. 28-52.

15. For example, M. John Farrelly, *Predestination, Grace and Free Will* (London: Burns & Oates, 1964).

lenge of the Donatist schism on precisely these grounds.[16] North African Christians had been divided since 311 on the question of who represented the authentic voice of Christianity: the Donatist schismatics, who claimed to be a pure people standing in the succession of bishops untainted by the sin of apostasy, or the Catholics, whose reputation was admittedly more sullied but who had maintained connections with the wider tradition and life of the church. The controversy had an impact on sacramental theology and practice and on the sacrament of baptism in particular, since the Donatists refused to recognize Catholic baptism as genuine, and thus they rebaptized Catholics who converted to Donatism.

Peter Brown, in his classic biography *Augustine of Hippo,* writes of how the catholicism of Augustine "reflects the attitude of a group confident of its powers to absorb the world without losing its identity."[17] Augustine held that the great weakness of the Donatist church was its inability to relate not only to the whole of the church but also to the world that the church stood to inherit in the fourth and early fifth centuries. Donatism's narrowness of spirit and its sectarian character stood in the way of the divine destiny of the church, which was to win the obedience of the entire Roman empire. Achieving this would in effect require that one be willing to tolerate the inevitable compromises that would necessarily accompany the triumph of Christianity as the new civil religion of the *imperium.* Thus the Catholic church had to be, and could only be, a church that would include both the pure and the impure. This conviction came to serve in Augustine's theology as the lens through which to rightly view the doctrine of the church. Did not the Lord himself teach that the kingdom of God is like a net let down into the sea that catches both good and bad (Matt. 13:47-50), or a field in which both wheat and tares are found (Matt. 13:24-30)? God so works through the *catholic* church, as his appointed instrument on earth, that even where its ministry is undertaken by sinful priests, it nevertheless objectively mediates the grace of God, since its power rests on the promise of Christ rather than on the worth of the minister.

To flesh out his understanding, Augustine relied on a variety of sources. The first was St. Cyprian of Carthage (c. 200-258), the great figure in earlier

---

16. On the Donatist movement, see W. H. C. Frend, *The Donatist Church,* 3rd ed. (Oxford: Clarendon Press, 1985); on Augustine's role in the controversy, see G. G. Willis, *St. Augustine and the Donatist Controversy* (London: SPCK, 1952).

17. Peter Brown, *Augustine of Hippo* (London and Boston: Faber & Faber, 1967), p. 214.

North African (and Western) ecclesiology, who had been compelled to examine the doctrine of the church in the early 250s as a result of the Decian persecution (249-251). Cyprian's ecclesiastical policy, which was grounded in his two main works, *The Lapsed* and *The Unity of the Catholic Church* (both dating from 251), had been to permit in principle the reconciliation of those who had become apostates under the persecution. Even clerics who had committed apostasy could, like the laity, be readmitted to communion under certain conditions, but they were permanently barred from resuming their clerical duties. To that extent, Cyprian's policy was ambiguous: later Donatists could appeal to Cyprian's moral rigor (indeed, to his policy of not counting the baptism of heretics to be valid); Catholics, such as Augustine, could appeal to his toleration of the imperfect in the ranks of the church.

However, Cyprian had also put great emphasis on the episcopal office as the principle of church unity (for Cyprian, bishops were the "glue of the church"), an emphasis that could be traced to older theological sources, such as Clement of Rome. But in Cyprian's hands it became the means of combating the influence of the "confessors," those who had stood their ground in the Decian persecution, and whose authority was being asserted by some within the North African church to be superior to that of the bishops. To this extent, the debate was between charismatic and institutional versions of authority. Cyprian, whose background prior to conversion had been in the law, and whose family roots were aristocratic, took a robustly "institutional" line: it is the Catholic church, understood as a visible, historical institution, that is the appointed representative of God in the world. Accordingly, Cyprian maintained that the sin of schism was utterly incompatible with Christian faith. "Outside the church, there is no salvation," Cyprian's most famous and influential saying, originally applied to this problem of schism (rather than to the relationship between Christianity and pagan religions) and thus to a situation *internal* to North African Christianity. For Cyprian, there can be no true Christian faith where there is not also a commitment to membership of the one church.

Augustine took precisely this view in his struggles with Donatism. One of his major arguments, for example, was that the sin of schism was a failure of charity on the part of the schismatic to live in union with the whole of the body of Christ. Appealing partially to one of Cyprian's arguments, he maintained that for this reason Donatist sacraments, though valid and needing no repetition, were of no effect, since grace works through charity:

[W]hen anyone comes to us from the sect of Donatus, we do not accept their sins, that is, their dissent and error; rather, these are removed as impediments to harmony. And we embrace our brothers . . . acknowledging in them the gifts of God, whether holy baptism, the blessing of ordination, [etc.]. Even if all these were present, they, nevertheless, did no good if love was not there. But who truly claims to have the love of Christ when he does not embrace his unity? And so, when they come to the Catholic Church, they do not receive here what they had, but they receive here what they did not have in order that what they had may begin to benefit them.[18]

The second major source for Augustine's early ecclesiological views was his philosophical commitment to Platonism. More specifically, one of the basic insights of the Platonism that Augustine had adopted on his way to conversion (and adapted afterwards), and that he retained throughout his life as a Christian, was the notion that the visible world is but a pale reflection of the world of true reality — that is, the eternal, heavenly realm of God's dwelling. As all that is visible is necessarily imperfect, and is thus flawed by strict metaphysical necessity, quite apart from the question of moral failure, it follows that any earthly, visible church can only be imperfect. Ultimately, the true church is the invisible one of the heavenly Jerusalem. Therefore, the true church is not to be identified simplistically with the visible church that was found, for example, in fourth- and fifth-century Hippo Regius, of which Augustine was bishop. Of course, this view was not unique to Augustine or to North Africa: almost all understanding of the church in patristic theology was colored to one extent or another by these philosophical ideas.

Later in life, Augustine added another claim, which became something utterly basic to his final theology and to his theological legacy. Beginning about 411, which, ironically, was the year the Donatist schism was finally settled, Augustine came to be preoccupied with a new question: the Pelagian controversy, which occasioned a further clarification of his ecclesiological views and engaged him to the time of his death in 430.[19] The Pelagian con-

18. Augustine, *Ep.* 61.2, in Augustine, *Letters 1-99*, ed. John E. Rotelle, trans. Roland Teske, *The Works of Saint Augustine* (New York: New City Press, 2001), pp. 245-46.

19. The literature on Pelagianism is vast. For a succinct overview of this original controversy, see Joanne McWilliam, "Pelagius, Pelagianism," in Everett Ferguson, ed., *Encyclopedia of Early Christianity*, 2nd ed., 2 vols. (New York: Garland Publishing, 1997), 2: 887-90;

troversy was arguably more fundamental than either of the first two, because it was a dispute about the doctrine of grace and thus was located at the very center of Christian faith. As such, Augustine's response was to have extraordinarily far-reaching consequences for the overall shape of the theology, including the ecclesiology that he bequeathed to the church of the Latin West.

Pelagius was by origin and training almost certainly a "Celtic Christian" who left his native Britain to become active in Rome in the early fifth century. He was about Augustine's age, and he traveled from Rome to North Africa with other influential refugees after the sack of that city by the barbarian armies of Alaric in 410. He preached a severe, moralizing message of Christian perfection, apparently wishing to see the example of the monastic movement taken up and imitated in the church at large.

Augustine's initial impression of Pelagius's teaching was its similarity to Donatist theology. According to the Pelagian model, the church was to be an assembly of the pure, a church to be defined by its rejection of the world. This was a view that, by 411, Augustine had spent almost two decades resisting, since it made his sense of an ecclesiastical "catholicity" that could embrace the whole of life inconceivable. From this point of view, it is hardly surprising that, when he learned of Pelagius's preaching in the region, Augustine immediately chose to set himself against the Pelagian theology. It initially seemed that this was the old foe reappearing in a new form, and that, as such, it could be easily dispensed with. However, as the controversy progressed, Augustine's reflections on the implications of Pelagian teaching deepened, with the result that many of the most basic themes of Augustine's final theology emerged over the next two decades, which in turn were to have incalculable effects on the centuries of theology that followed.

In the end, the problem with Pelagianism was not merely that it taught a version of the narrow ecclesiology that Augustine had long despised; what troubled Augustine much more was the specific way Pelagius and his followers approached the question of human salvation. Over many years, Augustine had been preoccupied with interpreting the Pauline Epistles. He explained them in a daring way, developing a distinctly pessimistic view of

---

or, for a more expansive treatment, see Jaroslav Pelikan, *The Christian Tradition,* 5 vols. (Chicago: The University of Chicago Press, 1971-1989), 1: 292-307, 313-31. More detailed and specialized accounts are provided by Robert F. Evans, *Pelagius* (London: Adam and Charles Black, 1968), and T. Bohlin, *Die Theologie des Pelagius und ihre Genesis* (Lundequist: Harrassowitz, 1957).

human sinfulness, drawing in this way on what was already a characteristic theme in the Christianity of North Africa (the idea of original sin, for example, is found in Tertullian). As a result, Augustine leaned strongly toward the view that salvation comes about, not because human beings choose to believe and obey, since their moral character is so compromised, but because God chooses obedience and salvation for them. In short, by way of Augustine's exegesis of Paul, the ideas of predestination and the necessity of the sovereign grace of God came to the fore in his thinking.

The theme that emerged in Augustine's writings after 411 was not, however, entirely novel. As early as 395, the first year of his episcopate, Augustine had been presented by a fellow Christian Platonist with the problem of how to reconcile Malachi 1:2-3 with the regulative idea of the goodness of God: "I have loved Jacob but I have hated Esau," the prophet had said. How, then, can God be good?[20] Christian Platonism from the time of Origen had been tempted to respond to this problem by appealing to the ancient Platonic doctrine of the preexistence of souls. In this view, God loves Jacob and hates Esau because Jacob and Esau had lived before, and so came into the world, not only as children of Isaac, but as souls with previous moral histories who had freely obeyed and disobeyed God in their previous existences. God's "hatred" is disciplinary rather than predestinating, so that God's goodness, the principle of human freedom, and Malachi 1:2-3 all stand together.

But Augustine responded already in 395 by breaking ranks with the more radical strand of the Christian Platonist tradition and insisting that humanity is totally dependent on the will of God, dependent even on God's will for the gift of faith itself, so that in the Christian life we can possess nothing that we have not first received. God himself and God's goodness are ultimately inscrutable. Thus Augustine affirmed the theme of the absolute sovereignty of God and pushed to the periphery his earlier insistence, as a Platonist, on the freedom of the human will. Sixteen years later it was precisely this theme of the freedom of the will in relationship to the sovereignty of God that Augustine encountered in the arguments of Pelagius: the latter maintained that it was possible, by the exercise of free will in a life of heroic virtue inspired by the example of Christ, to live the Christian life in its fullness. Not only that, but because Christ commands perfection (Matt. 5:48), perfection can only be obligatory; and if obligatory, it must hence be possible. It was on the basis of these ideas that Pelagius preached his message of rejecting the sinful

---

20. Brown, *Augustine of Hippo*, pp. 153-55.

world and of the moral renewal of the church amid the collapse of the Roman empire.

Pelagius himself was readily dealt with in the context of North Africa, which had long taken a more pessimistic view of human nature and consequently was quite ill-disposed to receive his ideas. By 416, five years after he had first come to Africa, a council held at Milevis condemned him, though Pelagius himself had apparently seen the writing on the wall, for by then he had fled to seek support in more hospitable places. Even prior to Milevis, Pelagius had arrived in the Holy Land, where he enlisted the support of no less a person than the bishop of Jerusalem and a number of other eastern bishops in his cause against the North Africans.

The controversy was to continue for years. The North Africans, resolute in their opposition to the Pelagian "heresies" of the continuing goodness of creation, the freedom of the will, and the eternal importance of human efforts, turned to the bishop of Rome, and especially to the imperial court, for a decision against the Eastern authorities. Ultimately, their network of political influence prevailed: Pelagius and his followers were condemned on the authority of the emperor Honorius in 418. Even this did not end the matter. To the end of his life, Augustine was engaged in polemics against Pelagian sources, the most notable of whom was an Italian bishop, Julian, who had been exiled after 418 but who, like Pelagius before him, had powerful ecclesiastical allies in the East, and who never gave up his struggle for the Pelagian reading of the gospel.

For Augustine himself, the whole controversy had a number of important ecclesiological implications, and if the ideas he worked out in his anti-Pelagian writings were not consistently defended in subsequent centuries, many of them did have a lasting impact on the life of the Latin church. For example, one need only think of his detailed explorations of the idea of original sin — and of the insistence on the absolute necessity of infant baptism that it entailed — to begin to see how far-reaching were the implications of the Pelagian controversy. A whole theology of Christian initiation and of the Christian life was shaped in this way. More than a thousand years after Augustine's death, the Council of Trent would continue to speak in terms that Augustine had set at the center of Latin theology:

> If anyone says that recently born babies should not be baptised even if they have been born to baptised parents; or says that they are indeed baptised for the remission of sins, but incur no trace of the original sin of Adam needing to be cleansed by the water of rebirth for them to ob-

tain eternal life, with the necessary consequence that in their case there is being understood a form of baptism for the remission of sins which is not true, but false: let him be anathema.[21]

Thus the Christian life, from its beginnings in baptism, is set first under the dark shadow of sin, and only then positively under the seal of God's sovereign grace, administered in the sacrament of baptism by the church, quite apart from the willingness or otherwise of the child who receives it. Baptism gives witness to the central idea that grace alone accomplishes human salvation.

As I have already suggested, Augustine's understanding of salvation by grace is closely connected with his understanding of predestination, which he again worked out chiefly on the basis of his long study of the Pauline Epistles. Among the more important of Augustine's writings along these lines is his late work *The Predestination of Saints*, a book addressed to alarmed Christian leaders in Gaul, Prosper of Aquitaine and Hilary of Poitiers, who had written for clarification when they had heard about Augustine's views. In reply, the old man makes clear the leap that is required by his view of "all or nothing" grace in order to embrace the predestining will of God:

> Faith, then, both in its beginning and in its completion, is a gift of God, and let it not be doubted by anyone who does not wish to contradict the most evident sacred writings that this gift is given to some, but to others it is not given. Why this gift is not given should not disturb the believer, who believes that from one man, all have gone into condemnation, a condemnation undoubtedly most just, so much so that even if no one were freed therefrom, there would be no just complaint against God. It is evident from this that it is a great grace that many are delivered and recognize, in those who are not delivered, that which they themselves deserved, so that "he who glories may glory" not in his own merits, "but in the Lord." As to why God delivers this person rather than that one: "How incomprehensible are his judgments, and how unsearchable his ways."[22]

21. Council of Trent, "Decree on Original Sin," Session Five (17 June 1546), 4, in Norman P. Tanner, ed., *Decrees of the Ecumenical Councils*, 2 vols. (Washington, DC: Georgetown University Press, 1990), 2: 666.

22. Augustine, *Predestination of the Saints*, 16, in Augustine, *Four Anti-Pelagian Writings*, trans. John A. Mourant and William J. Collinge (Washington, DC: Catholic University of America Press, 1992), pp. 237-38.

Grace and predestination are intimately linked, so much so that Augustine can go on to argue in the same treatise that predestination is simply the preparation for grace, whereas grace is the gift itself, bringing the eternal predestination of God to fruition in time (pp. 18-19).

Augustine's understanding of the church was not greatly affected by his "discovery" of the importance of divine predestination, but his earlier views were clearly reinforced. Decades earlier, in the process leading to his conversion, and above all in his episcopal struggle against the Donatists, he had made up his mind not only about what the Catholic church stood for, but also why it was necessary for it to contain both saint and sinner. His late doctrine of predestination is consistent with — indeed, massively buttresses — this earlier understanding. Since only God can know those who are his, it is not for humans to seek to narrow the scope of the Christian community to those who seem to *them* to be faithful. Even in the case of those already living godly lives within the church, in other words, the truth is that we do not know who will persevere to the end and who will fall.[23] God alone knows, for their lives are in God's hand, the God who freely predestines all things, including their perseverance to the end — or their falling away. Since God's will is unfathomable to the human mind, it is folly to assume that we can know those who are elect and those who are not.

This last point is an important one. The classic doctrine of election, and its correlatives in the doctrines of perseverance and the like, have been and are heavily criticized, on the one hand for their inhumanity, and on the other for their tendency to attribute the causes of human salvation and damnation to God alone. On both counts, the rational and moral plausibility of the predestinarian position is questioned. However, the classic predestinarian position is subtle: its genuine claim is that God is beyond human comprehension, which entails that the God of the critics may be more humanly conceivable, but also that, just for this reason, their God represents an idol of the mind to some extent.

The claim of the critics is that classic predestinarian theology asks us to speak nonsense about God, since the ordinary canons of human moral reason do not apply with respect to God. God is "good," even in monstrously damning humans for no moral failure of their own (note the notorious case of unbaptized infants in the Augustinian tradition). But this is not really an adequate representation of the claim of the predestinarian position. It's true

23. *The Gift of Perseverance*, 9, *Four Anti-Pelagian Writings*, pp. 286ff.

that Paul's famous argument in 1 Corinthians 1 concerning the foolishness of the cross is often cited in this light, particularly in regard to those strands of the Christian tradition that draw on or mirror the irrationalism often attributed to Tertullian's (spurious) dictum: *Credo quia absurdum* ("I believe because it is absurd"). Though it can be seen in this way, if we properly understand the argument, it runs much deeper.

To return to Paul, for example, his preaching of the foolishness of the cross seems to be foolishness only because it is in truth a proclamation of a wisdom that overturns "wise" human expectation and indeed reverses the entire human lot. Whereas the philosophers proclaimed the infinite distance between God and the world, the cross proclaims the extraordinary love of God for the world, affirming an astonishing solidarity with it that far surpasses the wisdom of the wise. Repeatedly in the history of Christian thought, theologians have had to return to this one theme in order to fend off some of the more imperious demands of reason, such as in the Arian controversy of the fourth century or in the Deist controversies of the modern period. Christian thought survives against such challenges, not because it clings to an irrationalist stance, but because in its clinging to what seems to be poor and foolish, it ultimately proves itself to be richer and wiser than the world's alternative.

The Transcendence of God and Feminist Theology

This is not to say that the classical predestinarian tradition got the question of the God of the church right. It did not. But the reason for this does not relate to arguments concerning free will and grace or divine sovereignty and love; rather, it relates to the actual content of the biblical narrative of the election of the people of God. We will need to explore the sense of this claim in what follows.

The classical position was closer to the heart of the matter than are the many varieties of contemporary theology that deny the sovereignty of grace and the transcendence of God altogether, and with it any meaningful sense of the priority of divine grace in the Christian faith. The position represented by Spong in contemporary Anglicanism is certainly one of these, but it is by no means the best known, nor by any means the most important. That distinction unquestionably belongs to feminist theology, which, as an extremely widespread movement, has been far more influential. There are so many varieties of feminist theology that it is difficult to generalize about it; but there is one common, central theological claim made in feminist Christian thought that we need to examine. This is the claim that the image of God as a sovereign being standing over against the creature is of questionable value. To quote one writer, the doctrine of God as a sovereign being is purely "a legacy of hierarchical and stereotypically 'male' understandings of power," and as such, it needs to be replaced.[24] In short, the problem is "the patriarchy."

Underlying this striking theological claim stands a broad-brush narrative account of human history that is widely told in feminist accounts of religion and in feminist studies generally. According to this account, there was a time in ancient human history when the reproductive role of women in the creation and preservation of society — and thus the centrality of women to society itself — was symbolized by and ritualized in a strongly matriarchal strand in human religion.[25] In this religious culture, the goddess figure flourished, serving as a representation or symbolic projection of female social power and, conversely, serving to legitimate the central place of women and of female sexuality in the social order. The main archaeological evidence cited for this is the profusion of female deities from archaic religions of the Neolithic and Chalcolithic periods, figurines that are typically naked and pregnant, with prominent breasts and vulva exposed, squatting in the birthing position.

What brought about the demise of this type of religion is disputed, but it is a broadly accepted theory that a shift to a radically new kind of religion occurred in a remarkable phase of human history. A number of scholars working in the area of the history of religions, and particularly comparative religion, speak of an "Axial Age" in human history, a pivotal point that took place in the middle centuries of the first millennium BCE, and marked a decisive break with the older fertility religions.[26] The shaping of virtually all

24. Carol P. Christ, "Feminist theology as post-traditional thealogy," in Susan Frank Parsons, ed., *The Cambridge Companion to Feminist Theology* (Cambridge, UK: Cambridge University Press, 2002), p. 82.

25. Gerda Lerner, *The Creation of Patriarchy* (New York and Oxford: Oxford University Press, 1986).

26. The phrase itself originates with Karl Jaspers, *The Origin and Goal of History*, trans. Michael Bullock (New Haven: Yale University Press, 1953), p. 1. Accounts can be found in John Hick, *An Interpretation of Religion* (Basingstoke, UK: MacMillon Press, 1989), pp. 21-35; and Ewert Cousins, "Spirituality in Today's World," in Frank Whaling, ed., *Religion in Today's World* (Edinburgh: T&T Clark, 1987), pp. 324-29.

the great religions of subsequent world history is traced to this period: Upanishadic Hinduism, the Hebrew writing prophets, the pre-Socratic philosopher-theologians of Greek civilization, Confucius, and Siddhartha Gautama all belong to it. Of special significance in feminist analysis is the argument that all the above represent, in different cultural contexts, the same turning away from the fertility cults of the past toward a stereotypically "male" type of religion, a type that survived into the future to shape the next two and a half millennia of human history.

For our purposes, as far as the theory of the spiritual patriarchy is concerned, the great event was the development of Hebraic monotheism, which, according to the theory of the spiritual patriarchy, marks a decisive "shift in emphasis from powerful goddesses [and gods] to a single male god."[27] Not the least of the implications of this is the elimination of any role for women in cultic ritual. Whereas in ancient Mesopotamian religion, for example, female priestesses served goddesses and male priests served gods, the Hebraic religion of the one male god only had room for a male religious leadership.

The feminist claim is that from the outset, then, the new religious order that emerged from the "Axial Age," and the assumptions governing community life in which it was grounded, were male in origin and in character. The God of the Hebrews was not only a male deity; fidelity to this deity also entailed, by definition, hostility to the fertility religions of the surrounding Canaanite cultures, and thus to the older matriarchal principle. Since religion and the social order go together, the practical function of Hebraic monotheism was to exclude matriarchy and hence to privilege the male and disempower the female.

> The prolonged ideological struggle of the Hebrew tribes against the worship of the Canaanite deities and especially the persistence of a cult of the fertility-goddess Asherah . . . hardened the emphasis on male cultic leadership and the tendency towards mysogyny, which fully emerged . . . in the post-exilic period. (Lerner, p. 178)

In a range of ways that had far-reaching implications, the hegemony of the Hebraic male God served to secure the hegemony of the male members of Hebrew society. Surviving remnants of the older fertility religion were systematically purged. All associations between fertility and the sacred were

27. Lerner, *Creation of Patriarchy,* p. 144.

transferred from the female to the male: Abram's seed is blessed in Genesis, so that women (in this case Sarai/Sarah and her handmaid Hagar) are mere means — in fact, *property.*

The profound evils associated with the lot of women in human history must be recognized, and women's situation globally still requires massive efforts for it to improve. Of this there is no doubt. What is in doubt, I wish to suggest, is the link feminists have made between religious principle and the feminist cause. The detail of the theory of religious patriarchy, in particular, is something that should not escape criticism. Its implications for theological understanding and for practice in the church are utterly revolutionary, so much so that certain versions of "Christian" feminism force one to honestly judge it to be another religion altogether. The infamous "Re-imaging God" conference, held in Minneapolis in 1993 under the auspices of the World Council of Churches, is an excellent case in point: participants made much liturgical reference to uninhibited female sexuality ("nectar" between women's thighs!) and of the function of the female principle of divine Sophia in reminding the world, not of the divine wisdom of the Hebrew God, but of sensual pleasure.

No doubt most Christian women on Planet Earth would soberly dismiss a good deal of this as untheological nonsense. The underlying claim, however, is more difficult for many to resist: the persistent assertion that "patriarchal" religion is inherently committed to the idea of transcendence because of a male penchant for hierarchical models of power. For just this reason, some feminists suggest, sovereignty is the key theme of patriarchal religion: ideas of the sovereignty of God over creation, of humanity over other animals and nature, of the soul over the body, and of the male over the female belong together as stereotypically "male." Conversely, they suggest, female religion is committed to mutuality, for example, via the idea of God as companion rather than Lord, or through an ecological emphasis on the solidarity of God with creation (extending to pantheism in some feminist approaches), or in an ecclesiology in which the main female emphasis is clearly to be found either directly in, or in close proximity to, the concept of community. The implication of such ideas for the people-of-God concept are immense: rather than seeing humans standing as the people God has chosen in an act of free grace, these ideas have reconfigured the people-of-God concept in terms meant to echo and embody the feminist ideals of solidarity and social inclusion, and to reject all associations with the sin of patriarchy.

The feminist theologian Letty Russell has developed this idea in her influential *Church in the Round*, a book that uses the analogy of a family in table fellowship as a key to the theology of the church. Russell's leading idea is that of finding liberation and the dignity of full personhood in community. Arguing from the premise that the idea of the church at table is basic to the ecclesiology of the New Testament, she develops what she describes as a "round table" ecclesiology of relationship:

> The round table in itself emphasizes connection, for when we gather around we are connected, in an association or relationship with one another. Feminist ecclesiology is about relationship. It continually asks how things are connected to one another, to their context, and to justice for the oppressed. . . . And it asks how to make connections across dividing lines of religion, culture, race, class, gender, and sexual orientation so that church and world become connected as a circle of friends.[28]

More daringly, Russell (a Reformed theologian by background) goes on to make a constructive case for the rehabilitation of the doctrine of election along these lines. For example, she maintains that election is both promise and problem in the Bible because, while people are indeed chosen by God, that very quickly leads to an "exclusive" emphasis on the privileges of election rather than on its responsibilities.

> From my perspective, the problems of patriarchy and of election go together. For, as we have seen, the web of oppression always includes a paradigm of domination and subordination. In the Bible we discover over and over a cycle of deformation that is in part owing to pervasive patriarchal social structures that turn the idea of election for survival and service into election for security and superiority. This pattern is . . . a cycle in which the oppressed become oppressors. (p. 164)

To salvage from such a wreck anything of lasting value would seem to be an impossible task, but Russell does so. What the prophets ultimately show, she argues, is that the idea of election is finally the idea of God's choice of fellowship with humans out of love — and for service. It is election that grounds

---

28. Letty M. Russell, *Church in the Round* (Louisville: Westminster/John Knox Press, 1993), pp. 18-19.

the "connections across dividing lines" that are so important (p. 165). To be elected by God is to be entrusted with the obligation to do justice and to care for those in need, to reach out to the margins, and to be "an egalitarian covenant community" (citing Amos 4:1-3; 5:18-24). In the Bible, the critique of society by the prophets repeatedly breaks open the narrowness of the covenant consciousness of the dominant and powerful, making space for the cause of the lowly and the weak in the life of the whole people of God. Therefore, rather than being an impediment to the realization of a "church in the round," the doctrine of election ought to serve as a crucial means to it.

Russell's account is of interest for several reasons, not the least of which is the light it throws on the significance of the prophets as well as the clear connection it draws between the doctrine of God and the doctrine of the church. However, it is misleading to suggest that the emphasis on relationship is somehow unique to feminist theological analysis (as we shall see in some detail in a later chapter) or that male relationality is by definition morally inferior to female relationality. The fact of the matter is, as "womanist" analysis regularly claims against white "feminist" thought, women, too, can be oppressors, certain that they alone are in the right and that it is they who represent the great cause of justice and truth in the world. This is something that a good many men have known all along, and, despite all the rhetoric, women naturally know it as well. One recent British survey of the dynamics of the modern workplace, for instance, suggests that 80 percent of British working women rank *female* bosses as the worse taskmasters, while fully 73 percent prefer working for male managers.[29] Though we should not accept such statistics uncritically, they are certainly not the kinds of figures one would have been led to expect on the basis of the main strands of feminist theory — and after decades of political and ideological activism.

The most interesting critique, however, is Angela West's study *Deadly Innocence,* in which she rather reluctantly arrives at the point of having no alternative but to argue against the abstractions of feminist theory. Too many of the central themes of the movement, she argues, fail to connect with reality. For example, feminism in general, and feminist theology with it, frequently appeals to the related ideals of female embodiedness and sisterly nonviolence on the (strikingly odd) assumption that male physical and sexual abusiveness is related to a characteristically male, original-sin-like denial

29. Helen Puttick, "Working Women Sick of Super Mothers," *The Glasgow Herald,* 13 June 2003.

of embodiment. The trouble with the theory is immediately apparent to men, of course, or at least to the average man with testosterone, whose own sense of "embodiment" has never been in doubt. However, West writes of it from the standpoint of the disappointed feminist initiate:

> [S]isterhood, as we began to discover, though it is full of power and ex-hilaration in the abstract, has a way of being difficult at the level of the particular. Bodiliness was good news, yes, but why was it that there was always someBody in a group of sisters who had problems with some-Body else? These sisterly differences were not really accounted for in the theory.[30]

As West presents the case, the problem that prevents feminism from reckoning with the reality of the human dilemma is quite simply that it is naively dishonest.

The feminist theological theory, broadly speaking, is that it is men rather than women who are the archetypal sinners, for it is men, in their hierarchical and violent relationships with others and with creation, who have ruined the purity and equality of "Eden." The human dilemma, in other words, is reducible to males' resorting to sexual violence, which means nothing less than the whole pattern and history of male domination that defines the patriarchy. This, in the experience of women, is the real source of the evil in the world.

What West does is take feminism, and particularly feminist theology, to task for its fablelike account of the origins of evil and its simplistic assessment of the nature of women. In her critique she calls to mind two test cases for the theory, one a story from the Third Reich and the other from West's own personal history as a British Christian feminist in the 1970s and 1980s. The first case draws heavily on the historical work of Claudia Koonz, which demonstrates, West argues, that the idea that there is a nonviolent "herstory" suppressed beneath the weight of the violent patriarchal "history" is at best a myth and at worst a dangerous lie.[31] What Koonz shows is that women did not merely contribute to the sins of Nazism as passive onlookers, but that they contributed actively to its atrocities. While they were neither the planners nor the prime instruments of the "Final Solution," women contributed

---

30. Angela West, *Deadly Innocence* (New York: Cassell, 1995), pp. 6-7.

31. West, *Deadly Innocence*, pp. 30-32, drawing on Claudia Koonz, *Mothers in the Fatherland: Women, the Family and Nazi Politics* (London: Cape, 1987).

to the ideology that underlay it: as Gestapo informants, for example, but most decisively and ironically through their active and extensive work in the Nazi women's groups, which had millions of enthusiastic members — a grotesque parallel to the women's conscious-raising groups of West's own experience, as she describes it.

Closer to home, West dwells at some length on the story of the Women's Peace Camp at the USAF/RAF base at Greenham Common in England, where an arsenal of NATO cruise missiles was aimed at the Soviet Union in the 1980s (West, pp. 14-29). The decision to place these missiles at Greenham Common was first made at a NATO meeting in 1981, during Margaret Thatcher's years as prime minister. This was followed almost immediately by a leftist protest march on the base — in the British socialist tradition. A small-scale peace camp of men and women was established, which by early 1983 had been transformed into a "women-only space," on the explicit understanding that the cause of peace in the world is specifically the concern of women, just as the problem of war is the fault of men. Women's political activism was seen at that moment in time as having huge significance for the future of the planet, since it alone, the thinking went, could stand against the massive buildup of nuclear weaponry that took place during the Reagan presidency in the United States. West observes:

> As the peace camp established itself, it came to represent that current understanding of feminism which was also fundamental to the project of feminist theology — namely, that women were possessors of the true spiritual qualities, those qualities that were necessary for peace, the preservation of the race, and proper care of the earth and its resources. Women's "essential and unchanging nature" embodied the values of procreation, warmth and security, solidarity, nurturance and creativity. And this essential female nature was seen as a challenge and a contradiction to everything that comprised patriarchal society and its military bastion at Greenham. (p. 17)

The mass appeal of such ideas at the time is demonstrable: by 1983, as many as 30,000 women (including Angela West) from all over Western Europe had converged on the air base in solidarity to "embrace the base."

As West's narrative continues, however, we discover that all was not well in the antipatriarchy. For, though the story of the Women's Peace Camp is extraordinary and admirable — surviving as they did for years in appalling weather conditions in squalid accommodations, against the financial, legal, and occasionally physical resistance of the military is no mean feat — the fact is that the ideal it represented was deeply marred by the reality of the power struggles, bickering, and straightforward sinfulness that existed among its most committed members. Central to the Peace Camp was the idea of a separate feminist culture, based on women's special nature and experience, and not least, their superior virtue qua women. But the truth is that the community in which all of this was to be expressed, and toward which the leading lights of the feminist movement at the time directed their energies, ended in a dramatic and public failure. West notes:

> The outcome of events at Greenham Common can be read as an ironic rebuttal of the idea that women have a special, non-violent nature. For it demonstrates that all the roots of violence, anger, rage, rivalry, guilt manipulation and scapegoating — all are present in women as they are in men. . . . The insight of the Greenham women was a truly radical one — but their investment in women's innocence was a fatal flaw that ultimately undermined the radical nature of the enterprise. (pp. 60-61)

In this light, a reexamination of the feminist polemic against the sovereignty and transcendence of the "God of the church" is in order. There are fictions in all theologies, but alas, the feminist case — and the argument made in feminist theology against the idea of transcendence in particular — resonates so deeply with prevailing secular attitudes and our general cultural hostility to ideas of moral, metaphysical, or religious absolutes, that its impact has been truly massive. For example, the influential feminist systematic theologian Sallie McFague argues, in her book *Models of God,* that all views of God are to be understood to project onto a kind of religious or valuational screen particular patterns of human social life: the ancient monotheistic model of God as Lord of heaven and earth merely projected onto this screen a dualistic, male-centered understanding of worth (the power of domination) that inhibits the true human growth and responsibility of both sexes.[32] Since this social distortion is the root of classical monotheism, its ultimate religious value has to be questioned. According to McFague, only a theological "model" that speaks of the community of God and creation can overcome this harmful dualism, and can relocate us in the total scheme of

---

32. Sallie McFague, *Models of God* (Philadelphia: Fortress Press, 1987), p. 68.

things as brothers, sisters, and fellow creatures. Consequently, the cosmos in McFague's theology becomes the "body" of God, that is, God's literal *bodily* self, since only this idea can root out the old destructive dualism and dethrone the God of classical monotheism, the Lord of heaven and earth, as a patriarchal idol.

Apart from its virtually libelous condemnation of everything male, what is interesting about McFague's theology is not simply the loss of transcendence it involves, or for that matter the potential latent within it for nature worship, but also the fact that the word "God" is used here principally as a means of regulating human life, not just in the context of nature and physical existence, but in the state. What is ultimately affirmed in all talk of God, she assumes, is a particular set of values, and what the feminist doctrine of God is meant to do is to underwrite, via the positing of a new set of values, a different kind of social order from the patriarchal one assumed to exist. For the word "God," once again, does not refer to a being entirely beyond the world of time and space (the very idea of that is, it seems, an inherently male abstraction).

In the words of one commentator, "Feminist dogmatic theology has agreed with the distinctively modern declaration that the realm of human affairs, historically conceived, is the beginning and end-point of our reflection and action."[33] The finite, temporal world of life and nature is, in this sense, all that there is, and both God and talk about God necessarily belong to it as a human idea and as human words. But if this is the case, why resort to religious belief or to theology at all? Though feminist theology is far from unique in this insistence, the truth is that the impact of this kind of claim on the fabric of Christian belief cannot help but be massive once it is accepted within the church itself: it runs deliberately and consciously contrary to virtually the whole of the Christian theological tradition. What we are left with is an odd kind of antiecclesiastical and ultimately anti-Christian teaching — and the conscious deification instead of feminist values.

The radical emphasis on immanence that characterizes feminist theology is a response to what feminism claims to be the distorted turn to transcendence in patriarchal religion; but the effect is to alter the shape and deepest content of Christian confession. This is obvious in the case of the concept of God, which is made to serve a this-worldly social function on the basis of the projection theory of religion (itself a product of antireligious

---

33. Susan Frank Parsons, "Feminist theology as dogmatic theology," in Parsons, *Cambridge Companion*, p. 127.

thought). More subtly, though, the claim also cuts off the need for and the very meaningfulness of talk about Jesus Christ as the mediator between God and humanity. In other words, if God is already part of the "creaturely" order, then all need for mediation between the "creature" and the Creator is redundant: it no longer serves, nor can it be made to serve, any real purpose. Accordingly, Christology in feminist theology's hands is not simply the old theology in an inclusive language and style, as most of its rank-and-file advocates seem to suppose; rather, in its very substance it is something utterly novel. As in the theology of John Shelby Spong, the Jesus of feminist theology is no longer the mediator between God and humanity, but instead becomes the paradigm of self-actualization and of contemporary liberalism's project of social inclusiveness, according to which only the flourishing individual matters — all else is dross. In the meantime, the historic and human specificity of the title "Christ" is transformed into a general symbol in the project of social liberation.

The God of the Church

A far more interesting response, both to the problematic Augustinian inheritance in the doctrine of election and to the assault on transcendence found in so much contemporary theology, can be found in the theology of Karl Barth. Significantly, and unusually among modern theologians, Barth actually makes the doctrine of election the very cornerstone of his theology. In Barth's work, election defines not only the content of "theology" proper, through the warp and woof of the doctrine of God developed in the labyrinthine volume II of the *Church Dogmatics,* but it also determines the shape of the doctrines of creation, Christology, and church that follow. Barth is loved neither by those who maintain the classical Augustinian line on election nor (generally speaking) by theologians thinking in the feminist mode, which is all the more reason to pay careful attention to his work at this juncture.

The point of departure for Barth's treatment of election in *Church Dogmatics* II/2 is the massive treatment of the "knowledge" and "reality" of God that he had already developed in II/1. The central argument is that the Christian doctrine of God is to be constructed in obedience to the act in which God defines or determines himself to be the loving one who wills to exist in fellowship with humanity, and who thus wills the salvation of the creature. This act, or "event," has a specific name in Barth's theology: Jesus Christ. All the errors in classical or contemporary approaches to the doctrine of God, Barth argues, have their roots in the attempt somehow to go past or beyond this name in theological definition. The result of this bypassing of Jesus Christ is that it eclipses the specific identity of God as human thoughts and words intrude.

In Barth's view, this is also the fatal flaw of classical Christian approaches to the doctrine of election that conceive of election in terms of the absolute power of the divine will, as it is abstractly conceived by humans, rather than concretely in terms of the actual event in which God makes that will known. Hence, Barth does not deny the force of the nineteenth-century antireligious arguments taken up in so much of subsequent theology: that the "projection" of a human reality onto the heavens — and the worship of that reality — is a genuine factor in all "religion." What Barth does deny is that Christian theology necessarily falls under the spell of projection, and that it cannot avoid being an ideological mirror of the social order. In short, Christian theology need not, and indeed must not, fall prey to the dictates of human religious sentiments and thoughts. By the power of the Spirit of God, and in obedience to the Word of God, it is possible for a Christian theology to be genuinely theological, so that what the church receives and proclaims in grasping hold of the name of Jesus Christ as the one mediator between God and humanity is nothing less than the truth of God. If this is not possible, Barth insists, then no Christian theology is possible at all.

The general shape of the Barthian position, its hostility to the siren songs of natural theology, and the corresponding turn it makes toward revelation are so well known that there is no need for me to belabor the point here. It flows from this general insight; but the richer theological implications of the argument are not so well known. These appear in the detail and depth of the Barthian treatment of the doctrine of God, which contrasts very sharply with the relative barrenness and lack of content found in corresponding classical treatments of the doctrine of God, or for that matter in such treatments as appear in the liberal tradition and its many varieties of contemporary adaptation.

Of special significance in Barth's theology is the idea that the triune God is knowable, for he has made known in Jesus Christ his own intrinsic knowability, opening up to the creature the possibility of a participation in the self-knowledge of the Father and the Son in the unity of the Spirit. This basic conviction, on the basis of which Barth works from beginning to end, issues in a range of startling reinterpretations of traditional themes. For example, God's omnipresence, which is usually treated in Christian thought in a technical, negative way as God's "non-spatiality," Barth interprets to strikingly different effect in *Church Dogmatics* II/1, where he argues instead that what makes the omnipresence of God conceivable is not the human negation of the finite but a *positive* theological reality. Barth argues that God necessarily possesses his own primordial space in the eternal fact of the "togetherness" of the Father, Son, and Holy Spirit. It is because of this strictly theological spatiality, he maintains, that God is also able to be present or together with the creation.[34]

Such innovations appear with frequency in the theology of Karl Barth, and as I have said, they lend a new depth of content to his theology at every turn. A similar point can be made with respect to the doctrine of election, which Barth ultimately develops in thousands of pages of theological exploration and argument. In fact, election requires so much development, in Barth's view, because it is "the sum of the Gospel" inasmuch as it bears full witness to the "eternal, free and unchanging grace" of God as something rooted in the very being of God.[35] God is not, as in classical accounts of election, known first of all to be omnipotent and then to be the electing God by way of logical deduction. In Barth's theology, the argument actually goes the other way around: it is only as the electing one that God is also omnipotent. Thus election, rather than omnipotence, defines the being of God (p. 45).

For Barth, there is no such thing as a general omnipotence into which the idea of election must be fitted as into an empty pigeonhole; instead, God has determined himself, in a "primal decision" (p. 50), to have a particular identity: it is to be the God who exists in relationship with the creature, or who wills fellowship with the creature for himself. All else must be understood in the light of this *particular* act, so that the activities of creation and providence, for example, must be understood in the light of the specific event of election rather than vice versa. However, Barth again claims that, to understand this aright — indeed, to understand it at all — requires yet another conversion of theological understanding, in obedience to the Word of God:

Who . . . is the God who rules and feeds his people . . . ? If in this way we ask further concerning the one point upon which, according to

---

34. Karl Barth, *Church Dogmatics,* ed. G. W. Bromiley, T. F. Torrance et al., trans. G. W. Bromiley et al., 15 vols. (Edinburgh: T&T Clark, 1936-1977), 2:1, pp. 440-90.

35. Barth, *Church Dogmatics,* II/2, p. 3 and passim.

Scripture, our attention and thoughts should and must be concentrated, then from first to last the Bible directs us to the name of Jesus Christ. It is in this name that we discern the divine decision in favour of the movement towards this people. . . . (p. 53)

The Christocentric character of Barth's theology is often noted (if seldom understood), but it is here that its import and impact appear most clearly in his thought. As we have seen, the classic account of election concentrates attention on a very different point, namely, the inability of humans to attain salvation because the weight of sin against which they struggle proves impossible to overcome. Being prisoners of their own sinful nature, they must rely utterly on grace — or else fall. In Barth's Christocentric account of election, however, there is quite literally none of this. Instead, he presents Jesus Christ himself as both the electing God and the elect man (pp. 94-194). In an adaptation of the two-natures doctrine of classical Christology, Barth maintains first of all that the "true God of true God" made known in the incarnate one, Jesus Christ, is none other than the God who chooses sinful humanity for participation in his own glory. He is "God with us," the one who does not forsake us but who comes to us in love. The one who does this is the "true God," and the true God is none other than the one who does this. Secondly, on the other side, Jesus Christ is the elect man, the faithful covenant partner of God, who is obedient to God in the "answer" of his human steadfastness, even to the death of the cross, and who is then exalted to fellowship with God in his resurrection.

Barth's approach to election thus issues in a very different account of the significance of the story of salvation than is found in the Augustinian and Calvinist traditions of predestinarian theology. His account of God does not allow for the distant, angry image of God found in the older theologies, nor does his account of elect humanity allow for the image of a lost group who are, by nature, corrupt beyond measure and pitiful in the extreme. Instead, God is love, and the humanity that is chosen, justified, and sanctified in Jesus Christ is faithful; this is the gospel as it is made known in the election of Jesus Christ, the electing God and the elect man. Although there is in Barth's treatment an emphasis on God's rejection of the paradox of sinful humanity, even this rejection he understands within the fundamental framework of God's choice of fellowship with humanity, so that there is, in the final analysis, no room in Barth's theology for anything other than grace.

Barth's account of election also has an ecclesiological dimension, and this is of fundamental significance in Barth's overall dogmatics. Further-more, a great strength of the Barthian approach is that it is able to handle the biblical theme of the "people of God" in a way that, unlike the classical ac-count, does not have the effect of distorting the main course of election in the biblical witness. We have seen that the problem in traditional accounts is that attention is concentrated on the individual who is called to faith and obedience, whereas the focus in Scripture is on the election of Israel and the genesis of the church as the people of God, brought about in the context of the gentile mission. These biblical themes are much more adequately inte-grated into the overall approach to the doctrine of election found in Barth's theology than they are in Augustinian theology.

I will more fully examine Barthian theology insofar as it relates to ecclesiology in the following chapter. For the present, what is of interest is the response Barth's theology provides to the assault of feminist theology on divine sovereignty. Barth is himself a critic of the classical theory, but his cri-tique of the classical approach does not have the effect of abandoning the notion of transcendence altogether in favor of a thoroughgoing humanism or a purely immanent and this-worldly God. Like feminist theology, Barthian thought maintains the community of God and creation; but Barth maintains that such a community is possible, not because God is not sover-eign, but precisely because he is. God's true "Godness," for Barth, appears in God's capacity to be present with and in the creature, which is, in short, grounded in God's true divinity. Transcendence is thus not to be conceived as a kind of metaphysical prison that isolates God from the world; rather, it is that divine *freedom* that alone enables God to reach out in love to the world in Jesus Christ. For God to become weak and little in the baby at Beth-lehem, or on the cross of Golgotha, Barth understands to be the true realiza-tion of divine power; transcendence does not mean isolation. God does not cease to be other than the world even while becoming subject to creaturely finitude.

The feminist claim has been that the very concept of divine transcen-dence is a projection of the stereotypical male models of power, and thus a creation of the patriarchy. On the basis of Barth's analysis, one might well re-ply, "If only it were so!" What wonderful creatures men would then be! To turn the argument around, if the feminists were correct in their adaptation of the projection theory to the patriarchy, then what Barth's theology would show is that "patriarchal" power can be humble, self-giving, and of astonish-ing beauty — quite the opposite of the feminist claim made. But this is to approach the whole question from a false starting point, from the human reality rather than from the standpoint of the reality of God as revealed in Christ. For Barth, the transcendence of God can only be known and understood in the act or event in which the deity of God consists, that is, in election. Therefore, rather than measuring God against social models of power, all expressions of power at the social level are to be measured against that divine norm.

What this entails ecclesiologically is almost as revolutionary as what it entails for "theology" or the doctrine of God proper. Whereas much of the church behaves as if its life were the point, Barth's doctrine of election ultimately allows us to see the existence of the church very differently. The reason the church exists is solely because there is a turning toward the creature that takes place in the very being of God, and not because there has been any such turning in the being of the world.[36] This is consistent with the rationale given for the existence of the people of God in general in Scripture: the God known in Christian revelation is the God who does not will to be without a people; who chooses not to exist in isolation from the creature; who, being in himself love, in the movement toward what comes into existence outside his own being, stands in a relationship of love with it. This love of God for the creature is not something secondary, but defines the being of God itself. Thus there is, in a manner of speaking, no God who exists without the people of God, and this, in the final analysis, is why there is a church. The church exists, quite simply, because there is a God, a God who is precisely the God of election.

36. John Webster has written an ecclesiological reflection on the doctrine of election that proceeds along these lines; see John Webster, "'The Visible Attests the Invisible,'" in Mark Husbands and Daniel J. Treier, eds., *The Community of the Word* (Downers Grove, IL: InterVarsity Press; Leicester: Apollos, 2005), pp. 104-5.

CHAPTER 3

The Body of Christ

The idea that the church is the body of Christ is among the most familiar of all ecclesiological claims. It is found repeatedly in Scripture, is regularly liturgized, and tends to be a favorite theme in catechetical settings with young people and adults alike. However, the idea that the church is the body of Christ is clearly subject to a variety of interpretations. At one end of the theological spectrum, the usage is purely metaphorical: the church is Christ's body in the sense that Jesus himself, as the ascended Lord, needs us as his "hands" and "feet" to continue his mission in the world. At the popular level, and especially in the latter half of the twentieth century, this idea has been adapted in such a way as to challenge the clericalism of the major church traditions and to affirm the baptismal ministries of the laity. It is also common to find the idea used in a rhetorical way to reinforce the idea that the church, as Christ's body, is a sphere of mutuality and unity: like the hands and feet of the physical body, the hands and feet of the body of Christ need one another if the church as a social organism is to function as it should.

At the opposite extreme from this metaphorical use of the body-of-Christ idea stands the theological theory that the church is the body of Christ in a realistic sense, as a "prolongation" or "extension" of the incarnation. In this view, which has been adopted by prominent representatives of a number of Christian traditions, the assumption of human nature effected in the incarnation during Jesus' earthly life has been extended, with the resurrection and ascension, to the social being of humankind, and the principal (but not necessarily exclusive) locus and agent of the resulting transformation is the church.[1] This view is frequently associated with the idea of the *totus Christus,* and its point is that Christians are not just placed in an external relationship to Christ, but they have been so engrafted into Christ by the power of the Spirit, or nuptially united with Christ by grace, that they are now Christ's own bodily members, bone of his bone and flesh of his flesh. Thus Jesus Christ is, in the strictest possible sense, not simply the head of the body (in which case we would be at a distance from him), but is himself *both head and body,* so that the church, together with its teaching, sacraments, and members, belong strictly to the doctrine of the "whole Christ."

Therefore, how we are precisely to interpret such language is a major problem. On the one hand, it is clear that talk of the church as the body of Christ represents something more than some of the other metaphors encountered in ecclesiology, such as the Holy Spirit sitting on the church like a hen on her eggs, cherishing her chicks-to-be.[2] On the other hand, allowing the words to be anything beyond metaphorical would seem to risk a confusion of Christ's person with those who come to him for salvation. To address the question requires not so much that we search for a linguistic theory to account for the use of the body of Christ in Christian discourse as that we grasp what the relationship between Christ and the church might be, since that is what Paul seems to refer to in his body of Christ figure.

The same theological questions are opened up when the problem of the eucharistic elements as the body and blood of Christ are introduced into the discussion: Are the risen and ascended body of Christ, the ecclesiastical body, and the eucharistic body of Christ one and the same, by way of a strict metaphysical identity of some sort, or should we take another approach? Augustine is often read as if he thought so, as in the following oft-cited sermon fragment:

> If you are the body of Christ and his members, then it is *your* sacrament that is set on the table of the Lord; and it is *your* sacrament that you receive. To what you *are* you respond, "Amen," and by responding

1. This view is found in the theology of Emile Mersch, e.g., in his *Theology of the Mystical Body,* trans. Cyril Vollert (St. Louis: B. Herder Book Co., 1952), pp. 197ff.; but it is also found in Anglican sources such as Oliver Quick, *The Christian Sacraments* (London: Nisbet, 1928), p. 123; and even in William Temple, *Christ in His Church* (London: Macmillan, 1925), p. 8.

2. From a sermon by the English divine J. Bradford, cited in Geddes MacGregor, *Corpus Christi* (London: Macmillan, 1959), p. 170.

thus you assent to the truth. For you hear the words, "the body of Christ," and you respond, "Amen." Therefore be a member of the body of Christ that your "Amen" may be true.[3]

It is difficult to see how this could be woven through the fabric of a whole theology; indeed, Augustine's use of language here seems rather more akin to the "hen brooding over her eggs" variety than it does to any strict use of concepts. Augustine certainly could not have *merely* meant to suggest that we receive ourselves in the Eucharist! Elsewhere we can see the point he presumably wished to make, but expressed more carefully: what is communicated with the body of Christ in the Eucharist is the spirit of Christ, from which the ecclesiastical body of Christ lives.[4] In this sense, it could be said that "our" sacrament is what is set on the table.

As in many ecclesiological questions, the issues at stake in talk about the body of Christ cannot easily be tackled on purely ecclesiological grounds, because the truth is that the doctrine of the church concentrates in itself a range of more basic theological assumptions. In this case, in fact, the primary issue is not so much what the *church* is as the body of Christ, or what Christians are as members of the church, but who the *Christ* is whose "body" the church is said to be, and whose body and blood are given in the Eucharist. Therefore, our treatment will eventually need to raise such questions. But first we turn to the question and quest of the "historical Jesus" and the problem of ecclesiology, and only then to the Pauline idea of the "body."

The "Jesus of History" and the Foundation of the Church

The question about the relationship of the historical Jesus to the Christian church of subsequent centuries, and the difficulties this question presents historically and theologically, has been a major theme in modern theological studies. Historical-critical New Testament scholarship has for more than two centuries shown a marked tendency to insist that the "Jesus of history" can only be known when approached by way of the science of history; ac-

3. Augustine, *Sermo* 272 [my trans.], ed. J.-P. Migne, *Patrologiae Cursus Completus: Series Latina* (Paris, 1878-1890), vol. 38, col. 1247 (hereafter *PL*).

4. Augustine, *In ev. Ioh.*, 26.13, *Tractates on the Gospel of John 11-27*, trans. John Rettig (Washington, DC: Catholic University of America Press, 1988), pp. 270-71.

cordingly, it has sought as a matter of methodological principle to resist the constraints imposed from the side of dogmatic theology and ecclesiastical tradition. Thus the whole of the historical-critical method of biblical scholarship implicitly presupposes the claim that the needs of religious faith as defined in Christian history effectively corrupt the memory of the historical Jesus within the believing community. Hence there is a gulf in much existing scholarship between historical-critical science and the content of faith.

On this reading of the problem of Christ and the church, Christology has been a product of ecclesiology rather than ecclesiology being a function of Christology. That is, it is the believing community that has really been central, and it has constructed an image of Jesus that fits with the demands of its faith. From the standpoint of historical scholarship, however, this faith has usually been claimed to have been a distorting influence on our understanding of the "real" Jesus. It will not only be necessary, but it will also be advantageous, for us to face this issue squarely, for the challenge from historical-critical scholarship has much to teach us about the character of ecclesiology and Christology alike. For the moment, however, we need to clarify the problem further.

In its most memorable formulation, the challenge to ecclesiology presented by historical-critical accounts of Jesus appeared in the context of Roman Catholicism early in the twentieth century in the work of Alfred Loisy (1857-1940). Loisy was a French priest — but also a modernist — who sought escape from and reform of the barren scholasticism of the time. According to Loisy's famous formulation, "Jesus foretold the kingdom, and it was the Church that came."[5] By this, Loisy meant to say merely that the church did not emerge fully developed in institutional form from the life and ministry of Jesus; instead, its structures developed gradually and organically over time. Loisy's view was that it was as such that these structures needed to be understood, and that is was only as such that they could, in principle, be legitimated. Eventually, of course, the ecclesiastical assumptions of the period would crumble under the assaults of Loisy's theological successors. However, in the case of Loisy himself, the statement in question constituted a major piece of evidence in his own excommunication, which occurred early in 1908.

---

5. Alfred Loisy, *The Gospel and the Church*, trans. Christopher Home (New York: Charles Scribner's Sons, 1912), p. 166. Originally published as *l'Évangile et l'Église* (Paris: Picard, 1902). Concerning Loisy, see Harvey Hill, *The Politics of Modernism* (Washington, DC: Catholic University of America Press, 2002).

The point Loisy was trying to make may seem to be a trivial one to us, but the response of the institution to his challenge was to resort to public anathematization. The Dogmatic Constitution on the Church of Christ from Vatican I, *Pastor Aeternus* (1870), had defined the church as instituted by Christ himself in the days of his earthly life, complete with a hierarchical priesthood and an episcopate united under St. Peter as its undisputed head. This was, of course, also the document that defined the infallible magisterial authority of the pope:

> [W]e teach and define as a divinely revealed dogma that when the Roman pontiff speaks *ex cathedra,* that is, when, in the exercise of his office as shepherd and teacher of all Christians, in virtue of his supreme apostolic authority, he defines a doctrine concerning faith or morals to be held by the whole church, he possesses, by the divine assistance promised to him in blessed Peter, that infallibility which the divine Redeemer willed his church to enjoy in defining doctrine concerning faith or morals. Therefore, such definitions of the Roman pontiff are of themselves, and not by the consent of the church, irreformable.[6]

This was hardly a document showing a ready willingness to compromise with the world, and its unyieldingness extended to the insistence that such Roman primacy has been "immediately and directly" promised to Peter and his successors, and conferred on him by the Lord Jesus Christ (chap. 1).

What is still ever so slightly ambiguous in the teaching of Vatican I is whether this "immediate" gift of primacy to Peter in the institution of the church took place all at once, or over a period of time. Loisy, wishing to exploit this ambiguity in an age of acute historical awareness, argued that the Lord might have conferred it over time: Jesus anticipated the kingdom, but the church, after all, did come. This possibility was rejected along with Loisy's condemnation. Indeed, the Roman Catholic Church's ultimate rejection of modernism (as seen, for example, in the decree of Pius X, *Lamentabili* [1907]) would include a blanket condemnation of all the most basic things for which Loisy stood. Indeed, *Lamentabili* essentially amounted to a syllabus of condemned propositions drawn from Loisy's works. This would be followed by further explicit statements that equated modernism with her-

6. Vatican I, Dogmatic Constitution on the Church of Christ, ch. 4, in Norman P. Tanner, ed., *Decrees of the Ecumenical Councils,* 2 vols. (Washington, DC: Georgetown University Press, 1990), 2: 816.

esy.[7] For two generations, in fact, the entire body of the Roman Catholic clergy globally was technically governed by an oath introduced in 1910 under Pius X, which bound them to reject the teachings of modernism.[8] Since Vatican II, of course, this kind of reaction to modern scholarship has been much rarer in the Roman tradition, but that is not my point at present. Suffice it to say, for the moment, that Loisy represents for us the wedge that has been driven in scholarship between historical-critical study of Jesus and the church, especially in biblical scholarship, a wedge that continues to split the two apart to this day.[9]

In this matter, all the available historical research confirms at least the general thrust of Loisy's own case, not to mention the fact that classical Protestantism had also insisted all along on something very similar on the basis of the biblical sources (in fact, "Protestantism" was one of the charges leveled against Loisy). In other words, Jesus himself did not "found" the church in precisely the sense that some theology would (even still) wish to claim. One representative reconstruction is that of Joachim Jeremias, who, though writing more than half a century after Loisy, maintained essentially the same view, though his conclusions were drawn on the basis of a much richer knowledge of the history of the period in question than was available to Loisy. Jeremias locates the self-understanding of the earliest community in connection with the tradition of the "remnant" of the people of God within first-century Judaism.[10] As we saw in chapter 2, though the word "church" is seldom found on the lips of Jesus in the synoptic Gospels, there is in fact a good deal of the teaching of Jesus that pertains to the gathering of the people of God for salvation, and to this generic notion of the remnant. Jesus speaks of them as a flock, as wedding guests, as a harvest of grain, or as fish gathered in a net, in each case differentiating the few from the many who surround them. In the Last Supper narrative, they are seen as participants in a new covenant, a new covenant that, following Jesus' passion, is taken to ground the existence of the group of disciples on into the era of the church.

7. Hill, *Politics of Modernism*, pp. 193-200.

8. See the documents in J. Neuner and J. Dupuis, eds., *The Christian Faith in the Doctrinal Documents of the Catholic Church*, rev. ed. (New York: Alba House, 1982), pp. 48-51, 226-31, 235-36.

9. A useful survey can be found in Gerd Theissen and Annette Merz, *The Historical Jesus*, trans. John Bowden (Minneapolis: Fortress, 1998), pp. 185-239.

10. Joachim Jeremias, *New Testament Theology*, trans. John Bowden (London: SCM Press, 1971), Part I, pp. 167-78.

The attempt to gather together and to renew the people of God was not in itself unique in its time. The theme was an ancient one in Judaism, and it was, moreover, a commonplace of Jesus' own religious culture. Thus the Pharisees, for example, presented themselves as the true community of God, as did the Essenes of whom we read in Philo and Josephus, and (assuming that they are not to be identified straightforwardly with the latter), so did the Qumran community. But what is distinctive of the community of Jesus is that it radically reinterprets the older theology of the "remnant" found in these other movements. As Jeremias presents the case, rather than assuming that only those who separate themselves religiously from what is "unclean" will be saved, Jesus opens the doors of the people of God even to notorious sinners, making his an all-embracing community of "boundless grace."

Here, it should be said, Jeremias's moralism trumps his exegesis: no community can be an "all-embracing remnant" any more than a geometric figure can be a square circle. However, this much at least is known: a community surrounding Jesus is present from the beginning. As we have seen, there is also evidence that Jesus himself provided regulations to govern the collective life of his followers. This is clearly relevant to the question of Jesus' own "ecclesiology," though it is equally clear that saying it is not admitting with Vatican I that the full-blown structures of the church of subsequent centuries must be recognized in what we know of the earliest community of the disciples of Jesus. Rather, these emerged slowly over time and were subject to regional variation as well as historical and theological development.[11] However, it is also clear that the extent and importance of this diversity can be unfairly exaggerated, and that many of the structures of later church order can be traced to "primal" forms in which they appeared in the New Testament period and in the time of the early church.[12] This is not to say that every feature of these later structures can be legitimated. For example, according to the Gospel of Matthew, Jesus warned his followers against an undue recognition of earthly religious authority. Among his followers, none was to be called "father," because the community had only one Father in heaven; even more radically, perhaps, none among them was to be called "teacher"

11. Useful overviews of the early developments can be found in Eduard Schweizer, *Church Order in the New Testament* (London: SCM Press, 1961), and Colin Bulley, *The Priesthood of Some Believers* (Carlisle, UK: Paternoster, 2000).

12. Aidan Nichols, *Holy Order* (Dublin: Veritas, 1990), provides a vigorous and intelligent defense of this more traditional posture.

(*rabbi*), for they were all brothers and sisters who have only one teacher (Matt. 23:8-10). Yet some *are* called "father" and "teacher" in later years, while others are not, and the distinctions thus drawn cause one to wonder whatever happened to the words of Jesus in the church.

Thus the earliest community of Jesus appears, like Jesus himself, to be characterized by a certain egalitarianism and critical of existing patterns of life, particularly as found within the organized religion of the time, though also as found in the structures of society generally (e.g., with respect to wealth). Jesus and his disciples stand in opposition to a variety of "institutional" features of contemporary Judaism: scribes, Pharisees, Sadducees, and the official temple priesthood were all subject to his criticism. Furthermore, the disciples themselves were apparently called to an ascetic renunciation of property and family in the service of Jesus (e.g., Mark. 10:28ff.), seemingly joining him in becoming itinerant preachers of the kingdom and even charismatic miracle workers. While there may have been a precedent for this kind of activity among the disciples of John the Baptist, such a religious stance was obviously not mainstream, nor was the movement surrounding Jesus during his lifetime obviously of a kind that could readily be institutionalized. Certainly, such evidence as we have of a pattern of community life does not yet amount to an ecclesiology — this has yet to come — and far less does it amount to the foundations of a church that revels in its social privileges.

On this view, then, Jesus did not provide a ready-made blueprint for church life that the apostles themselves and the church in subsequent generations could simply reiterate, and in which the institutions of the patristic, medieval, or modern church could be immediately recognized. The position of Vatican I on the institution of a detailed form of ecclesiastical government by Jesus himself simply cannot be defended. Though it seems that Jesus did envision that certain communal patterns of life should obtain in his community, including conceivably some kind of special role for Peter, these were probably short-term and provisional in his view, for Jesus' expectation was evidently that the kingdom of God was about to come. Of course, it did not come. Instead, as Loisy reminds us, there developed over time the massive ecclesiastical system of Christian history, much of which, particularly in its grasp of power and wealth, bears only a tangential relationship to what we are able to say on the basis of a methodical historical study of the figure of Jesus himself: "Jesus foretold the kingdom, and it was the Church that came."

It is clear that this argument is destructive of a certain kind of ecclesiological concern, of the kind that seeks to claim an immediate authority of the Lord for an existing, comprehensive form of church order, and that consequently tends to see its maintenance as a basic task of faith, of such importance that the church itself would fall without it. The fact is that no such immediate authority for a specific pattern of ecclesiastical order can be established on the basis of what we know of Jesus. This argument is not, however, something destructive of ecclesiology *as such;* indeed, from one point of view, the possibilities that the criticism opens up amount to a tremendous liberation for the church and for the theology of the church. What Loisy, Jeremias, and others like them suggest is that the whole history deriving from Jesus, and embracing many more than Jesus himself and his earliest followers, has to be taken as the real source of the institutional structures that came to exist in the church of subsequent centuries. This entails that, while our structures are necessary, they need not be and cannot be either uniform or absolute, given the varied cultural and historical circumstances in which the church has had its existence. Above all, in their present form they are not strictly dominical, nor can they be, to that extent at least, sacrosanct. For they derive not simply from Jesus' institution, but from the long process of interpretation, application, and negotiation that constitutes the history of Christianity. The ultimate result is that such structures must also be, by nature, something changeable.

Thus the criticism made from the standpoint of historical study effectively clears away much of what is especially problematic in ecclesiology. In particular, it allows us to say and do something new rather than merely repeating what has been said and done in the past. This is a helpful point of departure, for there is nothing that makes the dawning of new light more difficult than the certainty that it is not needed.

At this point, we may introduce a more general Christological consideration, in the light of which it is far from obvious that the doctrine of the church requires the church to have been fully instituted by the figure of the "historical Jesus," or, at any rate, by the kind of institution that could ever be demonstrated on the basis of historical study. The attempt to show historically that Jesus, in "founding" the church, envisioned anything like the full-blown structures of subsequent centuries actually makes a basic Christological — as well as an ecclesiological — error.

At this point we can see the abiding importance of modern Christology; for, despite all its many weaknesses, modern Christology insists on something of massive importance: the genuine humanity of Jesus of Nazareth. Quite apart from what, in the terms of New Testament Christology and classical Christology, must be said of his divine nature, Jesus' human nature is to be fully and unreservedly affirmed. This was, of course, formally accepted in the ancient church. The rejection of the Docetic tendencies of the Gnostics in the second century, according to which Jesus only seemed human; the anathematizing of Apollinaris in the fourth century, and with him the rejection of the idea that Christ had a human body but no human mind; the definition of the Council of Chalcedon (451 CE) that the Lord Jesus Christ is "of one substance with us as regards his humanity"; the ensuing monothelite controversy and its resolution at Constantinople III (680-681 CE), when the integrity of the two "natural" wills of Christ, divine and human, was accepted — all this shows that the intention of the ancient church was to defend the authenticity of Christ's humanity.

What the church recognized was that it is because of Christ's humanity, which he shares with us and into which we are incorporated in his "body," the church, that we come to salvation. Thus, in the document that arguably contains the "highest" Christology in the New Testament, we also find the "lowest": "[He] has to become like his brothers and sisters in every respect, so that he might be a merciful and faithful high priest in the service of God, to make a sacrifice of atonement for the sins of the people" (Heb. 2:17).

What is not at all clear in classical Christology, however, is that the reality of Jesus' humanity is adequately understood. It is not only the consistent "metaphysical bias" toward divinity over against humanity (of which John Macquarrie has written extensively) that is the problem.[13] The problem is also that, even where its authenticity is acknowledged, the humanity of Christ is conceived of in a relatively ahistorical way. *That* Jesus was born at a certain time in history and so forth is of course acknowledged, but what is not acknowledged is that this "certain time in history" also made him the man he was. We understand ourselves as products of history: whether through cosmic and biological evolution, culture, or psychological development, we *come* to be. The ancients, on the other hand, appear to be content for the most part to assume that to be human is to possess a human nature, or a human nature of a particular kind (male, Greek, Roman, etc.). In the case of the ancient church, such an understanding of human nature in gen-

---

13. John Macquarrie, *Jesus Christ in Modern Thought* (London: SCM Press; Philadelphia: Trinity Press International, 1990), pp. 339ff.

eral issued in a Christology according to which, to be human, all Jesus Christ
as the incarnate Son of God needed was the possession of a human nature —
as that static essence common to all humans.

The weakness of the resulting Christology appears regularly in the tradition. R. P. C. Hanson, after an exhaustive study, speaks of the Christology of
as great a figure as Athanasius in the development of Christology in the following terms:

> [Christ] made no moral decisions; he could not exercise faith nor ex-
> perience temptation, the example which he gave was one of divine, not
> human, behaviour, or, to be quite exact, not of a man but of a divine
> Being acting in the "space-suit" of human flesh.[14]

These are, of course, the words of a critic, but there is some substance to the
accusation. It is also true that the defects of this kind of Christological approach were ameliorated in later life by Athanasius's *Tomus ad Antiochenos,*
once he had come to see the Antiochene light, as it were, and Athanasius's
Christological shortcomings were much more fully transcended by the later
debates of classical Christology. The trouble is, however, that a formal recognition of the reality of Christ's human nature is not the same as a material
recognition. In short, it is one thing to say as a matter of principle that he
was fully human and quite another to "flesh this out" in a developed understanding of his person and work.

The problem reappears in the Christology of Thomas Aquinas. Thomas
operated on the basis of a penetrating understanding of the theological synthesis provided by classical Christology, and he shows something of its
greatness; but he could also not escape its influence. (The relatively dynamic
understanding of human nature in Aristotle, Thomas's great philosophical
source, might have helped had Thomas more consistently applied it to the
problem of Christ's humanity — but he did not.) For instance, Thomas
would argue that, in his human mind, Christ possessed an "infused knowledge" and a "beatific knowledge," by which he knew not only God (3a., 10, 4)
but everything made known to humans by divine revelation, and everything
that pertained to human science (3a., 11, 1).[15] Furthermore, he knew all this

---

14. R. P. C. Hanson, *The Search for the Christian Doctrine of God* (Edinburgh: T&T
Clark, 1988), p. 646.

15. Thomas Aquinas, *Summa Theologiae,* ed. and trans. T. Gilby et al., 61 vols. (London: Blackfriars, in conjunction with Eyre & Spottiswoode, 1964-1981), 3a., 9, 3.

not by experience and discursive reasoning, as we do, but by a kind of immediate intuition through its direct infusion in the mind (3a., 11, 3). To translate this into concrete terms, Jesus might have taught his disciples the elements of Newtonian physics, or how to design a nuclear reactor, since he possessed in his human mind all knowledge by infusion. Thomas does not deny that Jesus could also acquire knowledge, since to be human involves having an active intellect capable of acquiring knowledge (3a., 9, 4). Yet he is unable to say why Jesus himself should have needed any such knowledge. For example, Jesus did not need to be taught.

What is clear is that it is as such that Jesus was conceived classically to have founded the church, complete with its hierarchy and institutional structures. He did not save the world by giving the gift of technological know-how, though he might have imparted it had he wished to. The plan of salvation was different: God's way involved the gift of the church, about which Jesus possessed full knowledge, which he was thus in a position to communicate to his disciples. To paraphrase, "Jesus possessed human omniscience, and thus, from the beginning, it was the church that came."

The real problem with any such Christology, of course, is the extent to which it offends a meaningful contemporary affirmation of Christ's true humanity. A text such as Luke 2:52, "And Jesus increased in wisdom and in years, and in divine and human favor," which once caused great unease, is accepted today as naturally as the idea that Jesus needed to eat, drink, and sleep (which likewise caused much hand-wringing among ancient Christian thinkers). The recognition of the limitations of Jesus — in his knowledge, for example — has been a feature even of relatively conservative Christologies for many years.[16] What Jesus "knew" in terms of scientific insight he thus knew as all others do: in science, as in culture, he was a creature of his time. He needed to learn to count; he did not know all prime numbers. What he knew of God he grasped as all of us do — by faith and by the agency of the Spirit working within him. Yves Congar writes of the *kairoi* that mark stages in Jesus' relationship with God, and of God's communication to him: the annunciation, the baptism in the Jordan, the temptation, the passion.[17]

---

16. H. R. Mackintosh, *The Doctrine of the Person of Jesus Christ,* 2nd ed. (Edinburgh: T&T Clark, 1913), pp. 397-98.

17. Yves Congar, *The Word and the Spirit,* trans. David Smyth (London: Geoffrey Chapman; San Francisco: Harper and Row, 1986), pp. 85-100. See Gary D. Badcock, *Light of Truth and Fire of Love* (Grand Rapids: Eerdmans, 1997), pp. 145-69, for a fuller account.

To say that "God was in Christ" does not, from the standpoint represented by such claims, mean that Jesus possessed all knowledge of every event that would come to pass; rather, he grasped by faith, and across a lifetime, what it was given to him to know, that is, the "mission" that his Father had entrusted to him. This perhaps included those who would follow; but about them, we must say frankly and freely, we ourselves know vastly more than did Jesus himself.

To say this is not to embrace some radical version of subordinationist Christology, or an adoptionism, or even necessarily some version of kenotic Christological theory according to which the divine *Logos,* as Son of God, was obliged to lay aside the divine "relative" quality of omniscience as a condition of the possibility of the incarnation. Instead, it is to recognize the depth of the glory and power of the incarnation, that God's wisdom should be thus expressed in human finitude and God's power in such weakness. The depth of the "hiatus" that God entered into — and that entered into God in Jesus Christ — should not be compromised or covered over with ready answers.[18] It is part and parcel of the story of salvation, and a fundamental source of its wonder.

What this means for the doctrine of the church is that it is futile, and deeply problematic from the standpoint of Christology, to look for some immediate institution of the church by Jesus of Nazareth, or to expect that its entire fabric should have been given by the hand of the Lord himself. This is not the way of God in Jesus Christ. For in Jesus, God commits himself to human history, finitude, and all the rest — including the risk of failure. So must the church that follows in his way.

The "Body of Christ" in the New Testament

What is unquestionably of greater interest than the status of the church in the teachings of the "historical Jesus" is the relationship between the Jesus of the resurrection faith and the Jesus of the doctrine of the church. We can begin to see this by referring to the Pauline idea of the "body of Christ," which in Pauline usage is as much a pneumatological as a Christological or ecclesiological idea. In one of the key New Testament sources for the doc-

---

18. Hans Urs von Balthasar, *Mysterium Paschale,* trans. Aidan Nichols (Edinburgh: T&T Clark; Grand Rapids: Eerdmans, 1990), pp. 49-88.

trine of the church, Paul's First Epistle to the Corinthians, we find this well-known text: "You are the body of Christ and individually members of it" (1 Cor. 12:27). The immediate context of Paul's claim is that in baptism the many have been made one by virtue of their inclusion in this body — Jew and Greek, slave and free (v. 13). Whatever could be said of the Corinthians' racial background or social status previously, and hence of earlier divisions, all are now one *in the body of Christ*. Several texts reflecting a similar teaching can be found in the New Testament, particularly in the Pauline corpus.[19] The clearest parallel is found at Romans 12:4-8, where Paul develops cognate ideas: we who are many have become one body in Christ, with gifts of grace appropriately distributed so that the body can function as God intends. Beyond this, there are references to the church as the body of Christ, with Christ as its "head" (using language that goes somewhat beyond that of 1 Corinthians and Romans) in Ephesians 1:22-23 and Colossians 1:18.

It is not uncommon for the "body of Christ" texts of the New Testament to be read in such a way as to buttress the ministry of the whole membership of a local congregation. In 1 Corinthians 12, for example, every member of the body is endowed with a gift of the Spirit, who gives to one the "utterance of wisdom," to another "faith," to another "gifts of healing," and so forth (vv. 8-9). And each one has a vital part to play in the functioning of the church, with a particular dignity deriving from the function he or she serves (vv. 14-26). The text is thus a favorite among movements that try to engage all individual members of the church in their ministries, particularly where there is concern that the gifts of all have been suffocated under the weight of the church's institutional ministry. Thomas O'Meara puts it this way: "The analogy of the body rejects the idea that some charisms and ministries are essentially superior to others in the eyes of the Spirit."[20] The implication is (and this in a Roman Catholic text on the theology of ministry!) that there is no true ministerial hierarchy, for all ministries are equal in God's sight.

However, one must exercise a certain caution at this point. The more painful and ambiguous truth is that "body" language is a staple of social and

---

19. The classic studies include Ernst Käsemann, *Leib und Leib Christi* (Tübingen: Mohr, 1933); John A. T. Robinson, *The Body* (London: SCM Press, 1952); and Ernest Best, *One Body in Christ* (London: SPCK, 1955). An overview of twentieth-century discussion of the body of Christ is found in G. Yorke, *The Church as the Body of Christ in the Pauline Corpus* (Lanham, MD: University Press of America, 1991).

20. Thomas F. O'Meara, *Theology of Ministry* (New York: Paulist Press, 1999), p. 168.

political conservatism, which historically has manifested a strong tendency to maintain that the role of the natural leader and of the born inferior, for example, are part of one "body" politic, one social reality in which each has a role to play, and within which each, accordingly, is "affirmed" for what he is. This is what is assumed beneath the undoubted piety of a text like the following from the pen of the aristocratic Ambrose, writing to his sister (and referring to Luke 7:44):

> We are all one body of Christ, the Head is God, and we are the members: some perhaps as the Prophets, may be the eyes; others the teeth, as the Apostles, who have filled our hearts with the food of the Evangelical preaching. . . . They are His hands who perform good works: His belly are they who bestow the strength of nourishment on the poor: some too are his feet also, and would that I might be counted worthy to be even His heel. He then who pardons the very lowest of their sins, pours water on the feet of Christ, and while he frees only the mean, yet washes the feet of Christ Himself.[21]

This is all well and good, but what we must recognize is that in this case "body" language secures the servant's lowly status in the society, as it does the high status of the noble and the powerful. A person might wish to be the other, but alas, Ambrose complains, he is not. Thus 1 Corinthians 12, which today is broadly assumed to speak of the value of each person, can just as easily be read as a proof-text for ecclesiastical privilege. Indeed, this kind of usage of the concept of the "body" was a commonplace in Roman political thought, and this was something that Paul himself had to have known full well.[22]

What, then, does Paul mean by his talk about the church as the "body" of Christ in his Epistles? It is possible, of course, that he means it in an egalitarian sense; yet, though one might hope that he does, this is a good deal less clear than one might wish it to be. Therefore, we need to consider a number of alternatives. First of all, as I have suggested above, there is the view that we will arrive at a proper reading only when we recognize that what we have here is a solid, unambiguous instance of the metaphorical use of language,

---

21. Ambrose, *Letter* XLI, 11, in Ambrose, *The Letters of St. Ambrose* (Oxford: James Parker and Co., 1881), p. 273.

22. Raymond F. Collins, *First Corinthians* (Collegeville, MN: Liturgical Press, 1999), pp. 458ff.

according to which ideas deriving from one sphere of discourse (common-sense biological observation) have been transferred to another (discussion of the church). In this view, what is important about the Pauline "body metaphor" is the suggestion of unity in difference in the social being of the church: all are one in the sense that they are part of the one "organism," which can be likened to a physical body.[23] Though the organism is characterized by *plurality* of gifts, offices, and functions, this plurality is not incompatible with the larger unity achieved when each does his or her part. However, as always in matters metaphorical, the image must not be confused with the reality; that is, the oneness in question is metaphorical only. The members of the church are not, after all, the literal equivalents of the members of the body — hands, feet, and so on — since they do not literally share one biological life. Cut my gangrenous foot off in surgery, and it will die, whereas, if all goes well, I will not; cut me off from the church, however, and both the other members of the church and I will continue to live, and perhaps some of us would be the better for it! One cannot stretch metaphors too far without falling into elementary logical errors.

As we have also seen, there is an opposing view, according to which the body of Christ and the church are literally identical in Pauline theology. This view would hold that, following the resurrection, Paul believed that Christ's body exists, and exists truly, in the form of the church. The Anglican biblical scholar John Robinson adopted this view in his book *The Body*, a classic monograph of this genre, where he went so far as to argue that the resurrection appearance of Christ to Saul on the road to Damascus was none other than a realization that the postresurrection body of Christ was the Christian community.[24] More recently, the Lutheran theologian Robert Jenson has suggested much the same thing.[25] For Jenson, what Paul means when he speaks of the church as the body of Christ is simply that "the risen Christ as a complete living human person has a body and that the church is this body," on the grounds that to "have" a body means to be available, to be an object for others. The church is for Paul "the object in which the risen Christ is available to be found" and is thus, in this precise sense, his "body."

---

23. Yorke, *The Church as the Body*, pp. 119-24.

24. Robinson, *The Body*, p. 58.

25. Cf., e.g., Robert W. Jenson, "The church and the sacraments," in Colin Gunton, ed., *The Cambridge Companion to Christian Doctrine* (Cambridge, UK: Cambridge University Press, 1997), pp. 209-10.

Jenson's position at this point is closely related to his argument that, in a post-Copernican universe, it is meaningless to speak of Christ's resurrected body as having ascended to a "place" in the Ptolemaic universe called "heaven," or that there it is spatially related to other bodies in the physical universe. Quite apart from its theological peculiarity — "Does Jesus take little walks up there?" he quotes the Lutheran Johannes Brenz as having satirically asked the Calvinists in 1562 — the shift to the Copernican universe makes any such "location" of Christ's body in the "beyond" an absurdity.[26] Rather than seeking a "naturalistic" explanation, Jenson wishes to approach the question of Christ's postresurrection body by way of the gospel itself:

> Where is Christ's body . . . ? [T]he only body of Christ to which Paul ever actually refers is not an entity in this heaven but the Eucharist's loaf and cup and the church assembled around them.
>
> "You are the body of Christ." Paul's teaching can be exploited for the similes it enables, and thus does Paul exploit it. But the teaching itself is a proposition and not a trope. That is, "is the body of . . ." is also a proper *concept* where Paul uses it of the church and Christ. (Jenson, p. 204)

All commentators agree that there is a metaphorical element in what Paul teaches, but the question is always how far into the realm of *being* the metaphor extends. Jenson's position is apparently robustly realist: the only "body" of Christ there is, is the ecclesial one, but this ecclesial body is the "real presence" of Christ, and is presumably to be grasped in Lutheran terms as "in, with, and under" the members of the church in their hearing of the Word. For others — and they are by no means only those of a Calvinist persuasion — the phrase "body of Christ" can only mean the body over which Christ, the head of the church, rules; no strict identity can be permitted without jeopardizing Christ's human identity. In this view there is no meaningful sense in the claim that a human body, risen and ascended or not, is identical with a multitude of other human bodies. It is difficult to resist the logic of this argument. "Does Jesus go home after church and have roast beef?" might be the Calvinist riposte to Jenson.

And yet Jenson has said something important. For the doctrine of the church is in the strict sense a *resurrection* doctrine, grounded in the basic

---

26. Robert W. Jenson, *Systematic Theology*, 2 vols. (Oxford: Oxford University Press, 1997-1999), 1: 203.

conviction of Christian believers in the continuing presence and activity of the Lord Jesus Christ — and not simply in events of the past. This continuing presence and activity is something that takes place "in the Spirit." For this reason it is a matter of apparent indifference to Paul, for example, whether he writes that "the Spirit of God dwells in you," "Christ is in you," or indeed, that "the Spirit of him who raised Jesus from the dead dwells in you" (Rom. 8:9-11). Elsewhere, in what have become increasingly well-worn texts, we find the Spirit seemingly equated by Paul with the risen Lord: "the Lord is the Spirit" (2 Cor. 3:17), and "the last Adam became a life-giving spirit" (1 Cor. 15:45). In effect, there is no Christ of any interest to Paul other than this one, the risen one who is "the Lord" of the church's faith. Nor is this an exclusively Pauline preoccupation; we can readily find a similar teaching in John's Gospel: "I will ask the Father, and he will give you another Advocate, to be with you forever. This is the Spirit of truth, whom the world cannot receive. . . . I will not leave you orphaned; I am coming to you" (John 14:16-18).

Part of the problem we face here is that the theology of the resurrection has become a battleground between the theological left and right, the terms of which have tended to distort rather than illumine faith. Consequently, questions of the sense in which Scripture is authoritative, of whether literal miracles occur in time, or of the supposed "orthodoxy" of particular theologians, churches, or ecclesiastical statements have become matters of obsessive controversy. Unfortunately, the ironic result has been that the real point of discussions of the resurrection of Jesus per se has been buried.

Talk about the resurrection of Jesus, for example, is not the same as talk about the resurrection of Lazarus. Indeed, even were we to agree that both resurrections were true "events" in history, it remains true that the events themselves are entirely dissimilar. The case of Lazarus is an instance of literal, historical resurrection, so that talk about the risen Lazarus is merely talk about a resuscitated corpse — something remarkable, to be sure, but hardly of universal saving import. The assumption has to be that the postresurrection Lazarus was in principle no different from those countless individuals today who have been resuscitated in emergency rooms and on the operating tables of modern hospitals.

The resurrection of Jesus is different. Talk about the risen Jesus is talk about a glorified Jesus, whose status is transcendent and not this-worldly. The risen Jesus is a figure who, to put it in the most modest terms available, belongs as much to the divine side of the divine-human relationship as he does to the human side, since after the resurrection he was present, not at home with his friends, but at the right hand of God. To put the same point another way: what the resurrection of Jesus amounts to is the transition of Jesus from the obscurity of first-century Galilee and Judea to the status he bears in the faith of the church as the Lord and Savior of the world. It is precisely the resurrection that grounds the whole existence of the church as the place of Christ's continuing presence and activity in the power of the Spirit. To put the point in formal theological language: there is no Christology without pneumatology, and no ecclesiology without both.

Something of this is reflected in the theology of Rudolf Bultmann, which has a surprising amount in common with Jenson's theology at this point. Bultmann, of course, is well known for having spoken of the resurrection of Christ in the *faith* of the church. However, for Bultmann, the basis for this insight is the fact that the death and resurrection of Christ can have saving significance only to the extent that they do not belong merely to the past but have been appropriated by faith. This appropriation in the moment of faith is Bultmann's principal theological concern, for even if it were possible for us to demonstrate by historical method that Jesus rose from the dead, this would not make the resurrection a saving event. For this to happen, it must be something that "constantly takes place anew in the present."[27] It does so through the preaching of the church, which makes the significance of Jesus' cross something directed at the individual, who must make a decision with respect to his or her relationship to God. In the event of faith, for Bultmann, God summons me in such a way that I must make the decision to die with Christ. In this way Christ remains alive, in that he is still living and active in what takes place in the faith of the church. But there is, for Bultmann, no literal resurrection of the corpse of Jesus from Joseph's tomb.

What a position like Bultmann's can help us see is the extent to which the resurrection has to do with the relationship between Christ and the church and, derivatively, between the risen Christ and his ecclesiastical "body." On this view, the ecclesiastical body of Christ not only belongs to Christ, but it *is* Christ in some sense. From the standpoint of New Testament exegesis, the strength of this interpretation lies in its recognition that the Pauline view of the relationship between Christ and the church is more than metaphorical, or something that is merely a matter of human "perspective," but that it is real. For Paul, it is not simply the case that we have access to God because

27. Rudolf Bultmann, *Theology of the New Testament*, trans. Kendrick Grobel, 2 vols. (London: SCM Press, 1952-1955), 1: 302.

righteousness has been forensically imputed to us by an external reckoning; nor is it the case that we count ourselves reconciled to God by a mental fiction. As even Bultmann realizes, there is instead a realistic claim to participation in Christ that is truly basic to Pauline theology, such that he can speak of *our* being buried with Christ in baptism (Rom. 6:4), of *our* having been crucified with him (Rom. 6:6), and equally, of *our* new life by virtue of *our* sharing in his resurrection (Rom. 6:4-5). Our relationship with Christ, in other words, is not merely a matter of supposition or of moral imitation, but of our sharing by God's power in the eschatological events of salvation.[28]

This does not take place without the Spirit. It is highly significant that the leading Pauline "body of Christ" text, 1 Corinthians 12:27, is located in the context of a discussion that is thoroughly pneumatological. The interpretative key to understanding Paul's thought on this point is undoubtedly verse 13 of that chapter: "For in the one Spirit we were all baptized into one body," an idea that Paul then develops through the verses following. Much of the difficulty lies in recognizing the role of all that the Spirit's presence involves in the life of faith, obedience, worship, and so forth. The church as the body of Christ cannot be considered apart from this, for the ecclesiastical "body" of Christ is something that is mediated by the work of the Spirit, and that cannot exist without the Spirit. In fact, this is what Augustine suggests in his sermon cited at the beginning of this chapter: "Be a member of the body of Christ that your 'Amen' may be true."

Incarnational Ecclesiology

Therefore, the problems of ecclesiology need to be handled together with the problems of Christology, not only because a failure in Christology will distort or diminish our ecclesiology, but also because handling the two together will lend depth to our Christology. Of course, this is the problem with treatments

---

28. In Pauline theology, our participation in Christ is based not on the Platonic-Hellenistic concept of *methexis*, according to which the higher principles "inform" the lower orders of being, but rather on God's eschatological acts of salvation, according to which the resurrection and eschatological futurity has priority over the "old self" of the "flesh." However, because the Spirit is given as eschatological "down payment," the new life can be said to have already begun — though we must still await its full disclosure. For a stimulating and classic discussion of this question, see Albert Schweitzer, *The Mysticism of Paul the Apostle*, trans. W. Montgomery (London: A. & C. Black, 1931), pp. 5-25.

of the "doctrine" of the church in theological scholarship, which treatments are often content to deal with the church in practical, pastoral, or even sociological terms. In fact, such approaches predominate in much contemporary theology, and nowhere more clearly than in English-language Protestantism. On the other hand, it must be said that balanced assessments of the importance of Christology for ecclesiology from the side of dogmatic theology are also hard to find, because, unfortunately, some of those who discuss it tend to be somewhat "over-committed" to the approach in question, and thus have lost a proper sense of critical distance in their treatments of it.

The Jesuit theologian Emile Mersch, for example, sets the incarnational basis for the ecclesiological idea of the body of Christ at the absolute center of his own theological reflection. Over several decades Mersch conducted a wide-ranging analysis of patristic and medieval sources, intending all along the way to rediscover and enrich traditional Roman Catholic teaching in such a way as to renew the theology of his day. He did this in ways, and to an extent, that occasionally seem plainly ridiculous.[29] But abstracting from some of the details, we can see that Mersch wished above all else to open up a fresh perspective on the detail of Christology itself as the key to the doctrine of the church. It is unfortunate that his scholarly work on the classical sources, meticulously conducted over several decades, is widely overlooked and scarcely mentioned today.

Mersch, in fact, established something very important through his life's work, namely, that classical Christian thought grasps the problem of ecclesiology in the closest possible connection with the doctrine of Christ's human nature. That is, classical ecclesiology is developed in connection with theological reflection on the human nature assumed by the Son of God in the incarnation. In this respect, Mersch appeals particularly to the theology of Cyril of Alexandria. According to Cyril, for example, "[t]hrough one of us, the Word has taken up His abode in all of us. He dwells in all in that one temple He took for us and from us, to have us all in Himself and to reconcile all of us, in a single body, with His Father."[30] Cyril's point is that the human-

---

29. The following statement is a good example: "The doctrine of the Mystical Body has been the remedy for the principal heresies of history, as it is today for Modernism." Emile Mersch, *The Whole Christ*, trans. John R. Kelly (London: Dennis Dobson, 1939), p. 577.

30. Cyril of Alexandria, *In Ioan.*, I, 9 (cited by Mersch, *Theology of the Mystical Body*, p. 197).

ity of Christ, which he speaks of in typical Alexandrian terms in this passage as the "body" assumed, is not a single, isolated humanity that is enclosed within its own history. Rather, the humanity of Christ is a universal reality, with universal soteriological significance, precisely because of the union of human and divine natures in the person of the Son of God. That is to say, it is part and parcel of the Cyrilline theory — and ultimately of the Chalcedonian dogma — of the "hypostatic union." Mersch, like Cyril himself and the whole mature Alexandrian Christological tradition, makes a great deal of the doctrine of the *communicatio idiomata* in this context, according to which the attributes of each of the two natures of Christ can rightly be predicated of the other on the basis of this union. Thus, for instance, the Son of God is said to have suffered death on the cross (in the human nature assumed), while the human nature assumed is said to have the divine capacity to communicate to us the eternal life and energies of God. It is for this reason that Christ's humanity has the life-giving, saving status that it has in the Christian gospel. Salvation comes by union with this humanity, this "body"; thus it is not by means of what Christ *does* so much as by the sheer fact of who Christ *is*.

How this theology of the humanity of Christ, or what Mersch calls the "mystical body," relates to the doctrine of the church is the next question. For it does not appear at all obvious that only Christians, in this view, can be counted as Christ's members, or that salvation can only be found within the church. In many ways, the theology seems to imply something very different, namely, that salvation comes about merely by virtue of a person's having a human nature in common with Christ. Ultimately, salvation is grounded not in the faith or the individual, nor even in incorporation into the church in baptism per se, but, in a strict sense, in the assumption of the totality of human nature by the Son of God. Mersch himself occasionally suggests as much, speaking of a mystical union with God in Christ that involves the whole human race (p. 240). Thus he can claim, in the end, that the purpose of the church is twofold: first, "to make clear what the hypostatic union of one of the members of the race with [God] signifies for all mankind"; second, "to manifest what is involved for [God] by the fact that, in assuming a human nature, [he] took to [himself] the entire race of men" (p. 547). The most that Mersch himself can allow for by way of an ecclesiological restriction of the membership of the body of Christ, it seems, is that the union with Christ of which he speaks, and which is grounded in the incarnation, is made thematic in the proclamation, sacraments, and worship of the church in a way that obviously does not happen among those outside it, and that it is by grace more fully communicated to, and deepened in, the church by these means. Mersch's fondness for Alexandrian patristic theology is reflected in this approach, which has little time for the clear-cut distinction between Christ and Christians that is characteristic of many alternative traditions in Christian thought — including, as Mersch himself recognizes, the bulk of the Latin tradition (p. 350).

Mersch's position is also remarkably similar to that of his contemporary, Karl Barth, who likewise adopts a strongly incarnational approach to the question of salvation and speaks accordingly in his ecclesiology of the church as witness. The two are seldom spoken of in the same breath, but there are in fact very large areas of correspondence between the theologies of Mersch and Barth. There are also obvious points of difference, principally in the extent of Christological concentration found in Barth over against Mersch, on the one hand, and in Mersch's rather less generous churchmanship (i.e., his narrow Roman Catholicism), on the other. But Barth's Christology, particularly as it is represented in the doctrine of reconciliation that he develops in volume IV of *Church Dogmatics,* leads immediately and repeatedly to the affirmation that the church lives to bear witness to what is true, not for the church primarily, but for the world.[31] The church, according to Barth, is to be understood as the "provisional representation" of the justification, sanctification, and calling of *all humanity* in Jesus Christ.

Barth's development of the problem of ecclesiology in *Church Dogmatics* IV alone comprises over six hundred pages of closely argued text, and in addition there are multiple sources across the whole range of his work, including the rest of the *Church Dogmatics,* that feature ecclesiology. There is obviously no way that I can examine all of this in detail here. But a general survey would have to include at least the following central elements, corresponding to the overall thrust of the Christological argument Barth constructs as the *Church Dogmatics* unfolds. First, in a way that flows in the argument from the "journey of the Son of God into the far country" in IV/1, by which the justification of sinful humanity is accomplished, the church is called and gathered by Christ through the Holy Spirit. Second, the Spirit builds up the church, causing it to grow into Christ its head in a way corresponding to the "homecoming of the Son of Man" in IV/2, and the sanctification of all humanity in him. Third, in IV/3, Christ sends the church into the world and

---

31. Karl Barth, *Church Dogmatics,* IV/1, §62; IV/2, §§67-68; IV/3, 2, §72.

empowers it with the Spirit to be a witness to himself, in correspondence to the calling of all humanity in the prophetic office of Christ.

For our purposes, it will be enough to focus very briefly on the third of these, in which the question of the mission of the church is handled in closest proximity to questions of Christology and pneumatology. In Barth's treatment, the witness of the church to Jesus Christ in its mission is properly Christ's own self-witness in the power of the Spirit rather than an act of the church as such. What primarily takes place in the witness of the church, Barth argues, is Jesus' own confession of the church as his body. It is *Christ's* confession, his owning of the church as his, that makes the church into his body, "His own earthly-historical form of existence" (IV/3, 2, p. 681). Barth can say: "Its confession of Him gratefully follows His confession of it" (p. 791), and "the being of the community is a predicate or dimension of the being of Jesus Christ Himself" (p. 754). It is never the other way around: nothing that the church does can of itself render it the body of Christ. In the sending of the church into the world as witness, Christ permits the church, with all its flaws and foibles, to speak *his* word among the nations and to call all people to obedience, bearing witness to the covenant between God and humankind that is fulfilled in Jesus Christ, who is the beginning of all God's ways and works and the end of all human life. The church knows that humanity in Christ has not been abandoned by God, but that it is loved, and that it has been reconciled (p. 771). In light of this, it knows itself to be sent in the same direction as he was sent, "i.e., into the world, in order that it may exist, not for itself, but for the world as He did" (p. 791). This is why the church can only pray, *Veni creator Spiritus!* For it exists only as Christ does all this in the event of the calling, upbuilding, and sending of the community through the outpouring of his Spirit.

However, what separates believers from unbelievers in Barth's theology is that the Holy Spirit has awakened faith within them, so that they *know* and *confess* Jesus Christ as the second Adam, in whom God's "yes" to humankind is once and for all announced. In Christ, not only is the Lord our God, but we also are those who confess that we are his people, God's faithful covenant partners, the erring children who in Christ have returned from the far country to the fellowship of the Father's house. But it is not possible to speak of the church as uniquely related to Christ on the basis of Barth's approach, except to the extent that the church has been "quickened," or made alive, by the activity of the Holy Spirit precisely to confess the name of Jesus in the world. To speak precisely, by Barth's reckoning, the church is the provisional representation of and the explicit missionary call to what in God's grace is the purpose of every person, and indeed — as Barth daringly suggests at one point — even the whole creation: *ja des ganzen Kosmos* (p. 793).[32]

It is interesting that Barth puts such great emphasis on the idea of the body of Christ in his ecclesiology, going so far as to speak of the church as the risen Lord Jesus Christ's own earthly-historical form of existence. The relationship between the church and Christ is not just an external or metaphorical one, nor is it possible to define it as a reality only for faith. Early in the ecclesiological sections of *Church Dogmatics* IV, Barth insists that in this matter we must resist any ecclesiological Docetism, and we must reckon seriously with the idea that the earthly-historical form of existence now enjoyed by the risen Lord is one in which human, historical visibility — and with it human fallibility, sinfulness, and all the rest — is unequivocally accepted by God (IV/1, p. 653). We can thus see that, for all his antipathy toward a pure historical-critical biblical method, Barth's theology is at this point remarkably well attuned to its results, for there is no avoiding human failure, finitude, or the exigencies of history. We are also to understand the being of the church as something invisible, or else we fall into the trap of giving the institutional entity a status that it does not deserve. The church, like everything else of significance in Barth's theology, has to be understood as an "event" in which God acts. Therefore, the being of the church as the body of Christ is never something that can be reduced to a static possession of the institution. It is always subject to the freedom of God, or, to put the same point more clearly, subject to the freedom in which God is God. The implication is that we must learn to recognize the act of God *in* the earthly-historical life of the church, and not to identity the act of God *with* it. Barth argues that the papal encyclical *Mystici Corporis* contains precisely this error in that it refuses to reckon with the notion that in the church the glory of God is present only in a clay pot. That encyclical divinizes the earthly institution, particularly in its juridical aspects (p. 659).

Nevertheless, Barth's theology takes the idea of the body of Christ with total seriousness; indeed, it easily serves as the dominant biblical idea on which he draws for his ecclesiology. Barth affirms that the incarnate, crucified, risen, and ascended Lord lives at the right hand of the Father; but he rejects the idea that the risen Christ is somehow enclosed or entrapped in a

32. Barth, *Die Kirchliche Dogmatik*, Zweite Auflage (Zürich: Theologische Verlag, 1979), IV/3, 2, p. 908.

heavenly form of existence. Rather, the risen Lord *also* lives in an earthly-historical form of existence in the Christian community. It is as such that the church is constituted as his body, of which he is the head (p. 661). Barth uses the language of the *totus Christus,* head and body, to flesh out this understanding:

> [In the light of Easter] He lives — and this is now the decisive point — as the *totus Christus.* And this means that, although he lives also and primarily as the exalted Son of Man, at the right hand of the Father, in the hiddenness of God (with the life of Christians), at an inaccessible height above the world and the community, He does not only live there but lives too (in the power of His Holy Spirit poured out from there and working here) on earth and in world history, in the little communities at Thessalonica and Corinth and Philippi, in Galatia and at Rome. He does not live primarily in their knowledge and faith and prayer and confession, or in their Christian being, but as the place in which all this can and may and must and will happen, in which they are Christians; as the air which they breathe, the ground on which they stand and walk. As we are told [in John 15: 4f.], they have no being or life apart from Him. . . . He *is* the vine, and they *are* the branches. (IV/2, pp. 658-59)

If asked to explain how it could be that the humanity of Jesus can remain intact while being both in heaven, at the right hand of the Father, and on earth in this peculiar fashion, Barth might well respond that Christian theology must allow the revelation itself to determine our thought about it, instead of insisting that available philosophical thought-forms be permitted to determine the content of the revelation. In other words, for Barth, what is distinctive about Christ's authentic risen humanity is precisely that it *can* be such, while the confession of the risen Jesus Christ as Lord presupposes just this content.

Barth draws his major pieces of supporting evidence at this point from Scripture, particularly from the Pauline Epistles (IV/1, pp. 662-68). He draws attention to texts such as those in Romans 6 and 7, which speak of the representative office of Christ in his death and resurrection. Strikingly, he writes, "It was the body of everyman which became a corpse in Him and was buried as a corpse with Him" (pp. 663-64). This approach is in keeping with Barth's entire theology, in which the doctrine of the incarnation — and Christ's representative work — plays such a prominent role. For Barth, the whole point of the gracious act of God in Jesus Christ is that it establishes a new humanity for all on the basis of Jesus Christ's new humanity, so that Jesus is who he is supremely in his being with and for others, as the one chosen and sent by God to be the Savior of the world and the head of the church. To fail to recognize Jesus' true being as such is to fail to recognize him at all.

The Resurrection, the Spirit, and the Church

We have seen that for all their differences, Mersch and Barth are alike in maintaining that the "total Christ" includes both head and members of the body, the church. This view rests on a strongly incarnational approach to theology generally, the cost of which, perhaps, is that on the basis of both theologies, one actually has some difficulty in specifying in what sense the church's relationship to Christ can differ from the world's. The reason for this is that, if Christ is the Son of God incarnate, and if by virtue of that simple fact all human nature has in some sense been included in the God-man as the soteriological "representative" of all humanity, then the real difference between church and world can only lie at the level of its recognition in faith, and perhaps also in the ethical consequence of this recognition. Thus the church knows what God in Christ has done, while the world does not, and the church lives accordingly, while the world may well not.

However, there is something profoundly unsatisfactory about this approach: unsatisfactory not so much that it tends to universalism (which should be welcomed, could it only be established!), but in that it tends to push the life of faith, and with it *the work of the Holy Spirit*, to the periphery of theology. One of the most frequent defects in theological systems is that they make the work of the Spirit at best an appendage to the work of Christ: in those terms, the work of the Spirit adds nothing. The more adequate view is that Christ came furnished with the Spirit, and that the Spirit, which was poured out after the resurrection, has its own proper mission in the economy of salvation, which involves not only the role of bearing witness to what Christ has already accomplished but also of inaugurating what he wishes still to do. We shall turn to this question in the following chapter.

Let us approach the present problem, instead, from another angle. In the final analysis, the potential problem with the approaches of Barth and Mersch is the polar opposite of the problem one encounters in the "Jesus of history" school, where Jesus appears to be too human, that is, *merely* human, and where no genuine theological considerations can be admitted. In Mersch and Barth, by contrast, the problem is that it is difficult to see in what sense Jesus can be authentically human. An individual man in whom all human nature is represented, so much so that "everyman" lives and dies in him, to use Barth's expression, is hardly a person among the rest of humanity. In short, the "incarnational" ecclesiology typified by Mersch and Barth seemingly threatens to destroy the very foundation on which it intends to build — by jeopardizing the reality of Christ's human nature.

In the case of Barth, at least, we can address this criticism by noting the extent to which Barth's theology contains an adequate pneumatological "moment." This is not always acknowledged; in fact, in an earlier study, I argued that Barth does not treat the problem of the Spirit with the insight it merits. My argument was that Barth's pneumatology is weakened by his excessive emphasis on Christology, deriving from the orientation of his theology as a whole toward the concept of revelation.[33] I now judge this to be a serious misreading of Barth's mature theology, though it is a plausible reading of much of his early work, and though I would still maintain that Barth's pneumatology overall remains inadequate.

One way of seeing this is by comparing Barth's theology to John Calvin's theology, to which Barth's theology bears some relationship. It is, of course, a point of fundamental principle in Calvin's theology that the reality of the historic and continuing (risen) humanity of Christ must not be jeopardized in any way: Jesus Christ the risen Lord still possesses the authentic human nature that he assumed in the incarnation, and in which he lived in the days of his flesh.[34] This was the issue that came to the fore in the eucharistic controversy that was the subtext of the rupture between Lutheranism and Calvinism in the sixteenth century. The Lutherans, wishing to appeal to no other miracle than the incarnation in affirming the real presence of Christ "in, with, and under" the elements of bread and wine, speak of the communication of properties between the natures of Christ, and of his human nature as sharing in the divine nature's capacity to be both in heaven and upon earth. In Calvin's treatment, Christ, though risen and glorified, is still creaturely in his humanity and does *not* possess divine qualities.

---

33. Badcock, *Light of Truth,* pp. 179-84. This is also the thrust of the criticism of Barth in Philip J. Rosato, *The Spirit as Lord* (Edinburgh: T&T Clark, 1981).

34. The argument here is taken from Calvin, *Institutes,* IV, 17.

In Calvin's theology, therefore, the risen body of Christ is contained finitely in heaven, from which he will come in that same humanity to judge the living and the dead. Accordingly, in his theology of the Lord's Supper, Calvin insists — against the Lutheran sources of his day — that the body of Christ is not ontologically omnipresent (ubiquitous), whether by virtue of the hypostatic union, the resurrection, or the ascension. Instead, Christ's human nature was and is authentic — and thus finite. In short, his body is a true human body that is limited to a single space and time, even in its heavenly existence. Hence, Christ is not present on the eucharistic table by virtue of its postincarnation or postresurrection ubiquity, as in the main varieties of Lutheran eucharistic theory. Instead, he is present in heaven and we are united with him, and so we come spiritually to "feed" on the true substance of his body and blood in the Supper only by virtue of work of the Holy Spirit.

> [G]reatly mistaken are those who conceive no presence of flesh in the Supper unless it lies in the bread. For thus they leave nothing to the secret working of the Spirit, which unites Christ himself to us. To them Christ does not seem present unless he comes down to us. As though, if he should lift us to himself, we should not just as much enjoy his presence! (IV.xvii.31)

The Spirit's work is the decisive factor, for our prayer does not bring Christ down to the table. Instead, the Spirit lifts us up to be with Christ where he is. The fundamental movement here is one of humans' *ascent to* Christ rather than of the *descent of* Christ. The theology is consciously and deliberately conceived in a way that highlights the importance of pneumatology, which has its own status and importance in Calvin's theological theory and in classical Reformed theology generally.[35]

A second point reinforces this first argument, which was drawn from Calvin's sacramental theology. For Calvin's insistence that we are made one with Christ by the power of the Holy Spirit, working through faith, appears also in his lengthy discussion of the Christian life in Book III of the *Insti-*

---

35. *Cf.* Joseph C. McLelland's exposition of the sacramental theology of Peter Martyr Vermigli (1500-1562), which closely parallels the theology of Calvin, in McLelland, *The Visible Words of God* (Edinburgh and London: Oliver and Boyd, 1957). Of special interest is McLelland's comparison of the theologies of the Reformed theologians Martin Bucer, John Calvin, and Peter Martyr, pp. 272-81.

tutes, where we are told from the beginning that, without the Holy Spirit, Christ would remain outside of us and be in fact useless to us (III.i.1). It is only by the working of the Holy Spirit that Christ shares with us what he has received from the Father for our sake, indwells us, and becomes our head, so that we are engrafted into him to be made one body. The activity of the Holy Spirit, the "bond of our union with Christ," is thus essential to the work of salvation. Significantly, it also underlies the theme of the church as the body of Christ. Calvin says:

> [U]ntil our minds become intent upon the Spirit, Christ, so to speak, lies idle because we coldly contemplate him as outside ourselves — indeed, far from us. We know, moreover, that he benefits only those whose "Head" he is [Eph. 4:15], for whom he is "the first-born among brethren" [Rom. 8:29], and who, finally, "have put on him" [Gal. 3:27]. This union alone ensures that, as far as we are concerned, he has not unprofitably come with the name of Savior. The same purpose is served by that sacred wedlock through which we are made flesh of his flesh and bone of his bone [Eph. 5:30], and thus one with him. But he unites himself to us by the Spirit alone. By the grace and power of the same Spirit we are made his members, to keep us under himself and in turn to possess him. (III.i.3)[36]

Calvin's position entails that the proper Christological referent in any "incarnational" approach to the doctrine of the church should not be so much the "historical Jesus," nor the doctrine of the incarnation, but Jesus as the incarnate and crucified one, the one who has been raised by God the Father from the dead, and who even then is "useless" to us without the Spirit that he pours out. Earlier in this chapter we had reason to reject the idea that Paul identified the risen body of Jesus with the church, essentially on the grounds that this grossly overstates and oversimplifies the connection between the two. We can see that Calvin, at least, might well agree. But this

---

36. In a fine study of Calvin's "mysticism," *Union with Christ* (Louisville: Westminster John Knox Press, 1994), pp. 84ff., Dennis Tamburello has pointed out how basic all of these images are in Calvin's thought, and how deeply Calvin drew at this point on his key medieval source, Bernard of Clairvaux. The centrality of the Spirit in Calvin's ecclesiology is also recognized in a study by the Roman Catholic commentator Kilian McDonnell, *John Calvin, the Church, and the Eucharist* (Princeton, NJ: Princeton University Press, 1967), esp. chs. 5 and 7.

does not mean that there is no connection between the two in Pauline theology at all. Indeed, quite the reverse is suggested by the fact that, for Paul and indeed for the writers of the New Testament in general, it is precisely belief in the resurrection of Jesus that entails belief in Jesus as the Lord of the church, raised to God's right hand, from whence he will come one day as the savior and judge of eschatological expectation. Apart from this whole nexus of belief, one might say, there would have been no church at all, nor any Christology, nor, in all probability, even any continuing memory of the "historical Jesus."

Eucharistic Ecclesiology

Among the more interesting and important contemporary theological approaches to the doctrine of the church appears in "eucharistic ecclesiology." This approach, which began in France with the Orthodox church historian Nicholas Afanassieff and the Jesuit theologian Henri de Lubac in the middle decades of the twentieth century, continues in our own time in the work of such ecumenical sources as John Zizioulas, Paul McPartlan, and not least, Joseph Ratzinger.[37] The central idea of eucharistic ecclesiology is that the church is most truly what it is, and can be best understood in its own intrinsic being, specifically in the eucharistic celebration. For example, according to Ratzinger:

> The Church is the celebration of the Eucharist; the Eucharist is the Church; they do not simply stand side by side; they are one and the

[37]. There is a considerable literature on this subject. On Afanassieff, the most accessible source is Aidan Nichols, *Theology in the Russian Diaspora* (Cambridge, UK: Cambridge University Press, 1990); among Henri de Lubac's many works, we can cite his *Catholicism*, trans. Lancelot C. Sheppard (London: Burns & Oates, 1950; San Francisco: Ignatius Press, 1988). The more recent sources include John Zizioulas, *Being as Communion* (Crestwood, NY: St Vladimir's Seminary Press, 1993); Paul McPartlan, *The Eucharist Makes the Church* (Edinburgh: T&T Clark, 1993); and Joseph Ratzinger, *Das Neue Volk Gottes* (Düsseldorf: Patmos, 1969). Miroslav Volf surveys Ratzinger's position in *After Our Likeness* (Grand Rapids: Eerdmans, 1998). It is interesting to note that Ratzinger, at the time that he wrote *Das Neue Volk Gottes,* was fresh from helping to draft the key Vatican II document, *Lumen Gentium.* Perhaps the best general introduction to the subject of eucharistic ecclesiology as a whole is Paul McPartlan, *Sacrament of Salvation* (Edinburgh: T&T Clark, 1995).

same. The Eucharist is the *sacramentum Christi* and, because the Church is *Eucharistia*, she is therefore also *sacramentum* — the sacrament to which all the other sacraments are ordered.[38]

Thus it is the Eucharist, rather than the Word of God, the ecclesiastical hierarchy, or the common confession of faith, that most clearly and most fully constitutes the church.

Put in these terms, the standpoint may seem an unusual one, for the church is surely not *simply* "the celebration of the Eucharist," since much that happens under the auspices of the church, from preaching and teaching through to pastoral counseling and financial transactions, are clearly not things that can be so identified. Yet the Eucharist unquestionably concentrates in itself a range of other theological themes — christological, pneumatological, soteriological, and ecclesiological. Furthermore, the modern ecumenical "project," faced as it has been with seemingly intractable problems arising from church history, has found in eucharistic ecclesiology a way to bypass certain otherwise insoluble aspects of older conflicts. In fact, much of the remarkable flowering of ecclesiology that has occurred during the past century has grown in this soil. This development has been found particularly in both Orthodoxy and Roman Catholicism; but through them eucharistic ecclesiology has come to prominence in recent ecumenism generally. This is nowhere more clear than in the well-known "Lima text" of 1982, *Baptism, Eucharist and Ministry*, which incorporates the key theme of eucharistic ecclesiology, that the church is to be defined *principally* as a eucharistic community:

> The eucharistic communion with Christ who nourishes the life of the Church is at the same time communion within the body of Christ which is the Church. The sharing in one bread and the common cup in a given place demonstrates and effects the oneness of the sharers with Christ and with their fellow sharers in all times and places. It is *in the eucharist* that the community of God's people is fully manifested. Eucharistic celebrations always have to do with the whole Church, and the whole Church is involved in each local eucharistic celebration. In so far as a church claims to be a manifestation of the whole Church, it

---

38. Joseph Ratzinger, *Principles of Catholic Theology*, trans. Mary F. McCarthy (San Francisco: Ignatius Press, 1987), p. 53.

will take care to order its own life in ways which take seriously the interests and concerns of other churches.[39]

The truth of the matter is that, in historic Christianity and in the worldwide Christian church today, the Eucharist is far from being a sign of unity. In fact, it could be argued that the Eucharist has become the principal sign and instrument of Christian *disunity,* since Christians manifestly do not universally share one eucharistic table, and many of them have no wish to share it. On the other side, the easy request for "intercommunion" and the mutual recognition of other churches' Eucharists is sadly inadequate as a response to the ecumenical scandal, because what that represents is the desire to pass over division as unimportant and the sign of unity as something that need not be expressed also in the "facts" of the church's concrete existence.

If what the Eucharist symbolizes is not just the body and blood of Christ but the unity of the ecclesiastical body in the one body and blood of Christ, then the actual unity of the church matters. For Christ is not divided (1 Cor. 1:13). The fact that a common eucharistic table has not been realized by modern ecumenism is, no doubt, a symptom of the incommensurability of the differing understandings of the nature of the church and of the Eucharist that can be found in worldwide Christianity. To that extent, the problem is understandable; theologically, however, there can be no final excuse: Christ is not divided. We should not consider it beyond the capacity of the churches to reach the vision of a genuine sharing in one bread that *Baptism, Eucharist and Ministry* represents, a sharing in Christ's body and blood that would also be the sacrament of the unity of the ecclesiastical "body" with Christ in one body.

In itself, the importance of the Eucharist in theological approaches to the doctrine of the church is hardly a new or strange theme. The "new testament" itself has its sacramental sign in the meal that Christ celebrated with his disciples on the night he was betrayed. We read in the earliest of the accounts (1 Cor. 11:25): "This is my body. . . . Do this in remembrance of me. . . . This cup is the new covenant in my blood." Centuries later, as we have seen, as he reflected on the relationship between the eucharistic and ecclesial body of Christ, Augustine would connect the two vividly, teaching that in the Eucharist the church sees and receives nothing less than what it is: the body of

---

39. *Baptism, Eucharist and Ministry* (Geneva: World Council of Churches, 1982), "Eucharist," p. 19 (italics added).

Christ. Furthermore, at the time of the Reformation, the "marks" or "notes" of the church came to be seen less in terms of the ancient creedal notions of unity, holiness, catholicity, and apostolicity so much as in terms of the preaching of the gospel and right sacramental belief and practice, especially in connection with the Lord's Supper. For the Reformation tradition, it is in these matters that the unity, holiness, catholicity, and apostolicity of the church are chiefly to be discerned and nurtured.

Equally, however, the Reformation insistence on the place of both Word and sacrament in "defining" the church helps us see that a thoroughgoing eucharistic ecclesiology is at best partial. It is true that the three synoptic Gospels present the institution of the eucharistic meal as a central moment in the story of Jesus' passion, as does Paul, and even John's Gospel in its way: "Unless you eat the flesh of the Son of Man and drink his blood, you have no life in you" (John 6:53). However, the Reformation insistence on the hearing of the Word of the gospel in faith as the central event in the life of the church is also entirely faithful to the New Testament's ecclesiological vision. For example, it alone explains the missionary expansion of the church of the New Testament period, for this expansion is fuelled by preaching and witness to Jesus as the promised Savior of the world. The celebration of the Eucharist in the earliest Christian communities, however central it was to their life, would make no sense were it not for this wider setting of proclamation, faith, and obedience.

Thus the church exists insofar as the event of the proclamation of the Word of God — and the hearing of it in faith — takes place. Rather than viewing it exclusively in the light of the institution narratives, as contemporary eucharistic ecclesiology tends to do, we must appeal in the foundations of our ecclesiology to the constitutive role of the Word of God and of the gospel itself. Therefore, if the church is to be successfully understood as a eucharistic community, the sense in which the theological meaning of the eucharistic meal is to be identified with the content of the proclamation of the gospel needs to be more clearly drawn out. Ultimately, one could go so far as to claim that the distinction between the church as "hearer of the Word," such as one typically finds in expressions of Protestant ecclesiology, and the church as "eucharistic community," which is more characteristic of "catholic" ecclesiological traditions, can only be an abstraction. Surely the two must be taken together.

In fact, there are also many instances of "church" to be seen in nonliturgical contexts, where, for example, people are active in service to the poor in the name of Christ, in peacemaking, in ecological groups, or in witness to those who do not believe. Perhaps we should go so far as to say that it is precisely such kinds of activity, activity that all too often takes place at the furthest fringes of the institutional churches, that actually *best* defines what the church of Christ really is. "My mother and my brothers are those who hear the word of God and do it," says Jesus of his true disciples (Luke 8:21). The idea that those who bear costly witness to the gospel on the margins are somehow "less" the "mother" and "brothers" of Jesus than those who go comfortably to Eucharist on Sunday and listen to the sermon, or less than those who lead it, can only be a distortion.

Nonetheless, there is much light in eucharistic ecclesiology, even if, as a matter of theological principle, we have to carefully weigh its central contention that the church "is" the Eucharist. First of all, as the sign by which the church remembers Christ's death, the Eucharist gathers together in its symbolism the entire substance of Christ's saving work. The body of Christ is "given for you," and his blood is "shed for you," while both are received in the act of personal and corporate faith called communion. Deeper still, the Eucharist is the sign of the total self-giving of God, proceeding from the ocean of divine love, out of which the glory of God was laid aside, and the one who was "in the form of God" humbled himself and "became obedient to the point of death — even death on a cross" (Phil. 2:6-8). As such, the Eucharist is also the sign of total human self-giving *to* God, in the service of the world that God loves. In other words, in and with Christ we offer our lives in obedience and loving service.

One further theme will serve to round out the discussion: the idea that the Eucharist is an anticipation of the heavenly banquet, symbolizing the fulfillment of the kingdom of God. The roots of this understanding are found in the institution narrative in Luke 22:14-20, according to which Jesus says:

> "I have eagerly desired to eat this Passover with you before I suffer; for I tell you, I will never eat it again until it is fulfilled in the kingdom of God." Then he took a cup, and after giving thanks he said, "Take this and divide it among yourselves; for I tell you that from now on I will not drink of the fruit of the vine until the kingdom of God comes. . . . Do this in remembrance of me."

Thus the Eucharist anticipates the eschatological fulfillment of Christ's work. Paul McPartlan, in his exposition of eucharistic ecclesiology in *Sacra-*

ment of Salvation, goes so far as to speak of the event of the Eucharist as "the assembly of the last day," drawing on the imagery of Hebrews 12:18-24, which speaks of the life of the church in terms of Mount Zion, the city of the living God, the heavenly Jerusalem. "The Church, properly speaking, is the heavenly gathering of all the nations for all eternity with Christ in the kingdom of the Father."⁴⁰ Thus, McPartlan argues, whatever bears the name of "church" on earth does so only in a secondary and ultimately derivative sense, because it can at best be a step on the way to this eschatological goal. It is thus a future gathering that is revealed in the Eucharist, rather than something already realized (p. 6). To those who would object to this on the grounds that such otherworldliness is profoundly unhelpful or even incoherent, McPartlan's response is that the future kingdom can indeed be thrown open in this way in the church's worship, because, where the Holy Spirit is present, ordinary rules do not obtain.

This gloss on eucharistic ecclesiology is of particular interest when we read it in light of the problem of the relationship between the eucharistic and the ecclesiastical "body of Christ." As we have seen, the great danger associated with the ecclesiological idea of the body of Christ is that it lends itself to a sacralizing of the earthly institution. However, what happens if we read, in the light of this eschatological theme, the idea that in the Eucharist the church receives what it is? The answer must be that, just as the body of Christ is contained in heaven, so also the church *awaits* its own fulfillment, when it will be made wholly one with the risen Lord. Thus does the idea of the church as the body of Christ ultimately represent what is present to faith and hope rather than to sight and to our experience. And hence the notion that the church in its present sinful form can be straightforwardly identified with the risen Christ is false, while the eschatological goal of union with Christ can be retained. We *will* be bone of his bone, flesh of his flesh, united with him in the fellowship of the Father's house, but we are *not yet.* In the present we must resist any suggestion that the church in its present situation in history has "arrived," and that its present life can be regarded as sacrosanct. The church is indeed the body of Christ, but it is so only insofar as it grasps its existence "on the way" to the final fulfillment. Therefore, the church as the body of Christ is entirely subject to the descent of the Holy Spirit, which is the "down payment" (*arrabôn,* 2 Cor. 1:22; 5:5; Eph. 1:14) on the inheritance for which we wait — along with the whole of the church in all ages.

---

40. McPartlan, *Sacrament of Salvation,* p. 5.

Cross and Resurrection in the Theology of the Body of Christ

To draw this discussion to a close, I can quote some words from Paul: "I consider that the sufferings of this present time are not worth comparing with the glory about to be revealed to us," he says in Romans 8. "For the creation waits with eager longing for the revealing of the children of God . . ." (vv. 18-19). In short, the church as the body of Christ awaits its glorification with Christ, but in the present it lives in patience, "groaning" (v. 23) in hope of redemption.

The problem that a text such as this introduces is not only the problem of eschatology, but, much more clearly, the mystery of suffering, which is so often the experience of the members of the church and has so often been a major feature of the church's corporate life in the world. We know of the former through personal experience; the latter we know in ways that are seemingly only folkloric and that are part of the common consciousness of Christians. We have an awareness of the persecution of the church in the formative centuries of early Christianity, or perhaps of the suffering of our forebears in the sixteenth and seventeenth centuries. Americans in particular seem keenly aware that this latter suffering was endured not only for the sake of the faith, but also that in some sense it had as its goal the political revolutions of modernity that made modern religious toleration possible.

The "folkloric" quality of such awareness, however, also insulates us from the harsh reality of what such life involved, as people lived under the fear of literal torture, enslavement, or death for questions of moral and spiritual principle. Unfortunately, it also insulates us from a more troubling fact: the suffering of the church in our own era. For example, there have certainly been many more Christian martyrs in the past century than there were in the whole patristic period, and certainly much more in the way of long-standing and "general" state persecution. Behind the "Iron Curtain," millions of Christians lost social rights — for example, the right to have their children educated, in some cases the right to housing or to the necessities of life — and though the politics of Europe have changed in recent years, such political and physical suffering for the sake of Christ continues today in other parts of the world.

Christian "insulation" from suffering may have other effects. While still a young man, I had the privilege of encountering a theological student from communist Hungary in Edinburgh, where we were both students, and he confronted me with a strange new argument. The church in the comfortable

West, he said to me, cannot comprehend the Christian hope or the content of Christian eschatology. Because of its wealth, it has little to hope for, and thus its temptation is always to assume that the kingdom of God has already come. Only those who suffer persecution can understand what it means to yearn for a future of God's making. My fellow student may well have been right. It certainly would explain why, in the richest civilization that has ever existed, the interpretations of eschatology being offered are so bizarre. Or, for that matter, it would explain why, by contrast, there seems to be no eschatological hope at all in so many churches of the privileged West. It is presumably a question that we might better avoid, or else one that seemingly leads to madness.

The political and social context in which the church lives is not the only influence that leads to such problems. The temptation is also theological. For a very long time the church has associated itself as the body of Christ so fully with the "body" of its risen Lord that it has kept the necessary element of suffering at bay. The excesses of the late medieval church were so egregious in this respect that Luther, for one, occasionally argued that suffering must be reckoned to be one of the most important marks of the true church.

> They must endure every misfortune and persecution, all kinds of trials and evil from the devil, the world, and the flesh . . . by inward sadness, timidity, fear, outward poverty, contempt, illness, and weakness, in order to be like their head, Christ . . . they must be called heretics, knaves, and devils, the most pernicious people on earth, to the point where those who hang, drown, murder, torture, banish, and plague them to death are rendering to God a service . . . because they want to have none but Christ, and no other God.[41]

With his typical iconoclastic genius, Luther called this mark of the church its "holy possession of the sacred cross," in conscious parody of the slivers of wood encased in reliquaries of gold that were taken to be the remains of the true cross in the medieval church, and as media of salvation. The critique of the abuse of relics was fair enough for most of the Reformation movement, and Luther's constant argument that Rome was merely after the Germans'

---

41. Martin Luther, *On the Councils and the Church, 1539,* trans. Charles M. Jacobs and Eric W. Gritsch, in Helmut T. Lehmann et al., eds., *Luther's Works,* 55 vols. (Philadelphia: Fortress Press, 1959-1986), 41: 164-65. See Robert A. Kelly, "The Suffering of the Church: A Study of Luther's *Theologia Crucis," Concordia Theological Quarterly* 50 (1986): 3-17.

money certainly proved popular. However, Luther's full alternative would prove too strong a meat for the Reformation movement to take in and digest. In the end, it was true preaching and the right administration of the sacraments that came to be codified as the functional marks that distinguish the true church from the false. Hence, it is not only the medieval church that has had difficulty in following in the way of the cross.

Unfortunately, a discussion of the church as the body of Christ lends itself to the glorification of the ecclesial body with the body of its exalted Lord. We have it on good authority, after all, that God has "raised us up with him and seated us with him in the heavenly places" (Eph. 2:6), on the basis of which the church is surely also entitled to its little glories in *this* world. Whether this is true or not, it is certainly how much of the church behaves. On the other hand, though, the risen Lord of the Gospels bears on his body the marks of his crucifixion (Luke 24:40; John 20:27), and the vision of the exalted Christ, whose body the church is elsewhere said to be, is described in the Apocalypse as "a Lamb standing as if it had been slaughtered" (Rev. 5:6). On the basis of such extraordinary texts, there should be no bypassing the reality of suffering in ecclesiology. The pattern of life into which the church is baptized is a cruciform one. "I carry the marks of Jesus [*ta stigmata* — the source of the word] branded on my body," says Paul (Gal. 6:17). We also must find a way to carry his marks as his ecclesiastical body, for the heavenly body of Christ, the "Lamb slain from the foundation of the world" (Rev. 13:8), is never without them.

Theologians, like the church itself, often have ingenious ways of avoiding the implications of being the body of the crucified one. Vladimir Lossky, for example, has argued, concerning the spiritual theology of the Christian East, that it is comprehensively a theology of glory, and that — quite explicitly — the Eastern ideal is one of union with Christ in his transfigured glory rather than one of union with Christ in his lowliness.

> The way which Christ, the divine Person, took, was that of a descent towards created being, a taking upon himself of our nature; the way of created persons, on the other hand, must be that of ascent, a rising up towards the divine nature by means of the union with uncreated grace communicated by the Holy Spirit. The spirituality of the imitation of Christ which is sometimes found in the West is foreign to Eastern spirituality, which may rather be defined as a *life in Christ*.[42]

42. Vladimir Lossky, *The Mystical Theology of the Eastern Church*, trans. members of

Or again, and even more surprisingly:

> No saint of the Eastern Church has ever borne the stigmata, those out-
> ward marks which have made certain great Western saints and mystics
> as it were living patterns of the suffering Christ. But, by contrast, East-
> ern saints have very frequently been transfigured by the inward light of
> uncreated grace, and have appeared resplendent, like Christ on the
> mount of Transfiguration. (p. 243)

This is interpretation rather than text, but there are grounds for Lossky's interpretation in the overall character of the Orthodox tradition, and his position is at the very least characteristic of some of it.

From the standpoint of Western theology, we have already encountered
the theme of the glorification of the church as institution in the encyclical
letter *Mystici Corporis*. Karl Barth, who was among its critics, argues that the
identification of the mystery of the church as the creation of Christ with its
visible, juridical organization was so comprehensive in the document that it
was completely pointless for Pius XII to call the church the "mystical" body
of Christ. There is nothing "mystical" left to see, says Barth, once the visible
church of Rome has been taken into view, and "hard to see how there can be
any further discussion with the official Roman Catholic doctrine of the
Church when it so obviously continues to harden in this way."[43]

Barth wrote these words in the early 1950s, only a few years after the encyclical had been published, and when the reforms of Vatican II still seemed
to be an eternity away. But Barth himself has his own version of this identification of the church, as the *invisible* body of Christ, with what is glorious and
beyond the reach of human frailty. In some of the most brilliant and problematic pages of his entire theology, the account of the "Election of the Community" in §34 of *Church Dogmatics* II/2, Barth argues that God's election of
fellowship with humankind takes a twofold form: the first is seen in the election of Israel, which expresses in its life the necessary truth of the judgment of
God on human incapacity, unwillingness, and unworthiness; the second is
seen in the election of the gentiles, in which what is expressed is "the mercy in
which God turns his glory to man."[44] The community in the form of Israel

---

the Fellowship of St. Alban and St. Sergius (Cambridge, UK: James Clarke & Co., 1957),
p. 215.

43. Barth, *Church Dogmatics*, IV/1, p. 659.
44. Barth, *Church Dogmatics*, II/2, pp. 206, 210.

expresses the judgment that God makes and that God himself wills to endure in Jesus Christ; the community in the form of the church expresses the justification that God effects in his judgment, whereby humanity has God as brother, servant, and physician, as well as leader, master, and king (p. 211).

Barth is not anti-Semitic. It would be fairer to say that, in some respects, he is trying to make sense of the suffering of the Jews and to protest against it as well as he could in the context of the dark years of the 1940s. He insists that the Jews are the covenant people of God, God's own people, and even that they are fellow heirs of the promise with the church (indeed, its primary heirs). But his theology is also saying more than this. It is, among other things, part of his extended, lifelong engagement with the Epistle to the Romans, in which he develops the relationship of gentile and Jew as a major theme. On the basis of Romans 9-11, Barth would go on explicitly to reject the whole idea of a "Christian mission" to the Jews: it would be pointless for Christians to convert individual Jews, since they already belong to the "church" in its most general sense as the "gathering of Jews and Gentiles" alike (II/2, p. 199).[45] What is necessary for Christians to do, instead, is simply *witness* to God's election of Jew and gentile in Jesus Christ, but they should not undertake this witness for the sake of the salvation of the Jew. It certainly should not take the form of the alternate repression, toleration, and conversion to "proper" Europeanism that has hitherto prevailed in Christian "missions" to Judaism. Every such strategy has been a tragic mistake. The only thing required is that the church be faithful to the gospel, thus making the synagogue "jealous" (Rom. 11:11, 14) — via the continuing witness of the church to the world that the King of the Jews is the savior of all.

No, the problem is the association of Israel with the cross of Christ and the judgment of God, on the one hand, and of the gentile church with the proclamation and realization of intimacy with God, on the other. The scheme is certainly powerful to read in the light of its historical context, as well as brilliant and fascinating, so much so that it leads to what is unquestionably among the most compelling discussions of Judas Iscariot in the whole of Christian theology.[46] But it is difficult to see in this any sense in which the church must come to share in Christ's sufferings, or any basis on which it would be possible for the church to say, with the apostle Paul, that it bears the marks of Christ on its body.

45. Barth, *Church Dogmatics*, IV/3, 2, pp. 876-78.
46. Barth, *Church Dogmatics*, II/2, pp. 458-506.

It can take many years for disciples of Barth to recognize that there is anything at all left to say in theology once Barth had spoken. But two recent contributions to the theology of the church that both belong broadly to the Barthian tradition do extend the Barthian claim, and I will mention them briefly to draw this discussion to a close. Both contributions seek to express the idea that the current situation of the churches in the West is one of suffering, though many of the churches themselves might well not be able to perceive the fact. The first is a rather rueful study by Ephraim Radner, *The End of the Church*, which argues its case on the basis of pneumatology, but which might just as well have argued on the basis of the theology of the ecclesiastical body of Christ: where Christ's body has been broken, and where its brokenness is willfully sustained, there can be no authentic Christian understanding of Scripture, no sense of holiness, no truly eucharistic worship.[47] The Spirit has been divided, and the consequences have been so devastating that the fundamental theological task today becomes one of recognizing the brokenness of the church and reminding Christians that their high claims made in celebration of the Holy Spirit's presence are merely "false clamors" (p. vi). Where the body of Christ is willfully broken, and broken again, the ecclesiastical body of Christ cannot live. In this case, the crucial task is to recognize that the needless division of the church — amid its rubble — places in question the status of Christ himself as the one "body" in whom all are reconciled to God.

The second contribution proves the more interesting and fruitful: Alan Lewis's fascinating book *Between Cross and Resurrection* is not a lament but a penetrating quest for understanding.[48] How, it asks, are we to understand the mystery of suffering in the light of the crucified *and dead* Christ, in the conviction that the day between cross and resurrection is the most important day of all? "Might not the space dividing Calvary and the Garden be the best of all starting places from which to reflect upon what happened on the cross, in the tomb, and in between?" (p. 3). Lewis's argument is that it is necessary for the church to be found in the brokenness and godlessness of the world, because this is precisely where God lay when Christ was in the grave (p. 370). Therefore, the loss to Western churches of so much of their social

47. Ephraim Radner, *The End of the Church* (Grand Rapids: Eerdmans, 1998). Radner surveys several such crucial ecclesial loci and shows how the life of the church has been disfigured by division.

48. Alan E. Lewis, *Between Cross and Resurrection* (Grand Rapids: Eerdmans, 2001).

and political influence, the seemingly relentless numerical decline of Christianity in its old Western heartlands, and its subjection to the abyssal threat of nonexistence need to be seen not as something theologically meaningless but in a new way, as a mode of its participation in the crucified one.

Something in the church must die for the sake of the gospel. Perhaps it is its old penchant for power. Perhaps it is its easy assimilation to the norms of Western liberalism. Perhaps it is a good many of the old orthodoxies. Lewis is not suggesting that the threat of annihilation must everywhere and always be a permanent feature of the church's existence; one senses that that would be too much. But what he does wish to do is to give the experience of the church in the Western world today its proper name, and to allow us to see that in this name lies the key to understanding who and what we are as the body of Christ at this point in our history. This name, of course, is Jesus Christ, the Lord of glory, whose broken body the church shares.

Traveling along this way, we go well beyond the theology of Karl Barth. Both of these writers show that there is room for an understanding of the body of Christ in terms that do justice to the fragmentary forms of its existence, in terms that make theological sense of its persecution and rejection by the Western world (persecution by the media, one of the institutions of modern liberalism, is certainly real), and in terms that address its uncertainty concerning the present and the future. These are, to be sure, features of the church's experience at the present time. Perhaps, with Lewis, we will be able to give this experience its proper name, so as to understand it and so to bring hope for the day of resurrection. We will return to these themes in later chapters.

What we have seen is that the idea that the church as the body of Christ has a range of profound implications that are not simply reducible to any simplistic consciousness of mutuality or any sentimental "community of individuals." The gospel, properly developed and fully explored, can make its own claims on the life of the church clear enough. To say "You are the body of Christ," that commonplace of Christian piety, turns out to have implications that are rich and revolutionary, as Augustine expressed it: "[I]t is *your* sacrament that is set on the table of the Lord; and it is *your* sacrament that you receive. To what you *are* you respond, 'Amen.' . . . Therefore be a member of the body of Christ that your 'Amen' may be true."

CHAPTER 4

Temple of the Holy Spirit

Ecclesiology as a Pneumatological Problem

We turn now to the idea of the church as the dwelling of God. As we have seen in previous chapters, we shall see that the biblical witness to the idea will take us into territory that is seldom explored in contemporary ecclesiology, in this case the theology of the temple. The ecclesiological adaptation of this idea is largely defined by Pauline texts, but the Pauline conception also needs to be viewed against the background of a much wider canvas: the contested theology of the presence of God and of the temple within ancient Judaism. This wider background is assumed in the variety of reinterpretations of the indwelling of God in the New Testament; these interpretations appear not only in the Pauline literature but, pervasively, in the New Testament canon. Constructive Christian theology needs to engage with this hugely important, yet oddly neglected, strand of the biblical tradition. It needs to do so not only in its treatment of the doctrine of the church, for which the theme ought to be of central importance, but also in its understanding of the theological significance of the Old Testament, its treatment of the nature of the Christian life, and perhaps also in its engagement with Judaism.

It may be that the relative neglect of the idea is due in part to an under-representation of the doctrine of the Holy Spirit in the structures of Christian theology as a whole. For while the idea of the indwelling of God certainly cannot be restricted to the work of the Holy Spirit, the idea is properly *appropriated* to the Spirit, to use a precise theological term. Blindness to the one will likely involve blindness to the other. Unfortunately, the truth is that the Spirit, though named in the church's Trinitarian confession, is something of a "poor relation" of the Father and the Son — both in popular Christian understanding and in formal theology alike. Therefore, my goal here is to try to remedy this as far as is possible, and ultimately to seek redress by outlining a doctrine of the church that is capable of accommodating the Spirit of God. An adequate doctrine of the church turns as much on the viability of such a pneumatological understanding as it does on Christology and the election of God.

The Temple and the Presence of God in the Old Testament

The idea that the Spirit of God dwells among, or "indwells," the people of God is deeply rooted in Scripture. The idea can be identified in a wide variety of Old Testament texts, from Exodus and the legislation of Leviticus through to the postexilic prophets. Paradoxically, this immanent presence of God in and among his people, which can lead to the extraordinarily intimate spirituality of the Psalms, for example, exists side by side with a tremendous emphasis on divine transcendence. The tension between these themes of immanence and transcendence is fundamental to Old Testament thought: the God who "dwells in Zion" is also the God who cannot be contained in any such place, being exalted in glory above all the earth. As we shall see, this tension, which is an important element in biblical theology generally, reappears in later Christian thought.

The narrative progress of the idea of the presence of God in the Old Testament begins, interestingly enough, with the story of salvation. In Exodus, which is a crucial biblical document for this theme, the presence of God is closely associated with the pillars of cloud and of fire that accompany the people of Israel in their deliverance from Egypt (Exod. 13:21-22). In Exodus, the assurance of this presence later comes to be associated with the ark of the covenant and the tabernacle (or "tent") and its other fixtures in the wilderness, including the institution of priestly (Levitical) service and its maintenance. It is concerning this that we read the divine promise: "I will dwell among the Israelites, and I will be their God" (Exod. 29:45). Thus did the completed tabernacle and the ark that it contains together become the place where "the cloud of the LORD" is ultimately found during the forty years of wilderness wanderings (Exod. 40:34-38).

This idea of the divine presence is taken further and given a reference extending well beyond the wilderness experience itself and into the legal institutions of Old Testament religion. This appears especially in the legislation of Leviticus, which has at its heart the idea of the reward offered by God for obedience to the commandments: "If you follow my statutes . . . I will place my dwelling in your midst, and I shall not abhor you. And I will walk among you, and will be your God, and you shall be my people" (Lev. 26:3a, 11-12). A certain tendency to antinomianism makes many Christians blind and deaf to this clear strand in biblical theology, but it is something that was and is absolutely basic to the mother religion of Judaism. The presence of God and faithfulness to the commandments are inextricably linked.

When the temple of Solomon was completed, we find the symbolism of the Exodus account taken up into a new religious setting. At the consecration of the temple, Scriptures says that "a cloud filled the house of the LORD, so that the priests could not stand to minister because of the cloud; for the glory of the LORD filled the house of the LORD" (1 Kings 8:10-11). From this time, the claim begins to be made that the presence of God is to be found decisively in the Jerusalem temple. This idea is reflected in the many biblical texts, especially in the Psalms, which speak specifically of "Zion" as the Lord's chosen habitation or dwelling place (e.g., Ps. 132).

Later in the biblical story, following national catastrophe and the burning of Solomon's temple by Nebuchadnezzar (2 Kings 25:9), by which the local limestone of which the temple was built would have been reduced to dust, the prophets respond to the tragedy of destruction and exile by calling for the reconstruction of the temple (Hag. 1:1-6) and returning to the theme of God's presence, telling of its renewal: "Sing and rejoice, O daughter Zion! For lo, I will come and dwell in your midst . . ." (Zech. 2:10).

However, the Bible does not provide us with a straightforward historical account of these matters, nor is biblical thought theologically systematic. In other words, our texts tend to represent a variety of religiously motivated "readings" of the story of Israel, both in its political and in its religious aspects. The Old Testament makes competing claims about the presence of God, claims that are often surprisingly difficult to reconcile. At one end of the spectrum stands the official temple worship, and the claim that God dwells uniquely in the temple. At the other end stands the far more generalized notion that the "breath," or Spirit of God *(ruach)*, is present in every living thing, so that biological life itself, it would seem, is a direct function of the presence of God's Spirit (Ps. 104:25-30). Even the insects ("creeping things") enjoy this gift.

Why, for instance, should the God of Israel need a temple? The thought is obvious enough, and the ancients were not religiously unsophisticated. Accordingly, important instances of theophanies that are entirely independent of the temple traditions are reported in the Bible, such as God's appearance to Abraham at the oaks of Mamre (Gen. 18:1ff.). There are major documents in Hebrew Scripture (and other closely associated Jewish writings in Greek) that appear to posit religious structures independent of the Jewish religious institutions of temple, Levitical priesthood, and sacrifice altogether: the documents of the canonical and deutero-canonical Wisdom literature. These speak of divine presence in a different way. In the Wisdom literature, God's presence is given through the gift of wisdom (*hochma*, or *sophia*): "[I]n every generation [Wisdom] passes into holy souls and makes them friends of God . . ." (Wis. 7:27).

At the heart of the Old Testament understanding of the presence of God, however, stands the temple. The temple is also the key to grasping the theme of divine presence in the New Testament, which takes up and reinterprets the temple idea. Thus, while providing a developed understanding of the concept of the presence of God in the literature of the Old Testament would take us well beyond the requirements of this study, we do need to examine the presence of God in the temple, for here we are dealing with a theme of direct relevance to our subject.

In fact, three main Jewish temple buildings, which were successively constructed over almost a thousand years and stood on roughly the same site in Jerusalem, punctuate the history of the biblical period.[1] The first temple is of special importance, for in this temple (alone of the three) the ark of the covenant was housed, an artifact associated with the figure of Moses himself and said to date from the Exodus. It contained the stone tablets of the Decalogue,

---

1. The existence of these separate buildings is well established in both biblical and extrabiblical literary sources. However, detailed archaeological evidence is unfortunately unavailable because the existence on the site since 691 CE of the Islamic shrine, *Qubbet es-Sakhra*, the "Dome of the Rock," prevents archaeological investigation of the site (not least because some Muslim sources maintain, against the massive weight of historical evidence to the contrary, that there never was a Jewish temple in Jerusalem). For succinct and still valuable treatments, *cf.* W. F. Stinespring, "Temple, Jerusalem," and G. A. Barrois, "Temples," both in G. A. Buttrick et al., eds., *The Interpreter's Dictionary of the Bible,* 5 vols. (Nashville: Abingdon, 1962), 4: 534-60, 560-68. Fuller accounts are William J. Hamblin and David Rolph Seely, *Solomon's Temple* (New York: Thames & Hudson, 2007) and, from an archaeological point of view, Leen Ritmeyer, *The Quest* (Jerusalem: Carta, 2006).

and it was kept in the "most holy place" of the temple. The importance of the ark is, first of all, its association with the foundational stories of Old Testament religion, the narratives of the Exodus and the entry into the land of promise, and its appearance at frequent intervals in the story of Israelite worship and military activity prior to the centralization of power in Jerusalem under the monarchy. Above all, however, the ark was religiously important because the presence of God was closely associated with it, to the extent that, according to some of our sources, it was the fact that the ark was physically located in the temple that made the structure the "house of the LORD."

According to the biblical record, construction of the first temple began in the reign of Solomon (1 Kings 5–6). If so, the temple possibly dates from around 957 BCE. But Solomon's temple was a contested institution, for it did not enjoy the universal support of "Israel" in the broadest sense.[2] For in-

2. A number of other "regular" and "irregular" Jewish shrines existed, both before and during the period of the Solomonic temple, in which variations on the worship of the Jerusalem temples was likely practiced. We read in the books of Samuel, Kings, and Chronicles, for example, of a major temple sanctuary at Shiloh (e.g., 1 Sam. 1). This complex of buildings, according to the biblical narrative, housed the ark of the covenant and a Levitical priesthood prior to the temple of Solomon. Similar, but less important in the overall biblical narrative, was a shrine at Nob, on the Mount of Olives (1 Sam. 21:1-6). Again, according to Judges 20:27, the ark was kept for a time in Bethel, the "house of God" (so designated by the patriarch Jacob in Gen. 28:19), almost certainly in a religious building of some sort; while, immediately prior to its transfer under King David's personal authority to the newly-captured Jerusalem, the ark is even said to have resided for some decades in the private house of a Levite, Abinadab, in the obscure Judaean village of Kiriath-Jearim (1 Sam. 7:1; cf. 1 Chron. 13:6). The latter site is known by a number of different names (Baalah, Baale-Judah, Kiriath-Baal), which makes this memory of times past in the Hebrew scriptures all the more fascinating, for they show that the place was — like Jerusalem itself — a long-established Canaanite holy place. Another Canaanite shrine at Gibeon also appears to have been used for Yahwistic worship. No less a figure than Solomon is said to have sacrificed a thousand burnt offerings there prior to the construction of the Jerusalem temple, and to have received there, rather than in Jerusalem, the revelation that was to define his life (1 Kings 3:3-15). Only the last of these sites is spoken of in the biblical narrative as in any sense irregular, in what is clearly a later judgment (1 Kings 3:3). In addition to these "official" sanctuaries, a number of others existed in "irregular" versions of Jewish religion. There is, for instance, the sanctuary at Dan, where it is said that an idolatrous Yahwistic cult was practiced (Judg. 18:27-31; 1 Kings 12:29-30). The most significant heterodox shrine, however, existed at Bethel in the time of the kings. Bethel was, of course, an ancient holy site of tremendous importance, and it is likely that the Bethel sanctuary in the time of the northern kingdom had its roots in an older sacred

stance, it is clear that the temple was built in order to centralize royal as well as sacral power in the new capital, Jerusalem, and to assert the fundamental connection between the two kingdoms (2 Sam. 5–7). Thus its function involved political symbolism as well as the institution of a particular religious system.[3] Naturally, this proved to be a divisive factor in the history of Old Testament religion.

Solomon's temple was not destined to stand forever, and in 587-586 BCE the entire complex was destroyed by the Babylonians; the temple site stood in ruins for decades.[4] Amid the rise and fall of the nations, Cyrus and the Persians overthrew the Babylonian empire in 539 BCE, and subsequently released the Hebrew captives. An expedition of the Jewish exiles returned to Jerusalem and to Judea under Zerubbabel, and by perhaps 516-515 BCE, this group had reconstructed a second Yahwistic temple complex (the principal biblical sources are Haggai, Ezra, and Nehemiah; the extrabiblical sources are 1 and 2 Maccabees). We know little about this physical structure, though it was probably based on the architecture of Solomon's temple, insofar as that was possible. We do know from extrabiblical sources in Maccabees and Josephus that it was heavily fortified. It is often assumed that its workmanship was inferior to that of the first temple, but this is unclear, especially since, according to the decree of Cyrus reported in Ezra 6:3-5, the formidable resources of Persian imperial revenues were used to pay the costs of construction, while the available artifacts that Nebuchadnezzar had taken from the temple were also restored. In any event, the second temple stood for some five centuries, making it the longest-lived of the three buildings by a considerable margin. Its treasures were also sufficient to warrant their plun-

---

complex. In any case, the Bethel sanctuary became the official rival of the Jerusalem temple under the divided monarchy in the northern kingdom of Israel (1 Kings 12:28-38).

3. From texts such as Psalm 72, it appears that the king had an important place in temple worship. Jerusalem itself was similarly celebrated for political-religious reasons (see, e.g., Ps. 48). King and temple were also closely associated at the literal, physical level, for the temple appears to have been part of a complex of royal buildings, which included the main palace (1 Kings 7:1-12; 9:1, 10-11). The biblical description of the temple buildings cannot be confirmed archaeologically, but, according to the Bible, Solomon employed Phoenician architects on the building, and parallels exist from the archaeology of Phoenician culture that make the biblical descriptions entirely credible.

4. A list of booty that the Babylonians carried off from the temple under Nebuchadnezzar appears in 2 Kings 25:13-17, and in Jeremiah 52:17-23. It is highly significant, as we shall see, that the ark of the covenant is not mentioned in the accounts of the plunder.

der twice in just over a century, first by Antiochus Epiphanes in 168 BCE (1 Macc. 1:21-24), and then by the Roman general Crassus in 54 BCE (Josephus, *Antiq.* XIV.vii).

Jewish scholarship speaks of the whole of the period after the exile and before the catastrophe of 70 CE as the period of the "second temple," but this division is more theological than literal. The reality is that the temple of Zerubbabel was entirely replaced by a final (third) temple, which was begun in the time of Herod the Great. The latter reigned under Roman jurisdiction (c. 37-4 BCE), and he undertook a range of monumental building work. Herod's temple was an impressive complex of buildings constructed in the Hellenistic-Roman architectural style, but with a traditional Jewish design and arrangement in the core building of the complex, the temple itself. There is surviving masonry from the foundations of the structure in Jerusalem, the so-called "Wailing Wall," that incorporates massive blocks of limestone up to five meters long, which still needs archaeological excavation.

Work on this structure was begun in about 20 BCE, and construction appears to have continued virtually to the time of the destruction of the entire complex by the Romans in 70 CE. Detailed descriptions of the buildings are provided by Josephus, among other writers (*Antiq.*, XV.xi-xii; *War*, V.v). Josephus is the key source because he was not only a Jerusalem native who had firsthand knowledge of the complex of buildings, but was also a Levitical insider who had been a priest of the temple. However, his writings date from well after the temple's destruction, probably while he was a resident of Rome as an exile at the end of the first century CE.

The importance of the third temple in the context of the religious and political institutions of Judaism during the time of Jesus is difficult to overestimate. Imperial Rome was, as a rule, surprisingly tolerant of the indigenous religions of the peoples of the empire, and Roman rulers actively pursued this policy with respect to the ancient religion of Judaism (particularly since there had been an ancient alliance between Rome and Judea during the time of the Hasmonaean rulers). Under the Romans, in fact, Judaea was technically a "temple state" in the sense that the very existence of the Jerusalem temple itself provided the reason for the existence of Judaea as a separate political entity within the Roman political order. Its very geographical territory was the amount of land deemed necessary to provide for the maintenance and worship of the temple.[5]

5. James D. G. Dunn, *The Partings of the Ways* (London: SCM Press; Philadelphia:

The temple was, however, always a contested religious institution. First of all, alternative shrines existed in ancient times. Even in the late biblical period, two major alternatives to the official worship of the temple existed — even in close proximity to the temple. The first was the Qumran community (the Essenes), who believed that the official temple worship was so corrupt that they needed to withdraw from it altogether — at least until the administration of the Jerusalem temple could be reformed. The second alternative, and by far the more important, was the institution of the synagogue, which was to become the central religious institution of postbiblical Judaism. As we know from the New Testament, the synagogue already existed as an important Jewish religious institution in the biblical period itself, at least during the last decades of the Jerusalem temple. Given its importance, the origins of the synagogue are surprisingly obscure: the extent to which the worship of the synagogues should be seen as either a rival or a complement to the official worship of the temple is a matter of considerable debate.[6]

Trinity Press International, 1991), pp. 31-35, notes a number of factors that we might mention in this connection. First, the significance of the temple secured the political as well as the religious power of the high-priestly families that controlled it. Second, because Israel was a religious state, the civil law obtaining under Roman authority was for the most part Jewish religious law. Third, the place of the temple at the center of Judaea and Judaism made it enormously important to the economy of Jerusalem. For example, the Romans made provision for the transmission to Jerusalem of a temple tax from every adult male Jew in the (Roman) diaspora, while pilgrims, offerings, and other sources of revenue also flowed on a daily basis to the city. Arguing from the standard integration of market and sanctuary in the cities of the eastern Mediterranean, Dunn goes so far as to speculate that the temple complex likely functioned as a financial center, making loans as well as serving as a repository of wealth. Fourth, the construction of the temple under Herod and his successors was for generations an important source of employment for artisans and other workers. Such factors augmented the strictly liturgical importance of the temple as the center of Jewish worship.

6. See Howard Clark Kee and Lynn H. Cohick, eds., *Evolution of the Synagogue* (Harrisburg, PA: Trinity Press International, 1999). What is unclear is the extent to which elements within synagogue Judaism saw the synagogue as a rival to the temple (analogous to the Qumran community with its worship). What we do know is that the rabbinic Judaism that survived the destruction of the temple by the Romans in 70 CE functioned entirely in the context of the synagogue. Thus it is clear that the synagogue was in principle capable of existing independently. This is conceivably a clue to understanding the character of the synagogue during earlier times, when temple and synagogue coexisted. We may conclude that the synagogue most likely developed as a result of the Jewish diaspora, perhaps initially in the context of the exile, and that mainly for historical and political reasons — and

What is clear is that one could be a good Jew without ever attending the temple, since there must have been many pious Jews of the Diaspora who could not and did not visit Jerusalem.

Yet, even against this background, it is still astonishing to encounter the idea — not at the fringes but in mainstream Jewish sources — that the presence of God was not found in either of the postexilic temples.[7] The claim appears several times in rabbinic literature, generally in connection with the theological doctrine of the *Shekinah,* a rabbinic word specifically denoting the presence of God (from the root verb *shakan,* "to dwell"). Though the specific argument that the *Shekinah* was absent is by no means universal in rabbinic sources, the general view of the rabbis is clearly that both the temple of Zerubbabel and the temple of Herod were religiously disappointing. How far this idea should be projected back into the biblical period of synagogue worship is an important, but open, question. For the present, we may note it as a distinct possibility.

The view of the temple as a disappointment could be the result of a number of factors: for example, the supposed corrupt administration of the temple could have been to blame; or the fact that the worship of God did not yield the fruit of political independence from foreign oppression may have implied its defects. But the disappointment certainly could be explained by the perception that the presence of God in the temple was simply lacking. Such a view might have been resisted by the temple authorities, of course, but there is a clear departure from the older theology of the presence of God associated with the temple in postbiblical Judaism, which, given what we know about temple as a disputed institution all along, may reflect much more ancient misgivings. For example, some rabbinic sources speak of the *Shekinah* as dwelling with Israel in its uncleanness, or of the *Shekinah* as going into exile with Judah.[8] This continuing divine presence with the chosen people of God is conceived of in such a way as to make it independent of the physical temple. The claim is obviously a response to the catastrophe of destruction, but it also amounts to a rejection of the theology of the divine

---

indirectly for religious reasons — the synagogue gained sufficient ground to become the mainstream embodiment of Jewish religious life after the catastrophe of 70 CE.

7. Talmud Yoma 21b, where the reference is to the *Shekinah;* see also Midrash Numbers Rabba 15:10, where the reference is to the Spirit (cited by R. E. Clements, *God and Temple* [Oxford: Basil Blackwell, 1965], p. 126).

8. Talmud Yoma, 56b; Meg. 29a; cited in "Shekhinah," in *Encyclopaedia Judaica,* 26 vols. (Jerusalem: Keter Publishing House, 1972), 14: cols. 1349-54.

presence that went before, and that associated it uniquely with the temple and its service.[9]

The question of *where* the presence of God is to be located was thus disputed. We know from biblical sources, for example, that the issue of where Yahweh's sanctuary was to be located was a central point of dispute in the ancient division of the northern kingdom of Israel from Judah. In later rabbinic theology, there is an interesting — and to some extent parallel — dispute concerning whether the *Shekinah* is primarily to be associated with Sinai and the giving of the Law or with the Jerusalem temple. The association with Sinai fits neatly into the theological ethos of rabbinic Judaism, after all, and hence into the Judaism of the synagogue, as opposed to that of the temple.[10] The former is primarily a religion of the Word and of ethical observance; the latter is a religion principally of priestly ritual and sacrifice. Such disputes, of course, are endemic to religion generally, and are not susceptible to final theological resolution, beyond perhaps observing with Isaiah that all the ritual in the world is as nothing compared to simple obedience to God's will (Isa. 66:1-2).

The Ark of the Covenant

What is absolutely indisputable in this matter, and rather more surprising, is that neither of the two rebuilt temples that stood after the original destruction of Solomon's temple by the Babylonians contained an ark of the covenant. This is enormously significant, for it was the ark that symbolized God's presence, and perhaps even mediated it in some way. This extraordinary fact, given that the ark is represented in the Bible as the throne of God, was clearly a major source of uncertainty concerning whether the presence of God was or was not to be found in the rebuilt temples of the late biblical period.

Though popular portrayals abound, what the ark was is rather difficult

9. Much later in Judaism the theme of the *Shekinah* as a continuing reality in the religious life of the Jews would be developed extensively in the Safed spirituality of the early sixteenth century. Thus Elijah de Vidas, *The Beginning of Wisdom,* trans. Lawrence Fine, in *Safed Spirituality* (New York: Paulist Press, 1984), pp. 131-32, says that the *Shekinah* is to be found in a very concrete sense in any synagogue, which is presented as a "substitute" for the temple (citing earlier sources, such as the *Zohar*).

10. A question discussed in Roy A. Stewart, *Rabbinic Theology* (Edinburgh and London: Oliver and Boyd, 1961), pp. 39-42.

to determine exactly, not only because it is not represented in any archaeological find from the period (naturally enough, since it was meant to be hidden from view), but also because the biblical sources that speak of the ark give us subtly different accounts of its form. What are often held to be the oldest traditions represent the ark simply as a box or container for objects of holiness (usually said to be the tablets of the Law). However, later traditions appear to represent the ark as Yahweh's throne (hence the divine title, "he who sits enthroned upon the cherubim").[11] What seems most likely to some is that a number of closely associated objects that are often taken together as "the ark of the covenant" need to be distinguished (Exod. 25:10-22): first, the ark or box itself; second, the *kapporeth* ("cover," "mercy seat" being a traditional Christian rendering); and third, the two cherubim, whose size is not specified.

The general arrangement is spoken about in Exodus 25: "The cherubim shall spread out their wings above, overshadowing the mercy seat. You shall put the mercy seat on top of the ark; and in the ark you shall put the covenant that I shall give you" (vv. 20-21). Some translations speak of the cherubim as made in one piece with the *kapporeth* (e.g., the New English Bible), but this is very uncertain. In any case, in the account of the building of Solomon's temple in 1 Kings 6-8, the cherubim are said to have been *reconstructed* in massive proportions, so that they filled the most holy place, whereas the covenant box is obviously assumed to exist already from earlier times (the *kapporeth*, for its part, is not mentioned in this passage, and was either unknown to the writer of 1 Kings or taken to be implicit in mention of the ark). This whole complex of objects is what is commonly spoken of as the ark of the covenant.

Strictly speaking, it is on the cherubim rather than the covenant box itself that Yahweh is represented as enthroned, so that the divine presence is located above the ark: "There I will meet with you, and from above the mercy seat, from between the two cherubim that are on the ark of the covenant, I will deliver to you all my commands . . ." (Exod. 25:22). This text suggests that one of the important functions of the ark was oracular, or possibly legal, in character (all law being divine in origin). Other traditions concerning the ark give it a military function, as in the destruction of Jericho in Joshua 6-7, or in the "song of the ark" in Numbers 10:35-36, which is likely

---

11. Menahem Haran, *Temples and Temple-Service in Ancient Israel* (Oxford: Clarendon Press, 1978), pp. 246-59; and Clements, *God and Temple*, pp. 28-39.

very ancient. The ark also unquestionably was taken to be symbolic (minimally) of the presence of Yahweh, who is enthroned on the cherubim (e.g., 2 Sam. 6:2). It was also most likely taken to mediate it in some way, for though not being itself an "image" representing God, it could still function in a "sacramental" sense as a means by which the God who is unseen and who cannot be represented becomes present. Thus, upon the completion of Solomon's temple, it was the physical placing of the ark in the temple that is said to have brought about the descent of the cloud of glory that represents the divine presence (1 Kings 8:6-11).

We can mention one further crucial function of the ark, something drawn from the liturgy of the Day of Atonement: "[Aaron] shall take some of the blood of the bull, and sprinkle it with his finger on the front of the mercy seat, and before the mercy seat he shall sprinkle the blood with his finger seven times. He shall slaughter the goat . . . and do with its blood as he did with the blood of the bull . . ." (Lev. 16:14-15). This implies that, by definition, this key ritual could not have been properly carried out in a sanctuary devoid of the ark and mercy seat. Yet for fully six centuries after the exile, the Day of Atonement was celebrated annually under these conditions in the Jerusalem sanctuary. Later rabbinical sources give an account of the liturgy, which was complete in all respects apart from the presence of the ark and the liturgical use of its cover, on which blood was meant to be sprinkled.[12] But this liturgy actually highlighted the *absence* of the ark, for the rabbis seemingly used a stone on which, by tradition, the ark had rested in the most holy place during the time of the first temple.

It is significant that the ark is not mentioned in the detailed accounts of the plunder of the temple by the Babylonians that appear in Scripture (2 Kings 25:13-17; Jer. 52:17-23), which has naturally led to a good deal of speculation concerning its fate.[13] As is well known, the Ethiopian Orthodox

12. See the account in E. P. Sanders, *Judaism: Practice and Belief 63* BCE–66 CE (London: SCM Press; Philadelphia: Trinity Press International, 1992), pp. 141-43.

13. Three possible explanations suggest themselves. The first is that the ark had been hidden — as an object too holy to pass into enemy hands; as we shall see, this is the traditional account. The second possibility is that the ark was not present in the Jerusalem temple by this time, but had already been destroyed; this view is unconventional, but could be conjectured on the basis of the biblical treatment of the sins of King Manasseh, who in a fifty-five-year reign introduced a fertility cult into the temple of Solomon, going so far as providing for male temple prostitutes (2 Kings 23:7) and placing an image of the Canaanite goddess Asherah in the temple (2 Kings 21:1-7) (*cf.* Haran, *Temples and Temple-*

Church claims to possess it, though, according to most accounts, this is very unlikely. Some Jewish sages, for their part, maintained that it was hidden by the good King Josiah under the temple pavements (Mishnah, *Shekalim* 6.1-2). This view has persisted right up to our time and has led to recent unauthorized excavations under the Temple Mount by radical Jewish religious groups searching for the object. Alternatively, according to 2 Baruch 6:1-10, an angel took the ark and hid it. A more important text in Maccabees speaks of a written record, according to which the prophet Jeremiah, in response to an oracle, personally hid the ark, the tabernacle from the Exodus wanderings (the remains of which presumably still existed), as well as the altar of incense, in a cave on Mount Nebo, whose entrance subsequently proved impossible for others to find (2 Macc. 2:4-6). Jeremiah, it is said, rebuked those who sought the place: "[It] shall remain unknown until God gathers his people together again and shows his mercy. Then the Lord will disclose these things, and the glory of the Lord and the cloud will appear, as they were shown in the case of Moses . . ." (v. 7).

Maccabees is an important text, for it represents the mainstream voice of Palestinian Judaism in the intertestamental period. It was certainly authoritative enough to have been included in the Septuagint (and the subsequent ancient Christian Bible). The association with Jeremiah is also highly significant, for it is Jeremiah who says of the future restoration:

> I will give you shepherds after my own heart, who will feed you with knowledge and understanding. And when you have multiplied and increased in the land, in those days, says the LORD, they shall no longer say, "The ark of the covenant of the LORD." It shall not come to mind, or be remembered, or missed: *nor shall another one be made.* At that

---

Service, pp. 276-88). The obvious implication is that the image was set in the most holy place, according to longstanding Canaanite practice, which would have required the removal of the existing contents of the inner sanctuary, i.e., the ark, the mercy seat, and the massive cherubim. However, this is not the conventional account of events, largely due to an important reference to the continuing existence of the ark under a subsequent reformer, King Josiah, who abolished the cult introduced by Manesseh and returned the ark to its rightful place (2 Chron. 35:3). The third possibility is suggested by 2 Esdras 10:22, an intertestamental work that, uniquely among all the accounts, laments that "the ark of our covenant has been plundered" (i.e., by the Babylonians), a text that at the very least shows that *some* Jews certainly did think that the ark had been carried off to Babylon. But this was very much a minority view, and it scarcely appears in the literature.

time Jerusalem shall be called the throne of the LORD, and all nations shall gather to it, to the presence of the LORD in Jerusalem. . . . In those days the house of Judah shall join the house of Israel, and together they shall come from the land of the north to the land that I gave your ancestors for a heritage. (Jer. 3:15-18, italics added)

The reference here is clearly eschatological, and the content of the prophecy obviously stands in tension with the account in 2 Maccabees 2:7; but the text (with the Maccabean tradition alongside it) may well account for what seems otherwise inexplicable: that postexilic Judaism did not reconstruct the lost ark. The fact that it did not do so can be explained not by the concept that the ark was "irreplaceable," as some have argued, but rather by the words and the immense authority of Jeremiah.[14] A similar prophetic influence in postexilic Judaism might also be inferred from Ezekiel, who gives detailed instructions concerning the rebuilt temple and its worship, but who conspicuously does not mention the ark in an otherwise exhaustive account of the reconstruction (Ezek. 40ff.).

Was the rebuilt temple seen as devoid of God's presence, then, since the ark was not present? Jeremiah's statement as reported in 2 Maccabees 2:7 seems to imply that "the glory of the LORD and the cloud" were absent, or at least not present to the extent or in the way desired. What is striking about this statement is that the books of Maccabees are almost certainly to be located at or near the center of institutional Judaism of that time: this means that the view that the presence of God was missing from the temple was a prominent one. Later rabbinical sources, as we have seen, also give an ambiguous answer to this question, and so do other sources in the Bible itself. On the one hand, there is the voice of Ezekiel, who in the context of the exile has visions both of the departure of the presence of God from the first temple (Ezek. 11:22-25) and of its definitive return to the rebuilt structure that he describes, complete with living (i.e., real rather than crafted) cherubim (Ezek. 43:1-4; cf. 44:1-3). On the other hand, a text such as Jeremiah 3:15-18 appears to associate the return of the presence of God much more explicitly with a more remote, eschatological future (though this may also be the point of the vision in Ezekiel). Since this future was to include the restoration of the twelve tribes and the conversion of the gentiles, and since these events had

---

14. Thus, e.g., W. S. McCullough, *The History and Literature of the Palestinian Jews from Cyrus to Herod* (Toronto: University of Toronto Press, 1975), p. 27.

palpably not taken place during the period of the second and third temples, it is unquestionable that at least some Jews must have taken the view, on the basis of prophetic authority: (a) that the presence of God was not found in the rebuilt temple, or at least not as it had been in the temple of Solomon; and (b) that consequently the rebuilt temple was not in reality the "true" temple of prophetic expectation. A final temple, then, accompanied by these other eschatological events, was still to be anticipated.[15] While not universal, such views are clearly identifiable in a range of Jewish texts from the period (e.g., Tobit 14:3-7).

What does all this mean for us? Minimally, it suggests, first of all, that certain of the claims of the New Testament concerning the concept of the temple should be seen against the background of these longstanding themes in Jewish eschatology. When, for example, the Epistle to the Hebrews interprets Jesus' death by way of a lengthy treatment of the temple liturgy, but all the while speaking of the "true" temple as one that is not of this creation (Heb. 9:11), and treating the earthly temple as a mere "shadow of the good things to come" (Heb. 10:1), it is engaged in a pattern of theological reflection that has surprisingly deep roots in the Jewish religion of the time. In other words, the treatment is not merely a stereotypically "Alexandrian" allegorical interpretation, as much superficial exegesis of the book of Hebrews suggests. The second and third temples were far from uncontroversial institutions. However magnificent and however many economic resources were devoted to sustaining worship in them, many Jews explicitly saw them as provisional and anticipatory. Anticipation can, of course, be enormously important in religion as in human life generally, but it is not the thing itself. The thing itself was still to come.

Second, prophetic expectations about the restored temple are closely connected with the promised renewal of the presence of God, and that realization is an important pneumatological theme of the New Testament. By contrast, our sources suggest its absence — or at the very least its relative absence — in the time of the second and third temples. Certain of the claims made in the New Testament concerning the presence of God will need to be examined in this light.

---

15. A point E. P. Sanders vigorously argues in *Jesus and Judaism* (Philadelphia: Fortress, 1985), pp. 77-90 (see esp. texts cited on pp. 86-87).

The "Temple" Theme in the New Testament: Paul and the Epistles

In view of these factors, it is scarcely surprising that the Jewish theology of the temple is transformed in the writings of the New Testament. In fact, it could not help but be reinterpreted, given the conviction of the earliest Christians that in Jesus Christ, in the outpouring of the Holy Spirit, and in the conversion of the gentiles, ancient prophetic expectations were being fulfilled. A comprehensive reinterpretation of the temple thus appears in New Testament texts that date from both before and after its physical destruction by the Romans.

Of special importance for us is the fact that in the Epistles of Paul, which constitute some of the earliest strata of the New Testament (and which were written while the Jerusalem temple still stood and functioned), the church itself, Jewish *and gentile,* is identified as God's temple. The extent to which the idea is pressed is striking. For instance, this is reflected in the fact that the technical term for the "most holy place" of the temple, *naos,* is explicitly used of the church, that is, of the people who comprise it. Thus has the temple idea, and with it the theology of the indwelling presence of God, come to be totally reconceived.

A number of texts can be cited, the most important of which appear in the Corinthian letters.

> According to the grace of God given to me, like a skilled master builder I laid a foundation, and someone else is building on it. . . . No one can lay any foundation other than the one that has been laid: that foundation is Jesus Christ. . . . Do you not know that you are God's temple [*naos*] and that God's Spirit dwells in you? If anyone destroys God's temple, God will destroy that person. For God's temple is holy, and you are that temple. (1 Cor. 3:10-11, 16)

Here all the basic lines of Paul's theological reinterpretation converge. He refers to the whole assembly of believers in Corinth, the church that has been built through the labors of various evangelists, or "builders," as Paul puts it (vv. 10-17). This church is the "temple" by virtue of the indwelling presence of the Holy Spirit, which makes it (in a statement highly significant for an understanding of Paul's pneumatology as well) nothing less than God's *naos.* As he presses the building metaphor, he asserts the foundational status of Jesus (cf. Eph. 2:20-22) and emphasizes the holiness of the church as temple.

The same idea that believers who have received the Spirit have become the temple of God is also reflected in 2 Corinthians, in an extraordinarily dense text that alludes to a range of Old Testament statements that relate, first, to the glory of God found in the tabernacle of Moses (Lev. 26:11; Exod. 29:45), then to the prophetic expectations of Isaiah (52:11) and Ezekiel (37:27) concerning the eschatological temple, and also most likely to the Davidic theology of divine sonship associated with the temple of Solomon (2 Sam. 7:14). Paul says:

> Do not be mismatched with unbelievers. For what partnership is there between righteousness and lawlessness? Or what fellowship is there between light and darkness? What agreement does Christ have with Belial? Or what does a believer share with an unbeliever? What agreement has the temple of God with idols? For we are the temple of the living God. As God has said:
>
> I will live in them and walk among them,
>   and I will be their God,
>   and they shall be my people.
> Therefore come out from them,
>   and be separate from them, says the Lord,
> and touch nothing unclean:
>   then I will welcome you,
>   and I will be your father,
>   and you shall be my sons and daughters,
> says the Lord Almighty.
>
> (2 Cor. 6:14-18)[16]

16. A more individualistic emphasis, however, is possible in another text from 1 Corinthians: "Shun fornication! Every sin that a person commits is outside the body; but the fornicator sins against the body itself. Or do you not know that your body is a temple of the Holy Spirit within you, which you have from God. . . ?" (1 Cor. 6:18-19). However, here it may more plausibly be argued that the word "body" is to be taken in the technical Pauline sense as "body of Christ," in which case, once again, the reference would be to the people joined with Christ rather than to the individual. Note also that the Greek text is strained and has been subject to editorial emendation; thus a few manuscripts read "your bodies" rather than the better-attested "your (plural) body (singular)." Historically, the idea that the temple of the Spirit is the individual — as opposed to the collective — "body" would prove to be immensely influential. For example, it was destined to bear fruit in various physical evidences adduced for the presence of the Spirit, not only in "tongues" and similar phenomena, but also in the remarkable spirituality of transfiguration that Eastern Christianity laid claim to, which we briefly discussed in the preceding chapter.

This explicit adaptation of the theme of the temple to the doctrine of the church needs also be set alongside a series of further affirmations in the Pauline Epistles regarding God's presence in the church and in the believer. Taken together, they show how deep the idea of the divine indwelling runs in Pauline thought. For example, we read in Romans 8 of a contrast between two modes of existence: in one, the law of sin and death reigns; in the other, "the just requirement of the law [is] fulfilled in us, who walk not according to the flesh, but according to the Spirit" (Rom. 8:4). Paul then continues with these startling words:

> [Y]ou are not in the flesh; you are in the Spirit since the Spirit of God dwells in you. But if Christ is in you, though the body is dead because of sin, the Spirit is life because of righteousness. If the Spirit of him who raised Christ from the dead dwells in you, he who raised Christ from the dead will give life to your mortal bodies also through his Spirit that dwells in you [*dia tou enoikountos autou pneumatos en humin*, that is, "through his indwelling spirit in you"]. (Rom. 8:9-11)

Very definite *effects*, then, follow from this indwelling divine presence.

Several further points can be made about the Pauline conception before we move on. The first is that Paul (like John: cf. John 14:15-18) appears to be ambivalent about whether it is the Spirit of God or the risen Christ who dwells in the church. In the above text the indwelling of Christ and of the Spirit are spoken of synonymously. Thus Paul is far less careful to distinguish between the various activities of the "persons" than Christians were destined to become in the centuries of Trinitarian orthodoxy, though the fluidity of the Pauline conception of Christ and the Spirit is obviously something that any attempt to develop a triadic theological understanding of God as Father, Son, and Spirit has had to accommodate (e.g., through the Trinitarian doctrines of *perichoresis* and appropriation and, equally, the principle of *opera ad extra trinitatis sunt indivisa*).

The second is that the Pauline use of the temple motif is not restricted to the concept of indwelling, nor does it always involve explicit reference to the "temple." To take a well-known example, Romans 3:24-25 speaks of "the redemption that is in Christ Jesus, whom God put forward as a sacrifice of atonement by his blood." The "sacrifice of atonement" is rendered as "a place of atonement" in the margins of the *NRSV translation*, which is undoubtedly correct, because, to be precise, the phrase translates a single technical word from Jewish Greek, the word *hilastêrion,* which is used in the Septuagint to render the Hebrew *kapporeth,* or "mercy seat," which we have already encountered in connection with the ark. The importance of Paul's use of this word in his approach to the meaning of Christ's death is difficult to overestimate, given the physical absence of the *hilastêrion* from the Jerusalem temple for centuries. The *hilastêrion* is also regarded as a locus of the divine presence in the Bible: "Tell your brother Aaron not to come just at any time into the sanctuary inside the curtain before the mercy seat that is upon the ark, or he will die; for I appear in the cloud upon the mercy seat. Thus shall Aaron come into the holy place: with a young bull for a sin offering and a ram for a burnt offering [i.e., on the Day of Atonement only]" (Lev. 16:2-3). A second reference is less direct, and less well known. In Romans 15, Paul uses technical terms from the temple cult to refer to his own ministry: ". . . because of the grace given me by God to be a minister [*leitourgon*] of Christ Jesus to the Gentiles in the priestly service [*hierourgounta*] of the gospel of God, so that the offering of the Gentiles may be acceptable, sanctified by the Holy Spirit."

Both of these themes, the first relating to the theme of atonement, and the second to the "priestly" character of apostolic ministry and of the church, are taken up extensively elsewhere in the New Testament. For example, we might refer to the tearing of the temple curtain from top to bottom at Jesus' death in Matthew 27:51, which relates Matthew's understanding of the meaning of Jesus' death to the sacrificial system of the temple and, theologically, to the Day of Atonement ritual itself. It is also reasonable to infer that the tearing of the curtain in Matthew symbolizes a removal of the barrier between the people and the presence of God that was in some way effected by Jesus' death. It is interesting that Ephesians speaks of the breaking down of the "dividing wall" (the wall separating the gentiles from the people of God in the Jerusalem temple?) and of our free "access" to God through the death of Jesus Christ (cf. Rom. 5:2) — all in the context of a treatment of the church of Jews and gentiles as the temple and dwelling place of God (Eph. 2:14-22; 3:12). In the temple, not only were gentiles denied such access, but so were the great mass of the Jews; only the priests were entitled to enter the inner courts of the temple complex, and only the high priest could intrude into the most holy place — and then only once a year.

This last point is famously taken up in the Epistle to the Hebrews, according to which the old sanctuary was defective precisely because, in it, the way into the most holy place was barred (Heb. 9:8), whereas in the heavenly sanctuary that is not made with hands, into which Christ has entered on our behalf (Heb. 9:11-12), the way to the divine presence is open to all who wish to come. "Therefore, my friends, since we have confidence to enter the sanctuary by the blood of Jesus, by the new and living way that he opened for us through the curtain . . . let us approach with a true heart in full assurance of faith, with our hearts sprinkled . . . and our bodies washed with pure water" (Heb. 10:19-22). The text explicitly refers to the work of the high priest on the Day of Atonement in Leviticus 16, with this crucial difference: now there is free access to the true sanctuary, rather than an access open only to a priestly intermediary in the earthly shadow or copy of it.

The priestly character of the church is an idea developed through the length and breadth of these arguments of the Epistle to the Hebrews, but it is probably better known from the language of "living stones" being built into a "spiritual house" that is used in 1 Peter 2. This is, of course, the great sponsoring text for the idea of the "priesthood of all believers," which is such a crucial idea in the theology of the Lutheran Reformation:

> Come to him, a living stone . . . and like living stones, let yourselves be built into a spiritual house, to be a holy priesthood, to offer spiritual sacrifices acceptable to God through Jesus Christ. . . . [Y]ou are a chosen race, a royal priesthood, a holy nation, God's own people, in order that you may proclaim the mighty acts of him who called you out of darkness into his marvelous light. Once you were not a people, but now you are God's people; once you had not received mercy, but now you have received mercy. (1 Pet. 2:4-5, 9-10)

These ideas are not entirely new, for not only are a range of similar ideas widely reflected elsewhere in the New Testament, but in one of the many *Old Testament* texts that this New Testament passage presupposes, Israel as a whole is already spoken of as a "priestly kingdom" (Exod. 19:6). We need only observe for the moment that they have been very imperfectly observed in institutional Christianity through the centuries.

Temple and Indwelling in John

I must also mention briefly the distinctive theological reworking of the temple concept that appears in the Gospel of John, even though the connection with the doctrine of the church is indirect. In John, the temple theme is truly basic, but the primary *site* of God's dwelling is not the church, but Jesus himself, whom John presents as the new temple. Though the term is unconventional, Johannine Christology has been accurately described as "naomorphic."[17] For example, we can cite the famous text of John 1:14, "the Word became flesh and lived among us," as a text of immense importance in the history of Christology. However, this verse contains an unusual phrase that is not readily captured in translation. Literally rendered, the text reads that the Word became flesh and "tented among us" *(eskênôsen en hêmin)*. The theological reference in this doctrine of the incarnation's "charter text" is not merely to the Word's "dwelling" among us but to the ancient wilderness tabernacle *(skênos)* constructed by Moses, in which God dwelt and on which the Jerusalem temple was assumed to be modeled.

On the basis of this, the noted biblical commentator Raymond Brown speaks of a Johannine theology in which Jesus himself "serves as the Tabernacle."[18] The associated reference to the "glory" *(doxa)* beheld in the one who "tented" among us (v. 14) would be, in this view, an allusion to the divine glory present in the tabernacle and in the Solomonic temple in the biblical witness, but compromised or even absent from the reconstructed temples after the exile. The point is that the true hope of Israel, the renewal of the presence of God in its fullness, is found in Jesus himself.

In this connection, a text in John 2 is worth citing at length:

> The Passover of the Jews was near, and Jesus went up to Jerusalem. In the temple he found people selling cattle, sheep, and doves, and the money changers seated at their tables. Making a whip of cords, he drove all of them out. . . . He also poured out the coins of the money changers and overturned their tables. He told those who were selling the doves, "Take these things out of here! Stop making my Father's house a marketplace!" . . . The Jews then said to him, "What sign can you show us for doing this?" Jesus answered them, "Destroy this temple, and in three days I will raise it up." The Jews then said, "This temple has been under construction for forty-six years, and will you raise it up in three days?" But he was speaking of the temple of his body. Af-

---

17. This adjective was coined by W. J. Phythian-Adams, *The People and the Presence* (London: Oxford University Press, 1942). Among more recent studies, cf. Alan R. Kerr, *The Temple of Jesus' Body* (New York: Sheffield Academic Press, 2002).

18. Raymond E. Brown, *The Gospel According to John (i-xii)* (New York: Doubleday, 1966), p. 34.

ter he was raised from the dead, his disciples remembered that he had said this; and they believed the scripture and the word that Jesus had spoken. (John 2:13-22)

The core statement here for our purposes is verse 19: "Destroy this temple [*naos*] and in three days I will raise it up," a saying that the passage then interprets as a reference to Jesus' own body. This text is possibly based on the pericope in Mark 11:15-19 (assuming, with C. K. Barrett, that the evangelist knew the Gospel of Mark), but it is obviously given a different narrative location, as well as a characteristically Christological sense by the author of John. The point of this is clearly consistent with John 1:14, so that the Word who "tabernacled" among us is now spoken of in technical religious language as the new *naos* of God, which, by implication, replaces the old.

Thus in the Christology of John, Jesus is not "simply" the Word made flesh, but is specifically the "localization of God's presence on earth" (Brown, p. 33), so that he appears as the Word of God who "tabernacled" among us, and whose own body is therefore the *naos,* the most holy place in which God dwells.[19] Two millennia of incarnational theology have left us ill-equipped to accord such statements the theological importance they deserve in a religion born of biblical Judaism. In reality, however, one might well ask how a Jewish Christian, writing near the end of the first century, could express a more exalted view of Jesus than to speak of him as the *naos* of the tabernacling presence of God, long absent from the earth but now at last realized as the fulfillment of Judaism's longing.[20]

Later in his Gospel, John handles the related theme of the indwelling presence of God in those who have faith in Jesus in more familiar pneumatological terms, as Jesus promises that the Father will send the "Paraclete" to his disciples after his departure. The Paraclete is "the Spirit of truth, whom the world cannot receive, because it neither sees him nor knows him. You know him, because he abides with you, and he will be in you" (John 14:17). Another reference reveals what is at stake in such talk: "Those who love me will keep my word, and my Father will love them, and we will come to them and make our home with them" (v. 23). This theology of the

19. This idea is taken up somewhat idiosyncratically by Phythian-Adams, *The People and the Presence,* pp. 205-51, and by Yves Congar, *The Mystery of the Temple,* trans. Reginald F. Trevett (London: Burns & Oates, 1962), pp. 129-50.

20. Equally, of course, one might ask how a Jewish writer such as Paul could dare express a more exalted view of the church than be speaking of it as the *naos* of God.

indwelling of God, not only in Jesus but also in the disciples of Jesus, is a major theme of the fourth Gospel; and the same emphasis can be readily identified elsewhere in the Johannine corpus of the New Testament: "By this we know that we abide in him and he in us, because he has given us of his Spirit. . . . God is love, and those who abide in love abide in God, and God abides in them" (1 John 4:13, 16b).

The connection between this latter idea of indwelling and the temple concept is at best indirect, but it appears that in the fourth Gospel, God's dwelling has become Jesus himself, and consequently that the place of God's dwelling is extended to the church gathered around Jesus. A range of associated ideas can be traced through the Gospel of John. In particular — and in obvious contrast to the synoptic accounts — Jesus appears at the temple repeatedly in John's Gospel in order to attend the great religious feasts of Tabernacles, Dedication, and Passover. But each of these feasts provides an occasion for a Christological reinterpretation of the temple and its liturgy.[21] Of these, the Feast of Passover is the best known and the most important, since the Passover festival frames the interpretation of Jesus' death given in the Johannine passion narrative. Thus, for example, in John 1:29, John the Baptist declares of Jesus, "Here is the Lamb of God who takes away the sin of the world!" And in John 19, Jesus' trial comes to an end and he is led away to be crucified at the very hour (noon) when many thousands of Passover lambs were being slaughtered in the temple courts on the Day of Preparation (John 19:14).

However, the "naomorphic" character of Johannine Christology is clearest in the case of the account of Jesus' visit to the Feast of Tabernacles.[22] Tabernacles was an ancient and important festival that commemorated the wilderness wanderings and was associated with the dedication of Solomon's temple (1 Kings 8:2). Accordingly, at Tabernacles a twofold liturgy was cele-

---

21. A possible reference to Pentecost is also found in John 5:1. See Brown, *The Gospel According to John*, p. 206, who points out that though the feast is not specified, Pentecost would explain the references to Moses in the ensuing discourse, since Pentecost was (in part) a celebration of the giving of the Law to Moses on Sinai.

22. In the account of the visit to the Feast of Dedication in John 10, the Christological point is less obvious, but is nonetheless possible. Dedication (Hanukkah) was a celebration of the consecration of the temple and its altars following their desecration under Antiochus Epiphanes (1 Macc. 4:59). In John 10, the Jesus whom John earlier presents as the tabernacling presence of God and as the new *naos* is now "sanctified" in the world by the Father (the verb *hagiazein*, which is the root here, appears in Num. 7:1 in the Septuagint of Moses' consecration of the tabernacle).

brated, and its themes are taken up in John's Gospel. This involved a daily procession for seven days to the fountain on the Temple Mount that supplied the Pool of Siloam, and the liturgical carrying and pouring of water from this source into the ground at the temple altar.[23] The background of this ritual is important because, in the wilderness, Moses supplied water from the rock (Exod. 17:1-7); more important, the prophets Ezekiel and Zechariah both speak of the theme of water flowing from the temple. The better known is the passage in Ezekiel 37, but of greater significance is Zechariah 9–14, which is a key text for all the Gospel writers, especially John.

In Zechariah, a major "temple" text, the eschatological triumph of God and the vindication of his people include the following elements: the arrival of a king riding on a donkey (Zech. 9:9); the outpouring of the Spirit when people behold the one they have pierced (12:10); the opening of a fountain to cleanse from sin (13:1); living waters flowing from Jerusalem to the Mediterranean and the Dead Sea (14:10); the destruction of enemies, the conversion of the gentiles, and the proper keeping of the Feast of Tabernacles to ensure rain (14:16-17); and not least, the idea that at the time of fulfillment, there will be no more merchants in the temple (14:21).

Second, we learn from Mishnaic sources that during Jesus' lifetime there was at Tabernacles a liturgical celebration involving the lighting of four golden candlesticks in the temple courts (Mishnah Sukkah 5:2-4; Brown, p. 344). It seems that the symbolism of light was used to commemorate the pillar of fire in the wilderness, but in any case, the "candlesticks" were evidently massive: each had four golden bowls with wicks made from the sacred garments of the priests, and the light produced is said to have been visible all over Jerusalem. That the ritual was associated with the drawing of water is also implied by the Mishnaic statement that the light ritual took place in the "house of water drawing," that is, the court featured in the water ritual mentioned above.

The Gospel of John alludes to both liturgies, the first in John 7:37-39, and the second in John 8:12-20. In the first one, Jesus speaks of the quenching of thirst by the water that he will give (the Spirit); in the second, he speaks of himself as the light of the world. The connection intended between Jesus, the "temple of his body," the Christian community, and the worship of the Jerusalem temple is mainly indirect; but it is at least clear that the Gospel presents Jesus as the fulfillment of these temple rituals, and his community as beneficiaries.

---

23. Brown, *The Gospel According to John,* pp. 326-27.

Unlike Paul, the author of John does not present the church itself as the new temple, since the temple has become a strictly Christological category in Johannine theology. Nonetheless, the followers of Jesus share in his being: they eat the body that is spoken of as the *naos,* and they share the life of the vine. The Johannine idea of participation in Jesus lends itself to an extension of the indwelling of God from him to those who become his disciples.

The Theology of Divine Indwelling

In a study published in 1977 and entitled *God as Spirit,* the Anglican scholar Geoffrey Lampe makes a case for the view that in the biblical concept of the indwelling of God we have something more basic to the overall thrust of Scripture, more rooted in universal human experience, and more amenable to religious belief in our time than the classical Christological doctrine of incarnation could ever be.[24] The doctrine of the incarnation, Lampe argues, involving as it does the descent of a metaphysical being from heaven to earth, its assumption of a human nature through the Virgin Mary, and its life and death as one of us, belongs not only to an archaic mythical understanding of the nature of the cosmos, but also to an archaic understanding of the concept of God. As such, it is one that we are unable to cling to any longer with integrity. Lampe suggests that we might have more success in conceiving of Jesus — and in relating his significance to people in our day — by viewing him in terms of a more general and less "mythical" understanding of the relationship between the spiritual and the natural, or between the divine and the human. This more general notion Lampe identifies as the concept of indwelling. "We are thinking of deity itself," he says, "becoming immanent in the spirit of man, that is to say, in man as active and related — of God, indeed, becoming immanent in man in order that man may be moved to respond as a free son and so to achieve transcendence in union with God" (p. 208).

The emphasis on immanence has a long history in Anglicanism, though Lampe does not draw on it greatly in his exposition.[25] The point, apparently, is less a matter of historical theology than it is of looking to the theological future. Lampe's claim is that the idea of divine immanence makes possible a

---

24. Geoffrey Lampe, *God as Spirit* (London: SCM Press, 1977).
25. E.g., J. R. Illingworth, *Divine Immanence* (London: Macmillan and Co., 1898).

historic shift away from the classical overemphasis on the transcendence of God and on the theology of the Word in Christian thought, and a corresponding shift toward the concept of the Spirit of God, the Spirit that indwells the creature and thus grounds a life "in the Spirit." The particular advantage afforded by the concept of Spirit, according to Lampe, is that it is fundamentally a relational idea rather than an ontological concept, and, as such, it is more amenable to constructive interpretation in our time.

In short, Lampe wishes to avoid what he sees as the outmoded obscurantism involved in the classical doctrine of the incarnation that effectively makes Christian faith not viable in the modern world. According to Lampe, the word "Spirit" connotes the general religious idea of an encounter with the holy in the depths of human existence — which is, after all, the core of all religious experience — and this is as alive and well in the contemporary context as it ever was. What is needed is mainly a way of interpreting this human experience, so that Christian proclamation can speak to it today and make sense once more. Lampe's argument would suggest, by implication, that what is needed within the church is a new emphasis on the encounter with God and a move away from the hitherto prevailing focus on the Word — and what goes with it, that is, the pervasive ecclesiological fascination with questions of doctrine, order, and so on.

On one level, Lampe's theology seems to displace Jesus as the central name confessed in Christian faith, and to replace his name with another, the Holy Spirit. If God is to be identified primarily as Spirit, and if the divine outreach to or presence in the world is inherently a pneumatological question, that makes all else peripheral. However, it would be wrong to jump to the conclusion that Lampe's theology can make no place for Jesus at all; rather, the argument is that there was a particular and unique relationship between Jesus and the Spirit that indwelt him, and that Jesus' own story of self-giving love in obedience to the will of God becomes, for those who follow him, the basic paradigm or pattern of life in the Spirit. The story of Jesus thus becomes the basic model for Christian life. In short, a Spirit Christology corresponds to the proposed emphasis on the Spirit as the medium and focal point of encounter with God.

Lampe's call for a new theology of the Spirit took up a range of standard motifs from Protestant liberalism, especially as represented in Anglican circles. For example, the names of his contemporaries John Robinson and Maurice Wiles come to mind immediately. It certainly echoed far and wide in the 1970s, though it is possible that this had as much or more to do with the desire to come to grips with the very different account of the significance of the Spirit brought into focus by the charismatic movement of the 1970s and 1980s than it did with any loss of the relevance of classical theological conceptuality. The charismatic movement, though in general it was fiercely traditional in its claims regarding Scripture and the creeds, for example, is nevertheless radically experiential; therefore, it is not at all surprising that some of those who struggled to understand it theologically turned to Lampe for help.

Furthermore, subsequent developments have in many ways strengthened Lampe's case for a renewed emphasis on the "spiritual" dimension of human existence. The rise of the idea of "postmodernity" to the status of cultural commonplace over the past three decades has brought into being a sympathy for new approaches to human "spirituality," and it has raised the profile of what might broadly be seen as "religious" experience to a level that it has not enjoyed for a very long time in the Western world. If modernity was antireligious, and thus sought to reduce all meaningful religion to what could be contained within and controlled by reason alone, postmodernity — by definition — seeks to move beyond this and to find a place for what modernity rejected. Thus, though institutional religion may still be out of fashion and not entirely amenable to postmodern affirmation, "spirituality" is very much "in."

Christian theologians might well respond to this postmodern openness to religious experience with a constructive elaboration of the doctrine of the Spirit, and in particular, with an informed and sensitive approach to the question of the spiritual life, capable of lending depth to what is otherwise a rather thin subject. To this extent, at least, Lampe was certainly on an important and legitimate track. However, his basic contention that the idea of divine indwelling through the presence of the Spirit is less problematic from the standpoint of contemporary thought than is the concept of incarnation is doubtful. It may be that this is a theological theme from which he can make cultural mileage; but what is far from clear is that the challenge involved in thinking through the possibility of such an indwelling of God has been met.

To begin with, though Lampe appears to assume the contrary, the notion of God's Spirit indwelling people is certainly as "supernatural" an idea as that of incarnation. Divine indwelling, in fact, could plausibly be said to make most sense in a world where spirits generally are thought to indwell people to negative effect (sickness, madness, evil temperament), and little if any in ours. For Lampe to fail to register this fact is a little surprising, given the arguments he uses against classical incarnational thought. And the difficulties loom ever larger on closer investigation. For even if we assume the concept of "indwelling" to be more viable than incarnation as a Christological category, we must then go on to ask what, exactly, he means by it. How, for example, is God's indwelling in Jesus the same as or different from God's indwelling in us? Or, to put the question another way, what is the difference between the way God "indwelt" the baby in Mary's womb and the way the Holy Spirit "indwelt" Mary? Why should the child be a savior figure — in Lampe's terms — but not his mother? Or closer to home, what is the difference between the Pauline statements that "God was in Christ" and that "God is truly in you" (2 Cor. 5:19; 1 Cor. 14:25)? Am I (in Lampe's terms) in some sense as divine as Jesus?

Such questions are hardly trivial, and they need to be probed further. One seemingly unlikely source that we might refer to for help is patristic theology, particularly to the great patristic theological tradition once centered in the Hellenistic city of Antioch in Syria, which flourished especially in the fourth and fifth centuries CE. The reason is that it was already characteristic of the Antiochene school, long before the modern period had dawned and the works of Lampe had been written, to conceive of the incarnation as an indwelling of God in Jesus. For the Antiochenes, however, it is abundantly clear that God's indwelling in Jesus is qualitatively different from all other instances of God's indwelling. For example, according to one of the fragments preserved from the (posthumously condemned) writings of the Antiochene theologian Theodore of Mopsuestia (c. 350-428), God's gracious indwelling in the saints and in Christ is alike an instance of God's *eudokia*, or "good pleasure." But there is this crucial difference: that in Jesus Christ, God dwelt "as in a son," whereas God's indwelling in others and in creation generally comes about through fundamentally different modes of divine *eudokia*.[26] The particular "good pleasure" of God in the case of Christ is utterly unique and unrepeatable. It is interesting that Theodore in particular

---

26. The texts are most accessible in J. Stevenson and W. H. Frend, eds., *Creeds, Councils and Controversies* (London: SPCK, 1989), pp. 291-94. See also Rowan A. Greer, *Theodore of Mopsuestia* (Westminster, MD: Faith Press, 1961), pp. 56-61; Frances Young, *From Nicaea to Chalcedon* (Philadelphia: Fortress, 1983), pp. 199-213 (esp. p. 210). For a general account of Theodore's Christology, a standard work is R. A. Norris, *Manhood and Christ* (Oxford: Clarendon Press, 1963).

used the concept of the temple in his Christology in order to attempt to work out the implications of these ideas.[27]

Unfortunately, there was a major problem inherent in the Christology represented by Theodore and the Antiochene school: in this Christology it seems to be logically necessary for Jesus the man to exist first, in order for God to indwell him. In fact, this is how the Antiochene school conceived of Christology: they explicitly defended the notion that Jesus was in fact "the Man" in whom God dwelt, and accordingly that he was "the Man" who uniquely among other humans turned himself fully to God's indwelling presence. To its critics this Christology appeared to assume that there were two active agents in Jesus, one divine and one human, which, in the eyes of the critics, amounted to the suggestion that that there were effectively "two Sons" of God in him as well.

In subsequent developments, focused especially on the case of the heretic Nestorius (c. 360–c. 451), the Alexandrian idea of the *unity* of Christ, theologically expressed particularly in the work of Cyril of Alexandria (c. 370-444) in the idea of a "hypostatic union," came to be established as the orthodox alternative to the perceived dualism of Antiochene Christology. In Cyril's idea of the hypostatic union, there is no "Man," or no human nature of Jesus, that can be considered at all apart from the one created and assumed by God in the event of the incarnation. Furthermore, there is in Jesus Christ no one other than the Word of God incarnate, and in particular no "Man" who can be treated in isolation from him. According to this view, the concept of indwelling utterly fails to do justice to the mystery of Christ. At the Councils of Ephesus (431) and Chalcedon (451), the idea of the hypostatic union was defined as part of the formal doctrine of incarnation: rather than indwelling a man, the divine *hypostasis* (person) of the Son of God assumed a human nature, so that both divine and human natures were united by the power of God in the *hypostasis* of the eternal Son.

Still, one has to recognize that the Antiochene tradition did survive for centuries, sustaining piety, worship, theology, and mission on the basis of its own distinctive ideas of the indwelling of the Son of God in Christ, and that, even allowing for the Councils of Ephesus and Chalcedon, most of its theological representatives lived in their day as perfectly orthodox theologians of the great church tradition. It would appear also that the theology is capable of integrating the "naomorphism" of New Testament Christology more

27. Greer, *Theodore of Mopsuestia*, p. 59.

seamlessly into Christian teaching than was the orthodoxy that actually tri-
umphed. In fact, in the form of Nestorian Christianity, the Antiochene
school survived long beyond 451 as a vast, though heterodox, Christian
movement existing outside the Chalcedonian Christological settlement. It
still survives, in much diminished form, even today.

Presence and Omnipresence

Well beyond ancient Antioch, the question of divine presence has long been
discussed with respect to another of the difficult problems of theology: the
classical theological attribute of divine omnipresence. That God is present
everywhere, according to the attribute of omnipresence, would seem on one
level to make the question of the possibility of divine presence *somewhere* a
trivial one. Rather like the ocean, which can fill a vast geological basin, as
well as the little sunken bottle that lies in its depths, God can be both everywhere and yet also, for this very reason, somewhere in particular. However,
precisely herein lies the problem: if God really is present everywhere, then in
what possible sense can it be said that God also can indwell one person,
more people, or a given place any more than the next? God is, after all, commonly supposed to do precisely this. In Jesus, for example, or for that matter
in the saints, God is said to dwell more fully than he does in the sinner.

This question, and this kind of approach to the question, was widely assumed in medieval discussions of the indwelling of God. Thomas Aquinas,
for example, maintains that God, as the cause of all things, dwells in everything in a generic sense *per essentiam, potentiam et præsentiam,*[28] that is, by
reason of the doctrine of creation and the attendant mode of divine indwelling that was subsequently spoken of as the "presence of immensity."[29] Yet,

---

28. Thomas Aquinas, *Summa Theologiae,* 1a., 43, 3.

29. "The *presence of immensity* . . . signifies that God is truly and intimately present to
all things, and this in a threefold manner: by *essence, presence and power.* He is present by
essence so far as he gives and preserves the existence of all things (creation and conserva-
tion), so that nothing could exist or continue to exist without God's presence. He is present by presence in the sense that absolutely nothing escapes his gaze but all things are naked and open to his eyes. He is present by power in the sense that all things are subject to
his power. With one word he creates; with one word he could annihilate whatever he has
created." Antonio Royo and Jordan Auymann, *The Theology of Christian Perfection*
(Dubuque, IA: The Priory Press, 1962), p. 566.

for Thomas, God also indwells the saints in a special way that surpasses even this presence, by virtue of a divine person's being "sent" to dwell with and in humans in a more intimate and intentional sense. Thomas seems to tie this special presence to the life of conscious faith. In spiritual creatures who apprehend by faith the truth of God, Thomas says, God comes to be present "as the object known by the knower and as the one beloved of the lover" (*cognitum in cognoscente et amatum in amante*). In a strikingly beautiful exposition, he speaks of how we are made like God by virtue of this specific kind of indwelling of the divine persons of the Son and the Holy Spirit:

> By grace the soul takes on a God-like form. That a divine person be sent to someone through grace, therefore, requires a likening [*assimilatio*] to the person sent through some particular gift of grace. Since the Holy Spirit is Love, the likening of the soul to the Holy Spirit occurs through the gift of charity and so the Holy Spirit's mission is accounted for by reason of charity. The Son in turn is the Word; not, however, just any word, but the Word breathing Love. *The Word as I want the meaning understood is a knowledge accompanied by love.* Consequently not just any enhancing of the mind indicates the Son's being sent, but only that sort of enlightening that bursts forth into love; the kind, namely, that *John* describes, *Everyone that hath heard from the Father and hath learned, cometh to me;* and the *Psalm, In my meditation a fire shall come forth.* [This] points to a kind of experiential awareness and this precisely is what wisdom is, a knowing that, as it were, is tasted. . . .[30]

Yet, despite the grandeur and apparent rigor of the argument, not everything is clear. For example, one perfectly consistent reading of Thomas's position would seem to be that God's special indwelling in the saints is so tied to their conscious acts of thinking of God and loving God that it can only ever be "occasional." While we are asleep, for example, or while engaged in any number of the tasks that typically sap human attention and energy, or that merely distract us from God, God cannot be present, since in these activities we are not conscious of him. This is presumably not what Thomas *wanted* to say, of course, since the overall thrust of his treatment of sanctifying grace is that, by virtue of God's indwelling presence, we are drawn beyond our natural condition to have a real share in the eternal life of God. A version of divinization is clearly the goal; yet the detail of his account of the

---

30. Thomas Aquinas, *Summa Theologiae*, 1a., 43, 6 *ad* 2 (italics in original).

missions of the Son and the Holy Spirit in the human soul can be — and on occasion has been — read in this more superficial way.

Still, the continuing vitality of the tradition Thomas represents is obvious. Recently, it has appeared prominently in the pneumatology of Yves Congar, who (as might be expected of a Dominican) relies extensively on medieval sources such as Thomas. In treating the indwelling of the Spirit, Congar judges that, since God must be spoken of as already both everywhere and nowhere (everywhere because he cannot be confined to one space, and nowhere for exactly the same reason), it is not possible to take the concept of indwelling literally.[31] Instead, what indwelling means must be understood in terms that can do justice to acts of personal devotion, obedience, and so forth on the part of the person concerned. What happens when God is said to "indwell" someone is that he or she is placed in a certain relationship with God, who becomes present in a specific and explicit sense as the object of love and knowledge. Thus, when the Spirit is given to a person, it is not that a change in God's location is somehow effected; rather, a change has come about in the person concerned, and in his or her relationship to the omnipresent God.

The major problem with the Thomist position, however, concerns just this assumption of divine immobility, according to which the Spirit is "sent" into the world without this actually involving any "movement" for God himself, and consequently, without any "sending" in the strict sense. For God exists outside all finite, spatial limits, and thus can neither change, nor indeed, move from one "place" to another. Therefore, whatever change or movement occurs in this sending can only occur in creatures. The result is that the Spirit is not sent in any literal sense, but rather that the creature is raised up to grasp a primordial presence that must be assumed to have existed always and everywhere. But the trouble with this claim is that it makes numerous scriptural and theological ideas of the sending (or giving) of the Spirit seem nonsensical: the Spirit is "sent," only never really. Rather like St. Anselm's God, who is loving only in terms of our experience but not in terms of his own, there is something religiously deflating about the notion of a God who is incapable of meaningful engagement and who is reduced to reliance on creaturely mutability to bring it about.[32]

31. Congar, *I Believe in the Holy Spirit*, trans. David Smith, 3 vols. (London: Geoffrey Chapman, 1983), 2: 83-84.

32. Anselm, *Proslogium*, in *St. Anselm: Basic Writings*, 2nd ed., trans. S. N. Deane (LaSalle, IL: Open Court Publishing, 1962), ch. 8.

If the trouble lies with the divine attributes of immutability and omnipresence, then one option would be to abandon these regulative ideas in favor of some version of process theory. This is a much-traveled road; indeed, in many ways the whole theology of process turns on the redefinition of the (mutual) indwelling of God in the creature and of the creature in God, so that neither is what it is without the other.[33] Because of this dynamic interchange, and particularly because of the theological association of the Spirit with the theme of indwelling, process theology might be thought to be particularly susceptible to pneumatological elaboration. Oddly, however, relatively little constructive pneumatology has emerged from process theology, possibly because of the general tendency of process thought to deal with "God" in the abstract rather than with the specifically Christian form of the doctrine of God, which involves the Trinitarian question.[34] Yet mileage has been gained in other fields of theology through a turn to process insights,[35] and since the main thrust of the philosophical position it represents is at least a realistic one, the result could be welcome in pneumatology. For the present — and by way of a conclusion — I wish to develop the argument along different, more strictly doctrinal, lines, by referring to Karl Barth's *Church Dogmatics*.

Barth's revolutionary approach to the doctrine of God, developed in volume II of the *Church Dogmatics*, is something we have already encountered in connection with the theology of election. That same treatment of God also contains an examination of the idea of God's presence and omnipresence that equally repays careful study.[36] Barth begins with an observation that on one level directly conflicts with the central thesis of process theology, namely, that there can be no mixture or confusion of God and the world in

---

33. I am thinking here of A. N. Whitehead's seminal Gifford Lectures of 1927-1928, *Process and Reality* (New York: The Humanities Press, 1929), esp. pp. 519ff., where, via a distinction between God's primordial and consequent natures, Whitehead sketches the implications of his metaphysics of process for a Christian doctrine of God.

34. Cf., e.g., Blair Reynolds, *Towards a Process Pneumatology* (London and Toronto: Associated University Presses, 1990). Unfortunately, Reynolds adopts the characteristically positive stance of process theology toward the abstraction of "Deity" rather than toward the triune God: "There is no need to posit separate persons in God and no need of a doctrine of the Spirit separate from a doctrine of God" (p. 153).

35. A good example is Philip Clayton, *God and Contemporary Science* (Grand Rapids: Eerdmans, 1998).

36. Karl Barth, *Church Dogmatics*, II/1, pp. 440-90 (§31.1).

their relationship (p. 446). God does not abandon his glory, but remains God in all his outreach to the creature. In other words, God is absolutely unique and is never to be confused with anything else.

In characteristic Barthian fashion, the argument proceeds to carve out a theology that is, much like Barth's God, also absolutely unique, yet that he claims is fully biblical and in that sense representative of the true voice of the Christian theological tradition! God's omnipresence in the history of Christian theology has traditionally been treated as a "relative" attribute of God. God's relative attributes are distinguished from the "essential" or "absolute" attributes of eternity — aseity and so forth — by virtue of their belonging to the sphere of God's relationship with the world rather than to the sphere of God in himself. Therefore, in the classical view, God, though in himself spaceless, is nevertheless present in all things that came into being in space and time with the act of creation. God is not, therefore, omnipresent to himself but only to the world, inasmuch as all created things are related to God as their creator and sustainer.[37] In the *Church Dogmatics*, however, Barth maintains that God's presence does not describe merely God's relationship to the cosmos. Instead, he argues that a primordial kind of "presence" has to exist in the strict and proper sense first of all in God himself before it exists in the created world. The outward manifestation and realization of this divine presence in the cosmos in what we call "omnipresence" would be inconceivable, Barth argues, were it not for the fact that God already in himself is the eternally omnipresent one (II/1, p. 462).

The main argument supporting this claim is found in what at first blush looks like an unlikely place: the well-worn Johannine claim "God is love" (1 John 4:16). This extraordinary text has, of course, been reduced to banality through overuse and the ravages of moralistic sentiment. But in Barth's exposition, which once again occupies several hundred pages of closely argued text, the Johannine statement begins to recover its revolutionary character, as in his treatment it literally defines the being of God. God is "the one who loves in freedom." It is not, then, merely that God appears as the loving one of Christian revelation to us, whereas in himself God must be conceived in "dispassionate" terms. Nor is the point of the text that we should be as inoffensive as the God of popular Christian imagination. Rather, the deepest implication of the "God is love" text is that there is a relationship of love in God

---

37. For a discussion, see Luco J. van den Brom, *Divine Presence in the World* (Kampen: Kok-Pharos Publishing House, 1993), pp. 170-230.

that is the source of everything that is, and against which everything that is must finally be measured. This primordial relationship — a relationship of ceaseless love between the Father and the Son in the Holy Spirit that exists from eternity, according to which one is present to another — exists eternally in God (or in God's "time," as Barth puts it in another theological revolution in these same pages) prior to the existence of a temporal relationship between God and creatures. Indeed, for Barth, that prior relationship is the necessary and unavoidable foundation for the series of relationships that come to exist in time. Without it, we would not exist.

The importance of the idea of divine presence in Barth's theology is matched by the richness of content accorded to it in his exposition: "God is love" means, ultimately, that in order for such a relationship to exist, there must be otherness and distance as well as unity and nearness in God (p. 463). But the implication of this claim is that there must exist in God a kind of "space," God's own space as opposed to creaturely space, within which such presence is realized. Therefore, the theme of the love of God, if consistently thought through, requires a thoroughgoing reconceptualizing of the whole problem of the doctrine of God. Barth says:

> The absolute non-spatiality of God, deduced from the false presupposition of an abstract infinity, is a more than dangerous idea. If God does not possess space, He can certainly be conceived as that which is one in itself and in all. But He cannot be conceived as the One who is triune. . . . He cannot be conceived in His togetherness with Himself and with everything else as well. But in this case, is He really conceived as God? . . . God's omnipresence in the Christian sense of the concept has the very opposite meaning that God possesses space, His own space, and that just because of His spatiality, He is able to be the Triune, the Lord of everything else, and therefore the One in and over all things. (pp. 468-69)

Hence, the reason that God can be and is present in the cosmos has to be traced, in Barth's view, to the fact that God is first of all present to himself. God is always "somewhere," and for this reason God can also be here (p. 471).

Elaborating on this central claim, Barth maintains that God's freedom is such that divine presence can be individual and particular as well as general — indeed, that it is supremely so. Barth goes so far as to speak of an indwelling "according to good-pleasure," picking up on the ancient phrase of the Antiochene school (pp. 472-73). God is never lifeless and inert in Barth's theology, but always dynamic and active. Thus can there be a differentiated presence of God in the world, according to which God's presence to one is different from what it is to another. This is true not only from the subjective standpoint of the person concerned, but objectively, or *for God*. Again, Barth picks up on two main biblical concepts in his argument. He maintains that the language of the "throne" of God in Scripture needs to be taken with the utmost seriousness. Rather than representing God in pictorial fashion, or in the manner of religious representation, the language speaks instead of something profoundly real — indeed, of reality as such: the primordial "space" in which God dwells and which is "the principle of space itself, real space *par excellence*" (p. 475).

Second, and even more interestingly, Barth uses the idea of the tabernacle, arguing that the sheer particularity of the "place" in which Scripture says God dwells, both in the Exodus wanderings and in the temple in Jerusalem, is essential to the distinctive biblical understanding of the presence of God (pp. 478-83). He rejects the idea that the special presence of God with one people or one person is due to a subjective recognition or appropriation of the general presence of God in all things, as Thomas argues in his theology. It is not that God is absent from creation generally; indeed, for Barth as for the biblical writers, God is everywhere present. But the point is that the *particular* presence of God in Barth's theological understanding precedes the general, for the purpose of God is particular rather than general. God is not some abstract essence or logical *causa sui* existing infinitely beyond the world. For Barth, God is in the deepest depths of his deity the personal, loving God whom humans encounter in revelation, the one who "loves" and "gives" his only begotten Son. God's purpose is eternally oriented to this rather than to everything in general and nothing in particular.

To put the same thing in more formal, Barthian terms, the inner basis of creation itself, and thus of the general presence of God in all creation, is that there should be a people called into fellowship with God, a people reconciled and sanctified and bearing witness to God's truth, love, and glory. The particular presence of God in the sanctuary of Old Testament conceptuality, in short, corresponds to the particularity of divine election, which is in turn the foundation for the general doctrine of creation and thus for the theme of the general presence of God in and to all that he has made (p. 479).

As one would expect of a Reformed theologian, Barth is critical of the notion that any one place on earth can be identified in any literal way as the place of God's dwelling. The temporal throne of God is only a sign or image of the eternal throne, or of the "real space *par excellence*," as Barth puts it, in which God truly dwells as Father, Son, and Holy Spirit. Turning to the New Testament, and citing John 4:20-26, he speaks of how "Jerusalem and Gerizim and all temples made with hands" are thoroughly relativized by Jesus. While God does not cease to dwell in the world in a particular way, the true basis of the particularity of God's dwelling is established in the Word made flesh. Barth does not advocate the destruction or neglect of the sacred spaces of Christendom, as if these were somehow by definition impediments to faith, but he does wish to insist that the inner mystery to which they point in their mute and confused ways is made openly known only in the one in whom God tabernacles, that is, in Jesus Christ, in whom we behold God's glory (p. 481).

Barth's final move in this discussion is also a characteristic and distinctive one. Developing the Christological theme of the fulfillment of God's dwelling in created space in Jesus Christ, and emphasizing the idea that Christology effectively commits the Christian church to the idea that God's presence is always tied to such space, he concludes that the existence of the church is unavoidably also something spatial (pp. 482-83). Even the eschatological goal must be conceived as such, not as an escape from the limits of space, but as a discovering of and entrance into the divine space itself, the place where God dwells, and where the goal is the "house not made with hands, eternal in the heavens" (2 Cor. 5:1).

Accordingly, though the church is not itself the goal, nevertheless its own existence as a visible institution in the world corresponds to its eschatological hope. The existence of the church in this world is thus irrevocably spatial. As we have already seen in connection with Barth's treatment of the church as the body of Christ, the church is necessarily something visible, with concrete and worldly dimensions. It is the visible church, and indeed the church as a worldly institution, that is the temple of the Spirit and the body of Christ. It is the church with all its flaws and foibles, and not some amorphous and unworldly ideal hidden from our sight.

What may seem especially surprising is that Barth wrote these things in the dark years of European fascism, particularly in view of the tragic failure of so many of the European churches to resist it, and in view of his own involvement in opposing Nazism. During what is known as the German church struggle, Barth became convinced that the Protestant churches of

Germany were in danger of full-scale apostasy, and over the years in question he worked to expose the theological dangers implicit in their stance. Therefore, for him to speak of the institutional church, apostate warts and all, as the body of Christ and as a worldly, spatial site of God's presence seems remarkable. After all, it was the institutional church that had failed horribly to recognize the evil that Nazism represented. But at the same time, it is also quite unremarkable that Barth should have done so. The sole basis of human reconciliation with God is the grace of God in Jesus Christ: the very "fleshliness" of the church, in its sinfulness, ignorance, and pride, becomes a kind of witness to God's longsuffering love, patience, and mercy. Just as in the case of Israel, which is elect not because of its obedience but *despite* its disobedience, precisely this church is what, by the power of Christ's Spirit, can be the body of Christ. Though it may fall away (as it manifestly has during much of its history, in Barth's estimation), God does not abandon it; for it is in the community gathered around Jesus Christ in Word and sacrament and united to him by faith and in the power of the Spirit that God chooses to dwell.

Even "Christendom," the visible, human realization of Christian civilization, can survive in Barth's theology as a theological concept in these terms. Though he was by no means uncritical of much of what it represents in human history, or unwilling to seek to correct it, Barth saw in the very worldliness of Christian life and of the existence of the Christian church in human history something of theological significance. For what is at stake in the concept of Christendom is nothing less than the very thing to which our proclamation in all times must bear witness: that God chooses to dwell with sinful humanity and not to abandon it. Though by no means a comprehensive affirmation of the theological goodness of all Christian civilization, since it is precisely sinful humanity with whom God dwells, the idea of Christendom is nevertheless an affirmation of the love of the good God.

The Presence of the Spirit and the Doctrine of the Church

The biblical idea of the church as temple of the Holy Spirit has important implications, given the background of biblical Judaism and the hope for the renewal of God's presence that it contained. While talk of the church as the temple of the Spirit naturally becomes domesticated through overuse, the idea is really a remarkable one. When we examine it more closely, a massive series of theological claims and questions arises, not least with respect to the Christian understanding of God, but also for ecclesiology proper. According to this view, the church is genuinely something on which the fulfillment of the ages has come.

The truth of the matter is that such a "Pentecostal" approach to the doctrine of the church is relatively rare in the field of ecclesiology, despite the depth of the scriptural material that, in principle, it could draw on in developing such an approach. Barth's theology is a good example of this problem: despite all its depth and sophistication — even in his treatment of the theme of divine indwelling — not only is the Holy Spirit's work basically controlled by and oriented to Christ's work in his theology (as the sealing and impressing of the Word of God on those who believe), but he conceives of the church, too, from an overwhelmingly Christological standpoint. The idea of a work of the Spirit in the church that is in any sense separate from or even subsequent to the Christological "moment" of the Trinitarian mystery is utterly foreign to Barth's treatment. Indeed, it is foreign to much of Western theology generally.

Over the past century, the rise of the various Pentecostal movements in global Christianity suggests that it may be necessary to draw a line under all of this and seek to move on. The fact that Pentecostalism has become a global movement with a membership numbering in the hundreds of millions in itself provides sufficient grounds for such a new approach. Indeed, if we were to fail to engage it, willingly and fully, we would surely be guilty of evading the responsibility of a proper ecclesiology to help the church live more faithfully — and to avoid the situation in which the church lives today.

Yet the reality is that such an approach is not really new, for it is, in principle, deeply biblical. This one fact means that, whatever the path that may have been taken by the tradition, the fundamental connection between Spirit and church has a certain canonical and therefore indelible primacy for Christian thought. Surprisingly, the structure of the ancient creeds also lends itself to such a pneumatological focus in ecclesiology. This is surprising, because both the Nicene Creed and the ancient Roman creed that became the baptismal creed of the Latin West, the so-called Apostles' Creed, were products of a church in which the doctrine of the person and work of the Spirit was often overshadowed by an enormous concentration on the person and work of Christ. Yet the third article of the Apostles' Creed, for example, runs this way:

Credo in Spiritum sanctum,
sanctam ecclesiam catholicam,
sanctorum communionem,
remissionem peccatorum,
carnis resurrectionem,
et vitam aeternam.
Amen.

I believe in the Holy Spirit,
the holy catholic church,
the communion of saints,
the remission of sins,
the resurrection of the flesh,
and eternal life.
Amen.

Thus were the life of faith and Christian hope brought within the sphere of the Spirit, who works through the medium of the church. The forgiveness of sins is received by means of the faith to which the church bears witness, not least in its sacraments. Accordingly, J. N. D. Kelly speaks of the clauses that immediately follow the *Credo in Spiritum sanctum* as "the fruits of the Spirit in action": he notes the close connection in early Christian thought between pneumatology in general and ecclesiology in particular.[38]

It is often said that the distinction between belief in the Holy Spirit, on the one hand, and the church, the forgiveness of sins, and the eschatological hope, on the other, are differentiated in the Apostles' Creed by a linguistic device: the word "in," which means exactly the same thing in the Latin text as it does in English, appears in conjunction with the Spirit (and earlier, God the Father Almighty, and Jesus Christ, his only Son our Lord). The church, on the other hand, and the other clauses that follow, are not things we believe "in." Grammatically, this claim is stretching a point, but theologically the claim is absolutely natural and absolutely necessary: belief in the church is not to be placed on the same level as belief in God the Holy Spirit.[39] Still,

---

38. J. N. D. Kelly, *Early Christian Creeds*, 3rd ed. (New York: Longmans, 1972), p. 155.

39. If I say that "I believe in parliamentary democracy, Canada, and the Queen," I mean that I believe "in" them all. The preposition is not grammatically required before every item in the list.

though they are not to be confused, the close connection between the Spirit and the church is clear. The framers of the Apostles' Creed, for example, had before them — over long centuries of use and adaptation — the option of drawing a rigid distinction between the Spirit and these other matters by imposing a fourfold or a fivefold division, as was done in other ancient creedal statements; but they did not. Nor did the (mainly Eastern) bishops who framed the Nicene Creed, which adopts a similar threefold structure, see that any such distinction was needed.

The direction taken in the creeds can thus be read in two very different ways. In one view, the Spirit of Christ is made into a kind of captive of his ecclesial body, subject to its control and limitations. The Spirit is found uniquely in the church — not outside it. Cyprian's well-worn claim that "outside the church, there is no salvation" serves as the classical symbol of such ecclesiastical overconfidence (though, as we have seen, the original context of the statement has in view the narrower problem of schism rather than the doctrine of salvation as such). In the other, more generous, view, the Spirit remains always the Lord of the church — with the Father and the Son. As Jan Lochman observes, recognizing this simple fact and returning to it regularly allows the connection between the Spirit and the church to serve as a corrective to some of the more prominent errors that afflict so much ecclesiology.

> Church history offers ample warning that wherever a dividing wall has been erected in doctrine or in practice between Spirit and church . . . distortions have resulted. These have endangered the different confessions of Christendom in different ways: in Roman Catholicism mostly by the domestication of the pneumatological themes in a rigid ecclesiology; in Protestantism by underestimating the value of a concretely committed ecclesiology. The weak point in both tendencies is the same: they both divorce the first two statements of the Third Article.[40]

This is also the reason that the suggestion we occasionally encounter in Eastern Orthodox writers that ecclesiology is a peculiarly Western obsession, and that all that is really needed is an adequate pneumatology — along with perhaps an anthropology and a vital awareness of tradition — is ultimately a very unhelpful one. Given the clear tendency in Christian history for the church to wander from the ways of the Spirit, for example, in seeking power

---

40. Jan M. Lochman, *The Faith We Confess* (Edinburgh: T&T Clark, 1985), p. 198.

or wealth (tendencies to which the Orthodox are surely no more immune than others), it is necessary to have some means of calling the church to account, by measuring it against some ideal ecclesiological standards. To have such standards in place requires that Christians make the effort to reflect on the nature of the church, and criticize both it and their understandings of it, in order to have sufficient resources to correct and recall the church to its roots in the love and service of God. In short, all of this requires an ecclesiology, a theological account of the church that is — or at least can be — taken seriously as the criterion against which to measure the mere *modus operandi* of the church's life.

Two further reflections will serve to round out our discussion at this point: the first I take from material we have already encountered in the theology of Karl Barth, and the second from the work of Yves Congar. In Barth's theology we have seen that much of the specific worth of the promise of God's indwelling presence is bound up with the fact that it is with sinners that he chooses to dwell. Barth's approach is certainly insufficiently pneumatological, but it is just as certainly not un-pneumatological either: the Spirit who indwells the church as temple makes sinful humanity its home, or, at any rate, sinful humanity as it is being reconciled to God and made anew. One cannot escape or evade this fact, either for God's sake (for as Barth shows us, there is no diminution of divine glory in this indwelling) or for the sake of the doctrine of the church (for, as is by now clear, a straightforward realism about these matters is fitting and necessary). Speaking metaphorically, what we can say is that the theology of the church as temple is possible only because, in the inner sanctuary of the temple to which we have access, the *hilastêrion* (the "place of atonement"), the "mercy seat," has been restored by the one who is both priest and victim, and who in his own body reconciles sinners to God. This theme, which is so basic to various strands of Christian mysticism and the evangelical tradition, and which is implicit in all eucharistic theology and practice, needs to be rediscovered in discussions of the doctrine of the church.

The second insight comes from Yves Congar, who makes a case for an understanding of the Spirit as the "co-instituting" principle of the church with Christ.[41] He develops this idea partly in order to bridge the gulf with the Eastern Orthodox, for whom pneumatology is truly central, and with whom Congar kept up a decades-long dialogue. But it also appears in

41. Congar, *I Believe in the Holy Spirit,* 2: 5-64.

Congar's thought as a way of avoiding a series of pitfalls that threaten contemporary Western, and particularly Roman Catholic, ecclesiology internally. Clearly, one of these pitfalls is the hierarchical authoritarianism that Congar, as someone who worked under ecclesiastical suspicion in the years prior to the Second Vatican Council, had good reason to fear. But the point Congar wants to develop goes beyond that: he argues that it is only if the Spirit is seen as co-instituting the church with Christ that what is truly important in pneumatology can be affirmed, namely, that the Spirit has a work to do in the economy of salvation that is neither separate from what Christ does nor reducible to what Christ does.

In this regard, Congar cites an image found in the writings of the second-century theologian, saint, and missionary to Gaul, St. Irenaeus: the Word and the Spirit are the "two hands of the Father." Ecclesiologically, the implication is that the Spirit does not come merely to animate an institution that is already fully formed (the body of Christ), but rather that the Spirit's work is authentically its own. Congar thus traces the work of the Spirit through the creedal marks of the church — its unity, holiness, catholicity, and apostolicity — and argues that none can be understood without an essential pneumatological as well as a Christological reference.

By the same token, however, Congar resists the notion that the Spirit's work in the church is somehow separable from the ecclesiastical body of Christ, as if individual spiritual experience were the norm and the regulated structure of the life of the church were an external encumbrance. The two hands of the Father are equally at work in the church: the incarnate and proclaimed Word of God, as the concrete historical ground of the church's existence, and the Spirit, as the wild energy of God that cannot finally be tamed. These two elements of "institution" and "charism" must come together.

That Congar should need to insist on the importance of the charismatic element in ecclesiology is not surprising, given the time at which he wrote, which was the heyday of the charismatic renewal movement within the Roman Catholic tradition in the Western world. But Congar is also speaking here in favor of the wider traditions of Christian mysticism, East and West, which in his judgment need to be integrated into the structures of the theology of the church. In short, ecclesiology must learn to embrace the dynamic movement of the Spirit in the church as spiritual life is awakened and as people are given gifts and tasks to do. Therefore, the many renewal movements that punctuate the history of Christianity are key to a proper understanding of the very nature of the church — the same church that has so often tried to ignore or reject them — and are not to be dismissed as threats to institutional welfare, inconveniences in ecclesial life, or embarrassing turns away from the theological center to religious enthusiasm — that "horrid thing."[42] The work of the Spirit, though often found at what appears to be the margins of the church, for instance, among those who from those margins struggle for repentance and reform, is really always at the center, so that our thinking about the church needs to learn obedience, and to follow where the Spirit leads. We will have reason to return to these themes periodically in the chapters that follow.

By implication, Congar's emphasis also applies to the Protestant world, in which corresponding distortions of ecclesial self-understanding are common. On the one hand, there are the many versions of Protestant scholasticism wherein a one-sided emphasis on the intellectual question of doctrinal purity occludes all other concerns. One can find grounds for it, for example, in the Reformation principle that a true church can be found wherever the gospel is truly preached and the sacraments rightly administered, or where doctrine and institutional order have been rightly set in place. On the other hand, there is the equally distorted vision of Protestant liberalism, in which human spirituality and self-understanding alone have importance, and in which doctrine and church alike are made to do obeisance to the demands of subjectivity. What matters in this vision is what each "I" is free to believe and do, rather than what the church believes and does.

What Congar is suggesting is something truly radical: that in a church in which the "two hands" of the Father can be found at work, there is no room for such abstractions, for both sides will be found to be present in ways that enrich rather than diminish the proper emphasis of each.

42. This representative sentiment draws on the famous words of the eighteenth-century Anglican bishop of Bristol, Joseph Butler, in an interview with the young firebrand John Wesley, whom he reprimanded for preaching illegally in his diocese: "Sir, the pretending to extraordinary revelation or gifts of the Holy Ghost is a horrid thing, a very horrid thing." John Wesley, *The Works of John Wesley*, ed. W. Reginald Ward and Richard P. Heitzenrater (Nashville: Abingdon Press, 1990), 19: 471.

CHAPTER 5

Communion

At this point we need a change of approach. I began by identifying the critical loss of ecclesiastical identity in face of the dominant liberalism of Western culture as a major problem in Western Christianity. If the function of ecclesiology is to help the church to live more faithfully, then this is an issue that cannot be sidestepped. The confusion of the values of liberal individualism with the Christian gospel is, to be sure, a serious issue. But we also need to acknowledge that the stresses that this confusion imposes on the churches in the global setting, in which Christianity is decreasingly Western in overall numerical composition and increasingly non-Western in theological character. The present crisis in the Anglican Communion over the inclusion of homosexual men and women in church office is symptomatic of the problem.

In response to this challenge, I attempted to explore the theological foundations of the doctrine of the church (in chapters 2-4). Taking our lead from Scripture, we have discovered that these foundations lie in God. The Christian doctrine of God — or, more particularly, the Christian doctrine of the triune God of grace — grounds an approach to the doctrine of the church that cuts across and contradicts many contemporary treatments of the church. Since these too often tend to yield to one or another version of the concept of praxis, and far too readily to the cultural context in which the church lives, ecclesiology has been substantially weakened in these theologies. Beginning with God, it has been argued, is the one thing most needed in a contemporary ecclesiology: it is the one thing that can breathe new life into ecclesiology as a *doctrine* of the Christian faith. In short, the church is more than a praxis or social process. To treat it as such theologically is to misunderstand its character entirely, for the church is a creedal subject, a subject on which practical theory can undoubtedly be brought to bear, but which finally cannot be captured by it. It is, in other words, the dogmatic or doctrinal dimension of the church that is most forgotten in contemporary ecclesiological discussion, and we urgently need to rediscover that.

Our reflections have thus far been mainly tentative and exploratory and have resulted, at best, in a series of approach roads to the life and witness of the church. This has partly been necessary because God is, properly speaking, in himself mystery. Since the church in a certain sense exists either "in God" or not at all, *its* theological character must also be something that cannot be finally or fully defined. Therefore, to speak of the Trinitarian basis of ecclesiology is to open up the question of the doctrine of the church to fresh discussion, rather than to seek once and for all to resolve the doctrine. But now the time has come to turn our attention to questions of a more concrete character. Here we must draw on our sources in the previous three chapters, as well as further dogmatic material, but we must also attempt to move beyond the exploration of these foundations to make more definite proposals concerning the nature, life, and witness of the Christian church.

The doctrine of the church stands at the intersection of two major movements found pervasively in the structure of systems of Christian theology. These have been and can be named in different ways, according to the philosophical and theological contexts in which the doctrine is discussed, and also according to the more specific themes that come into view in a theology as it develops. Ancient and medieval Christian theology, for example, typically spoke of these two movements in the Neo-Platonist categories of *exitus* and *reditus,* or emanation and return. The theology of the Reformation, particularly in its Calvinist form, spoke of them in more biblical — but also more philosophically limited — terms, as justification and sanctification. We shall speak more simply of the divine outreach or of the descending movement of God toward the world, and of the ascending movement that takes place in the human response on the basis of God's grace. The descending movement of the divine outreach is the movement from the triune God to the world, by which the cosmos is created and redeemed (in effect, this has been our principal subject matter in previous chapters). The ascending movement that takes place in the human response, by contrast, though properly something enabled and sustained by the Word and Spirit of God, is still in the "paradox of grace" something authentically human, a product of human effort, tradition, and faith.[1]

The first movement has, as I have said, already been treated through the concepts of election, incarnation, and indwelling by which we have explored the foundations of ecclesiology. The church as people of God, body of Christ, and temple of the Spirit corresponds to these Trinitarian "moments" of the divine outreach. As we begin to consider the life of the church more concretely in this chapter, we shall adopt a classical strategy, seeing in the life of the Christian church a mirror of the modalities of God's loving outreach.

In this chapter our theme will be the idea of communion, or the theological foundations of the life of the church as a "common life." This idea has an impact not only on the way local congregations worship, bear witness, and engage in ministry, but also on the way churches are structured and on the goals of ecumenical engagement and of Christian unity. The concept of communion, as we shall see, can draw on a range of theological sources in Scripture, philosophy, and theology; but it is most authentically rooted in the structures of pneumatology, for it is the presence and work of the Holy Spirit that constitutes the proper ground of the church's common life, its *koinônia* with God and within itself. I will examine the theology of Word and sacrament in the following two chapters. These three together — communion, Word, and sacrament — constitute three fundamental modalities of the life of the church. Each one also brings to particular focus a range of questions to which any contemporary ecclesiology needs to respond.

We turn first, then, to the problem of the theology of communion.

The Shape of Communion: New Testament Perspectives

The basis and scope of the idea of communion in Christian theology can be grasped initially by returning yet again to Scripture. The Johannine and Pauline strata of the New Testament must be our principal points of departure, though additional reference to the wider New Testament will also prove to be useful along the way.

One of the clearest themes of the Johannine tradition of the New Testament is that the whole content of the Christian life, as well as the life of the church, stands on the foundation of the love of God. "God so loved the world

---

1. D. M. Baillie, *God Was in Christ* (London: Faber & Faber, 1948), pp. 114-18.

that he gave his only Son," we read in the famous text of John 3:16. However, in Johannine theology the love of God is not a general religious principle in accordance with which God is conceived, or an attractive value to which the idea of God is conformed, but something that is known from the utterly singular, breathtaking act that stands at the center of the gospel itself, the sending by the Father of "his only Son" into the world. The theology of the love of God thus involves, in an embryonic way at least, the Trinitarian question, while its incarnational and soteriological content sets Christian faith apart from all other systems of thought, religious and philosophical. Here, too, is the ground on which the church rests. We find in the wider Johannine corpus of the New Testament that this alone establishes the particular communion, or *koinônia,* that lies at the heart of the church's existence:

> We declare to you what was from the beginning, what we have heard, what we have seen with our eyes, what we have looked at and touched with our hands, concerning the word of life — this life was revealed, and we have seen it and testify to it, and declare to you the eternal life that was with the Father and was revealed to us — we declare to you what we have seen and heard so that you also may have fellowship [*koinônia*] with us; and truly our fellowship is with the Father and with his Son Jesus Christ. (1 John 1:1-3)

While the moral shape of this ecclesiastical *koinônia* is a major theme of 1 John, the Gospel of John also contains rich seams of ecclesiological ideas, and the implications of God's love for the fellowship of the church are of particular importance. These are explored partly *in via,* through the account of Jesus that John's Gospel offers, and thus as the Gospel unfolds, and partly in the lengthy discourse and prayer of Jesus that appears toward the end of the text. Though a mainly pragmatic idea of participation in a common activity with Christ and God is certainly present (John 14:23; 15:15; 17:22), on the whole it is a more mystical or unitive idea of the fellowship of love that predominates, as in the central eucharistic metaphors of John 6, or in the themes of mutual indwelling and glorification that appear repeatedly in the Gospel.

The emphasis on this fellowship has a further crucial implication: that the fellowship of love that defines the relationship between the Father and the Son, and between the Son and the disciples, should also define the community of believers itself. "I give you a new commandment, that you love one another. Just as I have loved you, you also should love one another. By this everyone will know that you are my disciples" (John 13:34-35). And again, "This is my commandment, that you love one another as I have loved you" (John 15:12). Thus is the love with which God loves and that is expressed in the sending of the Son to be echoed in the community drawn by the Son into fellowship with God.

The emphasis on the Trinitarian structure by which God's love is shared with the church is, of course, among the distinctive features of the Gospel of John. But much of its point lies in the moral outworking of this love in human life, as those who live in fellowship with Christ show love to one another. The effect of the Johannine treatment is to show how inescapable this love is. Johannine theology, indeed, calls the church to a life of love to such an extent that it is possible to speak of the love Christians show one another as something by which the church can be identified — a kind of "mark of the church." While living a life of love is clearly not the only such mark — for it must take its place alongside faith in the one God has sent and in obedience to God's voice — it is nonetheless a distinctive and defining mark in the Johannine conception of the church. Hence it is no accident that the closest John's Gospel comes to the institution of a sacrament is in its account of the foot-washing in John 13: "[I]f I, your Lord and Teacher, have washed your feet, you also ought to wash one another's feet. For I have set you an example, that you also should do as I have done to you" (vv. 14-15). The act of washing one another's feet, literally and symbolically, reveals for John the very nature of faith in and obedience to Jesus Christ.

What is also distinctive and perhaps more disturbing about the Johannine reference, however, is that nowhere in the Johannine witness is it said that Christians are to love the world, or that they should love nonbelievers. God loves the world that Christians are expressly told *not* to love.[2] Christians are to love "one another" (John 13:34; 1 John 3:11, 14) or their "brothers" and "sisters" (1 John 3:17). While it could be argued that the "other" whom we are commanded to love can be someone outside the church, this is far from explicit. Nowhere does Johannine ecclesiology ever approach the notion of "social responsibility" that so dominates in modern ecclesial self-understanding, or even the compassionate imperative to reach out to the needy fellow human being of a text such as Matthew 25:31-40. The Johannine

2. Cf., e.g., John 3:16 and 1 John 2:15: contrary to popular belief, the verb in both cases is *agapaô*.

ethic is far more stark, and in many ways far more demanding: the church is defined by the love of members for one another, so much so that the *koinônia* it lives is a realization and sign of its *koinônia* with God.

A particular feature of the portrait of the earliest Christian community presented in the Acts of the Apostles may be relevant here. In a statement of great importance for the subsequent history of Christian utopianism — most obviously as expressed in varieties of Christian monasticism — Acts speaks of a religiously inspired community of goods in the earliest church: "All who believed were together and had all things in common [*koina*]: they would sell their possessions and goods and distribute the proceeds to all, as any had need" (Acts 2:44-45). This is a sponsoring text for the many attempts to establish ideal, intentional communities of one kind or another in Christian history, from the ancient monastic communities in Egypt and Cappadocia, to the great Benedictine Order of the medieval period, to the Taizé movement and the Iona Community in the twentieth century.

What this passage from Acts and the tradition of the ideal Christian community also helped to inspire in the decades following World War I and then again following World War II, was a commitment on the part of Christians in much of the Western world to construction of the modern welfare state.[3] Here Christian social thought took its communal ideas principally from a variety of secular political and economic sources, and sought to apply them, not to life within the church, but to the political and social order as a whole. "God so loved the world" was the theme, and some Christian writers of the period presented the social policy of the welfare state as the realization of an explicitly Christian vision of justice for all.[4]

Whether the result was a success for the church or a failure is surely a matter for theological as well as historical debate. One recent study suggests that in Canada, a representative microcosm of these wider movements, the influence of the Christian churches in society and their relevance to ordinary people was never higher than during the period of rapid social development that coincides with the foundations of the Canadian welfare state.[5]

3. The paradigm case is undoubtedly William Temple, who through his work as Archbishop of Canterbury at the Malvern Conference (1941), and in his most influential book, *Christianity and Social Order* (London: SCM Press, 1942), helped prepare the ground for the introduction of the welfare state in Britain after World War II. See John Kent, *William Temple* (Cambridge, UK: Cambridge University Press, 1992), pp. 148ff.

4. Harry Blamires, *The Will and the Way* (London: SPCK, 1957), p. 72.

5. Nancy Christie and Michael Gauvreau, *A Full-Orbed Christianity* (Montreal:

This may be entirely accurate, but the rest of the story makes for more complex reading: that is, the 1960s, which was the heir of this period, was just as obviously the era of the "death of God" and of "secularization theology," one of the basic forms of which argued that the successful expression of the values of Christian faith in the social order amounts to a sacralization of everyday life that has made traditional forms of Christian practice redundant. It was also a period of catastrophic decline in church membership. Perhaps the relationship between the two merits more theological attention than it tends to receive.

It might be interesting, even if only as a thought experiment, to ponder what might happen today were the church to follow more the Johannine than the Matthean strategy. As is well known, the financial pressures on the state for the maintenance of the social programs that Christians, among others, have supported in the past have grown exponentially. It is also well known that the social influence of the church has diminished radically in the Western world in the past fifty years. Suppose, then, that in the cause of justice as well as in seeking to live more faithfully as the church, we were to withdraw somewhat from the arena of public policy and instead insist on something humbler: Christian love within the church's own reduced sphere. Rather than seeking a direct influence on the polity of the state, suppose that the church were to seek something different: to be a just society in itself, in order to bear witness to the state concerning the nature of a true community. Merely working to give each of *its* members and those who come to it a modicum of human dignity would provide plenty of constructive work for the church to do. Could such a demonstration of the way Christians "love one another" be, in the end, a more effective witness to the world of the love of God than the attempt to directly influence policy in the political order?

In light of the problem, one can be forgiven for thinking that the operating assumption of the church is too often that the "true" community in which concrete love is shown and God's just cause asserted is the state. Perhaps this is a good thing, given the resources that the state is able to bring to bear on the issues, for example, of poverty, health, or education. But this is

---

McGill-Queen's University Press, 1996). As an aside, Adrian Hastings, "Temple, William," in H. G. C. Matthew and Brian Harrison, eds., *Oxford Dictionary of National Biography*, 60 vols. (Oxford: Oxford University Press, 2004), 54: 93, notes that William Temple was the first person to use the phrase "welfare state" in print (1941). At least to that extent, the "welfare state" would seem to be a church creation.

not necessarily the same as to say that this shift of the ethic of the Christian community from the church to the world has been a good thing *for the church*. Nor is it necessarily to say that it has been a good thing for the needy who exist within the church. Many of us have watched people in our local congregations sink helplessly after losing employment or health, while we assumed that it was the state's role to offer the support needed. Suppose for a moment that we were to follow the Johannine line instead. Suppose that, within the local congregation, there was an awareness of a Christian obligation to offer work to the young man who is learning disabled, for instance, or to offer food and support to the middle-aged woman who has lost a job, and thus to sustain community with those surrounding us rather than through a secular bureaucracy to an anonymous mass. What might this demonstrate concerning the love of God that "abides" in and among Christians? What might be the ecclesiastical result?

Such a view of the life of the church as a profound *koinônia* may not ultimately be feasible, but the loss of the clear sense of obligation within the church itself to care for one another is not desirable — either from the standpoint of ecclesiology or from the standpoint of the person in need. In the Third World, by contrast, where varieties of Christianity are growing at astonishingly rapid rates, one of the common features of the "boom" is that churches are able to provide the kinds of social support that the state cannot. The sheer "worldliness" of the church's contribution to its members' lives is hugely important, and it is one of the principal sources of its success in such settings. In urban Africa, for example, the church provides a sense of communal identity to people who have left their villages in hope of a better life. Similarly, among Pentecostals in Latin America, there is very often a sense that membership in the church is tied together with a range of social benefits, from the young woman who hopes to find a spouse who shares her values, to the cultivation of habits of frugality and self-discipline, to the urban poor who hope that, because of their faith, Jesus literally will give them a good job. And so Jesus might, for Latin American Pentecostalism is often very well-heeled, and people who belong to it learn to look after one another.

What would be required to develop any version of such an ecclesiastical strategy in the contemporary West is hard to say. It might be possible in areas of urban deprivation, by working through cooperative enterprises and the like; but the truth is that, since the financial and human resources to deal with deprivation are not generally present in local congregations in such areas, this is difficult to envision. The rich and the middle classes, for their part, live in their own worlds, very often isolated and certainly insulated from the needs of the poor. In any case, they already give far more than their "tithe" to the state, and frequently deem *its* welfare initiatives to be the fulfillment of their Christian witness.

What is certain is that any such strategy for an enhanced sense of *koinônia,* however we may construe it, would need to draw on the resources of Christian confession to a far greater extent, or in far deeper ways, than many of us now know how to do. "I believe in the Holy Spirit, the holy catholic church, the communion of saints," and also without a doubt, "the forgiveness of sins" — these words would need to become more than a recitation on Sundays. Yet an adequately pneumatological theology of communion can only be developed by giving attention to such "real" questions. How we treat one another matters deeply. The Spirit is the one who writes the law of love on our hearts, who brings new birth and new life, who inspires devotion and sacrifice, and who knits the varied members of the body of Christ into one, leading them to bear one another's burdens. Much of our problem in pneumatology and ecclesiology alike is that the intimate connection between the two and these ethical imperatives has seldom been developed in systems of doctrine. On the whole, it has been the work of the saints; the theologians have too often stood afar off.

The Johannine concept of *koinônia* with God and within the church is certainly striking, but it is in the Pauline literature of the New Testament that we see the concept of *koinônia* (and its cognates) used most extensively. The best-known example, due to widespread liturgical usage, is the triadic Pauline formula: "The grace of our Lord Jesus Christ, the love of God, and the communion [*koinônia*] of the Holy Spirit be with you all" (2 Cor. 13:13). It is noteworthy that here *koinônia* is associated with the Holy Spirit, which is such a major theme in Pauline theology. Paul also uses the concept of *koinônia* in connection with the Lord's Supper in 1 Corinthians 10. He says that, just as those who share in the sacrifices of the Jerusalem temple are made "partners in the altar" (1 Cor. 10:18), and just as those who share in pagan sacrificial meals become "partners with demons" (v. 20), so those who share in the Lord's Supper enjoy *koinônia* in the body and blood of Christ (v. 16). It is this *koinônia*, Paul then argues, that makes us one: "Because there is one bread, we who are many are one body, for we all partake of the one bread" (v. 17).

The importance of the idea of the believer's participation in Christ in

Pauline theology is unmistakable. In Romans 6, the baptized are said not only to be buried with Christ (v. 4), but to be united with Christ in his death and resurrection (v. 5), again crucified with him (v. 6), dead with him (v. 8), and finally alive with him (v. 8). In a well-known passage in Romans 8 we read of being joint heirs with Christ, of suffering with him, and of glorification with him (v. 17), a thought that is echoed in Philippians 3:10. As is well known, the believer can be said — in a distinctively Pauline idiom — simply to be "in Christ."

How these claims are to be understood with theological precision is a difficult question, and there must always be room for debate about the meaning of the words, not least because whole approaches to the gospel itself are at stake in different attempts to address the question. Whatever the approach we take, we need to insist on and try to grasp how robust the theology of *koinônia* appears to be in the New Testament texts. In the Old Testament, people never have "fellowship" with God in such a radical sense, for though people may walk with God, obey God, or even be indwelt by God's Spirit, God remains unapproachable.[6] By contrast, in the New Testament the God who is in human terms unapproachable has, in the sovereign freedom of grace, approached humans. The New Testament speaks of the mediator, Jesus Christ, and it is on the basis of his mediation and the outpouring of the Spirit that follows, that the Gospel of John, the Pauline Epistles, and, perhaps most daringly, 2 Peter 1:4, can speak openly of a twofold intimacy with God: of God with humans, first of all, but secondly and no less daringly, of humans with God.

This last text, which has been especially influential for the Eastern Orthodox, who in fact have tended to nurture a spirituality modeled on it, says that Christians are made to be "participants of the divine nature" *(theias koinônoi physeôs)*. The goal of that participation is to escape from corruption. To be sure, it is not that the believer is literally made divine; and yet she is being offered a fellowship, or *koinônia*, with God. Since to have fellowship, or *koinônia*, is to share something in common with others, and thus to participate in a common life, to have fellowship with God is to have something in common, not merely with other members of the church, but with God, and to participate in a measure in the nature of God through the gift of incorruptibility.

6. Frederick Hauck, "*Koinos* . . . ," in Gerhard Kittel et al., eds., *Theological Dictionary of the New Testament*, trans. G. W. Bromiley, 10 vols. (Grand Rapids: Eerdmans, 1964-1976), 3: 800-803.

As it is in John, so it is in Paul: beyond these mystical, or unitive, themes in Pauline theology, fellowship with Christ grounds a further fellowship, the mutual life of the members of the church. Thus, for example, intensely practical themes appear through the length and breadth of the Pauline Epistles. "Bear one another's burdens, and in this way you will fulfill the law of Christ," we read in a representative statement of the theme in Galatians 6:2, which contains a reference to both the fellowship of the church and the law that Christ commands. The importance of the simple discipline of mutual respect appears prominently also in what is arguably the most cerebral of the Pauline Epistles, Romans. Here, too, Paul places great emphasis on such virtues as toleration and an avoidance of superciliousness: "We who are strong ought to put up with the failings of the weak" (Rom. 15:1) and "Welcome one another, therefore, as Christ has welcomed you" (15:7) are representative statements. The fellowship of the church also has implications for Christians' use of material wealth, as they "contribute to [literally, 'participate in,' *koinônountes*] the needs of the saints," and "extend hospitality to strangers" (Rom. 12:13).

Such concrete biblical injunctions help account for that prominent tradition of thought that insists that as a community, the church is to be understood as a visible society, so that whatever else it may be as something "spiritual" or "invisible," one also needs to attend to its physical, relational, and institutional fabric. Because we are a human society, for instance, many of the basic questions at stake in ecclesiology concern the concrete relationships of members to one another. Whether in matters of ministerial order, in treatments of the relationship between church and state, or in the use of money, ecclesiology at some point must have a practical human reference. Treatments of the church that sometimes can seem fixated on particular structures that are claimed to have been established by Christ or by the apostles are also to this extent absolutely normal in ecclesiology, even if the historical claims made cannot be verified, and even though the claims made can at times seem to amount to irrational justifications for continuing division. The simple truth is that, in order to be a human society, a church requires an organized system of authority. Leadership cannot be provided where it has not first been defined, and in the world of the church, such definition must be theological. The temptation to make "universal" claims is endemic to such thinking.

Already there are indications in the New Testament of a concern for institutional welfare that is achieved through a definite ecclesiastical order.

Even at the relatively primitive stage of the Pauline mission, Paul appeals to his apostolic authority as an instrument of ecclesiastical unity. The Corinthian church, being led astray by the appeal of the false "super-apostles" of 2 Corinthians 11, is instructed (over the course of 2 Cor. 11–13) to repent and to await Paul's third visit to them, when he will use "the authority that the Lord has given" to make judgment concerning the church's affairs (2 Cor. 13:10). Later, in what most scholars regard as the postapostolic period and a deutero-Pauline layer of the New Testament, Timothy is in turn entrusted with authority to appoint "bishops" *(episcopoi)* and "deacons" *(diakonoi)* (1 Tim. 3:1-13), an instruction that appears in the context of the question of "how one ought to behave in the household of God" in the absence of the apostle himself (1 Tim. 3:15). Equally, we read in the Epistle to Titus of the appointment of "elders" *(presbuteroi)* in every town in Crete, an office that this Epistle apparently equates with that of "bishop" (Titus 1:5, 7).

The precise meaning of the language is, of course, hotly disputed — not least because the *"presbuterion"* appears as a technical term denoting a council in 1 Timothy 4:14. Metaphorical and literal wars have been waged over these little words since the time of the Reformation; however, it is a specialist debate that I choose not to enter into in this study. What is important in the context of my argument is simply the observation that the question of office-bearers of *some* kind is a matter of theological significance, and that they are to be deemed necessary for the ongoing life of the church. The step taken here is more than a postbiblical innovation. To be a people, the New Testament suggests, the church needs an organized system of leadership, a leadership that will serve as guardian of the faith and morals of the community, and as a channel of divine authority. This is also a pneumatological issue, and it is of central importance to the question of ecclesiastical communion.

The Nature of Community: Three Models

If the establishment of ecclesial *koinônia* is mandated by the New Testament, how do we understand what is required? Ultimately, this is a theological question, but we can begin by examining the concept of community in secular thought. Community as a concept has already been featured in our exposition of the biblical material; but the concept can be developed in a range of very different ways philosophically. There are important things to be learned from an exploration of its possible meanings, not least because one of the major alternatives offered has achieved such a dominant position in Western culture that we can scarcely escape its influence. Yet this interpretation, judged from both a political and a theological standpoint, is characterized by weaknesses that are just as inescapable. Our point of departure will be a study by Frank Kirkpatrick that is appropriately entitled *Community: A Trinity of Models.* Though it is not a theological study per se, this book opens up a range of perspectives on the concept of community, and it takes a specific approach that will be immensely helpful to us as we proceed.

Kirkpatrick begins by noting the fact that the word "community" is used with astonishing frequency in a wide variety of contemporary disciplines.[7] From theology to sociology, philosophy, medicine, social work, and politics, "community" is emphatically on the agenda. Yet, for all its usage, Kirkpatrick argues, "community" is among the least consistently used concepts in all of public discourse, and the twenty years that have elapsed since Kirkpatrick's analysis have not changed this basic fact. A "community" in common parlance can mean anything from a traditional village with long-established cultural traditions, to an established physical town or city neighborhood with a human history in its bricks and mortar, but often exceedingly little that is culturally common, to even a new housing development that is as yet entirely devoid of human inhabitants. A community can be a professional group, a largely anonymous collection of sportsmen or sportswomen (the "skiing community"), owners of Volvo automobiles or Macintosh computers, or, as we all know, a Christian congregation.

Though the primary sense of community in each case is basically a group of people who share something in common, from physical space to consumer products, interests, values, responsibilities, or beliefs, a range of implicit assumptions concerning the nature of what is common to them — and what having something in common might even mean — has to be factored in. These determine what any such mutual existence might mean. Clearly, for example, there is a vast difference between a traditional village, in which long-established patterns of behavior and belief structure individual experience, and the consumerist expressions of community forged on the basis of something as ephemeral as one's choice of an automobile brand. This suggests that we often speak at cross-purposes in referring to such different things as "communities."

7. Frank G. Kirkpatrick, *Community: A Trinity of Models* (Washington, DC: Georgetown University Press, 1986), p. 1.

What, then, is community, and can the concept really be straightfor-wardly transferred so freely from any one form of human togetherness to another, and finally to the doctrine of the church? For example, is one par-ticular "faith community" much like any other? The modern liberal state certainly treats them as such, tolerating and to some extent encouraging their existence insofar as the object of such communities can be reconciled with that of government itself: to foster the existence of free and flourishing individuals.[8] A church leaflet that recently came to my mailbox proclaimed just that: though it was distributed by a local Christian congregation, it no-where mentioned the apparently objectionable word "church," nor indeed the name of Jesus Christ; but it explicitly affirmed and promoted the quality of the life of this "faith community" among the many available local "faith communities." This was all no doubt well intentioned, but it reduced the "community" of the church to a lifestyle choice, an optional identity open to members of any civil society.

As we shall increasingly see, deep waters lie beneath the question of the nature of "community" in our time. Yet it would be difficult to think of an-other term that has been used with such abandon in recent theology. Libera-tionists, liberals and conservatives, Protestants and Catholics all lay claim to the word, using it as if its meaning were entirely transparent and unproble-matic. But the nature of community is not something that can be taken as self-evident, especially in theology, where the word has a specific set of meanings that bear directly on the nature of the gospel and the Christian understanding of God.

We will get to the theological question in due course. Operating from a philosophical standpoint, however, Kirkpatrick himself argues a good case for three basic approaches to the concept of community, approaches that stand in tension and compete for allegiance, and can, for the purposes of furthering our own discussion, serve as a typology of the concepts of com-munity that are operative in our time. Kirkpatrick calls them the "atomistic/ contractarian," "organic/functional," and "mutual/personal" models of com-munity. The three, he claims, cover the main intellectual ground, providing an overview of the major available notions of community. I shall point out in passing that Kirkpatrick's models require amendment in the light of more

---

8. The assumption would thus be that such "faith communities" are contexts in which the individual can flourish — or not flourish, in which case the modern state in-sists that the individual be free to leave.

recent developments in postmodern thought; but for the moment let us turn to examine the main lines of his argument.

Appropriately enough, Kirkpatrick begins with the dominant understanding of community in late capitalist society: the atomistic/contractarian view corresponding to the reigning political and social liberalism of the Western world (pp. 13-61). This position has deep roots in modern social philosophy, extending back into the work of early modern thinkers such as Thomas Hobbes and the more influential John Locke, and forward in our own era into the political philosophies of John Rawls, Isaiah Berlin, and Michael Ignatieff. The atomistic/contractarian view underlies and informs the development of a variety of social and political phenomena, including, for example, the specific forms of democracy that evolved in the Western world during the modern period, ideals such as freedom of the press and freedom of expression, as well as the contemporary concept of human rights.

According to this view, the basic starting point in human existence is the individual, who as both the source and goal of the position, can be abstracted from all relationship and said to exist in one or another version of an "original condition" (Rawls) to exist alone. Living in an atomistic state isolated from and in competition with other atomistic individuals, all are and can only be motivated by self-interest. In the Hobbist social vision outlined in *Leviathan* (1651), a classic work of political philosophy written in the wake of the English Civil War (1642-1646), the life of the individual in the state of nature has been famously spoken of as "solitary, poor, nasty, brutish, and short."[9] The remedy for this suffering is a form of voluntary association in which the self-interest of each is advanced through collective regulation, by the force of law, in a common political life.

In the atomistic/contractarian view, then, the human community amounts to an artificial construct intended to advance the cause of the individual. The idea of the "social contract," in which abstractly free persons consent or contract to live in the state under common laws, became a key theme in subsequent English political thought. In particular, it appeared prominently in John Locke's hugely influential *Second Treatise of Government* (1690), a work that was destined to leave its mark on a range of subsequent political thought, including that of the founders of the United States of America (the U.S. Constitution and supporting documents are heavily Lockean).

9. Thomas Hobbes, *Leviathan,* ed. Michael Oakeshott (New York: Collier Books, 1962), p. 100.

Lest one be tempted to say that Hobbes or — to a lesser extent — Locke presents an outdated view of human nature, it is important to recognize that certain of the basic claims made here are fundamental to capitalist economic and social thought, and this is certainly something that is seen as viable at the present moment in history. For example, the idea that the driving force in society is not mutual concern but individualistic self-interest was reasserted with enormous conviction in the 1980s and 1990s by the New Right, which instituted, among other things, a policy of tax cuts in the conviction that only by allowing economic self-interest to prevail could the needs of each individual be adequately met.

Under Margaret Thatcher, for example, the British welfare state was to be left to wither, not so much because the government under her leadership believed welfare spending to be wasteful of public resources (though she and it did think so), but principally because she and it, inspired by the liberal tradition of social thought, believed that the welfare state was counterproductive, a kind of distortion of reality. According to the political thinking of the New Right, people do not act out of mutual regard but for reasons of atomistic selfishness. Economic prosperity can only be advanced, then, by giving free rein to this driving force in social development. Hobbes and Locke, we might fairly conclude, are alive and well, for the atomistic/contractarian social vision they represent still has tremendous purchase in our world.[10]

In the religious sphere, individualism of a kind that directly parallels the development of modern political culture is also a potent force. The individualism of late capitalism is perfectly matched by the notion that the church is a "voluntary association," so that the important thing in its realization is

---

10. One of the major features of Thatcherism, as of the New Right in general, was the extent to which it consciously and unconsciously abandoned classical conservative polity in favor of a radical form of economic and social liberalism. The loss to laissez-faire liberalism of a genuinely conservative voice in politics was one of the real tragedies of public life in the late twentieth century. However, we should remember that nineteenth-century reforms such as the abolition of slavery under British law was chiefly the work of the high Tory (and evangelical Anglican) William Wilberforce. A profound patrician sense of duty to serve and protect the weak was one of the hallmarks of classical conservative politics (likewise Shafesbury and the Factory Acts), whereas "progressive" supporters of the expansion of personal liberties and of economic freedom (notoriously, e.g., J. S. Mill) were uncommonly silent in face of the economic barbarisms of the Victorian era. The major difference between the two camps then lay in the hierarchical and "organic" view of society maintained by the conservatives, versus the individualism of the liberals.

that each person makes his or her own decision to belong. Since this is the root of the church's existence, it follows correspondingly that the church can hardly betray the freedom of those individuals who choose to join. In fact, the point of the church's existence is on these terms, that is, largely identical with that of the liberal state. Since the foundation of its existence is the free individual, the purpose of its existence can only be to enable individuals to flourish further as free persons. Therefore, the Christian "community" becomes something that exists only derivatively, that is, on the basis of a religious version of the social contract, and then only as a means of personal religious fulfillment.

The church community can thus be something instrumental at best in liberal theory. What it cannot be is a good in itself, since this "space" is already occupied by the free individual. In effect, what has become universal is the particular. Endowed with absolute rights, the individual towers over all else in the liberal political tradition. The basis of the state — and of all law — lies here, and with it the final measure and limit of the church, which is neatly and succinctly put in its place by the theory, and definitively detached from the reins of political power. Since the church as a religious community derives from a prior act of consent on the part of its members, who voluntarily choose to associate as they do for private religious purposes (principally for reasons of religious self-interest, though there may be social gains as well), the church exists, in the strictest possible sense, purely as a means to that end.

Such an understanding — or misunderstanding — of the church is manifest as much on the theological right in Protestant circles as it is in left-wing ecclesiology. For example, the exaggerated theology of the church purely as *congregatio fidelium,* understood as a gathered community of individual believers who have experienced individual conversion, is common in evangelical Protestantism; and yet, in more liberal circles, precisely that same individualism commonly leads to an equally distorted emphasis on psychodynamic or critical theory as the means to the goal of individual fulfillment, a fulfillment that can, rather unsurprisingly, be commonly expressed in terms of categories such as self-realization.

However, if the operative maxim of the church in both cases is effectively that "people's religious needs need to be met," then a brief encounter with reality is in order. Amid the individualism of so much of the contemporary church, people's religious needs are very often *not* met. A whole series of assumptions concerning the church as a voluntary association are to this extent obvious failures, mainly due to the simple truth that precisely the same subjectivism, and just the same needs for personal fulfillment, can be expressed and met in a multitude of other ways. People's "religious" needs, particularly when presented in terms of the quest for authentic selfhood, can in all honesty be just as authentically expressed and met altogether *outside* the church as they can be inside the church, not the least because so much of the historic "baggage" of the church seems still to be inimical to the goal desired.

If religious behavior has its ground in personal experience and choice, what does one make of the settled conviction among psychologically balanced, healthy folk that a person does not need the church, either for a healthy sense of selfhood, or even to be a Christian, since the church is, after all, purely secondary? One commonly finds the assumption among "unchurched" people not only that they are as "good" as anyone else, but that they do not "need" institutional religion. From the standpoint of liberalism, the choice is as valid as any other. Similarly revealing is the frequent claim made by the "unchurched" that the church represents an alien imposition on individual aspiration.

For such reasons, people today go to the lengths of inventing their own religion, choosing from among the eclectic competing forms of devotion and practice in New Age spirituality and other new religious movements. A look at the "religion" bookshelves in a typical bookstore in the Western world today immediately reveals how advanced this view has become. On the basis of liberal theory, how can one do anything other than assent to the judgment, which has been made by hundreds of millions of Europeans and North Americans of (formerly) Christian extraction, that all of this is a positive good, since it is based on precisely the same set of assumptions as the argument used within liberalism to justify the existence of the community of the Christian church? In short, as all of the alternatives in contemporary consumer religion — church-related or not — stem from the same root, its varied branches must in a very basic sense amount to the same thing.

By contrast, the biblical idea is that it is *God* who chooses us rather than *we* who choose God. Thus the church does not exist because people elect to join it for reasons relating to personal fulfillment, but because God reaches out to the world in love, calling a people into existence as his own. From the standpoint of the individual — judging from the Bible at least — being summoned by God is often a crushing experience, and it calls into existence a new identity for the person in question. In the paradigmatic call stories of the Bible, the whole meaning of a person's existence is restructured by the mission that is entrusted to him: the person receives a new name.[11] That a person's name changes is symbolic of this transposition, for in the Hebraic world of the Bible, a human name signifies a corresponding human character: Abram becomes Abraham, Jacob becomes Israel, Simon becomes Peter. Furthermore, the agents of the transformation of the church, the Son and the Holy Spirit (the "two hands of the Father"), operate in a way that, while certainly not crushing the human desire for personal fulfillment, is certainly not merely a means to it. Instead, what they do is lay hold of us, and they gather us in so that we participate in the divine purpose and mission. There is no sign here of the spirit of consumer religion.

Therefore, the shortcomings of the atomistic/contractarian model suggest that an alternative approach to the concept of community is advisable. Taking our lead from Kirkpatrick, we can consider a second strategy, one that emphasizes the social whole rather than the individuals from which it is constructed. From this point of view, the problem with the atomistic approach is that it amounts to a peculiar kind of reductionism in that it refuses to recognize the greater reality made up by the parts, a reality that as a whole is more than simply the sum of its members. So it is that a nation, to use one example, has an ethos and a history that is in a sense independent of its individual citizens.[12] This is a position that is anathema to strict political liberalism, and one can anticipate a similar reaction from consistent liberal individualists in the church. But there is a point of real significance here that requires exploration.

In recent political philosophy, there has been a recognition of the weakness of the excessive individualism of liberal politics, not only as pursued by the New Right, but also as it appears in liberal democratic politics generally. There is, for example, a widespread recognition that the ecological crisis cannot successfully be tackled merely from the standpoint of individual choice or freedom, and that instead, a political approach that focuses on ho-

11. Hans Urs von Balthasar, *Theo-Drama*, trans. Graham Harrison, 5 vols. (San Francisco: Ignatius Press, 1988-1998), 3: 150ff.

12. Curiously enough, even the liberal state is forced to reckon with this, for example, in its policies concerning immigration, where newcomers are expected to become members of a society sharing a common history and common (liberal) values, rather than to remain mere individuals having only an accidental relationship to the whole. The irony here would seem to be that not even liberalism believes that it can subsist on its own terms.

listic patterns of behavior in whole cultures (including religious cultures) is necessary. Such "communitarian" patterns of thought thus seek to emphasize the intrinsic importance of community and attempt to escape the individualistic distortions inherent in the liberalism of our time. It is perfectly possible to see the issue of the relationship between the individual and the whole as the truly great issue of our time, and as the issue requiring attention right across the spectrum of political life — from the family to ecology to international relations and global economics.

One version of the several theological adaptations of this posture can arguably be found in the loose contemporary movement known as "radical orthodoxy." Radical orthodoxy is neither particularly orthodox nor especially radical, but what it does is press to its logical conclusion the postmodern point that the distinctive culture, language, and "form of life" constituted by the church is a matter of first importance in theology as a whole.[13] The underlying assumption, drawn from philosophical sources such as Ludwig Wittgenstein and Jürgen Habermas, is that all meaning is constituted by collective use of language, so as to be a specific form of social praxis. Therefore, for us to grasp the content of Christian discourse at all, we must attend to the concrete context in which theological words, symbols, and other communicative gestures are used. The life of the community in this sense is utterly basic to the content of theology, and it cannot be bypassed at any point, as it crucially is in theologies that turn on liberal theory rather than the life of the church itself. The individual and his or her experience is, in the strict sense, something purely secondary.

This second approach, which is based on a very simple idea but is oddly formidable in its main literary expressions, is also paralleled by less theoretically "pure" approaches that have likely been even more influential. Likewise, these seek to highlight the distinctive "form of life" constituted by the Christian community, as opposed to the community of the surrounding world, but they take their rise less from the question of theory than from questions of concrete practice. Stanley Hauerwas's theological project is the

---

13. The main source is John Milbank, *Theology and Social Theory: Beyond Secular Reason,* 2nd ed. (Oxford: Blackwell, 2005); see also Milbank, *The Word Made Strange: Theology, Language, Culture* (Oxford: Blackwell, 1997). A useful overview of Milbank is provided by D. Stephen Long, "Radical orthodoxy," in Kevin J. Vanhoozer, ed., *The Cambridge Companion to Postmodern Theology* (Cambridge, UK: Cambridge University Press, 2003), pp. 126-45.

most obvious example of this kind of communitarian strategy.[14] While occasionally showing keen awareness of the potential allies that surround him, particularly the philosophy of Alisdair MacIntyre and the theology of Karl Barth, Hauerwas has generally been content to address in an ad hoc, or "occasionalist," way the contemporary political and social situation of the church in the United States, seeking to goad it into living more faithfully as a Christian community in the often alien context of the American state rather than merely as a religious association of American individuals.

Something of this approach is found in the second philosophy of community explored by Kirkpatrick, the organic/functional model (*Community*, pp. 62-136). But at this point it would be more accurate to speak of a "family" of philosophical perspectives, for the sources that Kirkpatrick mentions are extremely diverse. Nevertheless, what thinkers such as Hegel, Marx, and Whitehead share, in Kirkpatrick's presentation, is a conviction that the basic "constituent" in question in any adequate understanding of humanity — or indeed of the universe as such — is the collective, or the whole, rather than the individual. The point here is that the organic/functional model of community sees the human community in general — and implicitly the community of the church — primarily as a system in which individuals have a functional role to play in the operation of the whole. This echoes the ancient Roman idea of the state as a "body," and its ecclesiological parallel in the "body of Christ" imagery of the Pauline Epistles. Here, as we have seen, an individual Christian is a "member" or "organ" within the one corporate body, having a particular function to play for the sake of the working of the whole. From this point of view, however, it is the "body" rather than the "member" that is the primary thing of importance, for it is the context within which the very existence of the Christian individual first becomes possible and sustainable. In other words, rather than being a product of the decisions of individual Christians, the individual Christian only exists to the extent that he or she is a part, an organ, of the body of Christ. It is from the whole that life is communicated to the individual member, rather than from the individual member to the whole.

We can readily see that this model of community has certain advantages,

14. E.g., Stanley Hauerwas, *A Community of Character* (Notre Dame, IN: University of Notre Dame Press, 1981); Hauerwas, *The Peaceable Kingdom* (Notre Dame, IN: University of Notre Dame Press, 1983); Hauerwas, *After Christendom* (Nashville: Abingdon, 1991); Hauerwas, *In Good Company* (Notre Dame, IN: University of Notre Dame Press, 1995).

particularly in its ecclesiastical application, over the atomistic/contractarian model just examined. The first is undoubtedly exegetical, in the sense that it allows us to make some sense of biblical texts such as the classic "body of Christ" passages of 1 Corinthians 12 and Romans 12. A second obvious advantage is the escape route it offers from the excesses of religious individualism. For example, we have already observed how foreign the latter is to the vast numbers of Christians in the world today in Africa and Asia, where traditional collectivist patterns of social thought, on the whole, still prevail. Furthermore, the collectivist approach has the advantage of grounding a critique of the dominant liberal social order, whether as represented in the behemoth of the International Monetary Fund and the countries of the G8, in the attitudes and ethics transmitted through the mass media, or in the political rhetoric of the leaders of Western democracies, which has included in recent experience a willingness to go to war for liberal principle. A third advantage is that such a collectivist approach might offer resources that would help us resist the fragmentation of the social world, for example, as seen in the individualism that abstracts sex from the family and the generations, economic self-interest from ecological responsibility, and so forth. The idea that our real identity is to be found in the communities to which we belong, including the community of humans across the generations and the community of creation as a whole, is something that needs to be heard in face of the persistent claim to the contrary found at so many levels of contemporary culture.

Still, the failure of liberalism to sustain community, or put more strongly, its definite propensity to erode it, should not blind us to the opposing shortcomings of collectivism. The communist and fascist forms of the "organic" model have, after all, been tried in modern times and found rather badly wanting. The marked tendency of collectivism to suspend individual interests and individual human dignity in favor of the claims of the whole of society (or those that particular regimes judge to be in these interests) has been its downfall. The same oppressive dynamic can also be present in ecclesiastical communities in which the common life of faith is so emphasized as to exclude all differences of theological opinion, moral practices, or forms of devotion. Where there can be no room in the church for the dignity of the individual person, who is always, at bottom, a subject created, loved, and redeemed by God, it is clear that something has gone wrong. Yet, though the great weakness of the collectivist approach is its repeated tendency in human history to deny the value of the individual within the whole, its strength is that it can serve as a corrective to the excesses of liberal individualism.

It should not be entirely surprising that, after he has explored this dialectic of the liberal individual and the social collective, Kirkpatrick proposes a third model of community, the mutual/personal model, which he says overcomes the limitations, while also managing to retain certain of the advantages, of the previous two (pp. 137-220). Therefore, it is the model that interests Kirkpatrick the most. To develop it, he draws extensively on the thought of the twentieth-century Scottish moral and political philosopher John Macmurray (1891-1976). Macmurray, whose ideas have recently undergone a small renaissance, was active from the 1930s to the 1960s, most recently as professor of moral philosophy at the University of Edinburgh (1944-1957).[15] According to Kirkpatrick,

> [Macmurray's] philosophy . . . can match Whitehead's for its comprehensiveness, coherence, and adequacy. But because it centers itself upon the primacy of persons, and especially persons in relation to each other and to God, it provides the basis for a third, distinct model of community (despite having many things in common with some versions of the organic model) which is not only metaphysically satisfying but is religiously consistent with the biblical view of community (p. 145).

In his philosophy, Macmurray distinguishes broadly between three possible approaches to reality. The first is the *mechanical,* which is essentially the position of materialist or scientific cause-effect determinism. Second, there is the *organic,* which characterizes the world at its deepest level as a living material-spiritual whole within which each of us as a constituent part has a role to play and an appropriate value in accordance with it. Macmurray most likely has in mind here the version of Hegelianism that had been current in British philosophy in his youth, and that had so profoundly influenced British theologians, too, from Charles Gore and Hugh Ross Macintosh to (the young) William Temple and even John Macquarrie. Third, there is the *personal,* according to which the concept of the person is the most fundamental concept describing human reality. This concept involves — and indeed requires — relationships of mutuality and reciprocity. Therefore, the self is not primarily the "thinking substance" of Cartesian-empiricist metaphysics, nor the purely determinist product of socioeconomics as in Marxism, but a

---

15. The best biographical source is J. E. Costello, *John Macmurray: A Biography* (Edinburgh: Floris Books, 2002).

personal reality constituted as such by its active relationship with the world, and principally by the quality of its personal relationships with other persons in the world. This makes it unique, and makes the position that recognizes its uniqueness inherently distinguishable from the other, less adequate forms of self-understanding.

The key to Macmurray's thought is what he calls the "self as agent." According to this focus, it is action rather than consciousness that is primary, so that we know ourselves first as agents with regard to both external objects and to other agents who act upon us. Macmurray thus sets himself against the tradition of most modern philosophy, which involves a commitment to the primacy of consciousness or thought, and instead stands more clearly in the line of such thinkers as Fichte and Marx. We know ourselves as thinkers only by way of abstraction, when we stand back from the more primal activity of relating ourselves to the world practically, and therefore morally.

There is much in Macmurray's philosophy that need not detain us, though we can at least mention some of the conclusions he draws because they are relevant to our exploration: his rejection of mind-body dualism on the grounds that both are aspects of the unitary "self as agent"; his view that the concept of the personal includes within itself as "moments" both the material and the organic views of reality (though transcending both); his view that to be a person is to be a "person in relation," the most basic form of which is perhaps the parent-child relationship.

What is of greater relevance to our present purposes is to explore the implication of Macmurray's idea that to be a "self" at all is to exist in relationship to another, and thus ultimately to engage with other persons. This is the root of the concept of community in Macmurray's philosophy. He claims that there is no personal reality at all without a wider framework of mutual relationships within which the "self" can first of all come into existence, since "the Self is constituted by its relation to the Other; . . . it has its being in its relationship; . . . this relationship is necessarily personal."[16] Personal existence is thus, by its very nature, communitarian in quality. In the strict sense, we must conclude, there is no such thing as that modern abstraction, the "individual." Indeed, for Macmurray, the dignity of any person is integrally connected with existence in community. Self-realization comes about only by way of relationship with the other.

One major feature of Macmurray's philosophy is his active interest in re-

16. John Macmurray, *Persons in Relation* (New York: Harper and Brothers, 1961), p. 17.

ligion: he connects his philosophical system to a considerable extent with the values of the Christian religion. In fact, late in life, in retirement, Macmurray went so far as to live in a Quaker religious community. In an early work he argues:

> The field of religion is the field of personal relations, and the datum from which religious reflection starts is the reciprocity or mutuality of these. Its problem is the problem of communion or community.[17]

This contention remained constant in Macmurray's philosophy to the end. All religion, he maintained, is inherently bound up with what makes us persons, rather than just material entities or organisms. The priority of agency is related to this distinction. Crucially, it is implicitly recognized in all the great religions, and certainly in Christianity, through the emphasis on ethics and specifically on care for the other and for the community as a whole that lies at the core of religious practice and belief alike. Religion is intended to foster such relationships and to provide a means of healing when these relationships become broken. It also provides a formal communal bond by which the goal of establishing and maintaining relationships can be realized in ritual.

Accordingly, in the Christian religion, Macmurray maintains, the primary goal of such communal practice — and in fact the basic content of the message of the gospel itself — is the affirmation and establishment of community. Christianity, he claims, achieves this by conceiving of the world as the act of God, by seeing all people as creatures of the one God, and by setting forth, through the words and example of Jesus, the ideal of a universal community of mutual love.

The weakness of Macmurray's treatment of Christianity will also be apparent from this account: in short, his understanding is far too general. He has little in particular to say about any community with God mediated by the events of incarnation, atonement, and outpouring of the Holy Spirit. These are, in any reasonable account, the central preoccupations of the Christian tradition and of Christian proclamation, and they can hardly be bypassed in a Christian account of community. It is perhaps in keeping with this that, for all his interest in the human community of the church, Macmurray's thought has so little by way of an identifiable ecclesiology. Of

17. John Macmurray, *The Structure of Religious Experience* (London: Faber & Faber, 1936), pp. 30-31.

course, Macmurray was a philosopher rather than a theologian, so it may be asking too much to expect a lengthy engagement with the warp and woof of Christian doctrine. But it remains true that his philosophy would require substantial theological adaptation in order to be fully serviceable in a theology of the church.

What Macmurray does show is that the idea of community is far from the straightforwardly unambiguous thing it is assumed to be in so much contemporary theological parlance. His philosophy demonstrates the extent to which the concept is contested and contestable, and that there are issues of far-reaching importance at stake in any claim to establish and sustain a human community. The definition of the term, and the underlying assumptions that give it meaning, vary so greatly that it is difficult to see how a naïve approach can generate anything other than confusion, and thus ultimately threaten the collapse of community.

To this extent, Macmurray can help us to comprehend the opposing extremes of individualism and collectivism that beset the church in our time. Why is it, for example, that the full inclusion of homosexual individuals in the life of the church is of such importance to liberal individualists in the North American churches, while it cannot be of any real interest at all to the African church, which conceives of the problem of community very differently? In the communitarian view of Western liberalism, the goal is to avoid discrimination and marginalization; in the communitarian view that is so deeply embedded in African culture, the inclusion of homosexual persons actually contradicts the condition of the possibility of any human community's existence, for communities exist only insofar as there is a created natural order in which males and females bear offspring in each succeeding generation. Africans see the sustaining and defending of this community against the assaults of Western individualism as a vital question of political, philosophical, and religious principle. In the one case, the community is the place in which the individual finds recognition and affirmation; in the other, the community is the objective order within which and through which "individuals" can exist at all.

Macmurray's philosophy of the person in relationship clearly takes us well beyond the dominant liberalism of the Western world, with its one-sided focus on individual rights and entitlement. For Macmurray, rights and entitlements are in themselves abstractions: no legal "right" could exist at all were it not for the fact that there was, prior to it, a human community within which persons in relationship already had their being and, consequently, their own particular dignity. This is what all law recognizes — or should recognize. On the other side, however, Macmurray also seeks to show that a version of communitarian thought is possible in which individuals are not mere cogs in the wheel of history, or incidental actors in the life of the community as a whole whose personal aspirations can be overlooked. Though the community does not derive from a contract on the part of sovereign individuals, it also has to be said that the individual is more than an epiphenomenon or a byproduct of the whole.

A genuine community, Macmurray's philosophy suggests, can only exist where there are persons capable of relating freely to one another. A fascist or a Stalinist political viewpoint certainly emphasizes the value of community, but the distorted emphasis on community in each case amounts to a lie that is far worse than the distortions of liberal individualism: they represent a crushing of the individual person and an attempt to submerge his or her interests for the sake of the whole (by which, paradoxically, they claim that the individual is made free). It is for this reason that Macmurray wishes to combine both the atomistic/ contractarian and the organic/ functional model in his own "third way," and thus to find room in social polity for the needs of the individual *and* of the whole community, because in the final analysis the two are codependent: you cannot have one without the other. Christian theology would do well do seek a similar balance in its own approach to the life of the church.

Community in Christ: The Theology of Dietrich Bonhoeffer

Among the many modern theological approaches to the concept of community, Dietrich Bonhoeffer's contribution is of special interest, partly because it illustrates certain of the themes found in Macmurray's social philosophy. Bonhoeffer was fiercely opposed to fascist collectivism, and he famously collaborated in the plot to assassinate Hitler, the crime for which he was executed during the last days of World War II on Hitler's personal orders.[18] However, this does not mean that Bonhoeffer was a liberal individualist. If we had to choose between the three models we have surveyed, we would certainly find it most appropriate to describe Bonhoeffer's position in terms of

18. Eberhard Bethge, *Dietrich Bonhoeffer*, trans. Eric Mosbacher et al. (London: Collins, 1970), pp. 263-81, 409-91, 626-702, 827-29.

the mutual/personal model. But Bonhoeffer's theology of community is also of interest because it paradoxically illustrates how important an adequate pneumatology is to the subject. It illustrates this despite the fact that Bonhoeffer attempts to ground Christian community in Jesus Christ. However, in order to work out the implications of this idea, Bonhoeffer took recourse in pneumatological ideas.

Bonhoeffer succinctly formulated his thesis during the difficult years 1935-1937, while he was at the underground seminary of the Confessing Church at Finkenwalde in Nazi Germany: "Christianity means community through Jesus Christ and in Jesus Christ."[19] Bonhoeffer's theology developed over three decades of momentous change, but the specific context of this statement was the life of the Confessing Church, with which he was intimately associated, and whose existence as a distinct ecclesiastical body had come about because of the "Nazification" of German Protestantism in the mid-1930s. To say "Christianity means community through Jesus Christ and in Jesus Christ" meant in that situation that Christian faith required taking a step away from one community, that of the German *Reich*, with its insistence on Hitler's central *Füherprinzip* and its implications for the existence of a *Reichskirche*, and into another, separate *congregatio fidelium*, which would be an authentic community that confessed Jesus Christ alone as Lord. According to the Declaration of the Confessing Church's Synod of Barmen (1934), "Jesus Christ, as he is attested to us in Holy Scripture, is the one Word of God which we have to hear, and which we have to trust and obey in life and in death."[20]

Bonhoeffer's treatment of the Christological basis of Christian community was consequently linked to another distinctive theme in his theology, the better-known theme of costly discipleship. In Bonhoeffer's treatment, "life together" and the "cost of discipleship" are not different things. The Finkenwalde seminary was illegal under Nazi law, and its members risked imprisonment (indeed, many were imprisoned when the seminary was closed by the Gestapo in 1937). To be together as a group of people in that

---

19. Dietrich Bonhoeffer, *Life Together*, trans. Daniel W. Bloesch and James H. Burtness, in Wayne Whitson Floyd, Jr., ed., *Dietrich Bonhoeffer's Works*, 9 vols. (Minneapolis: Fortress, 1996-), 5: 31.

20. *The Barmen Theological Declaration*, 1, trans. Douglas S. Bax, in Eberhard Jüngel, *Christ, Justice and Peace*, trans. and ed. D. Bruce Hamill and Alan J. Torrance (Edinburgh: T&T Clark, 1992), p. xxiii.

place thus presupposed a willingness to stake one's life on faith in and obedience to the God revealed in Jesus Christ, to reject the Nazi gods of blood and soil, and to repudiate the Nazification of German Protestantism in the *Reichskirche.* It is no accident that *Life Together,* the book from which the "Christian community" quotation is taken, and what is undoubtedly Bonhoeffer's best-known work, *The Cost of Discipleship,* were written at the same time. The two works stand together.

However, Bonhoeffer also saw beyond the immediate needs of the church in the political situation of the Nazi state, and he claimed that the problem of community is in a certain sense the key question of all Christian theology. In other words, his theology at this point is more than "contextual"; in fact, it was precisely because he saw the universality of this basic claim that Bonhoeffer was able to speak to the situation in which he lived. In short, the Christological basis of Christian community, and the fact that what Christology grounds is precisely a community characterized by radical obedience to the Word of Jesus Christ, is what is especially noteworthy in his treatment.

As a disciple of Karl Barth, Bonhoeffer wished to avoid any suggestion that general theories of community should in any way determine the content of the doctrine of the church.[21] Theology has its own logic, and that must be pursued to its end. As the years progressed and Bonhoeffer's respect for Karl Barth grew, his emphasis on the importance of genuinely theological foundations intensified. Consequently, in his exposition of the existence of the church in *Life Together,* Bonhoeffer emphasizes that the foundations of Christian life are discerned in Holy Scripture, and he is concerned to work out the shape of that life as cultivated by ordinary Christian practices such as private prayer, family Bible reading, the public worship of God, and participation in the sacraments.

Bonhoeffer writes about all this in a modest and matter-of-fact way, and

---

21. Bonhoeffer's 1927 work *Sanctorum Communio,* trans. Reinhard Krauss and Nancy Lukens, in *Dietrich Bonhoeffer's Works,* vol. 1, can be and often is read in a different way, emerging as it does from Bonhoeffer's education in the classic liberal Protestantism of the schools of Ernst Troeltsch and Adolf von Harnack. However, even his youthful *Sanctorum Communio* he wrote under the looming shadow of Karl Barth. In it Bonhoeffer was already moving away from a purely sociological to a properly dogmatic perspective on the problem of the doctrine of the church: in fact, the work's stated purpose is to sketch a *dogmatic* framework for the sociological problem of the church, or to put it another way, to provide a dogmatic foundation for discussion of the entire problem of Christian sociology.

his point is that there is, in the strictest possible sense, no room for anything "greater" than such simple acts of faith and obedience in the life of the church. It is only by virtue of our being drawn into a relationship with God in Christ, by the work of the Spirit in our hearts, that we are also drawn into relationships with one another in the Christian community. *Gemeinsames Leben,* or Christian "life together," is not our achievement, nor can it be adequately comprehended on the basis of secular theory. It not only stands on something other than the Nazi ideals of race and soil, but also on something other than more "respectable" issues such as class, political or economic platform, gender, and social theory. The roots of the community of the church lie not in human existence or in human works but in the gospel of God's grace in Jesus Christ that the church proclaims and believes. Theologically, for Bonhoeffer, the church can only be comprehended from the standpoint of faith; therefore, it is not, in the deepest sense, a purely "sociological" reality.[22]

What emerges from Bonhoeffer's treatment is thus a rather more complex position than is, at first glance, suggested by the Christological thrust of his statement quoted above: "Christianity means community through Jesus Christ and in Jesus Christ." In other words, the ostensibly Christological point ultimately yields in the structure of Bonhoeffer's theology to a more differentiated treatment of the Christian life as a whole. Bonhoeffer is characteristically Lutheran in his concentration on the Christological "moment," and this makes it understandable; but, rather like Lutheran Christocentrism itself, his position as stated is certainly not *complete.* What is required — as in all theology — is parsing though a series of subsequent statements. (This is even necessary for us here in order to do justice to the complete vision that Bonhoeffer himself attempted to sketch out.) What he sought was above all a return to the central concerns of the gospel itself. Criteria and concerns internal to the gospel reveal how the church is to live it in the world, and the resources of the gospel alone sustain the church in that task. Bonhoeffer pointed to the necessity of a costly following of Jesus, the crucified one, especially in face of the failure of the national Protestant churches of Germany to obey the Word of God in living such a life. But doing so requires that we fall back again and again on grace, on the forgiveness of sins, on the fellowship

---

22. In this sense, it is correct to say that Bonhoeffer continued to pursue the line of thought he initiated in the early *Sanctorum Communio* well into the next decade of his life, and he drew on it in the challenges he faced during those years.

of the community, and on the simple disciplines of common worship and private devotion.

In other words, Bonhoeffer's theological vision is far more than straightforwardly Christological. Fundamentally, it represents a particularly searching account of the Christian life. And as a theology of the Christian life, it could with greater justice be termed pneumatological than Christological, for though he seldom mentions the Holy Spirit in his overall theology and does little to develop it as a separate theological theme, the pneumatological problems of faith and obedience, or worship and witness, are everywhere present at the core of Bonhoeffer's theology. This is also true of the faith that he lived, and to which he so urgently called his generation.

Bonhoeffer's position can also contribute something else to our understanding. Though it may seem that we are a long way from the specific problems faced by Bonhoeffer, his argument in fact drew on a range of experience that makes it remarkably pertinent to the crisis of Western Christianity today, and especially to the crisis of mainline North American Christianity. Our problem is not the threat of fascism, of course, but quite another: the atomistic individualism of the modern liberal state. In the position developed at Finkenwalde and in *Life Together*, Bonhoeffer did not appeal to notions of the dignity of the individual person, or to any "declaration of the rights of man." His appeal was to Jesus Christ and to the Christian's obligation to obey Jesus Christ in life and in death. It is here that the true dignity of the person is founded: in the love with which he or she is loved by God, and in the direction that God's command is able to give to human life in the service of God. This also means that the dignity of the person is founded on those same principles that ground the common life of the Christian community. The two — the authenticity of the Christian community and the worth of the individual within it — are to be taken together in Bonhoeffer.

A few years before the crisis of the mid-1930s in Germany, Bonhoeffer had spent a year of study abroad at Union Theological Seminary in New York (1930-1931), where he had discovered that the danger to the church does not come only from fascism. At the end of his time in New York, Bonhoeffer sent a report back to his church authorities on the state of Protestant theology in America in general, and at Union Theological Seminary in particular.[23] Union Seminary was at the time the leading "mainline" theological

23. The abbreviated English translation is available in Dietrich Bonhoeffer, *No Rusty Swords*, ed. and trans. John Bowden (London: William Collins Sons, 1970), 1: 82-87.

school in North America, with luminaries such as a youthful Reinhold Niebuhr on its faculty, and the detailed report that Bonhoeffer wrote about the seminary, its faculty, and the theological students they taught makes for fascinating reading.

Bonhoeffer's basic argument was that the logic of American Protestantism had led it effectively to deny the importance of theological truth in order to make room for community — where "community" meant a religious expression of American social principle. The primary thing for Bonhoeffer's fellow students in New York, and for the mainline churches he visited, was not to be serious about theological truth, for any genuine commitment to truth would conflict with the ideal of individual equality. In short, to be religiously "relevant" meant to adapt oneself to the dominant political order. This meant that for American Protestantism the most basic obligation in all thinking about the church was to make everyone in the church belong without distinction. Bonhoeffer observed bluntly:

> [I]n the conflict between determination for truth with all its consequences and the will for community, the latter prevails . . . they do not see the radical claim of truth on the shaping of their lives. Community is therefore founded less on truth than on the spirit of "fairness."
> (p. 83)

Bonhoeffer's analysis was largely ad hominem, and it was certainly youthful (he was twenty-five at the time), but it was also remarkably acute. For anyone who has experienced the contrast even today between the rigors of a European theological education and the norms of typical North American seminary study, it is still very pertinent. The American social experience was one of being thrown together in a situation in which people from a multitude of cultural backgrounds had to learn to get along with one another. In order to do so, it was necessary to leave one's particular culture behind for purposes of public association and to participate instead in public life as a free and equal person. Bonhoeffer judged that American Protestants had transferred their cultural assumptions about the civil community to the religious community: by making the values of the state the values of the church, they had effectively sacralized the values of the state and impoverished the life of the church. The average American pastor, Bonhoeffer argued, has received a theological education largely concerned with social context and the pastoral needs of the individual church member. From a strictly theological standpoint, Bonhoeffer judged that education to be almost unimaginably thin. The result was that the community spirit among students and in the churches they go on to pastor "in the last resort . . . rests on [their] fundamental individualism" (p. 84).

It is salutary to view the contemporary concern for inclusiveness in the church against this background. Its advocates are inclined to view this concern as something new, radical, and innovative. But in light of Bonhoeffer's analysis, the desire for an inclusive church looks instead to be strangely old, servile, and unimaginative. Though the problems are defined more through the lenses of feminist, queer, or black theory today, as opposed to the radical politics of America in the economic and social context of the early 1930s, it is still the question of social inclusion that dominates as *the* great ecclesiological good. Meanwhile, its social significance is still the same: to reinforce the reigning polity of the liberal state, giving religious expression to its central principle of individual freedom and equality in the form of civil religion.

Both Macmurray and Bonhoeffer have pointed to the need for striking a balance between the individual and the community, between personal fulfillment and the weight of tradition, between freedom and responsibility. What both their arguments suggest is that the idea of the church must rest on something more than the individual. The claims of community, tradition, and responsibility must be weighed against personal freedom. But on what principle? And how can these claims be ordered theologically so as not to crush the personal dignity of the individual members of the church?

Spirit and Church in the Renewal of Roman Catholic Ecclesiology

In order to further our theme, we are driven to the astonishing developments in Catholic ecclesiology over the past century. In Roman Catholicism, more than in any of the other Christian traditions, there has been a renewal of ecclesiastical self-understanding involving the twin concepts of Spirit and communion at its heart. This is a vast subject that deserves extended treatment. For the sake of this study, I propose to examine only a handful of major theological contributions, so that we can move on to a more substantial discussion of our own.

We can begin with the encyclical letter of Pius XII, *Mystici Corporis,* which argued not only that the (Roman Catholic) church is the mystical body of Christ, but also that the means by which the risen Lord Jesus unites that church to himself as his mystical body is none other than the Holy Spirit (51, 54, 77, 78). Clearly drawing on sources such as Möhler and Scheeben, who had advocated such a turn in Roman Catholic ecclesiology in the preceding decades, Pius XII maintains that, by the Spirit, Christ and his bride, the church, together constitute a supernatural unity. The two can, he says, rightly be spoken of together as a single whole, "the whole Christ" (78). It is in light of this living unity that the Holy Spirit is said to serve as the prime inward principle of all supernatural growth and life — in short, as the "soul of the Church" (54, 68).

This is a problematic claim, as we have seen and will see again, but it is also one that is pregnant with possibility. The theory that the Spirit can be understood as a kind of "soul" that animates the church as its "body" is found much earlier in the tradition, most notably in St. Augustine, and sub-sequently as an occasional thesis in medieval ecclesiology.[24] However, it is not, by any stretch of the imagination, a mainstream patristic or even medieval theory of the church. Since it was announced in the authoritative vehicle of a mid-twentieth-century papal encyclical, the theologians soon busied themselves in finding multiple sources for it, and then announced that it was a theological commonplace.[25] Their enthusiasm is understandable, since the new departure in Roman Catholic ecclesiology provided by *Mystici Corporis* provided the opportunity, long since desired, to escape the excesses of the stagnant, hierarchical, and juridical ecclesiology previously emphasized in modern Roman Catholic teaching — for instance, in the theology of Vatican I. The goal was to return to a more patristic vision, in which, as one representative of the relieved theologians and heirs of the period puts it, "the Church was not primarily a visible and hierarchical society endowed with a magisterium, but an organic fellowship with Christ."[26]

24. The sources in Augustine are two sermons on Pentecost: Sermon 267.4, *PL* 38:1231; and Sermon 268.2, *PL* 38:1232. Despite what is often said of the "Augustinian" pedigree of the theory of the Spirit as soul of the church, the idea is very difficult to find in Augustine outside of these two texts, and this despite the fact that the protracted Donatist controversy gave Augustine ample occasion to use it. It is merely a device in Augustine, not a theory.

25. See, e.g., P. de Letter, "The Soul of the Mystical Body," *Sciences Ecclésiastiques* 14 (1962): 213-34.

26. Marie-Joseph le Guillou, "Church," in Karl Rahner et al., eds., *Sacramentum Mundi*, trans. and ed. Cornelius Ernst et al., 6 vols. (London: Burns & Oates; New York: Herder and Herder, 1968), 1: 313-16.

The trouble with the theory as stated is that any doctrine of the church that insists that the Holy Spirit exists within it in such a way as to serve as its "regular" animating supernatural principle, or "soul," risks an identification of the work of God the Holy Spirit and the workings of the church. In other words, the problem with the theology of the "soul of the Church" idea found in *Mystici Corporis* is not only its tendency virtually to equate the invisible body of Christ with the visible institutions of the Roman Catholic Church, but also that it can appear to subject the Holy Spirit to ecclesiastical control. The converse, which would be to insist on the church's submission to the Spirit's leading, is also implied, but it is a lesser theme in the practice of church politics, and a lesser theme in some official Roman Catholic theology of the period. For instance, it is difficult to see how one could ever criticize the path taken by the church if one were earnestly to believe that the Holy Spirit is its singular principle of supernatural animation. It can seem as though, in effect, the Spirit proceeds *ex Patre ecclesiaque*, given his service to the magisterium of the church.

It is likely that the risk of confusion, and the danger of making the Spirit the servant rather than the Lord of the church, kept classical Western sources such as Augustine from making the idea of the Spirit as "soul of the Church" regulative in their ecclesiologies. Instead, those sources used it primarily as an occasional image. In other words, the theory announced by Pius XII is principally modern, a product of the reactionary anti-Protestantism and antimodernism of the Roman Catholic tradition during the period between the Reformation to the dawn of the Second Vatican Council.

Is there, then, an escape from this trap, a way of reenvisioning the insight that the "soul of the church" idea represents, so as to allow for the freedom of the Spirit over against the church, and for the sinfulness and fallibility of the church over against the lordship of the Spirit? One potential source of help in this matter is the influential German pneumatologist Heribert Mühlen, who argued in the 1960s that what we need in order to grasp the relationship between the Spirit and the church is a new theological and philosophical category that corresponds to the mode of relationship involved.[27] Mühlen called this relationship "personological," and he argued that the relationship is established first of all between the Holy Spirit and Christ in his

---

27. The main works are Heribert Mühlen, *Der Heilige Geist als Person in der Trinität bei der Inkarnation und im Gnadenbund: Ich-Du-Wir*, 5th ed. (Münster: Aschendorff, 1988), esp. *Una Mystica Persona*, 2nd ed. (Paderborn: Verlag Schöningh, 1967).

human nature, then between the Holy Spirit and the church as the fruit of Christ's incarnate work, and finally between the Holy Spirit and the individual as one of the baptized. None of these relationships can be adequately understood through concepts such as causality, for what that would overlook is precisely the personal dimension of freedom that is basic to personal reality, not only in the case of the humans to whom the Spirit comes (including the humanity of Christ) but also in the case of the Spirit of God himself.

Mühlen's theology also shows the importance of an appeal to questions of Trinitarian principle in any treatment of the work of the Spirit in the church. His argument is that, in order to do justice to the person of the Holy Spirit and to the personal character of those in whom the Spirit dwells, it is essential that the Spirit be understood in strictly Trinitarian terms. The Spirit's work in the church, he maintains, is properly seen as that of one person — that is, the third person of the Trinity — with, among, and in many persons, that is, the members of the church. But this role of the Spirit as the one in the many is ultimately grounded in the relationship of the Spirit to the other two divine persons in the eternal Trinitarian life, for here the Spirit is something common to the Father and the Son (using the Augustinian-Western theological model), and ultimately the Spirit of both, *qui procedit ex Patre Filioque.*

According to Mühlen, it is for this reason that the Spirit's presence in the church is so structured as to preserve — indeed, to ground more fully — the individual freedom of the creatures concerned. In other words, the Spirit does not intrude on the natural qualities of personhood in indwelling the human being. We might say, in effect, that the Spirit does not "possess" humans the way demons do. Rather, since Mühlen's theology conceives of the Holy Spirit in Augustinian terms as the mutual love of the Father and Son, who are united precisely in their differentiation by virtue of their joint "breathing forth" of the Holy Spirit of love, so also the Spirit's activity *ad extra Trinitatis* is such that it respects the personhood of the human creature.

I should make one further observation. In Mühlen's view, the Spirit is the Spirit of Father and Son, breathed forth in common by the two in their Trinitarian life as the corporate "we in person." In the same way that human lovers become ever more themselves in their outpouring of love for one another, so it is in the life of the triune God; indeed, the first is true fundamentally only because of the second, since we are made in God's image. Therefore, the Spirit's specific personal quality from eternity to eternity is to preserve the freedom of the Trinitarian persons of the Father and the Son while also uniting them as their corporate "we." This capacity for attaining a further "personological" union of individuals in a whole that is something more than the sum of its parts is reflected in time in the particular manner of the Spirit's indwelling of the church and the believer, and in its effects in the creaturely experience of grace. The latter is ecclesiologically and corporately structured in Mühlen's exposition. According to his argument, it could not be otherwise, since this would require that the animating principle of the church's life, the Holy Spirit, would have to be someone other than who he is, other than the corporate "we" of the Father and the Word; accordingly, his relationship to the church would be something less than authentically "personological."

The advantage of Mühlen's theological approach is that it allows us to see how the presence of the Spirit can be said, on the one hand, to bring life in its fullness, so that instead of a diminution of human dignity and of the human person, the human person and his or her dignity is fully affirmed, and on the other hand, to grasp how this life must be by definition something corporate or relational rather than purely private. For Mühlen, what it means to say is that the person is brought into fellowship with God, and why it is that the person is restored to wholeness in the fellowship of God, is that his or her personhood is here supremely actualized and deepened in *koinônia* with the triune God, who is fully personal and fully relational, and with others in God, in and through the life of the church. The call of God to faith, love, and obedience is a call to a new relationship above all, a relationship that is fully personal. Precisely because it is fully *personal*, it is also fully *ecclesial*. It is as such that the call is to life "in the Spirit." Mühlen's position is a brilliant piece of constructive pneumatology.

Unfortunately, the difficulty with Mühlen is possibly as great as his insight. The problem is that the position he advances is so closely bound to the Western Trinitarian tradition, and to the *Filioque* doctrine in particular, that it is curiously unserviceable as a basis for an ecclesiastical communion embracing the major forms of ancient Christianity, Latin and Greek, which diverge radically on the question of Trinitarian and pneumatological doctrine. In this case, rather ironically as it turns out, the idea of the Spirit as the "we in person" of the Father and the Son and thus the personological principle of ecclesiastical communion is identified with the principal cause of a millennium of schism between the Christian East and West. Therefore, the view that Mühlen offers cannot be a complete one, nor is it sufficient to do service in an ecclesiology that extends much beyond the confines of the

Latin tradition — and of Roman Catholicism. In other words, though it is brilliant, it falls short of achieving what, on its own internal standards, it clearly should.

If the problem with Mühlen's theology is that it says a little too much, then perhaps we can find recourse in the rather less theologically ambitious form of pneumatological ecclesiology developed by Yves Congar. As I have already noted, Congar argues a similar case for the relationship between the work of the Holy Spirit and the doctrine of the church. Like Mühlen's argument, Congar's is grounded in classical Trinitarian theology, in this case the theory that the temporal missions of the Trinitarian persons can be traced back to the eternal processions, and thus to the eternal relationships between the persons. Rather more successfully than Mühlen's, Congar's approach is expressly designed as an ecumenical proposal.[28] He says:

> The Church . . . is the fruitfulness, outside God, of the Trinitarian processions. We *see* the Church in the manifestations of its ordained ministry, its worship, its assemblies, works and undertakings. We *believe* that the profound life of that great body, which is both scattered and one, is the culmination and the fruit, in the creature, of the very life of God, the Father, the Son and the Holy Spirit. . . . This idea can also be extended to the authentic unity, holiness, catholicity and apostolicity that is sought and that exists in the ecumenical movement — insofar as this is God's, it is also dependent on the Trinity and is the fruit or the term, outside God, of the processions of the Word and the Spirit.[29]

In a conscious concession to the Christian East, Congar maintains that the Spirit is the "co-instituting" principle of the church with Christ, thus highlighting the ongoing and dynamic source from which the church lives as much as the historical and institutional. Furthermore, Congar suggests, one of the problems with the magisterially sanctioned theology of the Holy Spirit as the "soul of the church" is that it seems to imply that the Holy Spirit is ultimately the "I" of the church. If, however, the principle that makes the

---

28. While Eastern theology cannot accept this theory as it stands, it might accept it in a lightly modified form, i.e., through a more differentiated doctrine of the processions and the eternal divine energies of the persons (a theory that is distinctive of the theology of the Christian East).

29. Yves Congar, *I Believe in the Holy Spirit,* trans. David Smith, 3 vols. (London: Geoffrey Chapman, 1986), 2: 8.

church one is the Holy Spirit, how can Christ, whose body the church is said to be, also be its "I"? The tidy solutions of Latin Trinitarianism prove to be inadequate.

Congar himself maintains that the Spirit, in his "co-instituting" role, has a series of critical functions in the life of the church, all of which are seen as the "fruit" in the creature of the divine Trinitarian relationships that are expressed in time in the Spirit's mission. Unsurprisingly, in Congar's exposition these functions include making the church *one* as the principle of communion; *holy* as the principle of holiness and as the Holy itself; *catholic* as the principle of wholeness; and *apostolic* as the principle of faithful witness. For example, with respect to the holiness of the church, he speaks of the need for an ecclesiastical "hagiography in and through beauty" by which we can be drawn to love not only the church, but also God: "[W]e can say that the saints reveal the Spirit, that is, they reveal God as gift, love, communication and communion" (p. 58). Finally, Congar maintains that the Spirit grounds the communion of the saints, which is in a sense the very life of the church, in the sense that the Spirit's work, like the Spirit's very being, is one of sharing and participation: sharing, in that through the Spirit the love of God "has been poured into our hearts" (Rom. 5:5); and participation, in that what is given to one member of the community is given for the benefit of others (p. 59). Experience of the Spirit can be intensely private, as in the case of the mystics; but it is also always ecclesial, for the gifts of the Spirit are inherently meant to be shared. The mission of the Spirit is always ecclesial in its orientation or goal.

All of this has potentially radical implications for the world of Protestantism, which, in its many forms, has seldom reckoned seriously with the fundamentally ecclesial dimension of the Spirit's work, or with the implications of the personal quality of the Holy Spirit for the concept of communion. The particular genius of Protestantism, it would be fair to say, lies in its ability to champion the conscience of the individual in his or her need to grapple with God. In Luther's language, "conscience," condemned by sin and laden with guilt, needs to find a gracious God, the God who justifies the ungodly. All of this is certainly true, but the real problem with it, like much else in theology, is that it is not true enough. For the challenge presented to Protestantism by the theme of communion ecclesiology, which is grounded in nothing less than the gift of the Spirit, is that the individual cannot find a gracious God, and cannot hold onto this God, apart from the communion of saints, to whom the Spirit of sharing and of participation has been given.

Protestantism's great problem — perhaps one ought to be more emphatic and call it Protestantism's great sin — is that it ultimately fails to reckon with the communal aspect of Christian faith. Because of this, it denies the principle of unity in its practice, for its very logic tends to the establishment of the countless sects and countersects of its history. The problem it has here was greatly exacerbated by the rise in the eighteenth and nineteenth centuries of evangelicalism on the one side, and of liberal Protestantism on the other, both of which responded to the crisis of the Enlightenment by increasingly emphasizing the dimension of individual religious experience. There are exceptions to this general tendency within Protestantism, but the overall record of the Protestant movement on this matter is dismal.[30] The problem is that the principle of the church's existence in the work of the Holy Spirit is understood basically in individualistic terms. The Spirit is conceived of as the one who dwells in the "heart" rather than as the one who dwells in the "body" of Christ, and because of this also in the individual heart, that is, as the Spirit given to Christ as the "anointed" one and then mediated by Christ as the "head" of the "members" of the body. There can be no true movement toward unity within Protestantism, or any authentic realization of unity between Protestantism and the rest of the Christian church, until there has been a struggle to grasp and to be grasped by the full scope of the pneumatological principle of communion.

It is not as if by contrast all were clear sailing on the opposite side of the ecclesiastical divide, that is, in the Roman Catholic tradition. The idea of the church as a communion has certainly been given clear endorsement, not least at the Second Vatican Council in a number of key texts, and a theology of the Holy Spirit as source of the church's common life was powerfully reaffirmed there. However, even with this endorsement and definition at Vatican II, the doctrine of the church as communion has been subject to a variety of interpretations over the years that have followed, and the huge stresses that have emerged within Roman Catholicism over it are undeniable.[31] The German theologian Cardinal Walter Kasper enumerates several of the com-

---

30. The case of John Calvin, who was capable of arguing at length against the ready willingness to entertain schism that had already emerged in the Protestantism of the Reformation era, comes to mind: Calvin, *Institutes*, IV.i.12-29; but cf. IV.ii.9-10, which is by no means as irenic.

31. Dennis M. Doyle, *Communion Ecclesiology* (Maryknoll, NY: Orbis, 2000), provides an excellent overview of this debate in recent Roman Catholic thought.

peting approaches in an essay on the theme of communion, drawing attention to elements as varied as the yearning for a more authentic form of collective life among young people, which is such a positive thing, but which is also susceptible to ready abuse; the goal of the active participation of all the baptized in the life of the church; and the move away from concentration on the visible, hierarchical structure to the notion of the church as a mystery that can be grasped only by faith.[32] What is unsaid here is the fact that, for others in the magisterium, there is clearly a preference for a *communio* theology centered in the central powers of the church. This is a position that, as Miroslav Volf has reminded us, is profoundly represented in the personal theology of Joseph Ratzinger, now Pope Benedict XVI.[33]

The church as a mystery of faith is Kasper's own emphasis. The word "mystery" here is used in a technical sense to denote something given by God as a sacrament of grace. Accordingly, Kasper's basic assertion is that communion ecclesiology has to do fundamentally with fellowship with God through Christ — in the power of the Spirit. For Kasper, this is the key to an adequate understanding of the relationship between the church and its sacramental life: we need to be "vividly aware" of what it is that the church lives from, that is, its fellowship with God in the communion of Word and sacrament (p. 155). The social and hierarchical structure is at best a necessary concomitant to this; where this fact is obscured by ecclesiastical triumphalism, it can become, at worst, a deadening impediment to it.

Taken further, the theme of communion might have much more radical implications for the Roman Catholic tradition. Kasper himself argues that, for Roman Catholics, it might well imply the need to abandon "the one-sided 'unity' ecclesiology of the second millennium of the church" in favor of a renewed emphasis on the "*communio* ecclesiology of the first ten centuries" (p. 157). Others have called for such a shift of emphasis, perhaps most notably Hans Küng, but seldom has its theological basis been outlined with such clarity. Drawing on pneumatological, Trinitarian, and ecclesiological themes from Orthodox theology, Kasper maintains that the concept of "variety in unity," rather than the unity achieved by virtue of a monolithic institutional structure, is organically related to wider and more profound themes

---

32. Walter Kasper, *Theology and Church*, trans. Margaret Kohl (London: SCM Press, 1989), pp. 148-65.

33. Volf, *After Our Likeness: The Church as the Image of the Trinity* (Grand Rapids: Eerdmans, 1998), pp. 29-72.

in Christian theology, so much so that it is difficult to see how the mono-lithic ecclesiological emphasis can be sustained.

For Kasper, the plurality of the three persons in the Trinity thus needs to be defended against the tendency to reduce the mystery of the Father, Son, and Holy Spirit to the oneness of the divine substance. Furthermore, this pe-culiarly Latin overemphasis on the unity of God has had historical parallels in the repeated overemphasis on the institutional unity of the church, which is achieved through submission and obedience to ecclesiastical authority at almost any cost. But both are ultimately un-Christian, for they are ultimately un-Trinitarian, and they tend toward the distortion of the diverse life of the people of God. From this emerges Kasper's own agenda for the church:

> . . . more collegiality, more say in things and more co-responsibility, greater permeability of information, and more transparency in the de-cision process than we have at present in our church. In this respect not all legitimate expectations have been fulfilled since Vatican II. . . . [We] are only at the beginning, in our reception of the council. (p. 161)

Ecclesiology and the Way of the Spirit

A problem remains for the ecclesiology of communion: clearly, the churches are not one. Thus, if we say that the Holy Spirit is the theological ground of ecclesiastical communion, this would appear to mean that such division is not "of the Spirit." According to these terms, the problem affects the churches not at the periphery of their life — for example, in matters of dif-ferences in philosophical emphasis or in matters of liturgical preference — but at the very core of their existence, in matters relating to what it actually means to be the church. In short, if there is no ecclesiastical communion, can there be a church at all?

There have been and are a variety of standard responses to the problem thus raised. The most obvious is to say that, since only one *ecclesia* possesses the Spirit as the principle of its unity, all the rest are to be rejected as partial, schismatic, heretical, or simply reprobate. This view is found in all the Chris-tian traditions to some extent, in varieties of cultural-ecclesiastical chauvin-ism and in formal theologies alike. The theology also has an excellent pedi-gree: Augustine used just this argument in his protracted struggle against the Donatist church of North Africa (though, to be fair, the theological argument completely failed to convince the Donatists, and the movement was put down only by imperial repression). Because of Augustine's influence, however, versions of the argument appear and reappear throughout the Western theological tradition, including in early Protestantism.

The theology is also characteristic of a strand of Roman Catholicism that is represented by the encyclical letter of Pius XI entitled *Mortalium Animos* (1928). There Pius strictly forbade the "subjects" of the holy see of Rome to engage in any way in the work of the nascent ecumenical movement of the early twentieth century on the grounds that, since there was only one true church of Christ, the sole basis for Christian unity could only be the return of the dissidents to that one fold (p. 10). In short, he was saying that the new "pan-Christian" movement was nothing less than a threat to the very foundations of the Christian faith (p. 4).

Subsequent Roman Catholic theology has softened this hard-line stance. The documents of Vatican II, above all, not only welcomed the ecumenical movement and encouraged Roman Catholics to contribute to it, but also taught positively that "all who have been justified by faith in baptism are members of Christ's body, and have a right to be called Christians, and so are deservedly recognized as sisters and brothers in the Lord by the children of the catholic church."[34] The opening this kind of language has provided for Christian dialogue and for the cause of Christian unity is among the most important theological developments of the entire modern era, transcending as it does centuries of bitter theological hostility, in the name of which literally millions died during the European Wars of Religion, and in the name of which people can still die in appalling ways.[35] Although it is true that many in the "separated churches" have not welcomed this development — and that a good many Roman Catholics have not either — it is something that we can only embrace and something on which we must learn to build, for Christ's sake as well as for our own.

The importance of the new departure made at Vatican II for all Christians also appears in another of the distinctive ecclesiological themes of that

34. Vatican II, *Decree on Ecumenism,* in Norman P. Tanner, ed., *Decrees of the Ecumenical Councils,* 2 vols. (Washington, DC: Georgetown University Press, 1990), 2: 910.

35. While I was writing this section, an ordinary Catholic schoolboy, Michael McIlveen (15 years), was murdered in Ballymena, Northern Ireland, for purely sectarian reasons in a savage beating with a baseball bat (a common weapon in sectarian violence in a country where baseball is simply not played). Those arrested for the murder were, it seems, an equally "ordinary" group of Protestant youths ages 15-18.

council, a theme of particular importance in the present context. According to the Dogmatic Constitution on the Church, *Lumen Gentium,* while the fullness of Christian faith would require full communion with Rome,[36] there are Christians who are not in such communion but in whom the Spirit dwells nonetheless, with whom, consequently, the Roman Catholic Church "is joined," and with whom, indeed, it shares "a true bond in the Holy Spirit."[37]

In fact, this view is oddly similar to the standard one taken within Protestant circles on the question of how to relate belief in the Holy Spirit as the source of ecclesial communion to the problem of church disunity. Rather than deny the presence of the Spirit to the fractured world of Protestantism, or to the churches as a whole, Protestants historically have taken the view that the true church — and therefore its true unity — is in principle invisible. Among the great expressions of this idea in Protestant theology is *The Westminster Confession of Faith,* chapter 25, which stands out as a model of clarity:

> The catholick or universal church, which is invisible, consists of the whole number of the elect that have been, are, or shall be gathered into one, under Christ the head. . . .
>
> The visible church, which is also catholick or universal under the gospel . . . consists of all those throughout the world that profess the true religion. . . .
>
> The catholick church hath been sometimes more, sometimes less visible. And particular churches, which are members thereof, are more or less pure, according as the doctrine of the gospel is taught and embraced. . . .[38]

It would not be quite fair to say that the communal aspect of the work of the Spirit in the church as an institution has been denied here: for Prot-

---

36. A point powerfully reiterated by Pope John Paul II, Encyclical *Ut Unum Sint* (25 May 1995), though John Paul II also insists, in this remarkable document, that this would not be achieved without profound cost for Rome or for the papacy itself; thus he invites all Christians to help Roman Catholicism reshape itself in ways that would assist the cause of unity.

37. *Lumen Gentium,* 14-15, in Tanner, *Decrees of the Ecumenical Councils,* 2: 860-61.

38. *Westminster Confession of Faith,* ch. 25, in *The Confession of Faith* (Edinburgh and London: William Blackwood & Sons, 1959).

estantism as well as for Catholicism, the objectivity of the promise of Christ is operative in the church's ministry, even though the minister might be at times faithless or wicked. However, it would be fair to say that the objectivity of the communal work of the Spirit is strictly relativized: these things are subject to the qualification of the "more or less," rather than being matters of absolute certainty. A certain reserve about the life of the visible church is evident here, so that the kind of confidence in the visible institution expressed in *Mortalium Animos,* according to which "the mystical Spouse of Christ has never been contaminated" (10), as a statement concerning the *empirical,* or visible, church (which is clearly its referent in this encyclical), is simply unthinkable. Expressed theologically, the Protestant position is that the unity of the church consists in Christ alone; to say anything else is to take glory from Christ the head and render it instead to a fallible and finite human institution.

What is "under-represented" in Protestant ecclesiology in general is the imperative to unity grounded in understanding of the Spirit as the bond of the church's unity — and as the ground of Christian *koinônia.* The effect is to deny the communal dimension of the Spirit's work and to focus instead on individual experience of the Spirit. In this view, the Spirit comes to the individual, who then "congregates" with others; thus the church readily disintegrates into an aggregation of religious individuals. Rather than existing as a single whole, it becomes a pragmatic arrangement by which a person's religious "needs" can be met. As the modern era progressed, Protestant circles increasingly came to draw on their agreement on the principle of religious liberty, or freedom of conscience, as a basis for common life. However, the schismatic history of Protestantism in all its forms shows how unsuccessful this is as an ecclesiological ideal; for, if nothing else, the problematic question of *what* precisely it is that we are "free" to believe persistently arises. The theological principle of *koinônia* reveals all of this as finally unbiblical, while even a cursory examination of the theology of the Holy Spirit shows it to be an untheological and unsatisfying solution to the problem of unity in the end.

Having said this, however, I must immediately add that the Protestant standpoint has always had one major advantage over the classical Roman Catholic conception: it was always capable of recognizing that individual Roman Catholics could be saved and even, to cite John Calvin once more, that there are sound "churches" to be found within Roman Catholicism in which the Word of God is genuinely preached and in which the sacraments are to some extent present.[39] This was a far more generous view than the Church of Rome took during the centuries between the Councils of Trent and Vatican II, and we should remember that as we attempt to assess the relative merits of the two traditional ecclesiologies.

Today we may note the extent to which the ecclesiological position advanced within Protestantism and the one adopted by Vatican II occupy similar ground, for each in its way speaks of an ecclesiastical reality that is grounded in the presence of the Word and Spirit of God beyond the borders of those churches themselves. However imperfect its expression at the human level of liturgical or hermeneutical practice, or in explicit theological understanding, the grace of God is not to be denied where God's presence and activity comes to fruition in an authentic faith in Christ that is expressed in an ecclesiastical life, in gifts and graces, in witness and service, in self-giving love, and even in martyrdom for the sake of the gospel. It has finally been expressed that this has been present on all sides of the ecclesiastical divisions of Christian history, and in this recognition there is real cause for ecumenical optimism.

Is it possible to go further than this and suggest something very different: that the work of the Spirit, as the "bond" of the church's unity, is so profound as to provide not only the ground of Christian unity but also the basis for the agonies of the church in its *disunity?* Is such a thing theologically possible? In what follows, I wish to suggest that it is, and that we can only grasp the full depth of the pneumatological ground of ecclesiastical communion if we are prepared to risk thinking in just these terms.

Let me begin by recalling one of Karl Barth's arguments that we have already encountered in the preceding chapter. Barth argues that God is capable of being present to the world because he is already present to himself. According to Barth, such presence requires that there be a primordial spatiality in God within which this divine presence of God to himself can be realized. In short, as the one who is Father, Son, and Holy Spirit, there is relationality in God, a relationality that demands that there be in God a "here" and a "there," a "first" and a "second," an "I" and a "Thou." Therefore, rather than existing as a barren abstraction beyond all limitation, God exists in infinite freedom in a kind of eternal self-limitation: thus there is a here and a there, an otherness and a distance, in the life of the one God. Such self-limitation

---

39. Calvin, *Institutes*, IV.ii.12: "[W]hen we categorically deny to the papists the title of *the* church, we do not for this reason impugn the existence of churches among them."

does not mean that the being of God is inherently conditioned by the existence of the world; rather, it means that the persons of the divine Trinity are mutually defined. The Father, for instance, is not the "All" or the "One" of philosophical theism, but exists precisely as the one called "Father" only with respect to the Son and the Holy Spirit, and is defined by his concrete relationships with the other two persons.

Thus, in Barth's treatment, the unity of God as Trinity is not monadic but instead both differentiated and relational, which entails that the divine unity is something infinitely capable of embracing difference. It is unfortunate that, in his examination of the theme of God's presence, Barth did not provide a properly pneumatological elaboration of his ideas, for they might have helped us in the present instance to conceive of the grounds of ecclesiastical communion in such a way as to embrace otherness and distance in the life and history of the church. This is a question of great pneumatological importance, given the fact that, according to the Christian tradition, the one in whom God is present in the life of the church is the Holy Spirit, who came upon the church at Pentecost.

Analyses of the church as a communion could well learn from Barth that the question of unity must be answered in such a way that it is capable of handling difference, since the primordial theme of divine unity in the eternal Trinitarian life does precisely that. What this suggests is that the ecclesiological idea of unity — or the idea of communion in ecclesiology — must also be developed in such a way as to allow for difference. The unity of the church is symphonic, or, to borrow a word from Trinitarian discourse, it is *perichoretic:* it is involved in a ceaseless exchange of diverse traditions, energies, and gifts among those who comprise it. In short, the catholicity of the church, which is both a wonderful gift and an onerous task, demands that we recognize and accommodate our unity as *unity in difference* — sometimes even painful difference.

Accordingly, catholicity does not point to the superficially more attractive alternatives of either a unitary, visible, hierarchical structure, which, to be effective, must be as autocratic as it is ruthless; or of a seamless, invisible unity, which, precisely in order to be seamless, can only be "invisible," an ideal essence hovering above the real. These lesser alternatives simply will not do the subject justice. The triune God — Father, Son, and Holy Spirit — in reaching out to the world, spans a bottomless moral and metaphysical chasm in order to reconcile all things to himself. The church, as the product of this initiative and as bearing witness to it, must seek in its structures and in its own communion a similar generosity. Therefore, the communion of the church in the power of the Spirit is a much richer and, to some extent, a "riskier" business than is suggested by the approaches that preoccupy so much of the ecclesiology of the tradition. It must be capable of embracing not only stresses such as change, disagreement, and diversity, but also the deeper anguish of loss and death. We will begin to see something of what this might mean shortly.

To grasp the point, we must first focus once more on questions of Trinitarian theology — and specifically the role of the Holy Spirit in the economy of salvation — and to what this reveals concerning the more general "way" of the Spirit in the triune God's being and working in the world. This, in turn, will illuminate the character of the Spirit's work as the principle of communion. One specific question will allow for our exploration of the Trinitarian question, drawing both from Scripture and from the theological tradition. The question is located at the center of all Christian theology: the problem of Christology.

According to the Gospel of Luke, Jesus, as the one conceived in the womb of Mary by the power of the Holy Spirit, is the Son of God (Luke 1:35). Baptized by John in the Jordan, he receives the Spirit "in bodily form like a dove" (Luke 3:22). In the power of the Spirit, he is tempted by the devil (Luke 4:1); likewise empowered by the Spirit, he appears in his public ministry of preaching and healing (Luke 4:14-15).

It is not possible within the constraints of this book to comment in detail on all the pneumatological aspects of this "pneumatic Christology," according to which Jesus, empowered by the Spirit, treads the path of his Father's will to the end. This idea became a source of considerable confusion in the Christological tradition. The same general question appears in a number of ways in all Christology, but for our purposes it can be put in the following terms: How is it that the Lord Jesus Christ, the Son of God who pours out the Spirit upon the church from heaven, should be said in his earthly life to need the grace of the Spirit in order to fulfill his ministry?

Classical Christology dealt with this question in two principal ways. One route it took was the theological shortcut of outright adoptionism, according to which an ordinary man named Jesus was brought, presumably because of his moral merit, into a special relationship with God, who gave him power through the Spirit to preach and work miracles. In the end, and as reward for his ultimate act of obedience, God also raised him from the dead and exalted him to his right hand. The church, very early in its history, rejected this option as incompatible with the doctrine of the incarnation. A second option, it turns out, was nearly as unsatisfactory; but it came to be tolerated within theological orthodoxy. Soon it became clear that it is possible effectively to ignore the numerous biblical references to the work of the Spirit in and on Jesus' humanity, and concentrate instead on the action of the Word, which, according to the rapidly developing tradition of Christological thought, had assumed the human nature of Jesus into a personal or "hypostatic union" with itself. In this view, Christ truly had no need of the Spirit (just as he had no need of physical food, according to many of the authors in question), since as the Son of God he already possessed the fullness of grace and all spiritual gifts in himself, and could communicate them to his humanity continually. This view is profoundly represented in classical Christological orthodoxy, and was formally dogmatized by the documents of the Council of Ephesus (431).[40]

The trouble with this view is that it is difficult, if not impossible, to reconcile it with the clear teaching of the New Testament that Jesus experienced real moral and religious struggle, that he needed to pray, that he needed to get away by himself in order to set himself to do the Father's will, and so forth. The image of a Son of God who effortlessly engaged the powers of death and hell on Golgotha does not fit well with the image of the man who prayed in anguish in Gethsemane, his sweat becoming "like great drops of blood falling down on the ground" (Luke 22:44). This latter text may be disputed as far as the manuscript tradition is concerned, but the point of the text is not disputed today. Whatever must be said about Jesus concerning his divinity, he was at the very least this: a real human being who sweated, struggled, and truly suffered in facing death. At this point even conservative theologians break with the tradition of Cyril and Ephesus, insisting that any compromising of Jesus' humanity in any Christology is as great an error as the compromising of his deity.[41]

40. The key text is the Ninth Anathema appended to Cyril of Alexandria's *Third Letter to Nestorius*, which was dogmatized by the Council of Ephesus in 431; text in Tanner, *Decrees of the Ecumenical Councils*, 1: 60.

41. E.g., Yves Congar, *The Word and the Spirit*, trans. David Smith (London: Geoffrey Chapman, 1986), pp. 85-100. Of course, the position of Ephesus on this question is also transcended by the position of Chalcedon, which, in its affirmation that Jesus Christ is consubstantial with us as regards his humanity, ultimately grounds the approach taken here. In effect, the need for the Cyrilline Anathema that was dogmatized at Ephesus to be reinterpreted was established by the Christological definition of Chalcedon.

What is missing from the older Christology, and what is very often still missing from the new, is a sufficiently subtle doctrine of the triune God, according to which God's power is not diminished, but rather most gloriously expressed, in his becoming weak and suffering the death of the cross. By a similar logic, that Jesus Christ, the incarnate Son of God, needs the gift of the Spirit does not mean that he is somehow less than God or inadequate as Savior of the world; rather, it is that God, in "speaking his Word" into time and into human nature in Jesus, is able to be one with himself even in this ungodlike existence. That the Son can remain "one being with the Father," even and particularly in the anguish of death, should alert us to the possibility that the richness of God's being and the unity of the Father and the Son is also capable of containing and embracing difference and alienation. Hans Urs von Balthasar, for instance, speaks of the need to reckon with the depth of the *kenosis* of God in the cross of Jesus Christ, insisting that here there is a specific "theo-logic" established by God himself that contradicts the continuities of theological reasoning in much Christian thought.[42] For it was in his self-emptying in the suffering and death of Christ, when silence swallowed the Word of God, and revelation broke off, that the Word of God was most authentically spoken, as von Balthasar argues:

> In his self-emptying, God does not divest himself of his Godhead, but rather . . . [gives it] precise confirmation. . . . [The] God-Man can surrender himself to God abandonment, without resigning his own reality as God. . . . By becoming man, he enters into what is alien to him and there remains at the same time true to himself. (*Mysterium Paschale*, pp. 80-81)

The possibility of such a divine unity with itself in abasement, or of a theology of glory in what is by definition inglorious, is founded on nothing less than the inner-Trinitarian love of God the Holy Spirit, who in the divine freedom unites these "opposites" in himself, overcoming their contradiction and revealing himself truly as "the Giver of life." It is for this reason, too, that the Spirit rests on Jesus, the Lord who became a servant, mediating in his humiliation the will and presence of the Father. The work of the Holy Spirit should properly be deepened by our reflection on this idea; unfortunately,

---

42. The sources are numerous and lengthy, but for a brief account, see Hans Urs von Balthasar, *Mysterium Paschale: The Mystery of Easter,* trans. Aidan Nichols (Edinburgh: T&T Clark; Grand Rapids: Eerdmans, 1990), pp. 23-36, 79-83.

Christian theology has not generally recognized this possibility, and its history is much the poorer as a result.

From the standpoint of the twin themes of pneumatology and communion, the central point is that what we find in the story of the gospel is God's loving outreach to the world in Jesus Christ, in a love that is capable of stepping into the abyss of nonbeing so that God himself becomes subject to finitude and death. The implication is that it is not something foreign to God to be at one with himself in "otherness." The "way" of the triune God is not only such that God can be both "here" and "there" without contradiction, but that God can condescend to exist in the contradiction of sin and death, and yet precisely there remain one with himself. Jesus dies the death of the cross, crying out in anguish, "Why have you forsaken me?" Yet, from a deeper perspective, it is just this loss or sundering of relationship that God's outreach embraces, as that sundering comes to be "assumed" by a love that is deep and broad and high enough to take responsibility for it. In the mystery of the triune life, the "hell" of God-forsakenness is taken up through the death of Jesus into the unity of the triune God, as Christ "through the eternal Spirit offered himself without blemish to God" (Heb. 9:14). It is in this way that the power of death is broken in the gospel story, and God's great cause with humankind is vindicated.

Adapting these ideas to the concerns of a pneumatological account of *koinônia* thus requires that we pay careful attention to the Trinitarian framework within which such a pneumatology operates, out of which it comes, and which speaks in such extraordinary terms of the love of God for the creature. Clearly, the standpoint of the tradition is that ecclesiastical communion is indeed grounded in a great Trinitarian movement, by which we are made the body of Christ and given the gift of the Spirit. However, that Trinitarian movement is conceived in the tradition in far too one-dimensional terms; it particularly lacks a genuine encounter with the *pathos* of the cross. The *kenosis* of God, in which God steps into the bottomless void of death, is what alone can give it adequate depth. In seeking to avoid this singular path that God has trod, traditional ecclesiology lacks what is actually decisive: a properly theological content.

The whole problem of the communion of the church in the tradition is consequently understood in astonishingly superficial, theologically innocuous, and legalistic terms, as by a process of linear reasoning some are said to be one with God in the church, literally by virtue of their "joining," while the "other," the "alien," remains beyond communion. What the message of the cross can contribute to ecclesiology is (to use the term in Balthasar's sense) a properly "theo-logical" correction of this theologically primitive, linear reasoning. This is of paramount importance for the whole subject: the love of God, and with it the scope of what is capable of being brought into communion with God, reaches beyond the small grasp of our own community and embraces not only those who seem alien to us but supremely what seems strictly alien to God.

The first of these, the idea of communion with those beyond our community, is at least tentatively recognized in the new departure in Catholic theology made at Vatican II, which affirmed the Roman Catholic Church's "bond" with those outside the Catholic tradition. The same point was recognized — no doubt to a limited extent, but nevertheless for a much longer period of time and with some consistency — in the classic Protestant conviction that there are people and true churches known to God, if not to us, that exist in unlikely places. The Spirit "blows where he wills," in ways that we are not entitled to control. To define *the* church as this one or that one, as John Calvin rightly argues, is merely presumption.

However, there is also an anticipation of the second idea — that the communion of the Spirit extends to what is alien — to be found in the documents of Vatican II and in a diffuse range of theological sources, and this also requires comment before we move on. The Vatican II document, *Nostra Aetate*, which is concerned with the non-Christian religions, will serve as our point of departure:

> [Rejecting] nothing of those things which are true and holy in [other] religions . . . [the church] calls upon all its sons and daughters with prudence and charity, through dialogues and cooperation with followers of other religions, bearing witness to the christian faith and way of life, to recognise, preserve and promote those spiritual and moral good things as well as the socio-economic values which are to be found among them.[43]

This is a statement that is indefinitely "interpretable" (e.g., what constitutes the things that are "true and holy" in these religions of which "nothing" is to be rejected?). But what is significant is the clear turn away from the idea of the church as a unique ark of salvation toward a generous and open willing-

---

43. *Nostra Aetate*, 2, in Tanner, *Decrees of the Ecumenical Councils*, 2: 969.

ness to engage with the "other," and to do so precisely while and as a means of "bearing witness to the christian faith and way of life." *Nostra Aetate* extends such hospitality to a variety of the great religions by name, but pays special attention to Islam and to Judaism as children of Abraham and fellow heirs of monotheism.

In an earlier chapter, I made a case for the idea that the doctrine of election has its primary reference in the God who chooses not individuals principally, but a people and whole peoples. This, I argued, is the foundation of the idea of election in Scripture, and what finally grounds the gentile mission of the church. Neither *Nostra Aetate* nor my argument makes the missionary enterprise redundant or peripheral to the existence of the church. But what both have the effect of doing is insisting on a certain solidarity between God and the "other," which *precedes* and thus must be allowed to shape and inform the missionary task. The church is inherently "missional," as we shall see, but its mission is not merely to increase the sheer number of Christian converts. The goal is not simply to fill the choir stalls of heaven — or indeed, of earth. The goal could be more adequately expressed as purely and simply bearing witness to the God who chooses to dwell with humankind, and who in Jesus Christ has brought humankind into *koinônia* with himself — a *koinônia* that exists and has its basis "in God," whether people acknowledge him and it or not.

The extension of the concept of communion to the "other" potentially has an even more radical implication that was not envisioned by Vatican II or by Protestant ecclesiology, and is scarcely yet developed as a theological theory. The "other," the "alien" with regard to which God speaks his Word in time and thus defines his own being, must also refer in some way to those with whom we profoundly disagree, those we are tempted to call the "heretic" or the "unbeliever." The unity of God with the God-forsaken also extends to such a person, who is also a human for whom Christ died and someone who can share the communion of the Holy Spirit.

This is perhaps not something that can apply to all instances of the category of "heresy," such as what might appear on the lunatic fringes of the church, or such as appear purely as a means to personal gain; but it does apply to some of the "heresies." The Reformation of the sixteenth century is a good example. Though condemned early in its development by a variety of instruments, including papal bulls and full ecclesiastical councils, the theology of the Reformation serves at the very least as a corrective to the excesses of late medieval theology. Among those most captivated by the theology of

Martin Luther in our time, and who use some of his key theological ideas to greatest effect, are Roman Catholic theologians.[44] More generally, the documents of Vatican II show a readiness to accommodate various points of Reformation theology within the core of the Catholic tradition in a way that would simply have been inconceivable at the time of the Council of Trent or Vatican I.[45] Implicitly, at least, there is a recognition here that God's Word can be spoken not only to but also through the hated other, and that the one rejected may also be received as a brother.

In his treatment of the meaning of the cross in *Mysterium Paschale*, von Balthasar insists that the logic of God is not reducible to the structures of human reasoning or to philosophical expression. There is no way to "collapse" the fathomless content of revelation and the message of the cross into some dialectical system in which it is assumed that the mystery of God can be "understood" (p. 82). The target of von Balthasar's assault is almost certainly the philosopher Hegel, who can be and often has been construed as someone who presumed to "understand" the ways and works of God in just that way, "collapsing" the mystery into the limits of the philosophical system that he developed during the years 1807-1831. I have argued elsewhere that this polemic is unfair to Hegel and that it misrepresents both his intention and the express content of his system.[46] Even if we accept the force of von Balthasar's criticism, we can learn something from Hegel, something that may help us understand the central claim of the present discussion concerning *koinônia* and the "other." It is with this key insight that I will conclude this chapter.

As is well known, Hegel's philosophy is a bewildering and labyrinthine system, treating everything from then-current medical theory (e.g., phrenology), European politics, and advances in post-Kantian idealism in a comprehensive account of the history of ideas. Contained within it, too, is an informed — though selective — treatment of the content of Christian theology, which, among other things, strongly defends the principle of Trinitarianism as utterly central to Christianity, and criticizes its effective dissolution in "enlightened" religious thought. But the central importance of Hegel

44. Von Balthasar is a fine example; see *Mysterium Paschale*, passim.

45. The characteristically Lutheran doctrine of the "priesthood of all believers," for instance, is a major theme of *Lumen Gentium*, ch. 2, "De Populo Dei."

46. Gary D. Badcock, "Divine Freedom in Hegel," *Irish Theological Quarterly* 61 (1995): 265-71.

for our purposes derives from his methodological procedure, which is to take any single form of human philosophical consciousness and show how it breaks down of its own accord, yielding its place to another logical expression of the same core concern.

The reason for this procedure is simply this: the content of philosophical consciousness in Hegel's view is the infinite, or what is the same thing, the divine self-determining Spirit, the Absolute. To think the truth at all is implicitly to think absolute truth, and to think absolute truth is to think God. However, this infinite content is in principle incapable of being contained within the limits of finite logic, and consequently finite logic yields to the power of the infinite, and the truth "passes over" into another expression in human thought. This finite expression, in turn, must be subject to the same dynamic, so that the infinite content is expressed and re-expressed, and so on in a seemingly endless variety of ways. The burden of Hegel's philosophy is to attempt, first, to explore the dynamic by which this ceaseless expression and re-expression of ideas is produced; second, to attempt to grasp its logical development; and finally, to call the thinker to recognize its structures and to seek to mirror them in the structures of thinking itself. In short, it is to develop an infinite philosophical form that is adequate to the infinite content of thought. Above all, in Hegel's system one has to understand philosophy historically, and in relationship to the historical thread followed along the course of the Spirit's logical expressions in the world.

Therefore, in connection with the emergence of Protestantism from medieval theology, a Hegelian interpretation might be, first, that in medieval Catholicism the infinite truth of God is expressed in the mode of externality; however, being "defined" through conciliar decision and papal authority is its fundamental flaw, since the infinite is not capable of being captured in such external structures, or of being made the servant of the political order it represented. There is thus a breakdown from within medieval Catholicism: what is sought is a theological truth that can and does convince the individual rational conscience, and in which God in his Trinitarian outreach is grasped by the believing subject in the mode of inwardness. This is the insight of Protestantism, which Hegel sees, particularly in its Lutheran form, as a fuller realization of the truth of the Christian religion than was present in medieval religion, because in it the divine Spirit is apprehended immediately by self-conscious spirit. At this point Hegel's philosophy itself breaks off. But there is considerable evidence, particularly in his (posthumously published) lectures on the philosophy of religion that he saw the world of

Protestantism dissolving in the early nineteenth century through its affirmation of subjective and finite consciousness above its objective and infinite
content. A further expression is needed: for the strict Hegelian, presumably,
it would be one that we have yet to see, since Protestantism's dissolution
continues still, and has not yet reached its limit.[47]

Much of Hegel's system will perhaps seem fanciful, but it at least has the
advantage of allowing us to conceive of a development by which the "Spirit,"
as the Spirit of ecclesiastical communion, must move beyond one particular,
limited ecclesiastical expression of itself — and into another. The Spirit does
so precisely because it is wild and free, blowing where it wills, and not where
we may wish to direct it, nor solely in those areas of personal or cultural concern to which we wish to restrict it. It must find other homes, beyond the
old, in which it can also live and which it can shape in fuller ways. It is not
that the Spirit "departs" from one of its expressions and enters another; the
Spirit dwells in both, and in all. Rather, it is that the movement of the Spirit
is comprehensible only when we abandon the standpoint of "finite logic"
and instead follow "the way of the Spirit" into what seems alien, but which in
fact contains the same principle as we do ourselves. The Spirit's "passing
over" into what seems incompatible with it is, from this point of view, a fundamental dimension of the Spirit's work, and a fundamental possibility with
which the discipline of ecclesiology has scarcely begun to grapple.

In his theological exploration of the meaning of Holy Saturday, which,
like von Balthasar's exploration of the divine *kenosis,* chooses to linger over
and to meditate on the day when Christ lay dead, Alan Lewis speaks in the
following terms of the life of the contemporary churches:

> Christ's way to the fulfillment of his lordship leads through the
> servanthood and emptiness which culminate in Joseph's tomb. Death
> and burial are antecedent to his victory and glory. But, by contrast, the
> church has already had its triumphal history, its long, but passing, ep-
> och of grandeur and prestige, its generations of clerical ministers
> vested with power and crowned to greater or lesser degrees with supe-
> riority, dominance, and glory. The way for us forward now, in our
> Easter Saturday world, can only be a way back, a return to the cross,
> from power to service, from glory to self-giving. . . . This reversionary,

---

47. Such treatments are certainly rare, but not unknown; see, e.g., James Doull, "The
Logic of Theology Since Hegel," *Dionysus* 7 (1983): 12-136.

ecclesial pilgrimage, back from resurrection glory to the cross and its humility, must pass through the same grave of Jesus Christ on Easter Saturday. . . .[48]

Is this not very similar to the position represented by our "Hegelian" analysis — though Lewis certainly intended to say no such thing? On both accounts, in fact, the Protestant church, particularly but by no means exclusively in its "mainline" expression, has reached the borderlands of continuing viability. In Lewis's pictorial representation, there is now no alternative to a profoundly cruciform return to the source, through which it can find new expression. Lewis's account also tells us why this is so: it is the way of God himself, to which the church cannot refuse to be obedient. Hegel, however, also tells us why it is so — but allows us to recognize that all along the way the Spirit of God has, contrary to expectation, always been in the alien other, those we deemed "finally" heretical and schismatic, but who were, in truth, subject to similar limitations as ourselves.

What we also need to say is that the Roman Catholic tradition has, in effect, already seen this. In its extraordinary rebirth and renewal in recent decades, expressed decisively in the documents of Vatican II, but also and no less clearly in the renewal of its liturgical and theological life, it has seen itself in the other, affirmed its "bond" with it in the Spirit, and even, in a measure, incorporated it into its own life and witness. What the world of Protestantism now needs is a similar development that encompasses a recovery of the "catholic" principle, and then — who can say? If Hegel is right, some new thing must beckon us, something in which both expressions of the Spirit of communion can receive an even fuller, richer expression.

48. Alan E. Lewis, *Between Cross and Resurrection: A Theology of Holy Saturday* (Grand Rapids: Eerdmans, 2001), pp. 367-69.

CHAPTER 6

Word

At the end of the preceding chapter, I developed an argument for theological pluralism as something necessary for the deepening of authentic ecclesiastical communion, drawing in part on Hegelian philosophy and in part on the actual story of the church and its theological travails. It will be useful for us to bear this argument in mind as we proceed in this chapter to consider the problem of proclamation, doctrine, and the possibility of a common confession of faith. As we shall see, there must be such a confession, but the relationship between this "one" and the "many" theological positions that elaborate on it in the church is not what might be expected. If in the preceding chapter the movement was centrifugal, leading from the central core that focused on the concept of communion to a diversity of theological expression, in this chapter the movement will be centripetal, or tending from a diversity of expression back to the center — a doctrinal core. A large part of our task in this chapter will be to grasp something of the reason for this movement and the structures governing it; indeed, outlining the way communion and Word coexist in dynamic relationship is a major task of this book as a whole.

The argument will proceed in a number of phases. First of all, I will examine the idea of theological truth as central to the whole problem of the church. This in itself will be a somewhat unusual move, since the very concept of truth has been fundamentally challenged in modern times — and largely abandoned in modern theology. Clearly, that challenge requires a response. Second, it will be necessary to develop a theology of the Word of God, or more specifically of the Bible in its varied theological interpretation and use in proclamation, because the whole problem of the place of the

Word of God in ecclesiology comes into sharp focus at this point. Doctrine, faith, and proclamation are closely connected at the very heart of the life and witness of the church, and thus we cannot avoid them when we talk about ecclesiology. What we shall discover, however, is that the whole subject has surprising depths. What I will argue is that the one Word of God must be expressed in a variety of ways, and in a variety of theological systems, precisely so that its true theological unity will be realized. This, in turn, will serve to illuminate the nature of the church's common confession — over against the plurality of Christian theological systems. Third, I will examine the problem of Christian doctrine in the light of the crisis of liberalism, and I will present a certain core of Christian "orthodoxy" as the true end of an authentic theological pluralism.

Word, Truth, and the Doctrine of the Church

One of the most compelling features of historic Christianity has been its commitment to define and to uphold, particularly among its ministerial leadership, a standard of "right teaching," or orthodoxy. By its upholding of right teaching, the church is definitively understood as a place of theological truth, or in the words of the New Testament itself, the "pillar and bulwark of the truth" (1 Tim. 3:15).

This idea, though alien to wide sections of contemporary Christianity, is deeply rooted not only in the classical theological tradition, but also in the overall teaching of the New Testament. In fact, the word "truth" is commonly found on the lips of Jesus. In the Gospel of Matthew alone, the formulaic preface "I tell you the truth . . ." occurs no fewer than thirty times. That pattern is repeated not only in Mark and Luke, but also extensively in John, where it appears some twenty-eight times. It is among the most common of Jesus' expressions.

The ecclesiological extension of the concern for truth is equally obvious in the New Testament as a whole. Not only Jesus, but also his followers, have an interest in truth. The discourse of John 14–16 repeats several times that the promised Holy Spirit (the "Spirit of truth") will guide the believers into all truth after Jesus' departure (esp. John 16:12-15). This is a pivotal text for the theme, and it underwrites centuries of doctrinal formulation and conciliar decision. The documents of the New Testament repeatedly emphasize the idea that the Word of God that is preached by and believed in the church is truth, connecting the idea of truth explicitly with the content of Christian faith, which is a feature of much of the New Testament.[1] Thus, whereas it is possible to "suppress the truth" by wickedness (Rom. 1:18), the apostle Paul wishes only to live "for the truth" (2 Cor. 13:8); 2 Timothy speaks of conversion simply as coming to "know the truth" (2 Tim. 2:25).

Arguing on the basis of such texts, Hans Küng speaks in his theology of a basic and irreducible "weaving together" of faith and knowledge in the New Testament, particularly in John and Paul.[2] Indeed, Küng goes so far as to speak of the New Testament as "decisively concerned with truth," referring to the *speculatio facie ad faciem* and the eschatological hope of full knowledge found in the famous text of 1 Corinthians 13:12 as evidence of an interest in speculative knowledge even in the New Testament: "For now we see in a mirror, dimly, but then we will see face to face. Now I know only in part, then I will know fully, even as I have been fully known."

However, the extent to which any such speculative interest could be pressed is disputed. For instance, Emil Brunner argues in *Truth as Encounter* that the tendency to misunderstand the nature of theological truth is a basic feature of the history of Christian thought:

> Very early in the history of the church . . . the idea arose under the influence of Greek philosophy that the divine revelation in the Bible had to do with the communication of those doctrinal truths which were inaccessible by themselves to human reason; and correspondingly that faith consisted in holding these supernaturally revealed doctrines for truth. This Greek intellectualistic recasting of the understanding of revelation and faith has caused immeasurable damage in the church to the present day.[3]

In place of such an "intellectualist" reading of the truth of revelation, Brunner proposes a relational theology of personal correspondence, involving the God who demands and offers fellowship on the one hand, and the obedient trust — by which a person opens up to the loving self-offering of God in

1. Philippians, 1 Thessalonians, Philemon, Jude, and Revelation would appear to be exceptions.

2. Hans Küng, *The Incarnation of God*, trans. J. R. Stephenson (Edinburgh: T&T Clark, 1987), pp. 240-41.

3. Emil Brunner, *Truth as Encounter*, 2nd ed., trans. David Cairns et al. (Philadelphia: Westminster Press, 1964), p. 68.

Christ — on the other (p. 109). For Brunner, truth in the biblical sense means what is trustworthy, or personally reliable. God is not an *object* to be known, he argues, but a *person* to be encountered, a person who in this encounter creates, by the power of the Holy Spirit, the very possibility of a reciprocal response of the creature in faith and love. A double-sided giving of self to self is its hallmark. Truth as trustful self-giving has only the most remote connection with the subject-object structure of the standard philosophical conceptions of truth. The truth of God has to be expressed instead in *narrative* form, because the relationship between the divine self-giving and human self-giving is not a logical one, arising from the world of ideas, but is rather an event in time (p. 88).

For Brunner, it is for such reasons that it is impossible for ecclesiastical doctrine to express the truth of God in abstract formulas. But Brunner is by no means a voice crying in the wilderness. Paul Avis similarly argues that there is a difference of the utmost importance between a propositional-analytic view of theological truth and a personal-fiduciary understanding.[4] Avis's theology has the advantage of tracing this theme well back into the theology of the liberal Protestantism of the nineteenth century, thus demonstrating that many of the leading themes of the neo-orthodoxy of a figure like Brunner are not new at all.

One can perhaps question whether Brunner and Avis have done complete justice to the tradition of Christian orthodoxy, which always had to recognize that the Christian religion as a "system of thought" is not concerned merely with an abstract set of propositions. One can also argue that the propositions were important in it only because of the set of relationships they were *intended* to secure. If a lost child in the care of a beat policeman were to say, for instance, "That woman there is my mother," something objective and substantive would be stated as a propositional fact. However, the fact that it is stated at all is for the sake of the restoration of relationship: only if the child states the truth objectively to the policeman will the mother be able to take the child home. Similarly, an abstract proposition about God such as "three persons in one indivisible substance" may on the one hand be an attempt to state an objective fact taken to be divinely revealed; but the reason a person holds that it is true is not merely out of curiosity or for reasons of theoretical interest, but so that Christians

---

4. Paul Avis, *Ecumenical Theology and the Elusiveness of Doctrine* (London: SPCK, 1986), p. 7.

can pray, worship, and believe in God the Father, Son, and Holy Spirit meaningfully. According to those terms, there may be more to the "intellectualistic" tendencies of the Christian theological tradition than first meets the eye. For the present we may reserve judgment on this critique of the tradition.

Brunner argues his case elsewhere in more concrete terms: "A [person] becomes a Christian through the Word of God, which God gives to the individual through the Christian community."[5] This statement not only affirms the critical role of proclamation in the life of the church, but also recognizes the dialectic of the individual and the community in matters of faith, and it reveals another side of the relational quality of the theology of the Word of God. There is no doubt that it is the individual who believes, receives the promise of God's Word in faith, and is accordingly said to come to salvation, having been "begotten again . . . through the living and enduring Word of God" (1 Pet. 1:23 [my translation]). As in the well-known parable of the sower, what is sown is the Word, which on the good soil of a godly life produces a crop fit for the kingdom of God (Mark 4:14ff.). Yet, on the other hand, the Word of God is neither "received" nor "sown" in a vacuum. First of all, the Word as Scripture is written, preserved, exegeted, and handed on by the people of God, and so in a certain sense it can be said to have its proper "abode" within the community of faith. Furthermore, it is within the community that we hear it and come to believe. Even in the missionary context in which someone who has previously had no contact with the church might hear the Word as something surprising and entirely new, it must be assumed that there had already been, first of all, someone who was sent to proclaim it, and a sending community into which the convert could, in principle, be incorporated (Rom. 10:14-15).

The plurality of the "I" and the "we" that appears in Brunner's exposition of the nature of faith, and is central also to the dynamic of the church, is reflected notably in the Apostles' and Nicene Creeds. These begin in different ways, with the words "I believe" (or *Credo* in the Latin text) in the first, and "We believe" (or *Pisteuomen*, in the Greek text) in the second (*Credimus* in the Latin). The contrast between the use of the first-person singular in the Latin tradition, where the Apostles' Creed has its roots, and the first-person plural in the Greek tradition, from which the Nicene Creed derives, has been

---

5. Emil Brunner, *The Divine Imperative*, trans. Olive Wyon (London: Lutterworth Press, 1937), p. 300.

much commented on and has been traced to subtle distinctions in the Christological emphases found in the two traditions.[6]

It would also be possible to speak of a certain psychological interest and capacity for interiority in the Latin tradition, as exemplified in and shaped by the theology of St. Augustine, as opposed to the more metaphysical or objective orientation typical of the Greeks, as is seen in the theology of Origen or Athanasius, and of each as reflected in the two creeds. But there is also a more mundane explanation for the difference: the Apostles' Creed has its origins in a third-century baptismal creed of the Church at Rome, and thus in the liturgical practice of the pre-Constantinian church.[7] The *Symbolum Romanum,* as this early version of the Apostles' Creed is called, was used during the period of the most intense imperial persecutions of Christianity, a time when one's confession of the creed at baptism "rested on a personal decision as demanding as any an existentialist could imagine."[8] What is signaled by the Latin *Credo* is an intensely personal confession — of the faith of the church — in baptism. By contrast, in the Nicene Creed, the original version of which was approved under the Emperor Constantine's own watchful eye as an instrument of religious unity in the empire, it was the collective faith of the church on central questions relating to Christology and to God that was at issue, rather than the particular affirmation of any individual per se, so that the "we believe" of Nicea seems equally natural.

Our word "creed," it will be obvious, derives immediately from the Latin *credo,* and its use is a testament to the importance in the Western church of the Apostles' Creed. But a variety of words, in fact, are used in the ancient Christian tradition for what our word "creed" signifies, and they add much to our understanding of the meaning of such doctrinal summaries: "the faith," "the teaching," "the rule of faith," "the apostolic tradition," and "the symbol" are frequently used alternatives. The word "symbol" is of special interest because the word had an established usage in Hellenistic and Roman culture, which came to be adopted into ecclesiastical usage. The secular meaning was twofold: a symbol was a "token," as in the case of a broken shell or piece of pottery divided among friends which, when reunited, could identify their messengers; alternatively, a symbol could also be a "password," a

---

6. Heinrich Vogel, *Das Nicaenische Glaubensbekenntnis* (Berlin: Lettner, 1963), p. 21.

7. J. N. D. Kelly, *Early Christian Creeds,* 3rd ed. (New York: Longmans, 1972), pp. 100ff.

8. Jan M. Lochman, *The Faith We Confess: An Ecumenical Dogmatics* (Edinburgh: T&T Clark, 1985), p. 27.

word used in military contexts or by the police in the night. In both cases, the transposing of those usages to the life of the church is straightforward: a person's knowledge of the *symbolon* or *symbolum* identifies her as a Christian, as a sign or token by which she could be distinguished from those outside the faith. In other words, the "symbol" of faith was not to be openly shared and was not common knowledge. As late as the fifth century, long after Christianity had come to enjoy imperial favor, the ancient Christian historian Sozomen could write as follows of the Council of Nicaea:

> I formerly deemed it necessary to transcribe the [*symbolon*] of faith drawn up by the unanimous consent of this Council, in order that posterity might possess a public record of the truth; but subsequently, I was persuaded to the contrary by some godly and learned friends, who [convinced me] that such matters ought to be kept secret, as being only [required] to be known by disciples and their instructors, and it is probable that this volume will fall into the hands of the unlearned. I have not, however, entirely suppressed the information derived from my authorities . . . as to the decrees of the Council.[9]

While it is clearly assumed that the content of the symbol or creed was agreed on by the church as authoritatively true, the definition of the truth was not its sole function; nor, indeed, was the creed the principal means by which such theological truth was expressed. In fact, as we shall see, the primary expressions of theological truth must be taken to have been elsewhere: first of all, in theological writing; but, more particularly, in Holy Scripture and in those commentaries on Scripture that were intended and destined to translate ultimately into the church's proclamation.

The Critique of Theological Truth in Modernity

Before proceeding to examine the thrust of such material and its significance, it is important to note by way of introduction that during the modern period the teaching of the church has been subject to a prolonged and often violent criticism from a variety of quarters, both external and internal to Christian theology, over some four centuries. A polemic against traditional Christian

9. E. T. Sozomen, *Ecclesiastical History,* I.xx, *Sozomen's Ecclesiastical History* (London: Samuel Bagster and Sons, 1846), pp. 38-39.

doctrinal claims, for example, was a basic theme of early modern Deism. As announced by the "father of English Deism," Lord Edward Herbert of Cherbury, in his early manifesto of the Deist movement, *De Veritate* (1624), the Christian church must yield its claim to be the "pillar and bulwark of the truth" (1 Tim. 3:15) to modern reason.[10] Rather than acknowledge any such ecclesiastical claim, Deism spoke darkly of the menace of the churches' desire for power, particularly in the form of ecclesiastical "priestcraft," as the principal source of superstition, ignorance, and bigotry in society. For the Deists, this menace underlay all the old doctrines concerning incarnation, Trinity, salvation, and sacraments, which required submission to their priestly mediators — and thus secured their social and economic power. If people are ever to escape their clutches, they need rational evaluation of the claims of the church and sober dismissal of much of what it represents. Setting themselves against the "mysteries" of priestcraft and of traditional religion, the Deists proclaimed that Christianity, properly reconfigured, would not be "mysterious" in any sense, but a commonsense affirmation of a handful of religious and moral insights available to reason alone.[11] Accordingly, Deism taught a simple message of God as Creator, of Jesus as a teacher of moral wisdom, and of ethical purity in view of the hope of immortality.

The same basic atmosphere is found in the attempt to make faith accountable to "enlightened reason" in the eighteenth century, to have faith only insofar as it could be contained "within the limits of reason." The major difference is that by that time the impulse had become a popular movement that fed on the public distaste for the confessional positions underlying the disastrous wars of religion a century before, and was inspired with new confidence by a heightened awareness of the marvel of the modern science of nature.

Numerically, the churches were decimated during this period. By the early nineteenth century, Thomas Chalmers would note the dramatic impact of the changes in urban Scotland, one of the new heartlands of the intellectual, economic, and social revolutions of the time: he despaired of the impending "heathenism."[12] The extent of the crisis for the church during

---

10. Edward, Lord Herbert of Cherbury, *De Veritate,* trans. Meyrick H. Carré (Bristol: J. W. Arrowsmith, 1937).

11. John Toland, *Christianity Not Mysterious,* ed. Philip McGuinness et al. (Dublin: The Lilliput Press, 1997).

12. Thomas Chalmers, *The Christian and Civic Economy of Large Towns,* 3 vols. (London: Routledge/Thoemmes Press, 1995; first published 1821).

those decades can best be represented by a reference to the experience of an earlier generation, particularly the events of the French Revolution, when the people (the "third estate") rose up against the church and the nobility (the "first" and "second estates") and forced European history onto new tracks. In its aftermath, the Christian calendar was abolished, multitudes of French churches became stables, and an enlightened "cult of reason" was installed in the great French cathedrals.

It is difficult to underestimate the extent to which the lengthy polemic of modernity against Christianity has affected both the form and content of Christian thought over the past four hundred years. It is found not only in the fabric of virtually all antireligious polemic in the modern period, but it was also woven in some ways into the warp and woof of classic liberal Protestantism, which was largely constructed within the constraints of the modern critique of Christianity — and in answer to its "cultured despisers."[13] Evangelical Protestantism, with its pronounced tendency to flee from intellectual responsibility and its exaltation of individual religious conversion as a superior alternative to confessional orthodoxy, and the antimodernist movement in modern Roman Catholicism, with its reactionary stand against the claims of reason and its extremist recourse to magisterial authority, are equally reactions to liberal Protestantism. Of course, the truth is that the character of each position was in no small way determined by what it negated.

Even today, the influence of the polemic of modernism against religious belief — and particularly Christian belief — remains very strong. It is particularly profound in the academy, for most of the sciences are products of modernity and heirs of its traditions. Not only is this approach to religion generally discernible in a variety of academic disciplines, but it is also found in the scientific study of religion, particularly in modern biblical studies, which, as Brevard Childs has noted, has for two centuries explicitly attempted to "liberate" the biblical text from the constraints of the older traditions of Christian teaching, since it is only by being treated in this way that it can be understood through the methods of historical science.[14]

If the dominant assumption of the biblical studies inspired by Deist and

13. Friedrich Schleiermacher, *On Religion: Speeches to Its Cultured Despisers,* trans. Richard Crouter (Cambridge, UK: Cambridge University Press, 1988).

14. Brevard Childs, "On Reclaiming the Bible for Christian Theology," in Carl E. Braaten and Robert W. Jenson, eds., *Reclaiming the Bible for the Church* (Grand Rapids: Eerdmans, 1995), p. 14.

Enlightened reason has been that the truth contained in the Bible can only come to light when abstracted from the content of Christian faith, since the latter is seen as a distorting influence, the implication must be that Christian faith as traditionally defined is profoundly *untrue*. But if that is so, then the church is among the last places in which one ought to look for truth, so that the connection between a meaningful doctrine of the Word and the doctrine of the church is definitively severed. The only recourse would seem to be either a reactionary conservatism, or else a full-scale retreat from public truth to private opinion, from objectivity to subjectivity, and from marketplace and state to the sphere of hearth and home.

Part of the trouble for theology has thus been the dominance in modern scientific culture of an epistemological paradigm that is incompatible with certain of the claims of Christian theology. To take one example: the meaningfulness of the notion of divine purpose in creation has been challenged in science from the time of Galileo and Descartes, for in the scientific worldview they helped to create, natural purpose (in the form of Aristotelian teleology or "entelechy") is discredited as belonging to an antiquated, prescientific view of nature.[15] Such purposiveness cannot in any case be mathematized, and it is hence by definition strictly inadmissible in scientific knowledge. Throughout his works, René Descartes, the "father of modern philosophy," labored to demonstrate that a true knowledge of physical nature is exclusively found in the new mathematical understanding achieved in science.[16] This alone has rational warrant. The same basic claim is made in what was in its day a hugely influential work, Francis Bacon's *Novum Organum,* a book on scientific method explicitly intended to replace the old methodology represented by the corpus of Aristotle's logical work, the *Organon.*[17] These bold claims received important confirmation from the astonishing success of modern science in explaining and controlling particular natural phenomena and ultimately the natural world itself.

It has been only relatively recently that these assumptions have come to be widely questioned in Western culture, largely due to the widespread col-

15. E.g., Aristotle, *On the Heavens,* 271a33.

16. Desmond Clarke, "Descartes' Philosophy of Science and the Scientific Revolution," in John Cottingham, ed., *The Cambridge Companion to Descartes* (Cambridge, UK: Cambridge University Press, 1992), pp. 258-85.

17. Francis Bacon, *The Advancement of Learning and New Atlantis,* ed. Arthur Johnston (Oxford: Clarendon Press, 1974).

lapse of this ready sense of confidence in the competence of science alone to explain and control. The scenario evoked by the prospect of an unimpeded march of scientific progress is widely held today, perhaps even by a majority, to be both morally and politically unacceptable. The reasons for this are not difficult to discern, for among people's chief concerns at the beginning of the new millennium is the threat of further environmental degradation from yet more scientific "progress"; the very real possibility of the use of nuclear, biological, or chemical weaponry in future acts of war or terrorism due to the widespread dissemination of technology; the terrifying potential latent in the genetic revolution in contemporary biological science; and not least, the mind-numbing failure of Western technological culture to sustain the human spirit.

While nobody doubts the capacity of unimpeded natural science actually to tame and control nature, what people now doubt is whether such knowledge and power is by itself worth having. The result is that the all-encompassing claim to the dominance of science in the modern era is now widely disputed. In other words, exactly how science is itself to be tamed and controlled has become an area of tremendous uncertainty in the wider culture. However, the root of the uncertainty is nothing less than a sense of dissatisfaction with the assumptions and values of modernity itself, of which the modern science of nature is at once the chief product. In some ways, scientific progress has become modernity's chief contemporary liability.

Here we begin to enter on the social and intellectual condition generically known as "postmodernity," which is the dominant cultural context within which Christian theology is carried out in the Western world today, and in which the life of the church is lived. The important point for our purposes is that, if it is true that a crisis of confidence in the "old" intellectual and moral standards of modernity has dawned, then this may be a crisis similar to the crisis in confidence in the medieval order that altered the course of Western intellectual history in fifteenth-century Italy, and in northern Europe in the sixteenth century. If so, one of the great theological questions of our time must concern whether Christians will have the wisdom and the capacity to respond intelligently to these developments. In short, the advent of postmodernity presents the possibility of a massive renewal of Christian theological vision.

I do not intend to engage at length with "the postmodern condition," only to observe that the cultural ground has shifted significantly in recent decades and to note that there is scope today for theological exploration that makes new developments easier than they might have been even a generation ago. John Milbank, in an essay entitled "The Gospel of Affinity," has written of the need for Christian theology to be careful in its approach to postmodernity, not least because many of its claims amount to "confusions," while much of postmodern existence seems merely to be a self-manipulation into "a thousand shapes."[18] Postmodernity is not a cure for all theological ills, for to swallow it whole would bring on a cluster of new theological illnesses.

However, Milbank insists that postmodernity does present the church with new opportunities. His basic argument is that the posture of the church should be one of cautious engagement: "Not outright refusal, nor outright acceptance" (p. 9). The gospel has a logic of its own, a logic that is too often forgotten by a church that has had to survive the crises of modernity. What is needed in the postmodern situation is above all a rediscovery of the proper logic of Christian faith itself, and nothing less than a new and properly theological rediscovery of the gospel, since "neither a reiteration of Christian orthodoxy in identically repeated handed-down formulas nor a liberal adaptation to postmodern assumptions" can lead to such renewal (pp. 2-3).[19]

The explorations that follow will take a similar approach. Since a full-scale engagement of postmodernity is clearly out of the question, the option of using the postmodern situation in which the church lives as an opportunity for a rediscovery of the gospel has presented itself. In fact, this has been my strategy throughout this study. The way of theological renewal in the history of the Christian church has always led through a return to the sources of the church's life and witness, and to a reformulation of theological insight in ways that transcend them. Accordingly, what I have argued, and what follows below, is an attempt to plumb the resources of Scripture and of the theological tradition in the hope that the church can find theological renewal by way of a return to the center of the gospel. What we need is to hear the Word of God afresh and in some cases for the first time.

---

18. John Milbank, "The Gospel of Affinity," in Carl E. Braaten and Robert Jenson, eds., *The Strange New World of the Gospel: Evangelizing in the Postmodern World* (Grand Rapids: Eerdmans, 2002), pp. 2-3.

19. Milbank, "The Gospel of Affinity," pp. 2-3. See also John Milbank and Catherine Pickstock, *Truth in Aquinas* (London and New York: Routledge, 2001), for an arguement that a rediscovery of the roots of the theological concept of truth *alone* can provide the response needed to the crisis of truth in contemporary philosophy.

Scripture as "Site" of Theological Truth:
Moving toward the Center

The place of "right teaching" in classical doctrines of the church is clear, but the theme comes to special prominence in ecclesiology in the Reformation tradition. Whereas unity with the succession of bishops, for example, features prominently in ancient and medieval ecclesiology as a defining mark of the catholic church, the Reformation tradition was forced to break with such ideas for the sake of its overwhelming commitment to a theology of the Word of God. Because of that commitment, the idea of the unbroken succession becomes a matter of indifference, an *adiaphoron*. The best-known formulation of the Reformation position is found first in the work of the Lutheran theologian Melanchthon,[20] and it is expressed classically in Calvin's *Institutes:* "Whenever we see the Word of God purely preached and the sacraments administered according to Christ's institution, there, it is not to be doubted, a Church of God exists."[21] The church is thus essentially a "creature of the Word," living solely by the divine promise that it grasps by faith in Jesus Christ. The sacraments, too, are "visible words" in Reformation thought (though the underlying idea is Augustinian), for by virtue of Christ's command the Word of God assumes these concrete forms in the life of the church in baptism and the bread.

All of this not only secures the importance of the Word, and with it the centrality of doctrine in Reformation ecclesiology, but also, by implication, the ministry of preaching, and with it the adjunct ministry of teaching and doctrinal reflection. So it is that in the Augsburg Confession of 1530, the defining article on justification by faith leads immediately to an article concerning ministry: *Ut hanc fidem consequamur, institutum est ministerium docendi Evangelium* ("For obtaining such faith, the ministry of teaching the gospel has been instituted").[22] While it is not stated precisely what the phrase *ministerium docendi Evangelium* comprises, it is clear from the whole tenor of the Reformation movement that the work of both the preacher and of the scholar is under consideration. Calvin makes essentially the same

20. Philip Melanchthon, *Loci Communes D,* xii, in *Corpus Reformatorum* (Berlin and Leipzig, 1834-), 21 (1854): cols. 825-40.

21. Calvin, *Institutes,* IV.i.9.

22. Augsburg Confession, Art. V, in Philip Schaff, *The Creeds of the Evangelical Protestant Churches* (London: Hodder and Stoughton, 1877), p. 10.

move — from the Word to the ministry — in a second and parallel summary definition of the true church that appears in the *Institutes* shortly after the fuller and better-known definition already cited: "[W]herever the ministry remains whole and uncorrupted, no moral faults or diseases prevent [us] from bearing the name 'church'" (*Institutes*, IV.ii.1). He goes on to make the ministerial office of the "doctor," or "teacher," a permanent one, which, though less important than that of the "pastor" (by which he means the preacher), is nevertheless essential to it: "[T]eachers are not put in charge of discipline, or administering the sacraments, or warnings and exhortations, but only of Scriptural interpretation — to keep doctrine whole and pure among believers. But the pastoral office includes all these functions within itself" (IV.iii.4).

Once again, it would appear that the function of doctrine, whether taught or preached, is not merely cerebral in the Reformation tradition. To take one notable example, the fifth article of the *Augsburg Confession,* "On the Ministry of the Church," tells us not only that the churches, *magno consensu* (Art. i), teach that the ministry of the Word and sacrament was instituted by God for obtaining faith. It also immediately adds the following explanation: "For by the Word and the sacraments the Holy Spirit is given, as by instruments. . . ."[23] In other words, in Lutheran theology the purpose of the gift of the Word, whether as made audible in preaching or made visible in the signs of water, bread, and wine, is properly to be grasped by way of pneumatology. It is the coming of the Holy Spirit that counts in ecclesiology, and it is for the sake of it that everything else happens. The point was made with equal clarity, though for a rather different audience, in a later product of Reformed theology, *The Shorter Catechism* of the Westminster Assembly (1647), in what perhaps will seem disarming statements:

Q. *How is the Word made effectuall to Salvation?*
A. The Spirit of God maketh the Reading, but especially the Preaching of the Word, an effectuall means of convincing and converting sinners, and of building them up in holinesse and comfort through faith unto salvation.

Q. *How is the Word to be read, and heard, that it may become effectuall to Salvation?*

23. Augsburg Confession, Art. V, in Schaff, *The Creeds,* p. 10: *Nam per verbum et Sacramenta, tanquam per instrumenta, donatur Spiritus Sanctus. . . .*

A. That the Word may become effectuall to Salvation, we must attend thereunto with diligence, preparation, and prayer, receive it with faith and love, lay it up in our hearts, and practise it in our lives.[24]

It is common to treat the problem of the doctrine of the Word of God narrowly and technically, that is, in terms of a "doctrine of Scripture" or in connection with a "doctrine of revelation," examining theories of inspiration and disputes over the so-called single and double source theories of revelation (Scripture versus Scripture and tradition). But this is sterile ground that has been covered exhaustively by any number of writers, and in any case, it is an approach that misses the real theological point. What a text like the *Shorter Catechism* shows is that the point of discussions about the Word is that through it the work of the Spirit is accomplished in the church, so that, in practice, the real issue is about how the Bible is to be used in proclamation — in other words, how it becomes a "means of convincing and converting sinners." After all, it is only for the sake of this conviction that doctrines of inspiration and of revelation are developed at all, so that while these other questions have their place, they do not have *primary* place in the logic of a doctrine of the Word of God.

What the *Augsburg Confession* and the *Shorter Catechism* both show, therefore, is that in the key sources of Protestant theology and piety (sources that could be multiplied indefinitely), something more than a narrow biblicism is in operation. The vexed question of inerrancy, for example, is not in any sense a preoccupation: this is a modern problem that has been thrust up by the polemics of the Deists and of the Enlightenment. The fundamental idea in our sources is not that the Bible contains information (though this may well be assumed), but that it is a means of grace. The theology of the Reformation is not a Gnosticism. The key thing is that the *Holy Spirit* is given by the ministry of the Word, so that the Word in this way "may become effectuall"; but it is not, as it were, something that in automatic fashion can have any effect at all that is of saving consequence. To that extent, the Bible's authority does not lie in itself but in its *use*. The real point is its "effectuall" working, so at this point we are again thrown back on the structures of pneumatology. It is the Holy Spirit who takes the Word and makes it

---

24. *Shorter Catechism*, qq. 89, 90, in William Carruthers, *The Shorter Catechism of the Westminster Assembly of Divines* (London: Publication Office of the Presbyterian Church of England, 1897), pp. 14-15.

a means of grace in the faith and life of the believer. For this reason, it is not the Bible but proclamation, "the Preaching of the Word," that takes place within the church as the sphere of the Spirit's power, that becomes the instrument of God's action in the life of believers.

Near the beginning of the *Church Dogmatics*, Karl Barth speaks in similar terms of proclamation as the thing that makes the church the church, and of the Word of God as the thing that makes proclamation true proclamation. In developing this idea, he draws heavily on the theology of the sacraments, relating his theology of proclamation to the theme of sacramental realism:

> Proclamation and the Church are, of course, simply and visibly there just as the bread and wine of Communion are simply and visibly there and the distributing, eating and drinking of the bread and wine in Communion take place simply and visibly. They are not simply and visibly there, however, as that which they want to be and should be, as theologically relevant entities, as realities of revelation and faith.[25]

As in Reformed sacramental theology, it is necessary to draw a distinction between the sermon as an object of human thought or perception and the sermon as the proclamation of the Word of God. The true object of the sermon "can never in any sense be our possession." According to Barth, "[w]e have it as it gives itself to us."[26] It is only in this way, subject to the freedom of the God who gives himself in his Word, that the object of proclamation can be the Word of God as opposed to the words of men and women. Barth's point is that the act of proclamation, like the bread and the wine, needs to be understood as something that can *become* the Word of God in a realistic sense akin to the marking or inscribing of a new meaning on the eucharistic elements by the Word of God (citing Calvin). Barth returns here to a theme he announced earlier in his theological career: that it is possible to understand proclamation on the basis of what happens in the Eucharist, to the extent that a favorable comparison is drawn between the Protestant sermon and the Catholic Mass as a realization of Christ's presence.[27]

---

25. Barth, *Church Dogmatics,* I/1, p. 88.

26. Barth, *Church Dogmatics,* I/1, pp. 91-92. For a more extended treatment of Barth's theology of proclamation, see Joseph L. Mangina, *Karl Barth: Theologian of Christian Witness* (Aldershott, UK: Ashgate, 2004), pp. 29-56.

27. See, e.g., Karl Barth, *The Word of God and the Word of Man,* trans. Douglas Horton (London: Hodder & Stoughton, 1935), pp. 112-14.

Therefore, the Word of God as encountered in the proclamation of the biblical text is not our possession, nor is it something under our control. To use Barthian language, it has the character of "event," in the sense that its revelatory quality takes place solely in the freedom of the Holy Spirit, who comes to us in the moment of revelation.

All of this is merely formal: we are told something of *how* the Word of God comes to us, but thus far nothing of its content. Barth himself insists that what is needed is that the content of proclamation be the Word, and he proceeds to spell out its content over many thousands of pages. I have already explored something of the Barthian answer in this study. In order to advance the argument, and in order to turn it in a more constructive direction, I wish to look to a range of other sources, providing an ecumenical as well as a somewhat more historical vision of the directions in which it is possible to travel at this point.

There are a number of different ways of approaching this question. The theology of proclamation is obviously one possibility, which might involve an examination of the history of the sermon, or of sermons as theological "events." In order to constrain the discussion within acceptable limits, however, I wish to focus on the narrower question of "spiritual" interpretation of the biblical text, which I take to underlie its public proclamation as a theological question, and which could certainly be demonstrated to have given rise to an enormous range of sermonic "performances" in the history of the church.

"Spiritual Interpretation"

Let me begin with two quotations. The first is a rather difficult Pauline text from 1 Corinthians, where Paul explicitly links the activity of the Holy Spirit both to his own theological understanding and to the upbuilding of the church and the transmission of the gospel that he preaches.

> Now we have received not the spirit of the world, but the Spirit that is from God, so that we may understand the gifts bestowed on us by God [or better, "what God has freely given us" (NIV), *ta hypo tou theou charisthenta hêmin*]. And we speak of these things in words not taught by human wisdom but taught by the Spirit, interpreting spiritual things to those who are spiritual [or "interpreting spiritual things by

means of spiritual things," *pneumatikois pneumatika sugkrinontes*].
(1 Cor. 2:12-13 [NRSV])

The precise sense of this text in its setting in 1 Corinthians is disputed for reasons relating to both context and grammar; but in a more general sense, the text can plausibly be read as a summary of how Paul might have understood his own work, and that of the primitive church in general, in the task of preaching and teaching: "interpreting spiritual things to those who are spiritual" would thus amount to a kind of mission statement for the task of building up the church in Christian proclamation.

The second quotation, dating from around the year 230 CE, was written by one of the greatest of all Christian textual scholars and exegetes, the Alexandrian Origen. Origen is responsible for much that is highly speculative in the history of theology, but he was also extremely well traveled in ecclesiastical circles, and he knew at first hand the great Christian centers of Rome, Alexandria, and Antioch. As the first truly world-class Christian scholar, he was capable of thinking and writing with great precision. Among Origen's surviving work is the first full-scale Christian systematic theology, *On First Principles,* a controversial work that is, however, prefaced by what Origen assumes to be an entirely uncontroversial summary of the Christian faith. The summary represents the faith of the church as a whole, as Origen himself knew it from his studies and his travels. What he provides, then, is a digest of belief that is similar to the many early Christian "Rules of Faith." In this summary Origen writes most interestingly of the task of the interpreter.

> The kind of doctrines which are believed in plain terms through the apostolic teaching . . . [include] . . . the doctrine that the scriptures were composed through the Spirit of God and that they have not only that meaning which is obvious, but also another which is hidden from the majority of readers. For the contents of scripture are the outward forms of certain mysteries and the images of divine things. [*Formae enim sunt haec quae descripta sunt sacramentorum quorundum et diuinarum rerum imaginesi.*][28] On this point the entire Church is unanimous, that while the whole law is spiritual, the inspired meaning is not recognised by all, but only by those who are gifted with the

28. In Rufinus's Latin translation; unfortunately, the Greek is lost. Origène, *Traité des Principes,* ed. Henri Crouzel and Manilo Simonetti, 5 vols. (Paris: Cerf, 1978-1984), 1: 86.

grace of the Holy Spirit in the word of wisdom and knowledge. (Preface, 4, 8)[29]

In other words, Origen, rather like Paul, saw the task of theological interpretation in pneumatological terms. The point is in some sense to transcend a merely "human" reading, since God's wisdom far exceeds what human wisdom can tell. Thus it is not enough to wield human tools in the task. In fact, Origen appeals to two of the gifts of the Spirit of 1 Corinthians 12 (the "word of wisdom" and the "word of knowledge," v. 8) as alone capable of grounding a properly spiritual interpretation of the biblical text.

A confluence of Christian sources thus insists on the absolute necessity of the Holy Spirit's action for the Word of God, particularly as preached, to become a "means of grace." However, if the task of a Christian proclamation that is empowered by the Spirit depends on a spiritual reading of the text, what does it mean to speak of a spiritual interpretation of the Bible, illuminated and empowered by the Holy Spirit? What is it to say with Origen, or with Paul, that there is a meaning in the biblical text that is disclosed by the Spirit to the church in the ministry of interpretation and proclamation? What might this kind of disclosure look like in practice?

In order to attempt an answer to this question, we will need to examine some concrete examples of the practice of spiritual interpretation of the biblical text. Our first source, appropriately enough, is the apostle Paul, who in the Epistle to the Galatians provides, in his account of Hagar and Sarah, one of the charter texts of the ancient Christian tradition of spiritual exegesis.

> [I]t is written that Abraham had two sons, one by a slave woman and the other by a free woman. One, the child of the slave, was born according to the flesh; the other, the child of the free woman, was born through the promise. Now this is an allegory . . . [or, alternatively, "these things are spoken allegorically," *haitina estin allêgoroumena*]. (Gal. 4:22-24a)

Though this is the only use of the verb *allêgorein* (literally, "to say something other") in the New Testament, there are other prominent examples of the same exegetical strategy (the most obvious being 1 Cor. 10:1-10). The allegorical reading of the story of Hagar and Sarah in Genesis 21 was also known in

---

29. Origen, *On First Principles*, trans. and ed. G. W. Butterworth (New York: Harper & Row, 1966), pp. 2, 5.

first-century Hellenistic Judaism.[30] But Paul's treatment of the text is unique. As the exegesis unfolds through verses 24-31, Hagar and Sarah, the wives of Abraham, are no longer merely women, but they represent two covenants. Then the allegorical terms are shifted immediately, so that the women represent two cities, the slave Hagar standing for the earthly Jerusalem, a city that is in slavery with her children (Judaism under the Law), whereas Sarah stands for the heavenly Jerusalem, which lives in freedom (the new people of God, the church, which lives by the Spirit). One image is heaped on another: Hagar represents not only Jerusalem but also Mount Sinai in Arabia. We have become accustomed to seeing this kind of theology described by a rather imprecise term, the word "metaphorical." I am suggesting that Paul would have given it a more dynamic description, for though he uses the word "allegory," his phrase from the Corinthian correspondence, *pneumatikois pneumatika sugkrinontes,* would likely be more appropriate.[31]

A second example, chosen both because of the importance of the biblical text in question and because of the stature of the writer, appears not in the first but in the fourth century, in a fascinating text by the great Cappadocian theologian Gregory of Nyssa, entitled *The Life of Moses.*[32] Here, amid a lengthy account of the meaning of the Mosaic narrative, Gregory writes of the burning bush in Exodus 3, and of God's command from the flaming bush that Moses take off his sandals. Gregory's method in the treatise is first to sketch the story of Moses and then, as he puts it, "to seek out the spiritual understanding which corresponds to the history" (*Life of Moses,* Prologue, 15). He says:

> That light [from the flame] teaches us what we must do to stand within the rays of the true light: Sandaled feet cannot ascend that height where the light of truth is seen, but the dead and earthly covering of skins, which was placed around our nature at the beginning when we

30. J. Louis Martyn, *Galatians* (New York: Doubleday, 1997), p. 436, notes that, for Philo, Sarah was an allegory of "self-taught virtue" and Hagar an allegory of "imperfect training."

31. See the careful critique of the undifferentiated use and overuse of the word "metaphorical" in John McIntyre, *Theology After the Storm: Reflections on the Upheavals in Modern Theology and Culture,* ed. Gary D. Badcock (Grand Rapids: Eerdmans, 1997), pp. 269-77.

32. Gregory of Nyssa, *The Life of Moses,* trans. A. J. Malherbe and E. Fergusson (New York: Paulist Press, 1978).

were found naked because of disobedience to the divine will, must be removed from the feet of the soul. (*Life of Moses*, II.22)

The background here is clearly Gregory's understanding, heavily influenced by Origen, of the Fall (developed among other places in his *Great Catechism*), together with a more general reliance on the by-then well established tradition of Christian asceticism.[33] Both are simply assumed. More interestingly, however, Gregory immediately goes on to an extraordinary philosophical discussion of the concept of truth, which is based heavily on the Septuagint text of Exodus 3:14, *egô eimi ho ôn*. To be in possession of the truth, he says, is not to have a mistaken apprehension of Being, *ho ôn*. He then concludes that it was precisely this awareness that Moses attained at the burning bush: Moses grasped that true Being is

> . . . that which is always the same, neither increasing nor diminishing, immutable to all change whether to better or to worse . . . standing in need of nothing else, alone desirable, participated in by all but not lessened by their participation — this is truly real Being. (*Life of Moses*, II.25)

It was on the basis of this knowledge, Gregory tells us, that Moses was able to help others to salvation.

A final example of spiritual exegesis, or what was certainly taken for it in the Protestant tradition, is drawn again from John Calvin. I have chosen from the vast corpus of his exegetical work a text in his *Commentary on the Epistle to the Hebrews*. Calvin comments on Hebrews 9:19-20:

> For when every commandment had been told to all the people by Moses in accordance with the law, he took the blood of calves and goats, with water and scarlet wool and hyssop, and sprinkled both the scroll itself and all the people, saying, "This is the blood of the covenant that God has ordained for you."

Calvin's commentary runs as follows:

> If that was the blood of the testament then the testament is not ratified without blood nor does the blood avail for atonement without the tes-

---

33. English translation in Gregory of Nyssa, "An Address on Religious Instruction," in E. R. Hardy, ed., *Christology of the Later Fathers* (London: SCM Press, 1954), pp. 268-325.

tament. Both are necessarily joined together. We see that the symbol was added only when the law had been expounded. What kind of a sacrament would it be unless the Word preceded it? Hence the symbol is a kind of addition to the Word. Notice that this Word is not whispered like a magic incantation but proclaimed in a loud voice. . . . It is therefore a perversion and abuse of the sacrament and a pagan corruption where no explanation of the command is heard which is as it were the soul of the sacrament. Therefore the papists who take away the true understanding of things from the signs retain only the dead elements. . . .[34]

The reference to the eucharistic controversies of the Reformation era is unmistakable here, as is Calvin's distinctive conviction that the sacraments of the Jews were true sacraments of the one gospel of grace, rather than mere shadows of a glory still to come.

Furthermore, the matter does not end there. Calvin continues with an equally arresting argument:

The passage reminds us that all the promises of God are only profitable when confirmation of them comes from the blood of Christ . . . when we not only hear God speaking but discern Christ offering us Himself as a pledge of what is said. If only this thought came to our minds that what we read is written not so much with ink as with the blood of the Son of God, that *when the Gospel is preached his sacred blood falls on us along with the words,* both our attention and our reverence would be far greater. The symbol of this was the sprinkling mentioned by Moses, *although there is more content here than the words of Moses contain.* (p. 126 [italics added])

"There is more content here than the words of Moses contain": the words themselves are the bearers of a theological content that inherently requires further expression. Commentary, sermonic interpretation, and application in accordance with the overall thrust of the gospel of Jesus Christ, and in answer to the problems of the present, are needed if the words are to be properly appropriated. For when we hear the words so explained, Calvin claims,

34. John Calvin, *Comm. Hebrews,* 9:20, in Calvin, *The Epistle of Paul the Apostle to the Hebrews and The First and Second Epistles of St. Peter,* trans. William B. Johnston, ed. David W. Torrance and Thomas F. Torrance (Edinburgh: Saint Andrew Press, 1963), p. 126.

the effect is that we are covered with the blood of Christ. The words of the "testament," as we have just seen, are necessarily joined with the blood that makes atonement, so much so that the two are one, so much so that to hear the word of the gospel is to be sprinkled with it and cleansed. Further on, in his comments on the same Hebrews text, Calvin refers to the work of the Spirit:

> When there was a sprinkling of hyssop and scarlet wool there is no doubt that this represented the mystical sprinkling that comes by the Spirit. We know that hyssop has a particularly effective power of cleansing and refining, and in this way Christ uses His Spirit in place of sprinkling to wash us with His blood when He gives us a true sense of penitence, when He refines the depraved lusts of our flesh and when He touches us with the precious beauty of His justice. (p. 126)

Of course, there is much that is different in the hermeneutical methods and claims of the apostle Paul, Gregory of Nyssa, and John Calvin — of that there is no doubt. The overt Platonism of Gregory, for example, sets his approach apart from the much more overtly soteriological and Christological approach of Calvin, developed in the specific context of the Reformation of the sixteenth century (though a mild version of Platonism was also part of Calvin's world of thought). Both later exegetes differ from Paul, for whom the overwhelming theological "fact" to be interpreted was neither the relationship between the gospel and Hellenistic philosophical culture nor, certainly, the specific concerns of Reformation theology, but the extension of the people of God to the gentiles, and the subsequent mission that was at the center of his own apostolic calling.

However, there are also basic elements that are common to these three very different exegetes and the examples of spiritual interpretation that they provide. One of them is, quite simply, the fact of their allegiance to the biblical text as a source of theological truth, and this is certainly a matter of some importance. The key point, however, is that in each case the act of interpretation is tied not only to the biblical text, but also to the general theological vision of each theologian and exegete. Each has a theological worldview *in relation to which* he reads the text of the Bible, and each has a theology and set of theological concerns that the Bible illuminates. It is, in fact, the "theology" concerned that explains as much or more than the text itself about the content of the interpretation ultimately offered.

This is obvious in the Pauline exegesis of Genesis 21, where the biblical text in itself clearly does not tell us that Hagar "is" Jerusalem and Mount Sinai in Arabia; rather, she was clearly Sarah's servant and Abraham's concubine, who conceived his son Ishmael. However, this same reasoning could just as naturally be applied to the exegesis of Gregory and Calvin. In the first case, the Semitic custom of taking off one's shoes in the presence of God (as even Gregory himself must have known) is a sign of servility and simplicity rather than a signal that required the putting off of "the dead and earthly covering of skins" that was imposed on our primordial ancestors when they fell from a purer world of divine contemplation. Likewise, as even the most convinced Calvinist must recognize, there is no immediate polemic against "the papists who take away the true understanding of things" present in the Old Testament narrative concerning Moses' sprinkling the people with blood after the reading of the covenant (Exod. 24:6-8). Nevertheless, these were the paths taken when the texts in question were read "spiritually" by our sources, and vast ecclesiastical movements have followed in these same ways.

We can make two observations at this point — by way of transition to another, more substantial, concern. The first is a simple one: we must pay far greater attention to the actual practice of biblical interpretation if it is ever to be understood. Frances Young has recently shown that the standard reading of patristic exegesis in most English-language theology during much of the twentieth century was badly flawed, and it was flawed precisely because it ignored the evidence provided by patristic commentaries in favor of a particular hermeneutical theory deriving from the twentieth-century biblical theology movement.[35] In short, some of our theological judgments need to be more empirical and less programmatic. Second, the question might be asked how all of these theological positions can be deemed to be examples of "spiritual exegesis," for in the name of the Holy Spirit they lay claim to very different things. Does the Spirit teach different things, inspiring the messianic Jew in one way in one century, a Neo-Platonic Christian differently in another, and a French humanist turned Reformer in the sixteenth century to claim divine warrant for the argument he advances?

It is not possible to answer this question simply by referring to historical context, though, to be sure, historical context is important. Let me clarify

35. Frances Young, *Biblical Exegesis and the Formation of Christian Culture* (Cambridge, UK: Cambridge University Press, 1997).

this by making what was until recently a highly unconventional point about the modern historical-critical method of biblical exegesis, which I would like to say can be seen as entirely of a piece with the work of our three classical exegetes. One could even go further, alluding to the great Origen's claim that Scripture has a meaning that "is hidden from the majority," and is discernible only by those who have the knowledge to perceive it. Is a better depiction possible of the assumptions of the average parishioner, over against those of the historical-critical exegete? For again, it seems that in the latter case, we are faced with a kind of athlete of the spirit, delving into matters that elude the simple, discerning layer upon layer of hidden meaning in the text where others find only the literal sense of the words. And the inspiring "vision" in this case is nothing other than the conviction that historical context is the key to the meaning of the text.

I have already cited Brevard Childs's dictum concerning the demands of modern biblical studies with respect to the constraints of Christian dogmatics. In other words, the method assumes from beginning to end that Christian faith as it developed in the classical period, and as it came to be defined in ecclesiastical dogma, is a distorting exegetical influence. But what needs to be said is that it is not so much a *distorting* as a *competing* exegetical influence. After all, there is no such thing as a "value-free" interpretation. If the assumption is that the true interpretation of the biblical text can only come to light when it is understood, not in accordance with the canons of the church, but in accordance with the canons of Enlightenment rationality and the science of history, then it is self-evident that the text has been read from the standpoint of a worldview.

In a good many cases the worldview in question amounts to a "theology" that looks remarkably like that of the Deists of old: that God does not act in time except by moral persuasion, or that the world of theological meaning is purely inward, or "existential," in character. These are assumptions that are profoundly represented in contemporary biblical scholarship. In other words, the historical-critical exegetical method has a certain striking kinship with the methods of the apostle Paul, Gregory of Nyssa, and John Calvin in the specific sense that what unites all is not only a commitment to the text but also a willingness to engage with that text in terms of an overarching intellectual vision — in the light of which the text is read. The text in each case "speaks" when seen through the lens of an outlook that is neither identical with the text nor even strictly envisioned by the text. For the sake of that view, certain of the dynamics of the biblical narrative are highlighted, others perhaps suppressed, and other themes frankly posited or generated in the act of interpretation.

What this shows is that, in "spiritual interpretation," the theology of the interpreter is massively important. One is reminded at this point of the procedure of John Calvin, whom I have cited extensively and who saw his *Institutes of the Christian Religion* not as an independent work of Christian theology, but specifically as a contribution to the task of biblical interpretation. The relationship between Calvin's work and the Bible is often seen conversely, as if the *Institutes* constitutes a theology arising out of a close study of the biblical text — so that the hermeneutic, as it were, leads to the theology. This is true up to a point, but to put matters that way is ultimately to miss the real point: that the theology is itself a hermeneutic. The *Institutes* would have no reason to exist in Calvin's theology were it not for the hermeneutical task it is intended to inform and support. In other words, Calvin's *Institutes* exists because of the obligation placed on the church to proclaim the Word of God. Calvin's "Letter to the Reader," the preface to the 1559 edition, which looks back at the preparation of the work through five successive editions that were published over the previous twenty-three years, puts the point clearly:

> [I]t has been my purpose in this labor to prepare and instruct candidates in sacred theology for the reading of the divine Word, in order that they may be able both to have easy access to it and to advance in it without stumbling. For I believe I have so embraced the sum of religion in all its parts, and have arranged it in such an order, that if anyone rightly grasps it, it will not be difficult for him to determine what he ought especially to seek in Scripture, and to what end he ought to relate its contents.[36]

The ultimate implication of Calvin's position is very much like the argument from Barth that we encountered at the outset: not only is there no meaningful theology that cannot ground the proclamation of the Word of God, but there is no proclamation of the Word of God that really counts as proclamation apart from a theology that it contains.

---

36. Calvin, *Institutes*, "Letter to the Reader." A version of this claim is in fact found in all five editions of the *Institutes*, so that we are left in no doubt concerning Calvin's intentions: the theology is intended to provide the tool needed for a Reformed interpretation of the Bible.

Among the several questions this might raise for theology, the most important for our purposes concerns the relationship of the Holy Spirit to the task of "doing" theology, and to the achievement of the theologians when the theology has been "done." For while, in the history of theology, the theological interpretation of Scripture is appropriated to the work of the Holy Spirit, and even to the Spirit's charisms (Origen), the truth of the matter is that what such interpretation means in practice is that the biblical text has been read in the light of a theological system. In other words, theological systems matter, and not simply for intellectual or cultural reasons, as great theologians and their work tend alternately to generate or to sum up whole religious cultures (though this may be true); but they matter for reasons of the greatest importance, reasons that are closely related to the doctrine of the Holy Spirit and its place in the life of the church. In short, the theological vision of a church is crucially important, and the connection between it, the work of the Spirit, and the life of that church is something that merits careful attention.

What this means, of course, is that there can be no evading the question of the church's confession, which ultimately needs to be understood as a pneumatological problem (and no doubt possibility as well). Only as such can it be treated adequately within the structures of ecclesiology. Unfortunately, not all are inclined to understand the doctrines of the Spirit or of the church in quite this way, due to the ingrained tendency to see the Spirit's work as purely inward and rooted in feeling, rather than as something social and intelligible in character precisely because it is intrinsically related to the Word. Subjective experience has become such a key source of theological claims, and so dominating a factor in the arena in which it is to be worked out, that all else is abandoned. There is particular resistance to the intellectual dimension of the church's confession.

The Common Confession of Faith

In the preceding chapter I argued that the idea of *koinōnia* must be central to any pneumatologically informed ecclesiology, and I maintained that one of the principal reasons for the schismatic character of Protestantism historically is that it has operated with a deficient pneumatology. The tendency to operate exclusively with the idea of the Spirit who dwells "in our hearts" rather than with the Spirit who dwells "in the body of Christ," in particular, has yielded a problematic ecclesiology. It is interesting to ponder the historical trajectory of Protestantism in this respect, not least in light of the fact that the basis for grasping the Spirit's work as involving something more than an individual appropriation of the gospel is laid in Reformation dogmatics, and also developed in post-Reformation Protestant thought. Thus, for instance, the Puritan theologian John Owen, in his 1674 work *Pneumatologia*, argues that the work of the Holy Spirit must be treated, first, with regard to the human nature of Christ, second, with regard to the church as the body of Christ, and only third, with regard to the individual believer.[37] Unfortunately, the individual emphasis prevailed, which would seem to indicate a systematic flaw in Protestantism that its theologians were unable to overcome.

In this context, one of the welcome features of Wolfhart Pannenberg's treatment of the church in his recent *Systematic Theology* is that it returns to this theme, emphasizing the corporate work of the Spirit and the importance of the common confession of faith in the life of the church.[38] Pannenberg does not deny the fact that believing is a personal act. But for him, it is the *common confession* of faith that lifts an individual's allegiance to the name of Christ to the social level, which Pannenberg sees as the authentically pneumatological goal of all faith. As we have seen, to be baptized into Christ is to be joined with others, to be made part of the "body" that has many members, and to be included in the "people" that is God's own. Thus, while it may be true that the proclamation of the gospel can rightly be directed to individual persons, since the act of faith is deeply personal in character, the end is always to make the person part of the church as a wider fellowship that is united with Christ, its head, is indwelt by the one Spirit, and lives in unity of faith and love in the one community. This, however, requires a *common* confession, for this is what lifts faith above the purely personal into the social sphere.

Ultimately, what underlies this conviction in Pannenberg is not an abstract treatment of the nature of faith but a theology of the Holy Spirit that takes seriously the doctrine of the Spirit as it exists in relationship to both Father and Son, and that thus is unwilling to restrict the scope of the Spirit's work to the individual heart, mind, or conscience. Rather, for Pannenberg, it

37. John Owen, *The Works of John Owen*, vol. 3 (London: The Banner of Truth Trust, 1965), pp. 159-228.

38. Wolfhart Pannenberg, *Systematic Theology*, trans. Geoffrey Bromiley, 3 vols. (Grand Rapids: Eerdmans; Edinburgh: T&T Clark, 1991-1998), 3: 1-20, 110-22.

is essential to grasp the work of the Spirit with respect to both a doctrine of creation and the eschatological hope of salvation, since in this way the horizon of the Spirit's work is immeasurably expanded beyond the narrow world of the individual's religious experience. The Spirit is able, by virtue of his divine personhood, to "lift . . . [humans] ecstatically above their own particularity and thus enable them to grasp that which is beyond themselves and distinct from their own existence" (p. 17). The Spirit's work is thus related to the fact that, in Jesus Christ, believers have an existence with others, which lies outside themselves: they exist "in Christ." Pannenberg continues:

> Western theology has often failed to see this. . . . The special distinction of faith's recognition rests simply on its object, not on the nature of its perception. We find ecstatic phenomena of spiritual rapture elsewhere. This is not the specific thing. But the specific thing includes the fact that in the knowledge of Jesus Christ as the one Son and Messiah the Spirit binds together all believers into the fellowship of the church in unity with him and with one another.

There are echoes here in the Lutheran Pannenberg — indeed, deep echoes — of the Roman Catholic pneumatologists we encountered in the preceding chapter. Pannenberg's systematic theology is thus a profoundly ecumenical work, and profoundly challenging to all those individualistic tendencies within Protestantism that tend to the contrary.

This corporate, strictly pneumatological dimension of faith is basic to its very nature, and it is rooted in the covenantal dimension of believing. The doctrine of election, as we have seen, must imply at the very least that the gospel, in addition to being directed to the individual "heart," is also directed to societies and peoples, for the electing God of the covenant calls not only individual persons but groups of people to faith and discipleship: families, societies, cultures, and nations. God's faithfulness embraces these as well, and not simply the atoms from which they are constructed. However, this has implications for the attempt to define the content of faith. Faith is never strictly private, but is always ecclesial; therefore, doctrine, as a formal statement of the content of faith, also has an ecclesial character in the church's confession. From that point of view, it is worth noting the extent to which the church's common confession of faith is associated particularly with the liturgical life of the church, and thus explicitly with worship, rather than, for example, with lesser matters such as ecclesiastical polity or government. This is clear from the use of creeds in the liturgy, especially in the context of baptism, where the common confession is effectively a condition of membership in the church, and in the context of the Eucharist, which celebrates and realizes the church's relationship to Christ as its true bread and life.

Baptism is of special importance in this context because the very concept of a creedal statement is basically baptismal in origin. Historically, the rite of Christian baptism according to the dominical commandment of Matthew 28:19 led to the development of liturgically regular, Trinitarian confessions prior to baptism. By this the candidate assented to the church's faith, thus identifying himself not only with Christ but also with Christ's ecclesial body. Incorporation into Christ is inextricably linked, then, with the common confession, while even the efficacy of baptism as the sacramental sign of cleansing from sin and of new life is closely connected with a candidate's confession of the faith of the church. The dramatic quality of this event was unquestionably heightened in the early church by the fact that the candidate did not learn the content of the baptismal creed until well on in his or her catechetical preparation; even the very learning of the words was in a sense a baptismal act.

There is evidence of precedent for this in the New Testament. In Romans 10:9, for example, we read of a confession made with the mouth ("Jesus is Lord") in conjunction with believing in the heart that God raised him from the dead, which taken together are said to lead to salvation. Although baptism is not mentioned (indeed, in 1 Cor. 1:17, Paul denies that his apostolic commission included any responsibility to baptize his converts!), it is significant that a "confession" with the mouth (a verb deriving from the technical term *homologêsis* is used), that is, a *public* declaration, is required. A reference to this practice is also found in 1 Timothy 6:12, which speaks of Timothy's act of "confessing the good confession before many witnesses" (my translation), where the context is clearly baptismal.

Prior to the fourth century, liturgical creeds were mainly local or regional in character, so much so that it is even difficult to speak of a *general* form of Christian orthodoxy before the formulation, under the auspices of the imperial authorities, of the ecumenical creed of 325/381 (the Nicene Creed). So powerful was the normative status of local creeds that even the formulation of the Creed of Nicaea (325) was quickly followed by the production of local or regional *adaptations* of it (a factor that also explains the more clearly heretical "emendations" of the creedal text by bishops who were disappointed by the theology of the Council of Nicaea). In the second and third centuries, such local creeds were used by Christian teachers as evidence in the fight against heresy, combined with the "rules of faith" (whether they were oral or written, flexible or inflexible, is disputed) and with the claim of apostolic tradition and the succession of bishops.[39] In fact, however, much of the context for the use of these earliest local sources is shrouded in historical and liturgical obscurity, so that there is little that we can say with any confidence about it.

Two contributions may help us understand something of the theological significance of such creedal formulations. First, Pannenberg's thesis, which is indebted to a study by Bornkamm,[40] is that the defining element in Christian baptismal-creedal confession can only be understood in the light of what confession ("homology") meant in Greek law.[41] Whereas in the Old Testament the act of confession is an act of faithfulness to God and an offering of praise for his faithfulness, so giving God glory, Christian confession in the Hellenistic context, came to have the function of homology in Hellenistic law. What confession does in this context is to establish a contractual or legal relationship between two parties.

Pannenberg thus maintains that Christian confession had, for those being baptized, specific connotations of forensic witness. The effect was one of taking sides for and with Jesus in the matter of his claim to be the Lord and Son of God, in contrast to the earthly "lords" and even "sons of the gods" who ruled the Roman world. In the Old Testament, the covenantal relationship between God and the people of God would have made an attempt to *establish* such a relationship redundant. However, in the situation of the gentile church, things were rather different. Pannenberg refers particularly to Matthew 10:32-33 and its parallel in Luke 12:8-9, which together speak of a double confession, the first of Jesus by believers on earth, and the second by Jesus of those who believe before the Father in heaven. It is via such a confession that a binding relationship is established between believers and Jesus, by way of a kind of legal contract. Taking sides for Jesus by identifying ourselves with the confession of the church establishes a lasting fellowship with

---

39. Eric F. Osborn, "Reason and the Rule of Faith in the Second Century AD," in Rowan Williams, ed., *The Making of Orthodoxy* (Cambridge, UK: Cambridge University Press, 1989), pp. 40-61.

40. G. Bornkamm, "Das Bekenntnis im Hebräerbrief," in Bornkamm, *Gesammelte Aufsätze* (Munich: Kaiser, 1959), 2: 188-203.

41. Pannenberg, *Systematic Theology*, 3: 113.

him, as he then also "confesses" us before the Father in heaven. Although this argument would have to be balanced against the clear covenantal concept of the "people of God" in the New Testament, the thesis nonetheless represents a valuable contribution to an overall understanding of the significance of the confession of faith for at least some of the early Christians.

Second, the significance of the common confession of faith in the early church is illuminated by the sheer fact of the deliberate cultivation of extensive mutual interchange between geographically diverse Christian communities in the patristic period. In an essay devoted to the meaning of "orthodoxy" before Nicaea, Rowan Williams notes that there is a massive difference between the practices of heterodox groups and the mainstream church at this point.[42] He points out that there is absolutely no evidence, either literary or archaeological, to suggest that heterodox leaders and the congregations they established maintained regular links, whereas it is absolutely clear that the mainstream church tended toward the opposite extreme, one that might appear to us as "an almost obsessional mutual interest" (p. 11). The basic medium of this mutual involvement was the epistle, which from New Testament times down to the present day has served the interests of theological and pastoral exchange between churches in their varied locations in the world. Williams argues that the early church consciously saw these literary exchanges to be in keeping with the practice of the apostles, and to be vital to the continuing health of the church as a whole (p. 14). It is also closely related to the missionary character of the church, for missionary foundation suggests a history of personal contact, an awareness of which sustains further epistolary contact.

The mutual interest and regular epistolary correspondence of the pre-Nicene church fostered the idea of a normative Christianity. Whatever the role of local practice and belief, as expressed in local baptismal creeds, for example, the deliberate sharing of problems and insights had the crucial effect of generating a public discourse, and of highlighting the significance of what was common experience rather than the significance of private experience. The latter was the sphere of the heterodox, and especially of the Gnostics, whereas the mainstream Christian tradition evolved in a very different direction, the result of which was "catholicism." In such a context, faith is something that is precisely *not* private; rather, it is something that believers

---

42. Rowan Williams, "Does It Make Sense to Speak of Pre-Nicene Orthodoxy?" in Williams, ed., *The Making of Orthodoxy*, pp. 1-23.

hold in common, whatever the acceptable — though sometimes problematic — differences in local religious culture, theological emphasis, or liturgical expression might be.

All of this helps us understand the role of the ancient creeds in the
church's life of the patristic period. The common confession of faith is of the
essence, not just because of the threat of heterodox outsiders, or because of a
fixation with attaining theological knowledge, but because the very concept
of what believing the Christian faith means is bound up with the common
life, with what is by definition held in common with the whole of the
church. There is little room in such a context for religious individualism,
which is why the expectations of the early church in these matters appears so
problematic to so many people in our individualistic age — both inside and
outside the church.

This also explains why, for example, a document such as the famous
Christological definition of the Council of Chalcedon (451), the high point
of classical theological orthodoxy, is prefaced by an affirmation of the "saving" confession of faith found in the Nicene Creed (the Council of
Chalcedon regarded itself as merely clarifying the teaching of Nicaea). It is
not that the assembled bishops were foolish enough to take the view that, in
order to be saved, all one had to do was think the right things, to be "orthodox." Rather, the point of making a "saving" confession is that it identifies a
person with the faith of the church, which is the only Christian faith there is
in the patristic understanding. The saving confession also preserves from error, in the sense that it acts as a defense against the claims of the heretics. It
may well be that the church has often attempted to go too far by condemn-
ing ideas that might have been tolerated; however that may be, though, the
concern to define truth for its own sake is less central to the dynamic of the
patristic church than is commonly supposed. Much more important is the
sense, which the church had inherited from the by-then ancient Christian
tradition, that to believe at all is to belong to the fellowship of the church,
and this belonging involves the privileges and duties of living a common life
in the one "body."

Orthodoxy and Heresy

The very concept of a collective Christian orthodoxy, of course, has been subject to sustained criticism in modern times. As I have already noted, the En-

lightenment's critique of the "irrational" in traditional Christianity remains a force to be reckoned with, in both popular and more reflective Western attitudes toward the Christian religion — indeed, toward religion in general. The limitations of the kind of confessional orthodoxy that helped motivate the wars of religion is obvious; coupled with the dramatic success of the scientific method, those limitations generated centuries of intellectual crisis for Christian orthodoxy. Out of the pincer movement of these two great forces, the modern principle of freedom of religion developed.[43] Freedom of religion involves both freedom of conscience and toleration. The principle of freedom of conscience amounts to a way of controlling theological excess, since what is a matter of choice cannot be a matter of compulsion; on the other hand, the principle of religious toleration amounts to the relativizing of all such choices as finally unimportant, a matter of "reasonable" indifference.

Freedom of religion, as such, is in the strictest sense incompatible with the old idea of orthodoxy, certainly as that idea developed in Christendom from the late fourth century down to the dawn of the early modern period. In fact, the idea of choice that is enshrined in the very idea of *freedom* of religion is formally a vindication of the old definition of heresy, since the operative sense of the Greek word *hairesis* (from which "heresy" derives) is precisely "choice." In this sense, heresy could be defined as "an opinion chosen by human perception" rather than the one to be accepted on the basis of some central religious authority or text.[44] The modern view of religion is so far removed from the ancient and medieval view that the very possibility of an orthodoxy conceived along the old lines, a single body of religious truth defined by a religious leadership and imposed by law on an entire society, is today an impossibility.

We should not suppose that this modern view of religion has presented a threat to traditional Christianity only, for, as the historian John Henderson has convincingly shown, it is also profoundly hostile to fundamental themes in Islamic, Jewish, and Neo-Confucian religion as well.[45] In recent years, the hostility of Islam to the ideals of the West has centered mainly on the ap-

43. Joseph LeCler, *Toleration and the Reformation*, trans. T. L. Westow, 2 vols. (New York: Association Press; London: Longmans, 1960); see also Noel B. Reynolds and W. Cole Durham, Jr., eds., *Religious Liberty in Western Thought* (Atlanta: Scholars Press, 1996).

44. R. I. Moore, *The Origins of European Dissent* (New York: St. Martin's Press, 1977), p. ix.

45. John B. Henderson, *The Construction of Orthodoxy and Heresy* (Albany: State University of New York Press, 1998).

proach toward religion taken in the West since the Enlightenment, which has sought all the things that traditional Islam cannot abide: the separation of religion and politics and the consequent criticism of clerical power; the relativizing of religious ethics in favor of values that are free of religious "bias"; and the rejection of religious doctrine in favor of purely secular truth.[46] At least in this form, orthodoxy is taking a bitter revenge on the Enlightenment, a revenge that has as yet only just begun to be experienced in the heartlands of Enlightenment civilization.

The stresses imposed by such social change have also led to a reexamination of the concept of orthodoxy. For example, historians have informed us that what became Christian orthodoxy in the classical period, and continued broadly to be seen as such down to the modern era, was not simply "contained" in the Bible, awaiting discovery or elucidation. Rather, it developed painfully over time, and only after prolonged controversy had raised entirely new issues that had to be decided on in the light of Scripture, theological tradition, philosophical reason, and the particular needs of the time. Judged in the light of later standards of orthodoxy, in fact, early Christian writers frequently seem out of their theological depth. As John Henry Newman rightly perceived, the truth is that development in doctrine is something profoundly to be reckoned with, and that there is no point in simply looking to the past.

Newman's insights were especially attuned to the needs of an age of acute historical awareness, but they also represent a more honest appraisal of the situation than some theologians would care to admit. In fact, as Newman puts it, one of the principal causes of error in religion is "the refusal to follow the course of doctrine as it moves on, and an obstinacy in the notions of the past."[47] In other words, from the standpoint of historical science, there is at a purely empirical level no such thing as a timeless orthodoxy, a fully developed faith that can in any sense be taken to be divinely given. Instead, Christian doctrine grows from the seeds sown in Scripture and tradition into the mature organism it is actually *intended* to become. As has been noted by Hans Küng, the particular form of the claim to papal in-

46. W. Montgomery Watt, "The Muslim Tradition in Today's World," in Frank Whaling, ed., *Religion in Today's World* (Edinburgh: T&T Clark, 1987), pp. 230-49; Abdullah Saeed and Hassan Saeed, *Freedom of Religion, Apostasy and Islam* (Burlington, VT: Ashgate, 2002).

47. John Henry Newman, "An Essay on the Development of Christian Doctrine," in Newman, *Conscience, Consensus, and the Development of Doctrine*, ed. James Gaffney (New York: Doubleday, 1992), p. 179.

fallibility made in modern times almost certainly emerged from this notion of the necessary development of doctrine.[48] For if the deposit of "the faith that was once for all delivered to the saints" (Jude 1:3) can only be faithfully preserved by developing it into a fuller system, an authoritative court for adjudicating rival developments is required. Papal infallibility, the argument goes, is paradoxically needed because doctrine looks not so much backwards as forwards, and is by nature progressive rather than merely conservative.

Alternative accounts of the development of doctrine and of its progressive definition are, of course, also available. For example, in a seminal study published in 1934, Walter Bauer argued that the traditional view of orthodoxy as historically antecedent to heresy is almost certainly mistaken; instead, in many geographical areas during the formative centuries of the Christian church, what we call the "heresies" were the original manifestations of Christianity.[49] Bauer's thesis is that during the formative second century of the church, it was powerful pressure from the church at Rome, which imposed its view on the majority, that practically and historically defined the orthodoxy of the time. The hegemony of Rome emerged for the first time in the late second century in the context of the Gnostic controversy. In short, the earliest orthodoxy was a political rather than an intellectual achievement on the part of the church (or of one group within it), and it pertained at least as much to the realm of power as of truth. In these terms, there is no single, continuous stream of "authentic" Christianity that extends from the earliest church down to the present; there is also no one authentic form of belief, that is, beyond what a particularly powerful faction within the prevailing chaos seeks to impose on others.

From the theological point of view, Bauer overlooks the logic by which a common confession of faith becomes a compulsion, not simply emanating from the church at Rome but from the center of the gospel itself. From the strictly historical point of view as well, there are other versions of the emergence of orthodox Christianity that are by no means as radical or corrosive as Bauer's. For example, Richard Hanson, the Anglican historian of doctrine, argues rather more soberly that "it is clear that the way in which orthodoxy

48. Hans Küng, *Infallible?* trans. Edward Quinn (Garden City, NY: Doubleday, 1971), p. 150.

49. Walter Bauer, *Orthodoxy and Heresy in Earliest Christianity,* 2nd ed., ed. Robert Kraft and Gerhard Krodel, trans. Philadelphia Seminar on Christian Origins (Philadelphia: Fortress, 1971), pp. xxi-xxv, 111-46.

was achieved was a *process of trial and error.*" He maintains that this is entirely natural, given that it is precisely by way of trial and error that humans arrive at truth in any area of human knowledge.[50] Therefore, orthodoxy is by nature something *emergent* rather than something laid down or given in the past for all time.

Alternatively, there is a more conservative reading of the history of doctrine represented by eminent scholars such as Henry Chadwick, who presents the development of doctrine more in terms of those factors internal to Christian faith that necessarily tend toward the development of new expressions of that faith.[51] I sketched a more philosophically grounded version of this general thesis at the end of the preceding chapter.

"One body and one Spirit . . . one Lord, one faith, one baptism; one God and Father of all" we read in Ephesians 4:4-5, in a teaching that is hardly compatible with the dissonance of voices posited by Bauer as somehow normal, if not normative, in the church. While there is no doubt that there was such dissonance, the truth is that the different construals of Christian truth that are found in the second century, which is the period of greatest interest to Bauer, fall within a narrow range of theological possibilities that are generally explicable in terms of the relationship between the Christian faith and the surrounding culture. Thus, for example, second-century Gnosticism appears as an extreme adaptation of the gospel to Hellenism, but whether it may once have been in the numerical majority (as Bauer claims) or not, its denial of the Old Testament and even of the *God* of the Old Testament, its fantastic speculations concerning mythical origins and its hostility to the physical world mark it as ultimately incompatible with the internal structures of Christian faith, given the latter's historical roots in biblical Judaism.[52] The response that came in the church's condemnation of the Gnostic heresy thus amounts to far more than the imposition of Roman ecclesiastical authority. Whether by trial and error or not, the internal dynamism of Christian faith as rooted in the

50. Richard Hanson, "The Achievement of Orthodoxy in the Fourth Century AD," in Williams, *The Making of Orthodoxy*, p. 151. This was also the line of thought that Hanson developed in his magnum opus, his massive study of the Arian controversy, *The Search for the Christian Doctrine of God: The Arian Controversy 318-381* (Edinburgh: T&T Clark, 1988).

51. As noted by Williams, "Does it Make Sense to Speak of Pre-Nicene Orthodoxy?" p. 2.

52. Concerning Gnosticism, see Giovani Filoramo, *A History of Gnosticism*, trans. Anthony Alcock (London: Basil Blackwell, 1991).

Old and New Testaments was the thing at stake in this debate, and there can be no doubt that the correct side won the day.

Did the definition and defense of such standards of orthodoxy involve an unnecessary and unhelpful narrowing of vision on the part of the church? This claim is frequently made, and one suspects that it is made with greatest enthusiasm by theologians who themselves stand in greatest critical tension with the historic faith of the church. One must respond to this by saying that there is at once some truth in the claim, but that it is ultimately a misreading of the history of theology. Over against both must be set what I would describe as the profoundly minimalist tendency within classical Christian orthodoxy. Such minimalism is clearly in evidence in the ancient creeds: after all, it can hardly be said that the Apostles' and Nicene Creeds are constructed to close down all debate, or even to present a single comprehensive account of theological "truth." On the contrary, while they clearly do exclude certain errors, and are expressly calculated to do so, they also deliberately leave much unsaid. Even in what they do assert, the ancient creeds open up huge areas for debate, and they have succeeded in generating almost two millennia of theological reflection.

However, some scholars are so concerned about stressing the exclusivity emphasis in orthodoxy that they frequently miss this minimalism. For example, in his *The Construction of Orthodoxy and Heresy,* John Henderson claims that orthodoxy involves a progressive narrowing of the acceptable range of religious belief that, though achieved through an increasing intellectual precision, carries with it an increasing narrowness of outlook (p. 48). He cites as an example of this tendency the Chalcedonian definition of the faith (451), which, he claims, narrowed the definition of orthodoxy to an unparalleled degree (p. 47).

It is true that Chalcedon did exclude many who certainly saw themselves as belonging within the sphere of the church, both in Egyptian and in Syrian Christianity. But the truth is rather more subtle than Henderson apparently perceives. While it is indeed the case that the Chalcedonian definition excluded both Monophysite and Nestorian Christological theories and parties, it remains true that the Chalcedonian definition clearly attempted to be as accommodating as possible to the rival theories being argued — and to combine the best of both in a compromise formula.[53] Indeed, the imperial

---

53. Aloys Grillmeier, *Christ in Christian Tradition,* 2nd ed., trans. John Bowden et al. (London: Mowbrays, 1965-1996), 1: 488-557. The definitive study remains that of Aloys

legates present at that council saw to it that the previously hostile ecclesiastical parties represented particularly by the great sees of Antioch and Alexandria actually reached this accommodation. Those who were excluded in a
certain sense excluded themselves, by virtue of their inability to recognize
the value of the opposing view: "Alexandrian" Monophysites refusing to acknowledge the value of the theology of the "Antiochene" Nestorians, and
vice versa. Indeed, those who chose to remain outside the Chalcedonian definition in many ways insisted on a much greater narrowing of the definition
of orthodoxy than did Chalcedon itself. The Christological definition of the
Council of Chalcedon marks the high point of classical Christology. It
speaks of Christ as consubstantial both with humanity and with God the Father, of his two natures subsisting in one person — "without confusion,
without change, without division, without separation." This was an irenic
statement that was intended to reconcile rather than to divide. To this day,
the question of which side involved was the victor is a moot point, with the
possible exception of Rome and the Western church generally (which here
for the first time made a genuine contribution to the development of a precise theological vocabulary for the ancient church).

Thus Chalcedon effectively established the legitimacy of both sides of
the previous debate, whereas those whom it alienated were generally indis-
posed to tolerate such compromise of their more one-sided convictions.
What it thus achieved for Christian theological reflection was, as it were, the
positioning of markers in the waters through which the ship of faith must
pass, but allowing great latitude of interpretative navigation. The church has
proved itself able to allow such latitude over and over through the centuries,
beginning with Antiochenes, Alexandrians, and Romans, through Lutherans
and Calvinists, and down to our own day, when not only a Karl Barth can
breathe new life into the old words, but even religiously skeptical New Testament commentators can occasionally be heard to say that the "fully human"
Christ of Chalcedon dogmatically legitimates the historian's work on the
biblical texts concerning Jesus![54]

Dogmatic formulations can — and often do — have the potential to become too cumbersome; and crucially, when they are understood as the final

---

Grillmeier and Heinrich Bacht, *Das Konzil von Chalkedon,* 3 vols. (Würzburg: Echter-
Verlag, 1951-1954).

54. I have heard E. P. Sanders use this argument in a lecture on the historical Jesus to a
general audience.

word on a subject rather than a starting point for reflection and further consensus, they can become impediments to understanding. The ship of faith — to continue the nautical metaphor — at this point can easily become top-heavy, encrusted with ice, and in danger of being lost. Immobility and inflexibility bring theology to a standstill. This certainly happens at the point where one is so certain of one's position that one is willing to kill for it, or where one's limited awareness of the truth of God is closed to any new light. However, "fundamentalism" of this kind is more a moral than an intellectual problem, and it is as prominent a feature among the "liberals" as it is among the religious "conservatives." One does not have to be conservative to be close-minded.

In spiritual theology this is one of the great sources of the moment of negation, which is something necessary for all of us, not so much because our faith is false as because the truth of God is greater than we can grasp. Not even God can break through the shell of inflexible certainty without first bringing it to crisis. Openness in the awareness of truth, then — not only in the individual life of faith, but in the story of the church — and in the work of the theologian and of theology itself is an absolute prerequisite for progress in the truth. This is not so much because the human mind must seek new insight, though this is certainly true, but because the truth of God is something living, and it can only be had at all if it is not treated as a cadaver.

The Truth of God

To speak of truth in the present context has actually become an unusual theological move. In contemporary theological parlance, "orthopraxis" is everything. Yet, as we have seen, the category of truth is far from being peripheral to the New Testament, so that its disappearance from Christian theology, including the theology of the church, is difficult to defend. "Sanctify them in the truth; your word is truth," Jesus prays in John 17:17. The truth of God's Word is thus what separates the church for which Jesus prays (v. 20) from the world, and makes it fit to be sent into the world by him (v. 18). Truth is hardly an incidental extra in ecclesiology.

The Gospel of John also tells of an exchange between Jesus and Pilate toward the end of his trial: "Jesus answered, '. . . for this reason I was born, and for this I came into the world, to testify to the truth. Everyone who belongs to the truth listens to my voice.' Pilate asked him, 'What is truth?'" (John

18:37-38). Philosophically, as a man like Pilate might well have known, "truth" is a notoriously difficult concept to pin down: correspondence, coherence, and pragmatist theories vie for our attention; Platonists insist on its transcendence, and postmodernity seeks its deconstruction. But Jesus calls for an awareness of the truth of God, to which he himself is witness. Thus, while the immediate contrast in the text is between the Roman governor, whose difficulties arise from the conflict between political expediency and Roman justice, and the one whose coming into the world was for the sake of testimony to the truth, the issues run much deeper. It is interesting that in the Johannine narrative Pilate is unwilling initially to give up completely on the ideal of justice, and so he tries to find a way to cast back on the Jews the responsibility for the act of political expediency that follows (John 18:38-39). However, what he finally crucifies is identical with what is lost in the sin he commits: the truth, and the one who was born to testify to it.

As servants of truth, theologians have long highlighted the importance of the theme of truth in the Gospel of John, for it is there, above all, that Jesus' ministry — indeed, his very person — are oriented to it. Truth, though not explicitly mentioned in the Johannine Prologue (John 1:1-14), is nevertheless in view in it through the proxies of "Word" *(logos)* and "light" *(phos)*, both of which have closely related connotations. The word *logos* does not appear again in the John's Gospel after the Prologue, but the idea of "truth" repeatedly appears, for instance, at John 3:21 ("those who do what is true come to the light"), while obedience to God and access to the truth are closely aligned throughout the Gospel, for example, in John 7:17 ("Anyone who resolves to do the will of God will know whether the teaching is from God or whether I am speaking on my own"). At the apex of its usage, we hear in the upper-room discourse that Jesus is in himself "the truth" (John 14:6).

At this point we can return to Brunner's thesis in *Truth as Encounter:* his argument is that truth in Christian theology is not capable of being expressed propositionally, since it is a moral correspondence, an existence "in truth," far more than it is any proposition or system of thought. Brunner's debt to existentialism is well known, and that debt is certainly clear in this particular argument. The hostility to "the system" as incommensurate with the personal character of human existence is a common theme in existentialist thought. Just as philosophical existentialism replaces abstract metaphysical or epistemological reasoning with a life-philosophy, so Brunner wishes to establish the necessity of a theology that attends to the character of life lived under the gospel of grace. Accordingly, he argues that the truth of God needs to be expressed in narrative form.

> The decisive word form in the language of the Bible is not the substantive, as in Greek, but the verb, the word of action. The thought of the Bible is not substantival, neuter and abstract, but verbal, historical and personal. (p. 88)

So it should also be in theology: that the act of God and the corresponding acts of humanity in obedience to God come to the center in theological reflection.

There is a good deal of substance in Brunner's accusations, and in the alternative theological strategy he proposes. But there is also a good deal that is distorted and inadequate in it, for it is a misunderstanding of the tradition to speak of it as incapable of accommodating the personal character of God's outreach, and the correspondingly personal character of the human response. To begin with, formal "systems" of "theology" are not the sole ways in which theological content has been or can be expressed. Liturgy, mysticism, commentary, and, not least, proclamation also must be considered, and must be treated as fundamental modes of theological expression. Furthermore, there is an explicit attempt that was made even in ancient Christian "systematic" theology to acknowledge the personal character of God as a matter of both philosophical and theological principle. For instance, one could fairly argue that this was the main adaptation made to Platonic philosophy when Christian thinkers adopted it, baptizing it so that it became a basic Christian form of speculation. Pagan opponents certainly saw the issue, and Christian theologians made it perfectly clear that the personal quality of God that they had introduced into the native Platonism of the Hellenistic world was a philosophical improvement rather than a corruption of it.[55]

A more adequate view is suggested by the argument that appeared at the end of the preceding chapter, to the effect that the giving of the Holy Spirit to the church by the incarnate Word is oriented not only to a plurality of gifts (1 Cor. 12:4-11) and to a plurality of ministries (Rom. 12:4-8) but also to a plurality of theologies and theological systems (as the history of Christian thought abundantly shows). In my Hegelian excursus on the diversity of theological expression found in the many traditions of Christian theology, I developed the theory that such diversity occurs because the "way of the

55. Thus, e.g., Origen, *Contra Celsum*, VI.19, 64-69, in Origen, *Contra Celsum*, trans. Henry Chadwick (Cambridge, UK: Cambridge University Press, 1953), pp. 379ff.

Spirit" is to find expression in what *seems*, from the narrow perspective of one theological system, to be merely alien, so as to broaden the scope of the *koinônia*. The crux is that the Holy Spirit is not "resident" in one narrow system rather than in another, but rather that the Spirit can be found in both. A theology such as Nicholas of Cusa's "coincidence of opposites" is needed at this point, not just because what seems contradictory to us is in fact one in God's eternity and perfection, but also because what seems contradictory is also one in God's outreach, which also cannot be contained in any finite system.[56] Therefore, to speak of God as living means not only that God cannot be adequately "contained" within the logical rigor of Thomism, or within the rigid structures of post-Reformation Protestant scholasticism, it also means that God ultimately escapes capture in an existentialist theology — and in the dogmatics of a Brunner or a Barth. God's truth is forever new — and always "something more."

Methodological approaches to Christian theology that take up the challenge presented by these claims are surprisingly rare, but in an important recent study, *The Drama of Doctrine*, Kevin Vanhoozer has made a case for such a pluriform, or "polyphonic," understanding over that of the "monological" theological system.[57] Basing his theological argument ultimately on the existence of the canonical documents of the Bible, in which a variety of voices speak and yet make possible creative acts of faithful interpretation when heard in dialogue, Vanhoozer maintains that the nature of doctrine is such that it requires dramatic tension, action on a number of fronts and in a plurality of contexts, and from a number of dramatic persons (pp. 268ff.). He thus highlights the communitarian dimension of Christian theology, arguing not only that the canonical principle in a certain sense warrants a plurality of modes of witness to God's action in Jesus Christ, but also that the principle of catholicity is at stake in doing theology in this way, as we come to see theological truth in richer and deeper ways by attending to other attempts to grapple with it (p. 322).

Vanhoozer pays particular attention to the ideas of the Russian literary theorist Mikhail Bakhtin in this context. In a seminal study, Bakhtin maintained that the flaw in much conventional interpretation of the novels of

---

56. Nicholas of Cusa, *Nicholas of Cusa on Learned Ignorance*, ed. and trans. Jasper Hopkins (Minneapolis: Banning, 1985).

57. Kevin J. Vanhoozer, *The Drama of Doctrine* (Louisville: Westminster/John Knox, 2005).

Dostoyevsky lies in the inherited and thus ingrained "monological" tendency of commentators to resolve all of Dostoyevsky's narrative voices into one — such as can be articulated by a single narrator or thinker.[58] For Bakhtin, we must renounce the unity of the all-interpreting "I" in recognition of the existence of the other self and thus of the other interpreter, the "thou," whose voice cannot be reduced to that of the "I." Thus, alterity, the full and independent validity of the other, is utterly basic. For Bakhtin, the particular genius of Dostoyevsky's art lies in the way he recognizes this fact, precisely through the plurality of voices that are found in the one work. According to Vanhoozer, the unfolding of the "drama of doctrine" also requires a certain polyphonic dynamism. Though this doctrinal plurality is not limitless — something in particular rather than everything in general must be said in the teaching and proclamation of the church, since those acts are controlled by the *one* drama in which God engages with humankind in Jesus Christ — we might say that the nature of Christian doctrine is such that it can only be heard in stereo.[59]

58. The classic study is Mikhail Bakhtin, *Problems of Dostoyevsky's Poetics,* ed. and trans. Caryl Emerson (Minneapolis: University of Minnesota Press, 1984). See also Tzvetan Todorov, *Mikhail Bakhtin: The Dialogical Principle,* trans. Wlad Godzich (Minneapolis: University of Minneapolis Press, 1984); Michael Holquist, *Dialogism* (New York: Routledge, 1990); and Barbara Green, *Mikhail Bakhtin and Biblical Scholarship* (Atlanta: Society of Biblical Literature, 2000). In a notable misrepresentation, Bakhtin is fiercely critical of Hegel and of Hegelianism (which he tends to treat as representative of "monologism") and of the merging of multiple consciousnesses into a single system. Such a reading is perhaps explicable as a Marxian "gloss" on Hegel, for the tendency in Marxian interpretation is so much to emphasize the idea that Hegel (allegedly) makes history "walk on its head" rather than its feet, that it overlooks the truth of the matter: that is, that in Hegel's thought "history" has its own status — indeed, its own priority — over against the speculative "head." It is for just this reason that Hegel's position relies entirely on the existence of a multiplicity of voices and is anything but prescriptively and programmatically "monologistic" in Bakhtin's sense. For it is only after the many voices have spoken in a rather Bakhtinian cultural-historical "dialogue" that, according to Hegel, the philosopher can think at all. This is the point of the famous "owl of Minerva" dictum that we find in the preface to Hegel's *Philosophy of Right,* trans. T. M. Knox (Oxford: Oxford University Press, 1967): "The owl of Minerva spreads its wings only with the falling of the dusk." For Hegel, the philosopher can speak only *after* history has taken its course, and once its many voices have been heard. Indeed, philosophy itself is, in Hegel's hands, an attempt to attend to everything that has thus been spoken in a given epoch.

59. A similar view is developed in Hans Urs von Balthasar, *Truth is Symphonic,* trans. Graham Harrison (San Francisco: Ignatius Press, 1987). Likewise, von Balthasar's controlling argument is basically Christological rather than philosophical or literary.

There is a striking, poetic representation of the import of these ideas in Dante's *Divine Comedy:* in the *Paradiso,* nearing his goal, Dante at last meets his theological master, St. Thomas Aquinas. But the meeting goes in an unexpected direction, for Dante hears Thomas the Dominican extol the theological vision of none other than St. Francis of Assisi. Then, led further by Thomas, he meets St. Bonaventure, the great Franciscan theologian, only to hear him praise the life and works of St. Dominic (*Paradiso,* Cantos x-xii). The ultimate rebuke of the theological and ecclesiastical jealousies and disputes that divided the two great orders, Dominican and Franciscan, thus comes in heaven, where all such divisions are reconciled. Even more surprisingly, and as if to hammer home the point, Dante places Siger (Sigier) of Brabant among the same group of theologians in the "Sphere of the Sun," symbolizing divine illumination. Siger had been a colleague of Thomas at the University of Paris, where he taught as an interpreter of the Muslim Aristotelian philosopher Averroes. Siger had fled after being charged with heresy for teaching Averroist ideas such as the eternity of the world (he was murdered by his servant before he could be arrested and tried). Thomas had bitterly opposed Siger at the University of Paris; but in Dante's Paradise, Thomas acknowledges even Siger as a brother.

> This fire, from whom thy glance returns to me,
>   shines from a spirit grave in thought, who knew
>   Sorrow; for him death came too tardily;
>
> That's the eternal light of Sigier, who
>   Lecturing down in Straw Street, hammered home
>   Invidious truths, as logic taught him to.[60]

One way to understand this theologically is by way of the intimate connection between Christology, the doctrine of the Word of God, and theological understanding itself. For in the Christian tradition, it is because God reaches out to the world by his Word that humans can understand God at all: "No one has ever seen God. It is God the only Son . . . who has made him known" (John 1:18). However, the problem of the plurality of theological knowledge, and the apparently contradictory possibility of a common con-

---

60. Dante, *The Divine Comedy, Cantica III: Paradise,* trans. Dorothy L. Sayers and Barbara Reynolds (Harmondsworth, UK: Penguin Books, 1962), p. 139.

fession of faith, each represent two sides of the one divine action by which we are drawn into relationship with God. At the center of each of these is the Christological, or incarnational, mystery: that is, each is grounded in the central mystery of Christian faith itself, that the historical individual Jesus of Nazareth was the Son of God, the "Word made flesh." For the most basic claim of the gospel is that the Word of God was authentically and truly spoken in time in *this* human life. But this event in time was unique. We say this not out of any narrowness of outlook, so as to exclude other "revelations," but purely out of the conviction that such an expression of God's Word in time can only be understood as an act of God. The incarnation of God is not a human work, a human potentiality, or a human achievement.

In other words, if theological truth can be said to consist of the speaking of the Word of God into creaturely time, then we are bound to say that theological truth finds its unique and unrepeatable expression in the "Word made flesh," Jesus Christ. All other expressions of theological truth are modes of witness and are hence secondary, provisional, derivative, fallible, and, in principle, repeatable. The fallibility and repeatability of Christian claims extend through the length and breadth of Christian theology, from the Bible itself through to the creeds, and to the highest and lowest expressions of faith in quest of understanding: for the Word was made flesh only there, and then, and in this one, Jesus Christ; and though the church is the body of Christ, God's "speech" is not fully present here, or now, or in us. There is no ecclesiastical *alter Christus*. We cannot repeat — or prolong — the "speaking" of the Word into time in Jesus Christ. All we can do is to bear witness to it in ways that are inherently multiple and pluriform. In other words, faith in Jesus as the incarnate Son of God requires of the church that bears his name that it does not take itself too seriously. Above all, it must not misunderstand its own witness to the Word of God as the thing itself.

The doctrine of the incarnation, then, has to do with a unique event, the uniqueness of which ought to act as a safeguard against the kind of self-certainty and iron inflexibility that so often mars the face of the church. Here we take our stand on the side of the *act of God*, a "speech act" which is unlike any other and is by definition unrepeatable by humans. The other side of the incarnational coin, however, is nothing less than the *humanity* of the Word of God, and with it the historicity, the finitude — and, we might even say, the littleness of that humanity. We should not so freely overlook and misunderstand this great theme of Christ's true humanity, for among other things, it secures the particularly and peculiarly Christian approach to the goodness and dignity of the individual person, a dignity that exists despite our time-bound historicity, our fallibility, our littleness. God evidently respects this littleness, this fallibility, and this historicity. In speaking the Word into time, God allowed it to take the form of a human life. The expression of the Word of God in time recognizes and permits there to be a human being, who even in the case of Jesus Christ is not required to bear the burden of absolute knowledge, infallibility, or authority. How much more does this have to be said of the church! Whether expressed in Christian assumptions about the inerrancy of Scripture, the indefectibility of councils, or in dogmas relating to papal infallibility, the assumption is profoundly un-Christian, precisely because it is so badly out of step with the foundational event, the "becoming human" of God.

It is only when we grasp this idea that we can also grant the grounds for a converse movement, which has been our focus in this chapter. If, in the dynamic movement of the Spirit who comes through the Word, the truth of God must weave itself through the fabric of a thousand theological systems, and a thousand human cultures in the church's reflection and mission, and yet be contained by no one of them to the exclusion of the rest, then it is equally true that we must recognize something else that tends in the opposite direction, toward the center and away from the edges. Dante certainly grasped its significance in the *Divine Comedy*. Vatican II recognized it — despite its clinging to a very Roman obsession with structure and authority — in its affirmation of the true bond in the Spirit of all Christians, despite their many confessions and cultures. Here we must attempt to give it proper expression. It is a movement that takes place out of Christian theological diversity, a movement that takes place in the Spirit, who shines in upon the one Word of God, and that recognizes him in all the variegated forms of life and of thought that permeate the history and present experience of the church. It is the movement by which we together recognize that the one Lord Jesus Christ, in his divinity and humanity, transcends all our theological differences, and thus it is the movement by which we make the common confession: "Jesus is Lord."

By way of conclusion, and in order to illustrate the importance of these claims, let me refer briefly to the question of ecumenism. To speak of the ecumenical movement of our time as a movement of the Holy Spirit is accurate, and it represents something more than merely a pious gesture toward other Christians and churches. But it is not the only movement of the Spirit in our time, for the work of the same Spirit is found in the manifold theologies and theological interpretations of Scripture found in the churches that confess the name of Christ, and it is seen in those ecological and justice-oriented "missions" that consume so many of the energies of the people of God. This has to be taken for granted. What we need is a way to acknowledge this fact theologically, to integrate it into the structures of Christian thought, and crucially, to *relate* these two movements. This is the strength of the approach developed here. There is, as I have said, a "centrifugal" movement, by which the one Word of God, "shining out" through the Spirit, makes its home in countless forms of thought, languages, cultures, and historical epochs. But there is also a "centripetal" movement, by which the Spirit, "shining in" on the Word of God, awakens us to the unity that still exists in and amidst this diversity that it generates.

One of the great needs of the ecumenical movement today is to learn to distinguish between these two movements of the Word and of the Spirit, the "two hands of the Father," which together structure Christian life — and the life of the church. After all, ecumenism is located at the intersection of the two, where the fact of ecclesiastical and theological diversity meets the project and promise of Christian unity. Unfortunately, the history of Christian theology, and accordingly of the churches, is such that the various doctrinal positions of the churches constitute a massive impediment to unity.

What I would like to suggest in concluding this chapter is that the diversity of doctrinal positions found in the many churches should be seen principally as belonging only to the first of the movements described above, by which the one Word of God must find expression in manifold ways. Many of the churches in their diversity do not — as yet, at least — know how to participate in any real way in the second of the movements, the movement toward the center by which the Spirit, shining in on the one Word, draws us to the common confession. Dominated by an interest in the Word, who shines out through the Spirit in manifold ways, they are almost unacquainted with the problem and possibility of an interest in the Spirit, who from a beginning in the diversity of gifts and graces, of Christian experiences, cultures, languages, and theologies, shines in on the one Lord of the church. Therefore, what is needed for the ecumenical project is not a bare commitment to unity that is based on the existing positions of the churches in their diversity, but a theological renewal rooted in the work of the Spirit among the many forms and varieties of Christianity, which can lead them again to the center, to a common confession of faith, and to a realization of the *koinônia* with God that neither obliterates difference nor sacrifices unity. This communion is grounded in the God who as the Trinity of Father, Son, and Holy Spirit is both one and many, and who invites us by participation in the working of his Word and Spirit to share the divine Trinitarian life.

CHAPTER 7

Sacrament

The Sacraments: A Disputed Question

In the town of Paray-le-Monial, in the Burgundy region of central France, a remarkable Romanesque church dating from the eleventh and early twelfth centuries stands as testament to an ecclesiology that is now all but forgotten.[1] Built under the auspices of the Benedictines of Cluny and in the style of its own abbey church, employing the same masons who worked there, and constructed during the lifetime of Cluny's greatest abbot, St. Hugh (1024-1109), the church at Paray-le-Monial is arguably the most beautiful surviving example of Cluniac architecture in Europe.[2] Although Romanesque churches are frequently judged to be lacking in elegance compared to later Gothic designs, or at a more popular level as "dark" stops on the tourist trails of Europe, when taken at a proper pace, the church at Paray-le-Monial reveals the glory of its architectural style. The human fabric of the building itself is certainly impressive: it has stood for almost a thousand years, and it used in its construction major advances in medieval engineering, such as construction of a stone rather than a timber roof. An elaborate symbolism is

1. In 1875 the church was designated the "Basilica of the Sacred Heart" by Pope Pius IX.

2. The abbey church at Cluny was at its consecration in 1095 the largest church in Christendom. It survived for almost 700 years — until its destruction in the aftermath of the French Revolution. But the church at Paray-le-Monial gives us some sense of the architectural splendor of the abbey church at Cluny.

carved into the portals, columns, and spires of the structure. It is only when one enters the building, however, that the real genius of the building becomes clear, as its architectural statement becomes something entirely theological. Even on a bright summer's day, the interior is dimly lit, such that the only points of light available to its occupants come from those elements that are meant to radiate or reflect the glory of God and the illumination of the gospel: candles, occasionally the gold leaf of icons and statuary, and, of course, the stained glass that represents the story of salvation.[3]

In a crasser world, floodlights might be installed in such a building, and entrance fees charged, so that people could "really" see it and wonder at the strangeness of the medieval mind. As it is, we can be thankful that the good people of Paray-le-Monial seem to perceive the possibilities differently. And even if it is only because, to them, "it was ever thus," we are all in their debt.

An insight into the theological assumptions that made the church at Paray-le-Monial possible is provided in one of the earliest textbooks of medieval sacramental theology, Hugh of St. Victor's *De Sacramentis,* which he wrote perhaps two decades after that church sanctuary was completed.[4] In this work, sacraments of the natural law (e.g., the sacrifice of Abel), of the written law (e.g., the sacraments of temple), and of the law of grace (e.g., baptism) are categorized in a way that would become traditional; more surprisingly, some thirty Christian sacraments are enumerated and explored. What is obvious in the work of Hugh of St. Victor is that he represents a time in which a rather flexible and extensible understanding of the nature and number of the sacraments prevailed. It can occasionally be amusing to read the judgments of later Roman Catholic writers on Hugh's sacramental theology, but there was nothing unusual about the generosity of his position.[5] In-

---

3. My wife and I visited the church several times during a holiday in Burgundy during the summer of 1992. My wife was so moved by the church that at length — and as a Northern Ireland Protestant, of all things — she lit a candle and prayed for peace!

4. Hugh of St. Victor, *On the Sacraments of the Christian Faith,* trans. Roy J. Deferrai (Cambridge, MA: Mediaeval Academy of America, 1951). Concerning Hugh of St. Victor, see Roger Baron, *Science et Sagesse chez Hughes de Saint-Victor* (Paris: P. Lethielleux, 1957).

5. "He contributed notably to the elaboration of the definition of a sacrament in the strict sense of the term. It is true that he was not fully aware of the number of the Sacraments of the New Law, yet he treated extensively of all seven." D. Van Den Eynde, "Hugh of St. Victor," in *New Catholic Encyclopedia,* 17 vols. (San Francisco: McGraw-Hill, 1967), 7: 195. The point is accurate enough in a way, but it is surprising to see this theological tone still being sounded in the 1960s.

deed, as we shall see, even Hugh's thirty sacraments represent something of a "conservative estimate" for the time in which he wrote.

Though medieval theologians and the medieval church would shortly codify the matter far more conservatively, Hugh in fact speaks for an older tradition of sacramental theology that dominates the theology of the first Christian millennium. In it, the sacraments were understood much more generically than came to be the case during the second Christian millennium — and in the Latin tradition only, for the Eastern Orthodox have never formally accepted the restrictions of the second millennium of Latin sacramental theology. Furthermore, the generic sacramentalism that Hugh's theology represents was not merely a late medieval innovation in the Latin West. In the patristic period, Ambrose, for example, explicitly writes of the priest's use of spittle in anointing the ears of the catechumens in prebaptismal instruction, and of his speaking the Aramaic word *Ephphatha* ("be opened") (Mark 7:34), as one of the Christian sacraments of initiation.[6] Augustine, Ambrose's convert, spoke of a sacrament in terms that would define the shape of medieval sacramental theology: "Take away the word, and what is the water except water? The word is added to the elemental substance, and it becomes a sacrament, also itself, as it were, a visible word [*accedit verbum ad elementum et fit sacramentum etiam ipsum tanquam visibile verbum*]."[7] Again, Augustine says that "the visible . . . is the sacrament, the sacred sign, of the invisible . . . [*sacrificium ergo visibile invisibilis sacrificii sacramentum, id et sacrum signum est*]."[8] But Augustine was perfectly capable of using the technical word *sacramentum* to refer to a wide range of ritual acts that take place in the church, from saying the Apostles' Creed and the Lord's Prayer[9] to exorcism,[10] and he plainly felt no need to say how many Christian sacraments there are, famously declaring merely that the Christian sacraments are "more effica-

6. St. Ambrose, *De Sacramentis,* I. 1, in St. Ambrose, *Theological and Dogmatic Works,* trans. Roy Deferrari (Washington, DC: Catholic University of America Press, 1963), pp. 269-70.

7. Augustine, *Tractatus in evangelium Iohannis,* 80.3, in Augustine, *Tractates on the Gospel of John 55–111,* trans. John W. Rettig (Washington, DC: The Catholic University of America Press, 1994), p. 117.

8. Augustine, *De civitate dei,* x.5, in Augustine, *City of God,* trans. Henry Bettenson (Harmondsworth, UK: Penguin Books, 1972), p. 377.

9. Augustine, *Sermo* 228, in J.-P. Migne, ed., *Patrologia Latina,* 221 vols. (Ann Arbor, Mich.: ProQuest Information and Learning Company, 1996), 38, 1102. Hereafter *PL*.

10. Augustine, *Sermo* 227; *PL* 38, 1100.

cious, more beneficial, easier to perform, and fewer in number" than were the sacraments of the Old Testament.[11] Though "fewer in number," there are still clearly plenty of them by later standards. Likewise, Bernard of Clairvaux preached openly of actions such as the washing of feet as "sacraments."[12]

The Romanesque church at Paray-le-Monial is heir to this older sacramental tradition, constructed during the time of its final maturity, and before it fell into decline. Most likely, the church building itself — its use of light for instance — is intended to be understood in explicitly sacramental terms, along with the multitude of physical elements and liturgical actions that the structure was built to contain. This older sacramental theology was, however, not to last long, for a theology within which the church lives far less in the midst of these sacraments — and far more as the keeper and channel of sacramental grace — was about to emerge.

Around the year 1150, this innovation in sacramental theology appeared in a hugely influential book by Peter Lombard that was to have far-reaching consequences for the history of Christianity. Peter Lombard was an able traditionalist theologian of the cathedral school in Paris, a man ultimately destined for episcopal office, but who had distinguished himself as a young scholar and had enjoyed the patronage of no less a figure at the time than Bernard of Clairvaux. Lombard's main theological work, the *Sententiarum Libri Quatuor*, was a compendium of "opinions of the fathers," or *sententiae patrum*, which he organized loosely into a system of theology intended to consolidate the achievement of the previous millennium of Christian theology into a comprehensive vision. In the fourth book of the *Sentences*, drawing freely on older sources from the tradition, he made his most crucial contribution to the development of medieval theology, first, by defining a sacrament as a sacred sign that not only symbolizes grace but also "*causes* grace"; and second, by limiting the number of the Christian sacraments that do this to just seven: baptism, confirmation, Eucharist, penance, unction, ordination, and marriage.[13] Other rites that had been counted among the sacraments were relegated to the status of "sacramentals," or actions that are akin to the sacraments but do not share in

---

11. Augustine, *Contra Faustum Manichaeum*, XIX.13; *PL* 42, 355.

12. Bernard of Clairvaux, *Sermo in Cena Domini*, 4, in *Sancti Bernardi Opera*, ed. J. LeClerq and H. Rochais (Rome: Editiones Cistercienses, 1968), 5: 70-71.

13. Peter Lombard, *IV Sent.*, dist. I, cap. 2; dist. II, cap. 1, in Peter Lombard, *Sententiae in IV Libris Distinctae*, 2 vols. (Rome: Collegii S. Bonaventurae ad Claras Aquas, 1971-1981). On Lombard's position, see Marcia L. Colish, *Peter Lombard*, 2 vols. (Leiden: Brill, 1994), 2: 516-698.

the objectivity of the sacraments proper in that they do not "cause grace" in the same way. This was another move that Lombard made in his sacramental theology, and it was to be taken up and developed extensively in the theology of subsequent centuries.

It might seem as though Christian Europe, which had formerly tolerated what seems by these standards to be an extraordinary degree of confusion concerning the sacraments, now breathed a collective sigh of relief at this tidy enumeration of the sacraments' nature and number, for the theory of the seven sacraments was immediately and widely accepted in Latin Christianity (which then attempted, as we shall see, to force it on the Christian East). But the more likely explanation is simply that the theory of the seven sacraments answered a need that arose in the context of the new self-confidence that had emerged at the time in the Latin church, according to which the church became, in effect, God's vice regent on earth. The twelfth and thirteenth centuries, for instance, constitute the "classic" era of the Crusades, when the Roman claim to divinely instituted ecclesiastical and temporal power came to definitive expression. In the absurdly self-confident papal bull *Unam Sanctam* of 1302, all of this was neatly codified: the spiritual and the temporal "swords" were both asserted to belong to the church, with both being held specifically in the hand of Peter and his successors, so that the power of kings (wherever they might be, it seems) entirely depended on papal dispensation.

However, the "weapons" used in enforcing such claims were not mainly the arms of European kings, knights, and soldiers, but chiefly the sacraments, by which, it was thought, salvation could be alternately "bound" and "loosed" (Matt. 16:19), and the allegiance even of kings to papal authority secured. Given this emerging attitude of ecclesiastical self-certainty, it is hardly surprising that there was a perceived need for a fixed understanding of what the sacraments were and how they were to be properly regulated; for if the church was to wield such power through them, it had to understand their nature, and it had to control their use by a regular discipline.

Peter Lombard's definition of the seven sacraments thus matched the mood of the time, and it was quickly taken up by influential theological writers, including, notably, Thomas Aquinas: from his hands, after some centuries of reception, it would eventually find its way into the teaching of the Council of Florence, and thus into formal dogmatic definition.[14] In the context of a

---

14. The source from which it was taken, in the case of the Council of Florence, ap-

series of decrees governing "reunion" with the Greeks, Armenians, Copts, Bosnians, Syrians, Chaldeans, and Cypric Marionites, the *Bulla Unionis Armenorum* of the Council of Florence sets out the following definition:

> [F]or the easier instruction of the Armenians of today and in the future we reduce the truth about the sacraments of the church to the following brief scheme. There are seven sacraments of the new Law, namely baptism, confirmation, eucharist, penance, extreme unction, orders and matrimony, which differ greatly from the sacraments of the old Law. The latter were not causes of grace, but only prefigured the grace to be given through the passion of Christ; whereas the former, ours, both contain grace and bestow it on those who worthily receive them. The first five of these are directed to the spiritual perfection of each person in himself, the last two to the regulation and increase of the whole church. . . .
>
> All these sacraments are made up of three elements: namely, things as the matter, words as the form, and the person who confers the sacrament with the intention of doing what the church does. If any of these is lacking, the sacrament is not effected.
>
> Three of the sacraments, namely baptism, confirmation and orders, imprint indelibly on the soul a character, that is a kind of stamp which distinguishes it from the rest. Hence they are not repeated in the same person. The other four, however, do not imprint a character and can be repeated.[15]

As a summary statement of the sacramental theology of the medieval church, this is already an impressive piece of theology: precise, succinct, and powerful. A century later, the Council of Trent, while setting out essentially the same teaching, would sharpen it even further in response to the Protestant Reformation:

> If anyone says that the sacraments of the new law were not all instituted by our [Lord] Jesus Christ; or that there are more or fewer than

---

pears to have been Thomas Aquinas's short tract *De articulis fidei et ecclesiae sacramentis*. However, the main development of the theory in Thomas's theology appears in the *Summa Theologiae*, 3a., 60-90.

15. Council of Florence, Session VIII, 22 November 1439, in Tanner, *Decrees of the Ecumenical Councils*, 2 vols. (Washington, DC: Georgetown University Press, 1990), 1: 540-42.

seven; namely, baptism, confirmation, eucharist, penance, last anointing, order, matrimony; or that one or other of these seven is not truly and in the full sense a sacrament: let him be anathema. . . .

If anyone says that grace is not conferred by the sacraments of the new law through the sacramental action itself [*ex opere operato*], but that faith in the divine promise is by itself sufficient for obtaining the grace: let him be anathema.[16]

Thus the sacramental channels of the late medieval church were set in place, providing a ritual structure capable of covering all the needs of the church and its members. One of the things that is most impressive about it is the comprehensiveness of the theory — a fact that is also reflected in the dogmatic definitions of the Council of Florence itself:

For by baptism we are reborn spiritually; by confirmation we grow in grace and are strengthened in faith. Once reborn and strengthened, we are nourished by the food of the divine eucharist. But if through sin we incur an illness of the soul, we are cured spiritually by penance. Spiritually also and bodily as suits the soul, by extreme unction. By orders the church is governed and spiritually multiplied; by matrimony it grows bodily.[17]

In short, the claim is that in the doctrine of the seven sacraments, everything necessary is present; all needs are met; every eventuality in life and in the church is catered for by the sacramental channels appointed by Christ, and defined by his body, the church.

The trouble with this theory of comprehensiveness is twofold: from the standpoint of the older Christian tradition, "everything" is emphatically *not* there; from the standpoint of the new movements of the Reformation, *too much* is there. There are lessons to learn about the nature of sacramental theology if we ponder both sides of the critique.

In the first case, we could do worse than quoting from St. Bonaventure on the nature of the sacraments. Writing in the 1260s, Bonaventure would repeat the by-then standard teaching of the church: "[Christ] gave the sacraments as seven remedies against sickness. Through the administration of the

16. Council of Trent, Session VII, 3 March 1547, *Decretum primum*, Canones 1, 8, in Tanner, *Decrees*, 2: 684-85.

17. Council of Florence, in Tanner, *Decrees*, 1: 541.

sacraments he grants sanctifying grace and forgives sins, which are never taken away except within the faith and unity of Holy Mother Church."[18] Elsewhere in his theology, however, Bonaventure cannot escape the lure of the older sacramental atmosphere; indeed, he relies on it in order to work out his theology:

> The creatures of the sense world signify
> the invisible attributes of God,
> partly because God is
> the origin, exemplar and end
> of every creature,
> and every effect is
> the sign of its cause, the exemplification of the exemplar
> and the path to the end, to which it leads:
> partly by their own proper representation,
> partly from prophetic prefiguration,
> partly from angelic operation,
> partly from additional institution.
> For every creature is by its nature
> a kind of effigy and likeness of the eternal Wisdom,
> but especially one
> which in the book of Scripture
> has been elevated through the spirit of prophecy
> to prefigure spiritual things;
> and more especially, those creatures
> in whose likeness God wished to appear
> through the ministry of angels;
> and most especially, a creature
> which God willed to institute
> as a symbol
> and which has the character
> not only of a sign in the general sense
> but also of a sacrament.[19]

18. Bonaventure, *Lignum Vitae*, 40, in *Bonaventure: The Soul's Journey into God, The Tree of Life, The Life of St. Francis*, trans. Ewert Cousins (New York: Paulist Press, 1978), p. 164.

19. Bonaventure, *Itinerarium mentis in Deum*, II. 12, in *Bonaventure*, pp. 76-77.

There is, to be sure, no formal relinquishing of the doctrine of the seven sacraments in a text like this, and yet Bonaventure goes further than even Hugh of St. Victor did in arguing that, since God is the "end of every creature," every creature can become "the path to [that] end."[20]

From the other standpoint, it would seem that the number of the sacraments included in medieval doctrine seems rather arbitrary, for by what criteria are several of the seven, which have no explicit warrant in Scripture, included along with baptism and particularly the Eucharist as "sacraments" in the technical sense? A text like 1 Corinthians 10:1-22 assumes the existence of baptism and the eucharistic meal as specific "actions" that take place in the life of the church, and each can readily be traced to some scriptural institution by Jesus (e.g., Luke 22:17-20; Matt. 28:19). However, no comparable authority for rites such as confirmation can be found in Scripture. If, then, the number of the sacraments must be restricted, it would seem that the criteria distinguishing what is sacramental from what is not ought to be consistently applied. The fact that they are not so applied in the doctrine of the seven sacraments is the main objection to the theory that arises in the context of the Protestant Reformation.

We can begin with Calvin, the great systematizer of Protestant insight, who did not invent, but merely adapted to his own use, the medieval propensity to define the sacraments and to restrict their number. It was only in the second Christian millennium that the number of the sacraments came to be rigidly defined, and Calvin, like his Roman Catholic contemporaries, could no longer conceive of a situation in which such a definition was actually unnecessary. In a variety of other ways, the position he developed was also very medieval in spirit: for example, in his insistence on the addition of the Word of God to the sign or element; in his differentiated treatment of the sacraments of the Old Testament and New Testament; and in his use of the word "substance" in order to convey his own theology of the real presence of Christ's body and blood in the Lord's Supper.[21] In a number of senses, however, Calvin's theology also marked a radically new departure. For example, we can see this in his objection to ostentatious "ceremonies" as a mere substitute for true piety (I.iii.2); in his attack on the dogma of transubstantiation

---

20. The reference to the angels is almost certainly due to Francis's key visionary experience in 1224 of the six-winged seraph in the form of the crucified Christ, as a result of which he received the stigmata.

21. Calvin, *Institutes*, IV.xiv.3; IV.xiv.20-22; IV.xvii.19.

(IV.xvii.14-15); and most of all, perhaps, in his indifference to even ancient Christian ritual: "If anyone should like to defend such inventions by appealing to antiquity, I also am not ignorant . . . how soon after the apostolic age the Lord's Supper was corrupted by rust . . ." (IV.xvii.43).

However, in the need to define and defend "sacraments" as conventionally understood, Calvin remained firm. To redefine sacraments altogether is not his real goal. We only begin to approach this in a fragmentary form in the theology of Martin Luther, who, in one of the great texts of the Reformation, the 1520 treatise *The Babylonian Captivity of the Church*, makes the following observation:

> To begin with, I must deny that there are seven sacraments, and for the present maintain that there are but three: baptism, penance and the bread. . . . Yet, if I were to speak according to the usage of the Scriptures, I should have only *one single sacrament*, but with three sacramental signs. . . .[22]

Luther's reference here is almost an aside, a thought that he throws out and then quickly abandons as unworkable. Yet the point he makes is so unmistakably Christological, and the claim said to be so rooted in Scripture, that we are bound to ask how can it be a matter of such indifference. Luther had discovered, presumably from grappling directly with Erasmus's 1516 edition of the Greek New Testament, that in Scripture the Greek word that became the Latin *sacramentum* is a word with far richer connotations than its Latin version. The word is *mystêrion,* and though it is used very sparingly in the Bible, it is also used very specifically to refer, not to any ritual act of the church itself, but rather to the central "mystery" of the gospel. The classic reference is 1 Timothy 3:16:

> Without any doubt, the mystery of piety is great [*mega estin to tês eusebeias mystêrion*]:
>
> > He was revealed in the flesh,
> >   vindicated by the Spirit,
> >   seen by angels,

---

22. Martin Luther, *The Babylonian Captivity of the Church,* trans. A. Steinhäuser et al., in Helmut T. Lehmann, ed., *Luther's Works,* 55 vols. (Philadelphia: Fortress, 1959), 36: 18 (italics added).

proclaimed among Gentiles,
   believed on in the world,
      taken up in glory.

(1 Tim. 3:16 [my translation])

Here "mystery" obviously refers not to what we do in baptism, the Eucharist, or any other sign, but instead refers to that of which baptism and the Eucharist themselves are signs: the realization in time of God's eternal will to save, in Jesus Christ, the incarnate Son of God. However, it is significant that the ecclesiastical themes of mission and faith are also included in the "mystery" in the second stanza.

Luther did not carry this line of thought much further. As is well known, the Augustinian friar ultimately reverted to the standard Augustinian theory of the sacraments, arguing that the sacraments are "visible words," sensible instruments that, because they are authorized by the Word of God, become the means of grace in the life of faith, and instruments through which the Spirit is given — along with and under the authority of God's Word. Calvin would follow in the same path, offering as explanation what should strike us, in the light of what we have just seen, as a very curious argument from tradition: the word *sacrament* as commonly used among church writers is admittedly not biblical, but is by convention "applied to those signs which reverently [represent] sublime and spiritual things" (IV.xiv.2).

But were Luther and Calvin — and are we — right to abandon this line of thinking so quickly? After all, might it not be possible to ground the life of the church, much more clearly than we tend to, in Christ, the one whom Luther calls the "one single sacrament" of salvation? Unfortunately, sacramental theology has become a cause of massive division among the churches, with supporting theologies that are explicitly intended to divide rather than to unite. As I have argued, it is possible to understand the differentiation of theological positions and of liturgical practices as an opportunity for enrichment, according to the metaphor of the "centripetal" movement by which the implications of ideas are worked out ecclesiologically. But what is also needed is a corresponding "centrifugal" movement, according to which the "one in the many" is allowed to emerge; after all, this is precisely what is needed for such "enrichment" to occur. Reflection on the biblical use of the word *mystêrion* is of special importance here, for the *mystêrion* in the full New Testament sense is concerned precisely with what surmounts human division, or with what makes such division theologically redundant. The *mystêrion,* so conceived, should be supremely relevant to the problem of Christian division over "sacramental" practice and theology.

A survey of the New Testament use of the word *mystêrion* can well begin with its appearance in the teachings of Jesus. In the teaching concerning the purpose of the parables that appears in all three synoptic Gospels, Jesus says to his disciples: "To you has been given the mystery [*to mystêrion,* Mark 4:11; *ta mystêria,* Matt. 13:11, Luke 8:10] of the kingdom of God, but for those outside, everything comes in parables. . . ." "Secret," which has become the somewhat pedestrian English translation, does not do the word justice and represents a rather unfortunate "undertranslation" of the Greek. The *mystêrion* of the kingdom is not some puzzle kept hidden, but the great theme of the first three Gospels. To be "given" this is to be given something of immense importance that bears safekeeping.

I have already cited the crucial text, 1 Timothy 3:16, so we need only note that here the mystery is indeed great, since it embraces in one word the varied Christological "moments" of incarnation, resurrection, mission, and glorification. In Colossians 2:2-3, the author plainly states that "God's mystery" is none other than "Christ himself, in whom are hidden all the treasures of wisdom and knowledge," while in Romans 16:25, the mystery is the purpose of God spoken through the prophets, that all nations might believe and obey. This theme is relevant to our purposes because it relates expressly to the idea of the church. In Romans it occurs in the context of a benediction, which effectively summarizes the argument of the entire Epistle. However, the concept of the *mystêrion* is left hanging at the very end of Romans, so that the trail effectively runs cold.

The same idea appears much more extensively in the Epistle to the Ephesians. First of all, we read in Ephesians 1 of the *mystêrion* of God's will: "to gather up all things in him, things in heaven and things on earth" (1:9-10; the verb is *anakephalaiôsasthai,* "to recapitulate"). It is clear in Ephesians that the mystery has yet to be realized in its fullness, which is an important point, since it adds a crucial eschatological dimension to the discussion; nevertheless, the mystery is at least proleptically realized in the church. In fact, the realization of the eternal purpose of God in the church is a major theological theme of Ephesians. It appears again with special clarity in Ephesians 3, where in an "autobiographical" aside, Paul defines his apostleship in relation to "the mystery of Christ" (3:4), which is that "the Gentiles have become fellow-heirs, members of the same body, and sharers in the promise in Jesus Christ through the gospel" (Eph. 3:6).

We can now attempt a theological synthesis of the New Testament material, at least briefly. In the concrete reality of Christ's person and work, the *mystêrion* of God's eternal will is both revealed and realized. The church also belongs to this *mystêrion,* for in the church the saving work of God in Jesus Christ is also being brought to fulfillment. Christ's work is not yet complete, but it will be completed in the gathering of the church at the end time: Christ's person and work are such that they create an eschatological space for others, so that he is not and will not be without those whom he calls to himself. Long ago God purposed to bring all things into unity with himself. He gave Abraham the promise of a blessing to all nations, and through the prophets he made himself known as the God of all the earth. This he is now realizing in the creation of a people of God that includes Jew and gentile in one body, who together have one head in the one Lord Jesus Christ. Therefore, while the purpose of God in creation is not yet complete, the church is part of the *mystêrion* of that purpose. It participates — derivatively but decisively — in the *mystêrion* of God's great act of salvation in Jesus Christ.

The "Primordial Sacrament"

Luther's radical statement from the *Babylonian Captivity* of 1520 — "if I were to speak according to the usage of the Scriptures, I should have only one single sacrament, but with three sacramental signs" — will serve as our point of entry to a fuller discussion of this problem. The three signs Luther had in view here were baptism, Eucharist, and penance, though by the end of the same work in which he wrote these words, he had rejected penance as a sacrament, leaving only baptism and the Eucharist. Luther's theology at this point was evidently a theology *in via,* characterized by a certain theological fluidity or tentativeness; however, it was also a theology that was open to the Word of God and arose from a deep encounter with it, an encounter that led him to confess the centrality of the "one single sacrament," Jesus Christ, in life as well as in thought. We could do worse than to follow a similar approach in our own theological thought and work.

It is surprising that Luther's statement concerning the one sacrament of Christ has been passed over so often in the history of Luther scholarship. Of course, Luther himself quickly moved on to develop a heightened sense of the importance of the "structured" ecclesiastical life that a robust sacramental theology could provide, and his commentators have followed him along this path. Luther's objective in doing so needs to be understood over against the threat posed by some Reformation radicals, the most dangerous of whom denied the need for sacramental signs altogether and spoke of an immediate relationship with the Holy Spirit that made even the written Word obsolete. From this point of view, the oversight is understandable. However, the insight it represents has been taken up in a range of theology in recent years, much of it of ecumenical import. Since differences in sacramental theology loom large in the scandal of Christian disunity, theology has needed to seek news ways of conceiving of the sacraments in response.

By a considerable margin, the most important of these responses appears in the documents of the Second Vatican Council, which, while not formally taking the position that Christ is the "one single sacrament," seek a similar way into the problem of sacramental theology in their claim that the church itself, which has its being "in Christ," can be conceived in sacramental terms. The key document is *Lumen Gentium* (1964), which plainly identifies the church at one point as "the universal sacrament of salvation."

> Christ, when he was lifted up from the earth, drew all people to himself . . . ; rising from the dead . . . , he sent his lifegiving Spirit down on his disciples and through him he constituted his body which is the church as the universal sacrament of salvation [*ut universale salutis sacramentum constituit*]. . . .[23]

This ecclesiological use of the word "sacrament," which was a novelty in doctrinal definition up to the time of Vatican II, needs careful comment. It almost goes without saying that the intention was not to speak of the church as sacramental in the same sense as baptism, the Eucharist, and the other five sacraments of the Catholic tradition. The statement relates to the doctrine of the church, not to sacramental theology proper: in other words, the church was not defined in *Lumen Gentium* as sacrament number eight. Nor is the point that the church is "sacramental" in the technical sense that applies to those many physical aspects of the church's liturgy or practice that are deemed to be helpful to the Catholic faithful (vestments, candles, and so on).

The key to what is meant by the idea of the church as "sacrament of salvation" is most likely found where the idea is first announced, right at the beginning of *Lumen Gentium:*

---

23. *Lumen Gentium,* 48, in Tanner, *Decrees,* 2: 887.

Since Christ is the light of nations, this holy synod, called together in the [Holy] Spirit, strongly desires to enlighten all people with his brightness, which gleams over the face of the church, by preaching the gospel to every creature. . . . And since the church is in Christ as a sacrament or instrumental sign of intimate union with God and of the unity of all humanity, the council, continuing the teaching of previous councils, intends to declare with greater clarity to the faithful and the entire human race the nature of the church and its universal mission (*Lumen Gentium*, 1; Tanner, p. 849.)

The theme of the opening paragraphs of the document is thus that the light of Christ can be discerned in the life of the church. It is in this context that the church is defined as a sacrament of union with God and of the unity of humanity: *Ecclesia sit in Christo veluti sacramentum*. But the reference of the word "sacrament" to the church here is indirect: "the Church is in Christ as a sacrament," or better, "like a sacrament." In short, it is one thing to identify something as a sacrament and another to speak of it as "like" a sacrament. The document thus makes a distinction between the sacraments proper and the ecclesiastical "sacrament of salvation," for no good Catholic would ever say that the eucharistic meal is "like a sacrament," whereas such language introduces the ecclesiological themes of *Lumen Gentium*.

This reading of *Lumen Gentium* follows that of Walter Kasper, who has written of the origins of this idea in the debates leading up to Vatican II.[24] Of special importance is the *nouvelle théologie* that was developed in the middle decades of the twentieth century surrounding the theology of Henri de Lubac, the great French Jesuit who sought to find a way beyond the sterile clericalism and triumphalism of the Neo-Scholastic tradition by means of a "rediscovery" of more venerable sources in Scripture and the church fathers. In de Lubac's thought, the church is indeed the sacrament of Christ — so much so that, "strictly speaking, [the church] is nothing other than that, or at any rate, the rest is a superabundance."[25] His point is that the church, the visible institution with all its trappings, is in itself nothing; rather, in ecclesiology everything depends on Christ and on the relationship established by grace between the church and Christ. Thus, while the church is not

24. Walter Kasper, "The Church as a Universal Sacrament of Salvation," in Kasper, *Theology and Church*, trans. Margaret Kohl (London: SCM Press, 1989), pp. 111-28.

25. Henri de Lubac, *The Splendor of the Church* (London: Sheed and Ward, 1956), p. 156.

itself the object of faith, it is nonetheless, by means of its bond with Christ, the means by which Christ is made known and made available to the world.

This approach to ecclesiology within the *nouvelle théologie* of the middle of the twentieth century became very influential in European Catholic theology prior to Vatican II. It is not surprising, then, that once that council had been convened, the idea very soon found its way into draft conciliar documents. It proved to be controversial, because everyone recognized that the doctrine of the church had never before been handled dogmatically under the technical heading of a sacrament, and a battle ensued over whether or not the term should be used. In the end, the reforming movement won out, most likely because the phrase *veluti sacramentum,* which had wisely been inserted into the draft document by the German bishops, introduces the theme and thus frames all other references to it.

Along with Henri de Lubac, the other major Roman Catholic source for the idea of the church as a sacrament is Karl Rahner, who develops the idea repeatedly in connection with ecclesiological and sacramental problems alike. Rahner's treatment is associated especially with his development of the notion of the church as the "primal sacrament," the *Ursakrament* that grounds all others. As we have seen, this is the point Luther began to make, only to leave off. Rahner more fully outlines it as the potential basis for a renewed and ecumenical sacramental theology:

> This could give us . . . a new and broader basis for discussing the old question, so difficult historically, of the institution of all the sacraments by Christ himself: he instituted the sacraments, which are not attested by any express texts of Scripture, by instituting the Church; and he instituted the sacraments which were explicitly instituted, *as* moments in the institution of the Church. . . .[26]

Elsewhere, Rahner moves on to demonstrate how fruitful such an approach might be in ecclesiology.[27] Since it has now become possible to speak of the

---

26. Karl Rahner, "The Word and the Eucharist," in Rahner, *Theological Investigations,* trans. Kevin Smyth, 20 vols. (London: Darton, Longman & Todd; New York: Seabury Press, 1974), 4: 274.

27. Karl Rahner, "Membership of the Church According to the Teaching of Pius XII's Encyclical 'Mystici Corporis Christi,'" trans. Karl-H. Kruger, in Rahner, *Theological Investigations,* 2: 71-74. Rahner uses the concept of sacrament to try to move beyond certain of the main claims made in the encyclical.

church as the primal sacrament, he insists, then it must also be possible to approach the doctrine of the church from the standpoint of insights gleaned from the centuries of sacramental theology. Writing of the church as *Ursakrament,* Rahner argues:

> [S]he has a bodily nature which as such possesses an unmistakable, fully determined and juridically determinable form, and which actually causes the grace which it renders present in the historical here and now; and yet that bodily nature remains essentially different from this divine grace which will always be the sovereign mystery of God's freedom and can never be subdued by man. Hence there can be, as in the case of the Sacraments, a *twofold notion of the Church* which is due, not to the vagueness of notions or the inaccuracy of terminology, but to the very nature of things. (p. 73)

Just as in sacramental theology a sacrament can be valid yet not effective, so in Rahner's exposition of the doctrine of the church, the sign of the visible institution can exist without the effect of grace. Therefore, sheer membership in the visible institution is valid, but it is not effective as a means of grace. This further implies that the church remains the church (as sign) even when it is so sinful that the intended *effect* of the sign (the grace of God) is not received in its actions. Rahner's implication is that this kind of distinction, made on the basis of long-established principle in sacramental theology, can help us reconsider certain problems in the life of the church, from the perverse tendency to treat outward membership as a kind of magical cure for sin that requires no inward transformation, to the problem of the "whiskey priest" who is pathetic, broken, and even downright evil in some of his doings, and yet remains an objective means of grace in others. In a very rare reference to "the crucified God," Rahner speaks of this twofold dynamic:

> In the mystery of the valid Sacraments which nevertheless are actually empty of grace there . . . reveals itself once more the mystery of the crucified God: the God-emptiness becomes a real form of God's appearance in the world. The same as is true of the Sacraments is also true of the Church: she is the real, permanent and ever valid presence of God in the world. And this remains true even when she is the Church of the sinner; the presence of God is in her in a manner which leaves the mystery of God and the incomprehensibleness of his grace and free love intact. (p. 76)

Walter Kasper, in the essay already cited, makes one further point: that the sense of "sacrament" that underlies this new use of the word *sacramentum,* whether in *Lumen Gentium* or in the theologies of Henri de Lubac and Karl Rahner, can be traced to the New Testament word *"mystêrion"* — the very word that Luther noticed as having potentially revolutionary implications. Karl Barth, most famously in the final fragment of his unfinished *Church Dogmatics,* in which he famously rejected the idea of water baptism as a sacrament, has this to say of the *mystêrion:*

> In the New Testament [*mystêrion*] denotes an event in the world of time and space which is directly initiated and brought to pass by God alone, so that in distinction from all other events it is basically a mystery of human cognition in respect of its origin and possibility. If it discloses itself to man, this will be, not from without, but only from within, through itself, and therefore once again only through God's revelation. . . . The New Testament uses the term exclusively with reference to God's work and revelation in history, not to the corresponding human reactions. . . . Faith as a human action is nowhere called a mystery, nor is Christian obedience, nor love, nor hope, nor the existence and function of the [*ekklêsia*], nor its proclamation of the Gospel, nor its tradition as such, nor baptism, nor the Lord's Supper. Would this omission have been possible if the New Testament community had been aware that certain human attitudes, actions and institutions were freighted with the divine word and act, if it had ascribed to baptism in particular the quality of a bearer and mediator of grace, salvation, and its manifestation?[28]

The argument advanced here has troubled many a Barthian, but in fact the groundwork on which it rests was laid at a much earlier stage in Barth's work — indeed, throughout his work.[29] Already in the early 1950s, Barth had explicitly insisted that there is but one true sacrament:

28. Barth, *Church Dogmatics,* IV/4 (fragment), pp. 108-9.

29. At an earlier stage of my own life, I discovered an "oral tradition" among those who worked as junior colleagues with Thomas F. Torrance in the late 1960s at New College in Edinburgh. On his first encounter with the argument of the aged Barth in the *Church Dogmatics,* IV/4, Torrance had voiced the suspicion that Barth had succumbed to dementia! This story about Torrance may or may not be true, but it certainly reflects the problem that many Barthians had and still have with Barth's critique of baptism.

Was it a wise action on the part of the Church when it ceased to recognise in the incarnation, in the *nativitas Jesu Christi*, in the mystery of Christmas, the one and only sacrament, fulfilled once and for all, by whose actuality it lives as the one form of the one body of its Head, as the earthly-historical form of the existence of Jesus Christ in the time between His ascension and return? Has it really not enough to occupy it in the giving and receiving of this one sacrament, whose actuality it has to attest in its proclamation and therefore in baptism and Lord's Supper, but whose actuality it cannot represent or repeat in any other way either in its preaching or in baptism and the Lord's Supper? However we may understand these "sacraments" (and then, of course, the sacramental character of the Church and its action), what was it that really happened, that was hazarded and achieved, when particular sacraments, or a particular sacramental action and being, were placed alongside that which took place in Jesus Christ? . . . [At the time of the Reformation] no one took the opportunity to ask whether the presupposed concept taken over from the Roman Church was really legitimate. (*Church Dogmatics*, IV/2, p. 54)

Barth leaves the discussion hanging at this point, promising to return to it later. As we have seen, he did do so — and with typically ruthless logical consistency.

What is perhaps lost on those who fail to take Barth seriously at this point is the fact that Barth's theology offers an escape route from some of the more sterile features of Protestant sacramental theology — and a very welcome potential opening to ecumenical dialogue. On the one hand, though critical of the ecclesiastical sacraments, Barth does not deny the legitimacy of the rites of baptism or the Eucharist, nor, interestingly enough, does he say that these are the only rites that might conceivably fall under the general rubric of what people commonly call "sacraments." Barth includes preaching, the church, and the church's general "action" as conceivably being classed among these things. What is most unclear in Barth's theology, perhaps, is what the status of such rites would be. They "attest" the one "sacrament" of the gospel found in Jesus Christ; they must not be confused with it, as if human action could repeat or even adequately represent the action of God. Yet, as we have seen before and now here once again, the church is "the earthly-historical form of the existence of Jesus Christ in the time between His ascension and return." The implication is that the "earthly-historical" form of *its* existence is charged with theological significance. The reality and the sign, it may be, are to be carefully distinguished from each other, but is there not also some utterly basic sense in which they cannot be separated?

This is a subject that we will likely never answer as a point in Barthian interpretation, since the sources are so fragmentary. Instead, I would like to develop Karl Barth's central thesis in combination with those of Henri de Lubac and Karl Rahner (indeed, along with those of Vatican II) in an effort to sketch out an understanding of the church itself as "sacrament," and in an effort to develop a sacramental theology that coheres with the central thrust of the argument of this book. But I would like to approach this matter in a somewhat unusual way.

When I was a child, a saintly old neighbor by the name of Jim Dale picked me up with his car every week and drove me to church. My father did not attend church, and my mother went to one that I did not care to attend, so Jim took me along with him. Jim Dale was a good deal older than my parents — nearly sixty years my elder — yet I felt an affinity with him as a child, recognizing a holiness that came from his faith, and no doubt in some unformed way from mine as well. He was a simple man, barely literate by my standards today, who lived a very modest life. Yet I owe my Christian faith to that old man, Jim Dale, as much as I do to any of the scholars and Christian leaders I have been privileged to know, or indeed, as much as to any of the theologians I have read. For Jim Dale helped me to grasp what it might mean to love God, to believe in Jesus Christ, and to live in the power of the Holy Spirit. I still sense profoundly that I owe a debt to him, and that, in the light of his example, I have much still to live up to.

It is not a question that I ever thought to ask him, but it is almost certain that Jim Dale attended my baptism as an infant. He would have heard the promises made, seen the water poured and the Trinitarian formula invoked as I was washed with water in the sacrament of baptism and pronounced Christ's own forever. However, it has long seemed strange to me to suggest that the rite of washing with water should have obvious or necessary priority over that more longstanding and longsuffering "rite" by which Jim Dale turned up for his neighbors' child week by week over the years and taught that child by conversation and example the privileges and responsibilities of the Christian faith. The first I cannot remember, though I can "remind" myself of it as a fact, and by an effort of will I often do that. But the second, the faithfulness of Jim Dale, is (to use the language of the Council of Florence) something that has much more obviously imprinted indelibly on my soul a character that I could never lose. Even if I were to turn my back on the faith, its mark would still be on me. Others, I am certain, could relate much the same tale. The faith stories that we tell are filled with evidence of a broad sense that ordinary human acts, done in faith and in obedience to the Word of God, become the means of grace in our lives.

Unfortunately, it is not possible to account for this within the terms of the sacramental theology of the second Christian millennium. This is not merely because such ordinary acts of charity are not strictly numbered among the sacraments, but also because of the more general fixation of the church on the sacraments as ecclesiastical rites under the control of a ministerial priesthood, and the latter's habit of using them rather too freely as a means of keeping "the faithful" under its control. This was another of Luther's allegations in *The Babylonian Captivity,* where he argued that the sacramental system became over the centuries a tool of the "tyranny of the clergy over the laity," a means to their social influence and financial enrichment rather than a ministry of the gospel undertaken in humility and faith.[30] There was a good deal of truth in the allegation; unfortunately, Luther did not recognize that the ministry of the Word in preaching can equally become a tool of clerical "tyranny," and thus that the problem lay less in the sacramental system than it did in (some of) those who worked within its constraints. The more serious problem is the fact that the restriction of the means of grace exclusively to the appointed sacramental channels of the church proves to be easily manipulated. In short, power corrupts, and power deemed to be salvific is no exception to the rule.

The sacramental theology of the first Christian millennium fares better, for it was a time when the number of the sacraments was not fixed: though certain sacraments instituted by Christ and with clear roots in ancient Christian tradition have priority, a more general openness to "signs" is also evident. While individual acts of charity such as those of my old neighbor obviously cannot, in principle, be technically numbered among the sacraments, the concept of the sacramental is still elastic enough to accommodate such acts — for instance, under the broad heading of "footwashing." Generally speaking, however, there is still in the sacramental theology of the first millennium a tendency to restrict the meaning of the word "sacrament" to a

30. Luther, *The Babylonian Captivity,* p. 112.

range of specific church "rites" rather than to Christian practice in general. Sacramental actions usually take place within the sacred space of the church, for example, at the great church of Paray-le-Monial, rather than in the world. To take a concrete example, it is this tendency that eventually leads to the marriage ceremony being drawn explicitly into the rites of the church, so that the sacramental character of the institution came to be secured by the priest acting on behalf of, or along with, the couple, rather than by the couple as such in their sexual union.[31]

An adaptation of the idea of the "one single sacrament" can help us transcend some of these limitations in the tradition of sacramental theology. As we have seen, Barth wishes to speak of Christ himself as the sacrament; the Roman tradition, represented by Rahner and others, speaks of the church as the original, or "primal," sacrament of the presence of Christ, out of the heart of which the differentiated sacraments of the Christian religion arise. I would like to suggest that we conceive of the primal sacrament somewhat more generically, in a way that can initially be expressed as "those realities in which Christ continues to be present for the sake of the salvation of the world," thus drawing together the "one single sacrament" of Barth's Christological and Rahner's ecclesiological concerns, but also potentially broadening the scope particularly of the latter to include actions or events that lie beyond the church's control. Some of these have a privileged position: most obviously, though by no means exclusively, the "ordinances" of baptism and Eucharist mandated by Jesus himself. In fact, though, the number of those things to which the Word is added in such a way that they become extensions of the one sacrament is surely limited only by the freedom in which Christ continues to make such things into signs and instruments of grace. As Barth once put it, briefly but memorably, "God may speak to us through Russian communism, through a flute concerto, through a blossoming shrub or through a dead dog. We shall do well to listen to him if he really does so."[32]

On such terms, my old friend Jim Dale was to me a sacrament of faithfulness and of holiness: not merely a sign or a witness, but also by the power of God an instrument by which the grace of God became real and was received. Equally, the friend who visits at a time of bereavement can become, by the power of God, a sign and instrument of grace, and of grace that is objectively offered and received in faith. In the same vein, the Scottish theolo-

31. Joseph Martos, *Doors to the Sacred* (New York: Doubleday, 1981), pp. 399-452.
32. Barth, *Church Dogmatics*, I/1, p. 60.

gian John Baillie comments on the story of a simple Chinese woman carrying a baby in prewar Manchuria who became a Christian because a missionary gave up his seat to her on a bus.[33] For the missionary, no doubt, the gesture amounted to an ordinary act of courtesy, and perhaps a small act of witness; for her, being poor, Chinese, and female, it was revelation and a means of grace. It is nonsense to suggest that these things are not of central importance to the life of faith, and it is no argument to suggest that these are purely natural or moral events that, as such, can have no sacramental significance. For what are eating and drinking, or what is washing, if not natural events that are seized hold of in the sacraments of the Eucharist and baptism and made into something more than what by nature they are? For, in the end, is this not always how God acts in the world?

Throughout this discussion I have been inspired by Henri Crouzel's exposition of Origen's theology of the sacraments. Crouzel speaks of Origen's "acute sense of the essential dimension of the Church here below, which we call sacramentalism: the divine realities are already given to us, but in realities which are themselves perceptible, under the veil of an image." He continues:

> A more circumscribed notion of the sacrament was only to emerge in the High Middle Ages. One might say that for Origen the fundamental sacrament is the Christ, a man in whom "resides bodily the fullness of the Deity," and after him there are two other "sacraments," not quite so fundamental, the Church, a human society which is the body of Christ, and the Scripture, a human book which expresses the Word of God.[34]

To say this, however, is to use a language that "is not yet Origen's," for Origen has no theory of the sacraments, nor does he differentiate between a "fundamental" sacrament and others that are "not quite so fundamental." All this is exposition.

What this shows us is that it is possible to have a rich and subtle understanding of the relationship between sacramental sign and reality on the basis of a theology in which the sacraments have not yet been formalized. In many ways, in fact, the formalization of sacramental doctrine can act as an

33. John Baillie, "Truth and Love," in Baillie, *A Reasoned Faith* (London: Oxford University Press, 1963), p. 57.

34. Henri Crouzel, *Origen,* trans. A. S. Worrall (Edinburgh: T&T Clark, 1989), pp. 220-21.

impediment to understanding, not only in the sense that overdefinition has proven to close down alternative (and fruitful) perspectives on the nature and meaning of the sacraments, but also in the sense that they have proven to be an impediment to the unity of the church that those signs are intended to serve — which is a sure sign that they have been misunderstood, or rather *mistreated,* in far too many dogmatic definitions.

What is needed in face of this is an effort to get behind the problem of sacramental theology to its real possibility, to the core movements of grace that are at stake within it, on the assumption that theological renewal — and thus ecclesiological renewal as well — comes through a return to the "source," as well as to the great theological sources, that give it expression. For it is Christ who is active in his sacramental signs. Yet, astonishingly, to say this great thing is still to say only part of what needs to be said. Thus far, the focus has been on the action of God in human acts, or upon the communication of grace through human action in the church and in human life. But there is another utterly basic structure in the church's sacramental existence that has still to be explored, and to which we must now turn.

The Church: Realized in Signs

A way into this final aspect of the problem is provided by Edward Schillebeeckx, who in *The Eucharist,* one of his early books, argues not only that the Eucharist is the gift in which the giver gives himself in his real presence, but also one in which the church itself is realized as the body of Christ.[35] In a creative and daring theological move, Schillebeeckx speaks of a "real presence" of the church, as well as of Christ, that comes about in the eucharistic meal, citing what Augustine said: "'[W]e ourselves lie on the paten,'" together with "the whole patristic and scholastic tradition [that] was able to call the Eucharist the 'sacrament of the unity of the Church with Christ'" (p. 140). Thus the full sense of "the eucharistic body of Christ" is found in a "reciprocal real presence" of Christ to his church, first of all, and of the church to Christ in consequence. This is because the church, Schillebeeckx argues, comes into existence in this event, as it grasps by faith the self-offering of Christ to the world that it receives. Therefore, the sacra-

---

35. Edward Schillebeeckx, *The Eucharist,* trans. N. D. Smith (London: Sheed and Ward, 1968), pp. 137-44.

mental reality of the Eucharist cannot be conceived as separate from the community of the church, any more than it can be conceived as separate from the risen and glorified Lord (pp. 141-42).

We have already seen how this idea has been taken up and developed in the context of contemporary eucharistic ecclesiology, according to which the church is minimally conceived as a eucharistic community, or more maximally, according to some accounts, as identical with the eucharistic event. According to Joseph Ratzinger (now Pope Benedict XVI), for instance, it is possible to state flatly: "The Church is the celebration of the Eucharist; the Eucharist is the Church. . . ."[36] In my discussion of this idea in chapter 3 above, my argument was that eucharistic ecclesiology conceives the church too narrowly, for even though in a certain sense everything that the church believes and does is present in the eucharistic celebration, it is also true that everything the church believes and does can be present in service, mission, and proclamation. A further problem can now be identified in eucharistic ecclesiology. We have seen that the foundations of the doctrine of the church need to be developed using a balanced Trinitarian approach that does justice not only to the theme of the church as the body of Christ, which is certainly in view in eucharistic ecclesiology, but also to the themes of the people of God and the indwelling of the Holy Spirit, which are not in view here. The idea that the totality of ecclesiology can be adequately compressed into the dynamic of the Eucharist is thus unacceptable — no matter how venerable its source.

However, this is not to say that the idea contains no profound or fruitful insight. For example, one of the themes that needs to be rediscovered in Protestant ecclesiology is the sense in which it is not only possible, but absolutely necessary, to say that the church makes an offering of itself — in and with Christ — to God. Unfortunately, this idea, which is basic to the theme of the holiness of the church, does not mesh well with Protestant eucharistic theology. Therefore, to the extent that ecclesiology and the theology of the Eucharist belong together, Protestant theology finds itself impoverished in having no sacramental expression of its self-offering in and with Christ to God. It is perhaps for this reason that other signs of this oblation have emerged: the "altar call" of North American Protestant evangelicalism, for example, comes to mind, as does the aura of sanctity surrounding Protestant ministers in the eyes of the people of the church, which has developed de-

36. Ratzinger, *Principles of Catholic Theology: Building Stones for a Fundamental Theology,* trans. Mary F. McCarthy (San Francisco: Ignatius Press, 1987), p. 53.

spite the fact that there is said to be no difference between the clerical and lay "estates" in strict Protestant theory. The sheer infrequency of the celebration of the Lord's Supper in most Protestant churches might also be explained by this fact, along with the reluctance of the church as a whole to share in it. In other words, the notable unwillingness of some good Protestants to receive the bread and the wine might on this account be a kind of sacrificial oblation: "I am not worthy to come under your roof, but only say the word. . . ."

The tragedy of all this is that the sign of the church's oblation in and with Christ is already implicitly expressed in the eucharistic mystery, where it might be explored more fully. Protestant theology tends to resist all such conceptuality in its interpretation of the Eucharist. In hostile reaction to the excesses of late medieval piety, the Reformation's position was that the church has nothing to offer by way of sacrifice for sin, and thus no offering to make in its eucharistic celebration. Holy Communion thus came to be seen as a meal only — "the Lord's Supper." The Eucharist is thus a unidirectional event in the sense that the church is purely on the receiving end of the gracious promise offered to it by God in Christ, who in a mysterious manner feeds the church spiritually and renews it by the gift of his body and blood. However, it is perfectly possible for the church to understand the Eucharist as the event in which it offers itself to God, without in any way derogating the uniqueness of Christ's self-offering. After all, the "whole Christ" does include his body, the church: the church (or is it all humanity?) is said to have "died with Christ" (Rom. 6:8). On the strength of such scriptural warrant, Protestantism can hardly resist the implication that its very being as the body of Christ is bound up with *everything* the Eucharist signifies. Protestant persistence in ignoring this is not only distinctly odd, but also theologically perverse. It is one thing to resist an error; it is quite another to fail to see a legitimate point.

An interesting illustration of this failure can be seen in the Methodist tradition, and in the history of its later "reception" of one of the leading themes in the theology of its early leaders. Both John and Charles Wesley were keenly interested in fostering a renewal in Anglican sacramental theology and practice, and they turned to, among other things, the patristic tradition and the theology of the Caroline divines in order to try to deepen their understanding. We can find one of the more remarkable expressions of this in the hymns of Charles Wesley.[37] In his *Hymns on the Lord's Supper* of 1745,

---

37. Cf. J. E. Rattenbury, *The Eucharistic Hymns of John and Charles Wesley* (London: Epworth Press, 1948).

Wesley speaks openly of the way in which the church, in the event of Holy Communion, presents before the Father the one sacrifice made by Christ.

> With solemn faith we offer up,
>   And spread before thy glorious eyes
> That only ground of all our hope
>   That previous bleeding Sacrifice. . . .
>
> Father, behold thy dying Son,
>   And hear his blood that speaks above;
> On us let all thy grace be shown,
>   Peace, righteousness, and joy, and love;
> Thy kingdom come to every heart,
> And all thou hast, and all thou art.[38]

This theme, appearing in the heart of Wesley's eucharistic piety and intended for the renewal of mainstream Anglican devotion, represents a theology that is not entirely alien to the understanding of the eucharistic sacrifice developed in the context of the Counter Reformation. This was developed in answer to Protestant critique of the "repetition" of the sacrifice of Christ in the Mass, and came to formal expression at the Council of Trent:

> Hence the holy council teaches that this is a truly propitiatory sacrifice, and brings it about that if we approach God with sincere hearts and upright faith, and with awe and reverence, *we receive mercy and find grace to help in time of need.* . . . For it is one and the same victim here offering himself by the ministry of his priests, who then offered himself on the cross; it is only the manner of the offering that is different.[39]

Undoubtedly, the key differences lie in the language of propitiation, and also in the sense one finds in the hymns of Charles Wesley that *each believer* "offers up" the "precious bleeding Sacrifice" by faith, rather than the sacerdotal priesthood offering it on behalf of the rest. But there is no repetition of the sacrifice when we make such an offering; rather, there is a participation in the one sacrifice made by Christ, who offers himself in the here and now in

---

38. Frank Whaling, ed., *John and Charles Wesley* (New York: Paulist Press, 1981), p. 266.

39. Council of Trent, Session 22, 17 September 1562, ch. 2, in Tanner, *Decrees*, 1: 733.

the prayer of the church in the eucharistic mystery. There are, then, clear and important differences — chiefly, there is no caste of priestly mediators — but also there are clear affinities, so much so that it is perfectly conceivable that even a conservative Tridentine Catholic could sing much of the eucharistic hymnody of Charles Wesley without difficulty. It is no doubt for this reason that neither the Anglicanism of the time nor the movements found in the various forms of Methodism that developed after the Wesleys' deaths were able to live with the eucharistic theology of the Wesleys, and that as a result it was effectively lost to memory. The outcome has been that very few Christians have ever sung these hymns.

Interestingly, the radical thrust of Charles Wesley's eucharistic hymnody did not end there, for the church also shares in Christ's oblation, singing in the context of the memorial of his death:

> Jesu, we follow Thee,
> In all thy footsteps tread,
> And pant for full conformity
> To our exalted Head;
>
> We would, we would partake
> Thy every state below,
> And suffer all things for thy sake,
> And to thy glory do.
>
> We in thy birth are born,
> Sustain thy grief and loss,
> Share in thy want, and shame, and scorn,
> And die upon thy cross.
>
> Baptized into thy death
> We sink into thy grave,
> Till thou the quickening Spirit breathe,
> And to the utmost save.

(pp. 267-68)

Among the several things these stanzas show is that the totality of Christian commitment in Wesleyan theology in its original formulation is not merely moralistic, but basically Christological, soteriological, and pneumatological.

As such it must also be eucharistic, for it is in the eucharistic celebration that the church sacramentalizes the unity between itself as the ecclesial body of Christ and the body of Christ that was surrendered on the cross. Grasping the church's commitment in eucharistic terms, as Charles Wesley did, by way of the central dynamic of faith by which we "partake" of Christ's "every state" and are in this sense and for this reason "baptized into [his] death," sheds much light on the theological basis of the Wesleyan theology of "Christian perfection." Rather than a "second work of grace," which is what Christian perfection became in the oddly scholastic adaptations of the Wesleys' theology that emerged after their deaths, Christian perfection is a dynamic entering into the one saving event that took place in Jesus' death and resurrection. It could never be anything more.

What these hymns also show is that the idea of a eucharistic piety and a eucharistic ecclesiology is not entirely foreign to at least one strand of Protestantism. Clearly, the idea of the participation of the church as the body of Christ in Christ's sacrificial surrender is also not unknown in Protestantism considered as a whole. The failure to grasp the fruitfulness of this idea more widely has been damaging to Protestant theology and has tended to impoverish the fabric of its ecclesiastical life.

Charism and Institution

The idea that the church realizes in signs the substance of its own hidden mystery applies also to the pneumatological aspects of its existence. In short, the fact that the church is the temple of the Spirit requires expression in "sacramental" form. Indeed, in the strict sense, unless sufficient "charismatic" space is made for this expression, the fire of the Spirit is quenched in the church and its status as the dwelling place of the living God remains only an implicit possibility rather than something actual. After all, the Spirit of God is not the church's "possession"; rather, it is something to which the church is subject as it prays for the Spirit as Lord and life-giver to come. It is not that the church fully expresses the presence of the Spirit within it in any single form of its life; the freedom of the Spirit, which blows where it wills, is not compatible with any such notion. Nevertheless, the church in its visible structures can be a sign of what it is in its invisible foundations, precisely in those aspects of its life that are most clearly pneumatological — and that are for this very reason least under institutional control.

The constant struggle of the church in the history of the relationship between the sometimes wild freedom of the charisms and the church as a structured organization has repeatedly been to learn how to "contain" the new wine of the Spirit in the wineskin of the institution (Mark 2:22), or, in more common language, to find how to adapt to new situations in order to allow some sign of spiritual renewal to take root and grow. Forms of spirituality and ecclesial "styles" constantly arise and flourish, and the church finds them helpful for a while, only to find that after a time that they again prove stifling. For example, this is the situation in Protestant liberalism at this moment in history, just as it was in the Tridentine Catholicism of the first half of the twentieth century: each one began as a renewal movement, and both ended up as signs of death.

There are thus varied spiritual gifts that appear in the church: the phenomenon of the great mystics, the theologians with their deep and difficult works, the innumerable Christian quests for justice, and the many renewal movements that punctuate the history of Christianity. What does the church, in those *visible* structures that are somehow under its control, say about the *invisible* presence and working of the Holy Spirit within it, which is by no means controllable, in how it deals with the sometimes disturbing freedom of such things? All too often it has sought to suffocate the voices that have emerged from these movements of the Spirit, and in doing so it has "quenched" the light of the Spirit. What about the idea of the "priesthood of all believers," according to which all the members of the church have equal access to God, and according to some versions, all members have responsibility for ministry, according to their various gifts? How does the church reflect the common responsibilities and privileges of each of its members in its institutional structures of leadership and service, in which inevitably, as in any "visible" human society, not all are equal, and not all have the same privileges?

The basic datum of faith, according to which the church has become the dwelling place of God by virtue of the Pentecostal gift of the Holy Spirit, requires some kind of expression or realization in the actions and institutions of the church, and where that proves impossible, in the *reform* of those actions and institutions. *Ecclesia semper reformanda,* the old adage cited by every movement that is new in the church, should really be a permanent fixture in all ecclesiastical life. If it is not, if the church becomes so dominated by a powerful bureaucracy that all other lights and ministries are extinguished, or so dominated by a rigid and authoritarian dogmatism in which all difficulties are so neatly tidied away that all newness in the Spirit becomes unthinkable, then the wild and free fire of the Spirit has been put out. We must never allow ourselves to forget that such self-satisfaction is always possible in ecclesiology, and in ecclesiology of all kinds, from the most "conservative" to the most "liberal," and that, as such, it has proven throughout Christian history to be among the most deadening and dangerous features of our religion. When this happens, the visible "sign" that the church has become signifies nothing more than the quenching of the Spirit rather than the light of its fire burning bright.

The truth is that the freedom of the Spirit is never capable of being fully expressed in the church. It is never something that can be described as a static possession of the church; it is always a "happening," or an "event" (in Barthian language), when the Spirit "gleams over the face of the church" *(Lumen Gentium)*. But it can happen thus. Though the Spirit will always be "new wine," and the church's structures will always be — or at least will always be on their way to becoming — "old wineskins," there are moments of transparency when it becomes possible to discern in the life of the church that the Holy Spirit is its animating principle, so that the visible church appears in some measure as a "sign" of the underlying reality of the Spirit's power that is the source of its true life.

For all the apparent troubles of the church in the world, the Spirit, the source of the church's life, can be discerned in a multitude of ways in its life. It appears clearly in the Roman Catholic awareness of the new possibilities for the church that were unleashed when a new leader, a "caretaker," Pope John XXIII, announced a plan early in 1959 to convene the Second Vatican Council, and when the pope himself signaled that there was more to be said by the church than had already been said. In some ways, this "sign" of openness to the world and to reform is more important to Catholics than the documents that came out of Vatican II. It appears in the dynamics of modern ecumenism, which, for all its failure to achieve much by way of reform of the "old wineskins" that divide, still in a manner of speaking constitutes of itself a new ecclesial reality in which the Spirit who makes us one shines forth for all to see. It even appears amid what so often amounts to the drudgery of local church life, in its administrative minutiae and ministerial business, when suddenly a person or a family is touched by God because of it all and through it all. It is surely for the sake of these things that people persist with the church. For, despite all its banality and its faults, from time to time "something happens," and the glory of God is seen in its life. It is surely not because they revel, chapter and verse, in the documents of Vatican II on the magisterium, or because of the tremendous changes in their own church brought about by modern ecumenism, or because the pastoral round is always so enthralling.

The openness of the church at all levels is immensely important, for in it is found a kind of "sacrament" of the church's openness to the Spirit that dwells in it. This is what is signified when the church shows a willingness to hear every voice in the hope of hearing in it the Word of God, for with this willingness is found a readiness to throw open windows that might otherwise be barred, in order to let the wind of the Spirit sweep through. Somehow this openness needs to be reflected in the way the church is structured, and in an awareness that these are always provisional, and always for the sake of something else, something more. As in the "sacramental" theology of Origen, the visible must attest the presence of what is invisible. Rigid and authoritarian structures are a sure "sign" that the winds of the Spirit are assumed to be firmly leashed and under the church's control, whereas open structures are a "sign" of the opposite, that the Spirit is not the servant but the Lord of the church's life. The people of the church (and of the world) read these "signs" rather more readily than many of the church's institutional leaders seem to assume.

This discussion of the sacramental dimension of the doctrine of the church began with the Romanesque church at Paray-le-Monial, and with a recollection of the generalizing sacramental theology that was operative during the first Christian millennium, within the terms of which that church was built. It can end with some observations by the Reformed theologian Alasdair Heron, who noted twenty years ago not only that each individual Christian life, as a "channel of the everlasting mercy," is "essentially sacramental in its core," but also that the sole basis on which it is possible to speak of this sacramentality or any other is that Jesus Christ is the sacrament of union between God and humanity, "of the coming of God to man, and the raising of man to God."[40] In the secondary sacramentality of the church, this original sacramentality is reflected, confessed, and realized in our acknowledgment of the ways in which God comes to us, and of the disarming power and wisdom of the cross of Jesus Christ, by which and by whom we are reconciled to God.

---

40. Alasdair I. C. Heron, *Table and Tradition* (Edinburgh: Hansel Press, 1983), p. 158.

CHAPTER 8

Theology and the Renewal of the Church

Believing in the Church

Reinhard Hütter has argued in a recent study that the church in the cultural context of modernity faces a distinct and massive problem.[1] In the classical Christian tradition, the church was acknowledged as the setting in which it is uniquely possible to come to know God as the one who draws us into relationship with himself through the crucified Christ and the gift of the Holy Spirit. By contrast, the historical path taken by the church in modernity has emptied it of this foundational theological confidence. We find ourselves in a situation so fundamentally shaped by modernity and its doctrine of the free individual that the individual subject now stands even at the center of what passes for ecclesiology. Instead of the church appearing as the context in which we are shaped by the Word and Spirit of God, the church is here reduced to rendering functional service to the modern doctrine of the individual. Under the conditions of modernity, Hütter maintains, the individual has become the "end of the church" ("The Church," p. 25).

While the church's service to modernity in this respect might have made it culturally "relevant" in a certain narrow sense, when viewed from the standpoint of the doctrine of the church as a strictly theological theme, the

---

1. Reinhard Hütter, *Suffering Divine Things*, trans. Doug Stott (Grand Rapids: Eerdmans, 2000). The rather complex argument of this volume is also summarized in Hütter, "The Church," in James J. Buckley and David S. Yeago, eds., *Knowing the Triune God* (Grand Rapids: Eerdmans, 2001), pp. 23-47.

result is clearly problematic. The problem can be seen in several sectors of church life: on the one hand, in "the service-jargon pervasive in contemporary church growth talk," in which the market reigns supreme and the gospel must do it homage, or on the other, in something even worse — though it is, to be sure, a function of the same pressures — "the kind of free metaphorical constructivism characterizing especially North American Protestant theology in its more progressive representatives" (*Suffering*, p. 23).

Hütter maintains that what is missing from such approaches is any clear commitment to the church as locus of the distinct practices of the proclamation of the Word of the gospel of grace and the celebration of the sacraments, by which alone the triune God of the Christian revelation can be known, obeyed, and enjoyed. In Hütter's judgment, the importance of these practices has been generally belittled under the influence of modernity, as the religious experience of the individual has instead been refashioned and mediated by other means. The consequence is the pervasive spiritual and theological impoverishment of the church, which lives by Word and sacrament or not at all.

Hütter's treatment of the problem of ecclesiology has a number of important corollaries. The most memorable of these is that the church, to be set on a proper foundation in our time, needs to be reconceived as thoroughly "pathetic" rather than "poietic" in character. Speaking of the church as pathetic in this context means that it "suffers" the justifying and sanctifying work of God, being brought into existence by an action of God that lies entirely beyond its own control. Unfortunately, under the pressures of modernity, the church has both implicitly and explicitly tended to treat itself as a free poietic (creative, formative) construction of those religious individuals who comprise its membership, so that its structures, teachings, and practices come to be shaped by their demands. For Hütter, this distinction lies at the root of the contemporary ecclesiological problem: rightly conceived, the whole of the church's life, and even the whole enterprise of theological reflection, is fundamentally a *pathos* by which we "suffer" God's work in the world. Only in this way do we come to participate in the knowledge of the Father, who through the Son and the Spirit invites us into fellowship, and who by the divine initiative alone establishes that fellowship with us.

Drawing on the political ideas of Hannah Arendt, Hütter develops a further leading thesis. The church, he maintains, is nothing less than "the Spirit's public" (*Suffering*, pp. 39-41). In the sense intended, any "public" is defined by a set of normative convictions that are embodied in distinctive practices and directed toward a unique *telos*. In the case of the church, doctrine (in the sense of scriptural, creedal, and confessional teaching, or *doctrina definita*) and the core practices of proclamation and the sacraments constitute the church as a distinct public with the singular *telos* of knowing the triune God.[2] Such knowledge, and the conditions of its possibility, does not lie at our disposal or under our control; it is neither of our making, nor does it strictly belong to us. Instead, it is the work of the triune God. In Hütter's analysis, this has an additional notable implication: the whole enterprise of Christian theology itself has coherence only when it is clearly bound to those norms, which are rooted in the work of God in the church and constitute it as that distinct public. Any theology that might attempt either to justify or to criticize the teaching and practices of the church on grounds *external* to the normative convictions and core practices that make the church this public reveals itself to be a function of some *other* public, constituted as such by completely other normative convictions and practices.

In one sense, Hütter's argument is highly abstract; but we can acknowledge that there are many concrete examples of attempts to negotiate the practices of the church on grounds that are ultimately alien to Christian faith, some of which we have encountered along the way in this study. But we should also acknowledge that Hütter's argument is itself somewhat problematic. The most obvious, and in some ways the most important, of the questions that can be raised about it is the fact that it can scarcely be said that there has been no proclamation of the Word or celebration of the sacraments in the church in the modern world. Hütter's difficulty is presumably that the very meaning of the Word and sacrament has been compromised by being harnessed to serve a certain set of alien purposes, namely, the doctrine and demands of the modern individual rather than the summons to communion with the triune God of grace. However, a further problem is that the tendency to retreat into the particular discourse and practice that constitutes the church as a public seems oddly jarring when set over against the claim that those norms and practices that define it as such are none other than the work of God. Is the work of God ever purely "particular" in the strict sense, or could it ever be acknowledged as such in faith? Hütter's argument is

---

2. Less convincingly, Hütter maintains that the church, defined in this way, is not to be understood as a member of a genus such as "polis" or "civil society," but is instead to be set alongside such concepts as an alternate "public." The problem with this thesis is that the idea of a "public" as Hütter's theology defines it is also a genus (*Suffering*, p. 42).

hardly peculiar to him on that point; a succession of recent "postmodern" theologies have taken the same stance. However, all such "particularism," to give it a generic name, sits uneasily with the requirements of Hütter's own talk of the triune God, the revelation of whom and engagement with whom in the life of the church must surely, by definition, involve some intrinsic relationship to the absolutely universal. Thus, if universal claims are not inherently involved, then at least claims *concerning* the universal are.

From this point of view, the other distinctly odd feature of Hütter's analysis lies in the fact that, for all his talk of the distinctiveness of the norms and convictions of the church as a separate public, there is still in Hütter's theology a residual desire to find an Archimedean point from which to move the theological world, or a place to stand that does not collapse under stress. Writing as a Lutheran theologian, but educated in the post-Enlightenment traditions of European theological education, Hütter is unable to find this immovable point in the biblical canon any longer. Earlier generations of Lutheran theologians might have done so, but as a result of modern biblical exegesis, now "everything moves" in our treatment of the biblical text, because nothing in Scripture is impervious to the withering theological effects of the historical-critical method. For Hütter, it would seem, after modernity it is no longer possible simply to point to the biblical canon as the ultimate source of theological authority. Hütter is also critical of the Barthian alternative to traditional Protestant biblicism because, in his estimation, the theology of Karl Barth is "pneumatologically unstable" (*Suffering*, p. 45). Hütter means by this that Barth's constant tendency to require the reformulation and reappropriation of the content of Christian faith represents a denial of the "public" character of the church's convictions. These become, under the Barthian model, too much subject to the inventive wisdom of the theologian, and too little a function of the will and work of the triune God as encountered in what we suffer by participation in the sheer dynamics of ordinary ecclesiastical existence under Word and sacrament.

A Barthian riposte might well be that Hütter's theology makes the work of the Spirit in the church too much a matter of ecclesiastical convention and too little a function of precisely the freedom of the triune God with whom we have to do. Hütter's desire for a place to stand that does not yield under pressure may well have led to his own conversion to Roman Catholicism shortly after he wrote the works I have been referring to here. One can certainly say that, in a certain kind of Roman Catholic commitment, it is possible to find security in *doctrina definita*, which is set forth as the normative conviction defining the church as a distinct public. The trouble with such security is that the Roman Catholic tendency is to be rather too definite in matters of *doctrina* than the subject actually warrants, and to assume that the truth of the gospel and the channels of sacramental grace are rather too narrowly under the church's control. One might say that it is not only the *church* that suffers the work of the triune God under these conditions, but the converse: where such assumptions are found, the implication would seem to be that the *triune God* "suffers" the work of the church. Against this, the Barthian insistence that God is always "something more," implying that the teaching of the church is always and inherently something unfinished, stands as a helpful corrective. Whatever the limitations of Barth's approach, at least it serves as an antidote to the worst excesses of ecclesiological over-confidence.

Nevertheless, in broad terms, the argument that I am making in this book is comparable to Hütter's. For example, he certainly maintains that what is needed is for the church to engage in an act of remembrance with respect to its tradition, or, more specifically, in a theological rediscovery of the promises of God by which it lives (*Suffering*, pp. 176ff.; "The Church," passim). Similarly, my argument has been that a major ecclesiological *resourcement* is presently needed, a return to those roots and sources from which the church derives its life. There is nothing surprising about our having this need, since these sources and roots need to be rediscovered and reappropriated in every age, so much so that a great deal of the work of theological thought is precisely this: to think what has been thought before, to own it afresh, to see it anew, and, as necessary, to give it some new direction. Yet modernity's assumption that it is somehow beyond history, and that the tradition is something that can be looked on as a dark era that is best overcome and forgotten, makes this an extremely difficult task for large numbers of Western Christians. However, the problem for ecclesiology is that, without such a wider vision, there can be no adequate doctrine of the church and, for that matter, no genuine or distinctive *ecclesial* practice. Where the meaning of the biblical witness is severed from the theological tradition; where the communion of saints, which involves responsibility to previous generations who have handed on the faith, as well as to those who will follow, has become a matter of indifference; and where the hugely questionable particularities of contemporary liberal society, which is economically and militarily the most powerful culture that has ever existed, have been made the measure of the gospel of Christ, to the extent that it threatens the *oikoumenê* of the global church — where these things take place, we can hardly doubt that adequate ecclesiological principle is wanting.

A Test Case: Homosexuality

We can take this matter further and move toward a constructive — though perhaps painful — conclusion by making the argument much more concrete. We could pursue the same end in a number of ways, but for our purposes I will focus on an event that occurred in 2003, when controversy erupted in the worldwide Anglican Communion. The controversy was occasioned by the decision of Michael Ingham, bishop of the Canadian Anglican Diocese of New Westminster, to authorize a marriage-like rite of blessing for homosexual couples. This action (which had its parallels in other, mainly North American, ecclesiastical jurisdictions and traditions) took place against a backdrop of several related events: first, the overwhelming vote of the 1998 Lambeth Conference of the Anglican Communion *against* legitimating or blessing same-sex unions (Lambeth 1998, Resolution 1.10); second, the contrary *endorsement* of such a rite of blessing by successive diocesan synods in New Westminster in 1998, 2001, and 2002; third, the divisions within the diocese itself that were reflected in the existence of a protest group, "the Anglican Communion of New Westminster," consisting of several parishes that resolutely opposed the synodical decision and the rite in question, and who would go on to seek alternative episcopal oversight; and, finally, the attention of the media, who seized on the controversy as if it were effectively the only thing in religion worthy of newsprint and airtime.

In a pastoral letter of May 23, 2003, issued along with the rite of blessing in question, Ingham emphasized the needs of the couples concerned, writing that such persons have "full and equal claim, with all other persons, upon the love, acceptance, concern and pastoral care of the church."[3] Such an entirely uncontroversial insistence did not in itself, of course, render the decision any less divisive. Though the Canadian Anglican bishops as a group presented a united front on the question (which might equally be construed as fence-sitting), they were obviously deeply split on the matter, as were the

---

3. Anglican Communion News Service, "Rite of Blessing authorized in Diocese of New Westminster," 29 May 2003. ACNS 3453: http://www.anglicancommunion.org/acns/articles/34/50/acns3453.html (accessed 25 September 2007).

major ecclesiastical representatives of the Anglican Communion worldwide. On May 29, 2003, the Archbishop of Canterbury, Rowan Williams, judged the matter sensitive enough to warrant public comment. At the time, Williams mainly repeated the longstanding objection of the great majority of Anglican bishops worldwide to any such rite:

> [T]he public liturgy of the Church expresses the mind of the Church on doctrinal matters and there is nothing approaching a consensus in support of same-sex unions.
>
> In taking this action and ignoring the considerable reservations of the Church, repeatedly expressed and most recently by the Primates, the diocese [of New Westminster] has gone significantly further than the teaching of the Church or pastoral concern can justify and I very much regret the inevitable tension and division that will result from this development.[4]

The question whether a given theology can or cannot be adequately "liturgized," to coin a term, is an interesting one. Williams's point was that it is one thing to hold a controversial theological view, but quite another to assume that such a view can be made normative in the worship of God. The problem was not only that the decision was taken against the objections of the great majority of Christians globally, and specifically against the express hostility of the responsible organs of international Anglicanism, which had met synodically and rejected precisely the policy in question. The deeper difficulty was that, within the Anglican tradition, the historic role of the Prayer Book makes the *liturgical* unity of the church, rather than its *confessional* unity, a matter of first importance — indeed, on most accounts, a defining issue. Thus Williams's criticism, though seemingly a modest one, strikes at the heart of an extremely important theological concern.

Most interesting of all was a response issued shortly after Williams's statement that came out of the largest of the Anglican provinces in Africa. On June 2, 2003, Peter Akinola, the primate of the Church of Nigeria, formally severed communion with Bishop Ingham and the Diocese of New Westminster. Akinola did his cause no great service by referring to New Westminster's policy in rather immoderate terms; but he also returned in

---

4. Anglican Communion News Service, "Archbishop of Canterbury expresses sadness at New Westminster decision," 29 May 2003. ACNS 3454: http://www.anglicancommunion .org/acns/articles/34/50/acns3454.html (accessed 25 September 2007).

that statement to a more measured and important text that he had issued a year earlier at a meeting of the Anglican Consultative Council in Hong Kong, in which he anticipated a future synodical decision in New Westminster. The statement is worth quoting at length:

> While I appreciate that the New Westminster diocese and the Church of Canada may not be, in numerical terms, especially large ecclesial bodies [there are approximately 800,000 active Canadian Anglicans in total, versus around 17,000,000 Nigerian Anglicans], we value them as dearly as we value all our partner Provinces. We have a growing fear for the sense of loss which any sustained departure by them from our common path and mind must risk. We urge and pray that reflection will lead to reconsideration. It is hard indeed to see any action, which threatens our Communion to be justified as a "local mission priority."
>
> But there is also a further context of which I must speak, painful though it is. Many of us from the two-thirds world feel that the global north still seeks to retain its disproportionate power and influence in our Church just as in the world. It is significant that those dioceses most tempted to indulge themselves with unilateral actions, taken without consulting the wider Communion, seem so often to be among those materially most advantaged and to be in the global north. Should this not occasion reflection? Do we not see here, in the ready assertion of superior wisdom, a *new imperialism?*[5]

This is a fascinating comment, illustrating not only the changing political and theological character of global Christianity, but also something of the depth of the problem at stake in this particular impasse, which focuses the issue on something far more than the inclusion of homosexuals in the Christian community in the Vancouver area. Instead, the issue it raises more broadly concerns the relationship of what might be called the theology of inclusion to modern liberal political and social thought, on the one hand, and the pride and self-sufficiency of North American "mainline" Protestantism, on the other, including its evident inability to grasp that certain of the dominant cultural assumptions of a modern Western liberal democracy are neither normative for all humans nor especially Christian.

---

5. Anglican Communion News Service, "Church of Nigeria cuts ties with the Diocese of New Westminster," 2 June 2003. ACNS 3455: http://www.anglicancommunion.org/acns/articles/34/50/acns3455.html [italics added] (accessed 25 September 2007).

It is widely recognized that a major thorn in the side of Christianity globally stems from the fact that Christians in earlier generations acted as though the European experience were simply identical with Christian experience. Therefore, it is said that to become a Christian in Asia, the Americas, or Africa from the sixteenth through the nineteenth centuries typically meant to adopt, so far as possible, a "white" outlook. This association between Christian missionary expansion and the values of imperialism has marred the reputation of the modern missionary movement and of the churches that sponsored it among many hundreds of millions of people in the old heartlands of Christianity, where the peoples of European descent live. In fact, it constitutes an important part of the cultural case for the prosecution against the church in the present antireligious climate in these societies. But the truth is that it is not easy to escape these sins of our fathers and mothers. Akinola, for example, reminds us that cultural imperialism is a surprisingly subtle sin that can repeat itself in new and disarming forms. Andrew Ross, a historian of missions, has put the same point succinctly:

> Europeanism is still alive and well, flourishing in western intellectual circles which reject European political imperialism and Christianity yet still unquestioningly assume the experience of western European humanity to be definitive. . . .[6]

It is well known that this controversy (to which must be added, of course, the parallel event of the consecration to the episcopate of Gene Robinson, a gay man living in a long-term same-sex relationship, in the Episcopal Church of the U.S.A.) has generated great difficulties for Anglicanism globally. Among the more important products of the storm that followed was the publication of *The Windsor Report* in 2004, which was produced by a commission established by the Archbishop of Canterbury to examine the theological nature of ecclesiastical communion, and its implications for the present crisis.[7] Furthermore, many of the same tensions over homosexuality can be readily identified in other traditions (e.g., the Presbyterian Church, U.S.A.), so that, as in the case of Anglicanism, questions have arisen concerning how long individual churches can hold together under the strain.

6. Andrew Ross, *A Vision Betrayed* (Edinburgh: University of Edinburgh Press, 1994), p. xv.

7. The Lambeth Commission on Communion, *The Windsor Report* (London: The Anglican Communion Office, 2004).

What, then, does the argument I have been making in this book have to say to this difficult situation?

The first thing that our argument might contribute to the debate is to observe that the obsessive attention that some ecclesiastical circles pay to the question of human sexuality in general, and to homosexual behavior in particular, must be taken as a symptom of the central problem facing much contemporary ecclesiology. That is, the very self-understanding of the church itself, in the structures of its theology — or in what passes for theology in the church — has come to be shaped far more by the dictates of secular theory, particularly by its focus on the interests and tastes (or equally the "rights") of the individual, than it has been by the substance of the doctrine of the church. The result has been that the claims of the former, rather than those of the latter, tend to dominate discussion. The extent to which the ideals of modernity have been confused with those of the Christian faith is a subject I have referred to repeatedly in this volume.

In the present context, I might add that such confusion helps to explain the disturbing levels of incomprehension of the theological substance of a document like *The Windsor Report* that can be discerned among liberal Anglicans in North America, who have, on the whole, shown that they are exceptionally ill-equipped to deal with the doctrinal claims that it makes.[8] We might recall Dietrich Bonhoeffer's youthful critique of the ethos of Union Theological Seminary in the United States in the early 1930s (to which I referred in chapter 5 above) at this point. Bonhoeffer's frank criticism was that the importance of all genuinely theological claims tended to be set aside at Union Seminary for the sake of the secular goal of social cohesion, the American political ideal to which the mainline Protestant churches of the time did obeisance. Consequently, Bonhoeffer, who at the time was far from being any right-wing firebrand, found it next to impossible to engage in a serious theological conversation with his American peers; in point of fact, he

---

8. One might go so far as to claim that *The Windsor Report* develops a more robust ecclesiology for Anglicanism than has appeared since the time of Richard Hooker. For example, the *Report* begins by rooting the communion of the church in the communion that exists from all eternity in the divine Trinity. Because it argues that case in such unabashedly theological terms, many on the theological left in North American Anglicanism have labeled it as "fundamentalist," apparently for the simple reason that to take the distinctive language and conceptuality of Christian faith seriously enough to base an *ecclesiology* on it seems novel! This move is as alien to liberal ecclesiology as the attempt to base a politics on religion seems in the sphere of the modern state.

found a far more authentically theological atmosphere in the black churches of New York, where there was distinctly less reason to advocate the kind of civil religion that he discerned at the heart of the mainline. The global Anglican Communion experienced the same perplexity in encountering establishment North American Anglicanism at the Lambeth Conference of 2008.

For all that, however, we cannot deny that a constructive engagement with the needs and demands of gay and lesbian people, both within and beyond the church, is still necessary. What does my argument in this book have to say to them, and to the ongoing disputes within the church concerning their claims? This, too, must be discussed and decided on, even if its place is scarcely at the center of theological thought.

I propose to answer this question only briefly — by way of reference to two of the leading themes of this study. The first relates to what we might call the scope of the church, though in this instance it might as well be termed the scope of the body of Christ, or perhaps even the reach of the incarnation. The second is the question of the dialectic of Word and Spirit — and correlatively of truth and community — that we have encountered in earlier chapters. In order to make sense of some of what I will argue, I shall add to these questions a short excursus on the need to rediscover a certain strand of the distinctive thinking of the Christian theological tradition concerning human sexuality.

(a) The Scope of the Church

Among the several leading ecclesiological ideas I have explored in this study, one has special relevance to the problem of homosexuality in the church and to the disputes over it that rage at the present time. I featured it extensively in chapter 3, though the idea is so pervasive in Christian thought that it has occurred in a number of other contexts in my argument as well. It is the concept of the church as *the body of Christ*, which is developed ecclesiologically as well as Christologically in the New Testament itself, notably in 1 Corinthians 12. This idea is capable of serving as the basis of an entire ecclesiological vision, but I have cited two particular examples. For Emile Mersch, who drew extensively on patristic sources and especially on the Christology of Cyril of Alexandria, the Son of God, in being "made flesh," established a relationship between himself and *all* humanity, so that there is no human being and no human nature beyond his reach. For Mersch's contemporary Karl

Barth, the being of the church is similarly a predicate of Christ's being in the strict sense that it exists solely by divine election, and it is to be a witness of the covenant established in him between God and, not merely the church itself, but all humankind.

One assumes that it is obvious to all that the gay and lesbian individuals and groups who advocate a loosening of traditional Christian morality, or for its being made sufficiently flexible as to include them, are as much members of the human race as anyone else; thus they are, if Mersch and Barth are to be believed, beneficiaries with all humanity of the grace of God offered in Jesus Christ. Of course, the objection to the ecclesiological implications of the position this represents will also be clear: being a member of the church, it will be argued, requires more than that a person should be born and thus be a human being. It requires something more than the sheer fact of baptism, or at least it must do so on all but the most theologically irresponsible accounts of baptism. To be made one with Christ in a saving sense, and to be a member of his ecclesiastical body, requires faith and obedience, participation in the Spirit, and thus the very quality that faith, obedience, and the gift of the Spirit bring — that is, holiness. This is the very quality that the homosexual lifestyle is said to compromise — and, I should add, with massive biblical and theological foundation.

Much of the trouble that the debate over homosexuality in theological circles has occasioned, we need to recognize, concerns the denial of these last ideas rather than simply the "homophobia" of the more traditional church as such (though, to be sure, homophobia or something very like it can also exist). I wish to outline a rather unconventional case at this point, one that is likely to please neither a good many gay and lesbian Christian activists nor many of their more conservative opponents. I will argue that, while sexual holiness is indeed compromised by homosexual activity, this *in itself* is no sufficient reason for denying full membership in the church to gay and lesbian people.

My reasoning underlying this view is twofold. In the first place, the church as the "body of Christ" is such, neither by permanent human potentiality or possession, nor by virtue of its own sanctity. Rather, it comes about solely by virtue of its union with God in Jesus Christ, who makes us members of his own body in assuming human nature and thus making himself one with us, and by the union of faith, which takes place in the power of the Holy Spirit and makes us one with him. No human perfection can be thought to accrue to us by virtue of either of the two — at least not in this life. We are the body of Christ in the strict sense only in faith and hope, in the mystery by which we are, in all our sinfulness, incorporated into Christ and thus made righteous. There is, in the strictest possible sense, no difference between the homosexual "sinner" in this respect and any other.

In other words, it is most important for us to say that our place in the church stands on the basis of the forgiveness of sins rather than on the basis of a social liberalism that knows only the value of the individual. As we have seen from our examination of Reinhard Hütter's argument, the trouble is that, insofar as we make the latter the basis of the life of the church, we effectively deny the grace of God, or the need for it, since what we then are really affirming is that we believe is the modern dogma of the individual rather than the Christian doctrine of the forgiveness of sins. The final product of such reasoning can only be a betrayal of the one foundation both for the existence of the church itself and for our membership in it. A church so in thrall to the world that it has neither need nor room for the grace of God is, in short, merely "an assembly of the ungodly" (Calvin) and thus a church in name only. This is the first insight our study brings to bear on this vexed question.

In the second place, there is a great need to recall the theme of the brokenness of Christ's body that we have already explored in this study, and the correlative idea that the humanity with which God in Christ is identified is not some ideal humanity existing beyond the world that we know, but rather a humanity that exists in fragments, in sinfulness, in suffering, and in death. This idea, which I have drawn from the theology of Alan Lewis (among other places), suggests that the key to grasping the gracious ways of God with the world might lie in reflection on the *broken* body of Christ, the body of the one who came into a world of sordid imperfection and violence in the breathtaking fullness of the condescension of divine mercy. What the mystery of Christ's death for the salvation of the world shows is that it is precisely the sinful world, the godless and shameful world, that God chooses to reconcile with himself. Hence there is no cause for boasting of one's righteousness over another: "All have sinned and fall short of the glory of God" (Rom. 3:23) in some form.

What we need to recognize in the current crisis is that on all sides we should avoid the pretense that some are broken while others are not, or that some are godly while others are not. In a church that is always sinful, but despite its sinfulness is accepted and put in the right by God, there is indeed room for all. However, the further truth is that only in such a church is there room for anyone, for in a church that implicitly assumes that there is a humanity not marked by sin, there is in the final analysis room for nobody. In short, the church's being *simil justus et peccator,* in Luther's famous phrase, is of fundamental and abiding importance.

(b) Truth and Community

One of the more unusual suggestions that I have made in this study concerns the way we need to conceive of the dynamic relationship between doctrine and community, or truth and love, on the strength of a renewed understanding of the Trinitarian life of God. My argument via an analysis of the "people of God," "body of Christ," and "temple of the Spirit" ideas that I have drawn from the New Testament has been that the life of the church is grounded in the outreach to the world of the triune God. For this reason, there can be no adequate understanding of the doctrine of the church without attending to the prior question of what the roots from which the church derives its life are. For example, just as the Christian mission is not the church's own, but a participation in God's outreach to the world through his Word and Spirit, so the teaching of the church and the fellowship of the church are not our possession, but they come about through participation in the Word and the Spirit of God that are thus given. By reflecting on this dynamic, perhaps we can help the church see a path through this controversial matter.

In chapters 5 and 6 of this book, I have discerned in the work of the Spirit and of the Word a twofold movement that amounts to a kind of pulse by which a correlative expansion and contraction of outlook and practice in the life of the church takes place. According to the argument I have made, we must recognize, in the first place, a "centrifugal" movement by which the plurality of God's gifts is realized in the Spirit's work in the history and work of the church. Here there is occasion for trial and error, for development, for diversity and struggle, for impoverishment as well as enrichment, as we discover that God is always "something more" and even, from time to time, that God has been present all along in the "other," who had seemed so alien. In other words, the communion of the church in the properly theological sense involves recognition of the diversity of theological expression, and of ecclesiastical and spiritual style: what it is cannot be reduced to something monolithic or static, since the way of the Spirit is diverse and dynamic.

Along with this centrifugal movement, by which a plurality of theological stances and styles receives expression, there is, in the second place, a corresponding "centripetal" movement: in it God is acknowledged as the source, particularly in the recognition that there is a single mystery that is confessed by all, and that none can grasp finally or fully. Therefore, the very plurality of witness to the one mystery of God — at least for those who do not fixate narrowly on any one of the "gifts" — makes for a recognition of the source from which it derives and toward which it tends. Though the object of Christian faith is never something that we can possess or capture within the bounds of a single system, however coherent or highly developed it might be, it is nonetheless the one truth of God that must always be recognized as offering itself to us anew. While there should be no confusion of the small systems and practices by which we know God, and the God who is in a measure known through them, it is the one God rather than many gods who is thus known and confessed in proclamation and witness.[9]

There is no doubt that much of what has been argued on the theological left for the case in favor of the full inclusion of gay and lesbian individuals in the church is a product of the confusion of contemporary liberalism with the content of the Christian gospel. That it has led occasionally to misrepresentations of the Christian tradition, and thus to significant distortions of its implications, is to that extent and for that reason something to be anticipated.[10] Yet not all of it is so badly flawed. For example, it is perfectly clear that Christians themselves and the churches to which they belong have historically been more willing to overlook the sexual sins of heterosexuals than

---

9. At this point, a major difference between Hütter's position, in which the ordinary practices of the church assume an inordinate importance, and the one I am advancing in this book becomes clear.

10. A good example is from a paper written by Michael Ingham, "Sex and Christianity: Re-thinking the Relationship," http://www.anglican.ca/faith/ethics/wmc/ingham.htm (accessed 25 September 2007): "Once you question the connection between sexuality and procreation, and once you move the focus of sexuality beyond mere genital activity and into the realm of total interpersonal relationships, then traditional Christian teachings about sex appear to be quite limited and limiting." The paper in question prefaced an activist conference: "The Whole Message Conference: Inclusiveness in the Anglican Church of Canada," 13-14 April 2007. Astonishingly, the underlying argument that Ingham presents in the paper is that traditional Christian moral teaching about sex lacks any reference to the relational values desired, and sinks instead to the level of "mere genital activity." In an argument paradoxically delivered from the standpoint of the episcopal office, Ingham entirely overlooks the fact that the majority voice of the Christian tradition regards married love as a *sacrament,* and thus as an objective means of grace in the strictest possible sense.

they have been to overlook those of homosexuals. Other distortions of Christian practice more blatant than those occurring in a good many same-sex relationships have been tolerated, and it is a good thing that the duplicity of Christians over such questions is being challenged in our time.

The communion of the church and the outworking of Christian truth ultimately require that there be both a risky venture into new and unexplored theological territory, one that allows for the possibility of struggle and dissent and acknowledges the importance of difference, and a recognition that the work of the Spirit in the church is such that the central core of faith must finally be defended against trespass. If it is by trial and error that theological truth is extended and developed, then it is equally by living with those with whom we often frankly disagree that we can realize and deepen the *koinônia* of the Spirit. Hence it should not surprise us that disputes such as the one that threatens the worldwide Anglican Communion at this point in its history also have the potential to clarify the implications of Christian teaching, the conditions of the possibility of the unity of the church, and the nature of Christian moral obedience to the command of Christ. (*The Windsor Report* of 2004 and its aftermath are an excellent example of this kind of development.) Of course, it is unlikely that this potential will be realized without great cost, a cost that must be borne on all sides of the debate. But when has the course of Christian theology ever run otherwise?

(c) Homosexuality and Christian Ethics

In the suggestions above, I have tried to show that a constructive *doctrine* of the church contains resources that can help the church to live more faithfully in a given context. However, my suggestions will undoubtedly require some modest elaboration, given the controversial character of current debates in sexual ethics.

To begin with, the following question might well be raised by someone who objects to the argument I have pursued: "Is homosexual genital activity, then, not inherently sinful?" The answer of the Christian tradition is that it is indeed sinful, and I accept it, without any desire to squint at the relevant texts of Romans 1 in order to see them differently (the plain sense of Rom. 1:26-28 being really what is intended), or to suppress the worst that the Torah — in the book of Leviticus — might offer on the subject. However, I must add two critical observations to this point. The first is that much heterosexual "genital activity" in our world is also sinful, and frequently condemned in Scripture, for in being exploitative, faithless, violent, or merely in "using" another human being in sex (including in married sexual acts), humans pervasively "fall short of the glory of God." We are meant for something better, yet we persist in something worse. The second observation is that we all must recognize and acknowledge at some level that a mutual, faithful, and loving homosexual relationship exceeds in moral worth a heterosexual relationship that utterly lacks those qualities. In short, one is not qualified as sexually sinless purely by virtue of having a partner of the opposite gender. Surely nobody would be so morally obtuse as to suggest that physically abusive heterosexual relationships, for instance, are morally and religiously superior to homosexual relationships in which there is genuine mutuality and respect.

This does not mean that homosexual acts do not inherently fall short of the good purposes of God the Creator. According to the classical Christian conception of evil as *privatio boni,* homosexuality as such is precisely definable as an "evil" in the direct and undeniable sense that it fails to attain the full potentiality of the general structures written into created human sexuality. In this sense it does not represent something evil *in itself,* for on the classical Christian definition of evil, there is no such thing. Rather, it is a clear "privation of good." By definition, homosexuality is not merely incapable of, but strictly *unrelated to,* the procreative dimension — without which there would be no humanity at all — and to which all sexual differentiation in the created world is inherently ordered (which is not the same as exclusively ordered).[11]

In an age of profound ambivalence toward the value of procreation, one might also note here that the homosexual relationship also fails to attain to a full recognition of the mysterious otherness involved in being male and fe-

11. Furthermore, I might note at this point that a *heterosexual* relationship that is deliberately closed to having any children — purely for the sake of financial gain or personal career ambition — also "falls short" of the created potential of human sexuality. Though the use of artificial birth control methods and devices can obviously coexist with a responsible approach to the family and procreation, the rejection of any possibility of the birth of a child among large numbers of heterosexual couples shows the individualism of the contemporary West reaching its moral limit. It is interesting that the stance taken in such relationships is as frankly incomprehensible to much of the rest of the world as is the homosexual relationship, because in both cases sexuality is divorced from the *family* and thus from the existence of cultural traditions and collectivities that continue fundamentally to define human identity for most of the world.

male, and most decisively to affirm the wholeness of humanity signified by
the male-female relationship, specifically in sexual union. After all, it is for
this very reason that in the creation narrative of Genesis, "the two" (a reference not to mere individuals but to the male and female as sexually differentiated) can become "one flesh" (Gen. 2:24). But then it is also true that all human sexuality, like all human nature in general, is likewise flawed. We lust, we
seek to possess and to use, we betray, we delude ourselves and deceive others.
We are broken and sinful creatures, and it would be dishonest for any of us to
suggest that in the matter of our sexuality, which touches us so deeply, the
reach of our sinfulness is so shortened that it could ever be otherwise.

However, the church exists precisely for sinful human beings such as we
are, and so there is real common ground between us all. To return to our
concrete case, the problem for the Anglican Communion is that it is not this
kind of theological account of the problem, rooted in the biblical witness
and in the theological tradition, that underlies the movement for the "inclusive" church of gay and straight (along with those of bisexual and trans-
gendered "orientations," who are, let us make clear publicly, presently and
none too patiently waiting in the wings for their inclusion). Rather, their
case is underwritten by another vision and another set of values: the values
of that modern "Babylon" to which the church is captive. Therefore, the African provinces of the Anglican Communion would be well advised to hold
firm against the case that has been made, for it does not stand on foundations that can easily be sustained theologically. In fact, one could go so far as
to claim that the primary danger for the Anglican Communion lies not in
the vexed issue of attitudes toward sexuality and homosexuality per se,
which in so many ways seem scarcely worth the trouble taken over them, but
primarily in the sacralization of Western liberalism that the demand for the
"inclusive" church involves. To accept this sacralization as the measure of the
gospel and effectively as the content of salvation risks outright idolatry.

One of the curious features of the controversy that rages as I write is the
extent to which (to use the conventional language) the "liberal" church of
the West and the "conservative" church of the global South speak close-
mindedly and at cross-purposes in this whole matter, at a time when they
would have a good deal to gain by listening more carefully and respectfully
to one another.[12] After all, human sexuality in African culture is also com-

---

12. Note that the words "liberal" and "liberalism" are generally used in the political or
social sense elsewhere in this analysis.

promised: the soaring rates of HIV infection in supposedly "Christian" Africa, the related and ingrained cultural tendency toward the exploitation of women, and the inherited problem of polygamy in the African context make certain of the problems of the African Anglican provinces surprisingly akin to those of the Canadian and the American churches. Everyone has to confess that not all is what it should be; yet Christ has made *this* imperfect church his own, and so must we — in discipleship, obedience, and gratitude.

What we need most is confidence in the proclamation of the Word of God's grace, a knowledge that it is sufficient to allow for broken and sinful humans to hear and belong to the family of God, with a faith sufficient to tolerate those differences among believers that arise from the ebb and flow of human culture, and from the vagaries of practice. Perhaps some adaptation is possible of the Pauline principle, according to which we recognize the urgency of the demands of conscience that arise in changing contexts and thus refrain from imposing on others more than is needed (1 Cor. 8). But what we cannot do is acquiesce to what the theological left in North America has insisted on, for it makes a particular, powerful, and hugely problematic human culture the source and norm of theological judgment. Those functions and that place are reserved for one alone, and it is idolatry to bow the knee and worship instead what is, in the last resort, the work of human hands.

The State We're In

The difficult question thus raised, and with which we must conclude, concerns the relationship between the political consensus that has been reached in modern democratic liberalism on the one hand and the doctrine of the church on the other. Though this is a contentious issue, its importance for the church in the contemporary Western world (indeed, for the liberal state as well) is, I believe, difficult to overestimate. The problem we face is a subtle one. Following not only the work of writers such as Reinhard Hütter, but that of others of more established reputation, including John Milbank and Stanley Hauerwas, I have argued that the very identity of the church is compromised by its rather easy alliance with the central forms of social thought and political power that have developed in late modernity. But the church could also be said to have reason to be confused, not only because there are genuine parallels between some of its values and those of the liberal state, but, more important, because certain of the critical values of the liberal state in its modern Western expression arguably *derive from* the particular history of European Christendom. Here, at the close, we enter a new phase of the argument, very possibly the most difficult of all; this is not least because the secular order for its part commonly resists any religious content and particularly any religious constraint.

However, help can sometimes come from unexpected quarters. In an article published in the British newspaper *The Times*, shortly after the attacks by Islamic extremists on the United States on September 11, 2001, the chief rabbi of Great Britain, Dr. Jonathan Sacks, spoke of the dangers to religion posed by "universal civilizations."[13] Western culture, Sacks reasoned, has known several such civilizations: ancient Greece, the Roman empire, medieval Christendom and the Islamic civilization contemporary with it, the modern world centered around the ideal of Enlightenment, and now, what he terms "contemporary global capitalism." Arguing that since only God is universal, and thus that all human civilizations can only ever be purely particular, Sacks spoke of the idolatrous threat posed by civilizations that pose as something "universal" to all real faith in God. The Jews, he notes, have suffered much for the sake of *their* particularity at the hands of the universal civilizations that have risen and inevitably fallen over the centuries.

In Sacks's view, central to the tragedy of "9/11" is the fact that in that event two self-professed universal cultures, each profoundly threatening to the other, met head-on, each making its self-assertive claim, and they clashed violently. The results have been catastrophic for geopolitical relations and profoundly challenging for the Western and the Islamic worlds alike. Sacks's argument is essentially that what is at stake in the 9/11 event is that *both* sides mistakenly identify a finite form of human culture as something absolute. The appropriate response of people of faith to this crisis must be to recognize the futility of universalizing what is, and what can only ever be, merely a product of the ebb and flow of history. Since there can be no truly universal human civilization, Sacks maintains, both global capitalism and the Islamists can only be in the wrong, while each has much to learn from the particularity of the Jew about God and about human civilization alike. "We will make peace," he concludes, "only when we learn that God loves difference and so, at last, must we."

The person who has claimed to be the chief architect of the atrocities of

13. Jonathan Sacks, "Credo," *The Times*, 3 November 2001.

9/11, Osama bin Laden, has made a very different — but in some ways an equally arresting — point. In stark contrast to Sacks, bin Laden has claimed that the form of Islamism he represents is set explicitly against the forces of *Christianity*, and not against something as anonymous or religiously neutered as "contemporary global capitalism," or even the generic concept of "the West." Shortly after the attacks of 9/11, in an interview with the *Al-Jazeera* network's correspondent Tayseer Alouna (broadcast in October 2001), bin Laden repeatedly returned to this claim, noting that not only had President George W. Bush used the word "crusade" in reference to an American response to the attack, but also — and much more significantly — that it had been used extensively and repeatedly in the rulings, or *fatwas*, issued by a range of Islamic jurists concerning the interference of major Western nations in the Islamic world over many decades. On the strength of these *fatwas*, bin Laden went so far as to claim that Bush "carries the cross" in a global Christian crusade, against which it is imperative for all Muslims to rise up and fight.

Most people in the democratic West, including Jonathan Sacks, have dismissed such talk of a "crusade" against Islam in the policy of Western nations as propagandist nonsense. The Western media, for example, paid little attention to the word "crusade" (beyond references to Bush's use of the word in an unguarded moment). Christian religious thought has likewise ignored bin Laden's claim, effectively considering it the raving of a moral madman, despite the fact that the claim he makes concerning Christianity would be shared by vast numbers of Muslims globally, even those who — we can be thankful — reject his peculiar tactics. The British theologian Richard Bauckham, for example, responding to Sacks's column, has acknowledged the very common *perception* in the Muslim world that the United States and her allies do indeed represent "Christianity" in contemporary geopolitical struggles; but he maintains that the idea cannot be considered credible, least of all by Christians themselves.[14] The struggle is secular rather than sacred — on this the Western world appears to be united.

I need to note that the separation of politics and religion as a matter of principle in the contemporary West does make the Islamist assertion seem outrageously misinformed. Furthermore, from the standpoint of sheer numbers, the United States and her allies cannot literally represent Chris-

---

14. Richard Bauckham, *Bible and Mission* (Grand Rapids: Baker Academic; Carlisle: Paternoster, 2003), p. 2.

tianity today, for the majority of living Christians do not reside in the United States, or in the handful of nations allied with it in the war on terror, but rather in the so-called Two-Thirds World. Since in Islamic eschatology the entire earth is destined to embrace Islam as the solution to injustice and irreligion, the idea that those who suffer from irreligion and injustice among the world's poor should be turning in massive numbers to the religion of the Western imperialist "crusaders" is something that bin Laden would no doubt be unwilling to concede. Presumably, his grasp of these matters is as poor as that of many Western Christians.

On the other hand, it might be wise for us not to move too rapidly to the desired conclusion. After all, what if Muslims were even in some limited sense entitled to speak of a contemporary crusade of a residually Christian West against Islam? If so, the inability to engage with this point would surely represent a monumental failure, not least on the part of Western Christians. Could it possibly be that the avowedly secular West is, when all is said and done, a child of the Christianity that it so often is said to have abandoned? I wish to suggest that the answer to this is a quiet though qualified "yes," which becomes increasingly emphatic the more the question is approached from the standpoint of the premodern outlook of much Islamic thought. This surprising "yes," I want to add, also has certain major implications for contemporary ecclesiology, as well as for the question of the Christian churches' mission in the Western world.

The claim is perhaps surprising, but it is useful to note that it would not have occasioned such surprise a mere half century ago, when the broadly Christian roots of the democratic politics of the modern West were still openly acknowledged, an acknowledgment that featured commonly in political discourse. However, the idea has become so unconventional through the course of recent decades that it is necessary to explain and defend it. This is a massive subject, and it merits much greater attention than is possible in this book. For the moment, it will suffice for me to illustrate the point by referring to one of the major figures in the political history of the twentieth century, Winston Churchill, who repeatedly spoke of the struggles in which he was involved before, during, and after World War II as representing the cause of "Christian civilization."

Two of Churchill's especially memorable invocations of the idea can serve for our purposes as representative statements; neither one of them caused special cries of protest when he uttered them. The first was in a famous speech that he delivered in the House of Commons on June 18, 1940, on the eve of the anticipated German invasion, and in face of the known barbarities of Nazism. He said: "I expect that the Battle of Britain is about to begin. Upon this battle depends the survival of Christian civilization. . . . Let us therefore brace ourselves to our duties and so bear ourselves that, if the British Empire and its Commonwealth last for a thousand years, men will still say, 'This was their finest hour.'" Churchill's words on that occasion were then, and remain now, an extraordinary example of modern Western political discourse. Equally striking is his famous "Iron Curtain" speech, which he delivered in the United States on March 5, 1946, and which generated more than forty years of Cold War political discourse, in which Churchill referred to the Communist Party in the Soviet Union and its fifth columns abroad as nothing less than "a peril to Christian civilization."

Now it is true that Churchill's voice was only one among many at the time, and that his outlook represented very much the principles of patrician British conservative politics. It is also undeniable that, in any case, politicians today no longer speak that way. The mass emigration of peoples of other faiths from their traditional homelands to settle in Europe and North America during the past few decades has made such political language almost unthinkable in our day, whereas Churchill was a son of the ruling classes of a still imperial Britain. There is no doubt that we need to acknowledge all of this. On the other hand, the truth is also that, in someone of the stature of Winston Churchill, Islamists who rage against a new "crusade" are to be found in strange company.

If the post–World War II settlement was genuinely, as Churchill's words might lead us to think, the victory of "Christian civilization" over the threat of a new "dark age" in Europe, and if the recent triumph of the West over the Soviet empire and the threat of Stalinism again amounted to the vindication of the cause of "Christian civilization" — bringing, for instance, the dawn of a new era for those churches that had lived behind what Churchill called for the first time the "Iron Curtain" — then perhaps contemporary Islamists might not be entirely mistaken in claiming that their struggle is against precisely the kind of Christian civilization that these massive events in history have set in place in the modern West. According to these terms, it would seem that in some sense even a person like bin Laden understands the West better than it understands itself.

Christianity and the Liberal State

I am suggesting that the relationship between Christianity and modern democratic politics is similar to the one that exists between it and modern natural science, which represents a parallel case that I can cite in order to clarify the argument. It is widely recognized today that the science of nature that developed in early modern Europe and that, since the eighteenth century in particular, has been exported to the whole of the world, is a product of a specifically Christian civilization.[15] The fact that the universe could be understood at all rather than feared as holding hidden powers to be controlled and placated by magic, or alternatively, ignored as the work of an inferior deity, was itself a matter of Christian theological principle. For the universe is the creature of God, who brought it into being through his Word as a prolongation of his own inherent rationality into created space and time. Nevertheless, there is a difference between the uncreated Word and the "contingent" or "created rationality" of the universe that came into being through him. This world requires empirical observation and measurement to be understood, which finally would come to be developed in the modern scientific method. Such a science could never have been the product of Hellenism, according to which the rationality of the universe is fixed and eternal; rather, it arose historically in a Christian culture that finally learned, after the discipline of long centuries, to escape the lure of Hellenism, and to grasp that the doctrine of creation implies that the structures of the universe are a product of God's will. We must observe and describe them in order to know them, and not attempt to deduce them in godlike fashion from self-evident principles.

An impressive literature has grown up in Christian theology over the past few decades around the ideas I have summarized above. However, the cultural impact of Christian faith on the development of modern politics is not as widely discussed.[16] One of the likely reasons for this is the lingering antipathy felt in modernity toward the religious past, an ill-feeling that is

---

15. *E.g.,* Alister E. McGrath, *A Scientific Theology,* 3 vols. (Edinburgh: T&T Clark, 2001), 1: 135ff.

16. An exception can be found in a diffuse form in the work of Oliver O'Donovan, in, among other places, O'Donovan, *The Desire of the Nations: Rediscovering the Roots of Political Theology* (Cambridge, UK: Cambridge University Press, 1996); Oliver O'Donovan and Joan Lockwood O'Donovan, *Bonds of Imperfection* (Grand Rapids: Eerdmans, 2004); and Oliver O'Donovan, *The Ways of Judgment* (Grand Rapids: Eerdmans, 2005).

certainly reciprocated by many theologians. Yet the distortions that result from this lack of engagement with such a major development in secular experience are akin to those that can be seen in those theologies that retreat from science. Just as forms of Christianity that ignore the achievement of science have become religiously irresponsible, so a Christianity that recoils from proper political responsibility is something that, when weighed in the balance, can only be found wanting. Either it retreats in the ghetto world of private experience, hearth, and home, or it uncritically overcommits — because it has no properly theological foundations — to a secular order that is only ever a conditional and partial entity. Perhaps more importantly in the present context, we see equally that a science that breaks free from the kind of comprehensive vision that grounds scientific endeavor in human dignity before God can become dangerous and proud, as we ourselves attempt to "play God" with respect to created nature (including our own!). This pride and independence has a corresponding expression in the political sphere as well, in a politics that assumes human dignity to lie within *its own* proper sphere and that refuses the claim of God, which alone can ground the good.

Historically, it is at least clear that the modern democratic nation-state developed largely in the context of late Western Christian civilization, and that, like modern natural science, the political institutions inherited from this civilization have been widely exported from their older Christian heartlands to much of the world. Therefore, it is at least a *plausible* suggestion that, as in the case of modern natural science, so also in the political sphere, the development of democratic institutions derives from the Christian civilization in which they originally developed and took root.

Certainly Hegel, the philosopher from whom I have drawn from time to time in my analysis in this book, argued for just such a relationship, maintaining that the principle of political freedom that finally came to expression in the political institutions of the modern West is a uniquely Christian value, though it had to develop gradually and often painfully through successive movements in the historical progress of Christianity.[17] Perhaps the claim will seem less jarring when we remember that Karl Marx, for one, took his

17. The key discussion is G. W. F. Hegel, *The Philosophy of History,* trans. J. B. Sibree (New York: Dover Publications, 1956), pp. 413-37, 438-57. Hegel's political philosophy has frequently been misrepresented as "fascist." Over against that notion, see the measured discussion of the Hegelian position in Schlomo Avineri, *Hegel's Theory of the Modern State* (Cambridge, UK: Cambridge University Press, 1972), pp. 176-93.

old teacher Hegel at his word, though he famously reversed the structure of the argument so as to make history "walk on its feet." It was for this reason that Marx taught not only that the critique of religion is the prerequisite of all political criticism, or that the "inverted" consciousness that finds expression in religion is the key to understanding the inverted political world in which people live in misery, but also that the critique of Christianity as it had developed in modernity, was of crucial significance in this respect.[18] In Marx's analysis, it was Christianity specifically rather than (as is usually assumed in accounts of Marxism) religion in general that represented the "sigh of the oppressed creature" at the particular stage of human development that had been reached in modern capitalism.[19]

Though we do not have space here for a full account of Hegel's position in its original formulation in his philosophy of history, we can point out that the argument runs rather differently, as might be assumed in a philosophy in which history is widely supposed to "walk on its head." Hegel's argument, which should not be reduced to such gross Marxian oversimplification, is threefold. First of all, his claim rests on a particular appropriation of the Christian doctrine of the incarnation, which entails, Hegel observes, that since God is incarnated in a finite human life, there is in Jesus Christ a true unity of the absolutely universal with the sheer particularity of human existence. It is of fundamental significance that such a unity is thus known to be possible: this observation is crucially important in Hegel's analysis, because in his view it serves as the foundation for the special dignity of humans in the political institutions of modernity. In short, it is the human being who is thus conceived as the proper "site" of what is universal when expressed in time, so that in the political sphere it is the person, rather than the monarch, or even "the people" as a whole, that comes to prominence.

Second, it is central to Hegel's analysis that God should have given himself to be *known* in Jesus Christ: the divine *logos* made flesh. The rational

18. Karl Marx, *Critique of Hegel's "Philosophy of Right,"* trans. A. Jolin and J. O'Malley (Cambridge, UK: Cambridge University Press, 1970), p. 131.

19. What often seems to be left unsaid about Marx's early critique of religion is that, rather like his fellow Hegel student Ludwig Feuerbach, Marx argued that Christianity specifically represents the "essence" of all religion, inasmuch as in it the content of faith is none other than "deified man." The Christian religion is thus treated as the "consummate" form of the inverted human *self*-consciousness achieved in religion, in which the real object of consciousness is humanity itself (Marx, *Critique of Hegel's "Philosophy of Right,"* p. 30).

form of the self-expression of God in the incarnation is central to the exposition of the Christian religion offered. Whatever theologians or the church may have said from time to time to the contrary, God is revealed to rational consciousness in the Christian revelation precisely as the one who is not alien to humanity, since in Jesus Christ, the God-man, God himself overcomes the division between divine and creaturely being. Furthermore, the rational content of Christian revelation is in Hegel's (very Lutheran) view closely bound up with the Christian doctrine of reconciliation. In Christ, God tastes death, the apex of finitude, and in so doing he triumphs over it with life, so that nothing finite is left unreconciled to God. In this connection, Hegel cites the controversial phrase *Gott selbst liegt tot* several times, the source of which is a Lutheran chorale of the seventeenth century.[20] It is precisely as the one who reaches out to the world and refuses to allow it to remain an alien other that we *know* the true and triune God.

Third, and most important for our purposes, we need to consider Hegel's specific treatment of Protestant Christianity here, and particularly its specific relationship to the "spirit" of Enlightenment. It has long been characteristic of Roman Catholic criticism of the Protestant tradition that it highlights the principle of subjective freedom as a peculiarly Protestant religious aberration. Hegel also highlights the significance of this principle, though maintaining positively that the "faith" of the Reformation tradition and the "pure insight" of the philosophical tradition from Bacon and Descartes to Kant represent two sides of one movement, a historical movement that is distinctive of modernity and that alone could lead to the development of the democratic institutions of the modern nation-state.[21] The central point is that in both cases truth is known, not on the basis of external authority, but by the individual rational self, in such a way that the truth is "ownable" by consciousness as something in accordance with its own nature. (After all, it is in this way that the Hegelian form of "alienation" is overcome; the concept is developed in a distinctly different direction by Marx.) It is this idea, first of all expressed religiously, that marks the transition from the medieval to the modern world in the theology of the Reformation, and that

20. "God himself lies dead." Cf. Eberhard Jüngel, *God as the Mystery of the World,* trans. Darrell L. Guder (Edinburgh: T&T Clark; Grand Rapids: Eerdmans, 1983), pp. 64-65.

21. The significance of this is highlighted by James Doull, "Faith and Enlightenment," *Dionysius* 10 (1986): 129-35.

subsequently had to work itself out through the structures of Protestant Christianity and the several political, material, and economic cultures that it generated.

There is much in Hegel's treatment of these themes that cannot detain us, but we must note that the specifically *political* outworking of this core insight was, in Hegel's estimation, the burden of the massive societal changes that occurred during his own lifetime (1770-1831). The importance of this theme as Hegel's life project is also signaled by Hans Küng, who sees it as nothing less than the project that generated the Hegelian philosophical system.[22] But it is perhaps more strikingly reflected in a dictum of Karl Barth, who as a young scholar asked in all seriousness how it was that Hegel, a thinker for whom he evidently had great respect, did not become for nineteenth-century Protestantism something similar to what Thomas Aquinas became in the nineteenth century for Catholicism, that is, the thinker who reconciles the Christian theological and the secular philosophical traditions.[23]

Whether Hegel's political philosophy covers conventional ground or not, his view of the way that Christian religious ideas are related to Western democratic institutions is highly relevant to the world in which we live, in which the question of the Christian roots of our political institutions has been ignored and forgotten, on the one hand, and in which such democratic institutions are currently being imposed through military force on the soil of the very different religious culture encountered in Islam, on the other. In a passage that might well be set as required reading for all those involved in leading these efforts, Hegel mocks those who suppose that the state of affairs in politics is unrelated to what can be found in religion or, conversely, that the transition from a set of religious values to a series of political institutions is a straightforward affair.[24]

First of all, he maintains, there can be absolutely no coherent political reality without an underlying consensus in society about the basis of social order. Hegel says that this is provided by religion, everywhere and at all times,

22. Hans Küng, *The Incarnation of God: An Introduction to Hegel's Theological Thought as Prolegomena to a Future Christology*, trans. J. R. Stephenson (Edinburgh: T&T Clark, 1987), passim.

23. Karl Barth, *Protestant Theology in the Nineteenth Century*, trans. Brian Cozens and John Bowden (London: SCM Press, 1972), p. 384.

24. G. W. F. Hegel, *Elements of the Philosophy of Right*, trans. H. B. Nisbet (Cambridge, UK: Cambridge University Press, 1991), §270.

though often in distorted and half-formed ways. The trouble, he suggests, is that people naively suppose that the move from the religious to the political is an easier thing than it is in reality. The result is frequently an incoherent or fanatical gesture toward the problems of politics rather than anything of lasting significance.[25] Hegel maintains that what is needed is always a "momentous transition," which is often painful and always has to be worked through with difficulty, from the inner to the outer, or from moral value and intellectual principle to the far more mixed environment of political exigency in particular human contexts. Trial and error is needed; suffering is inevitable, sometimes on a vast scale; centuries of struggle, rather than weeks or months or even years, are sometimes required; a multitude of wrong turns will be taken; and dead ends will be pursued to the death before they are recognized as such.

Especially now, when the case study of the travails of global Islamic civilization presents itself because of geopolitical events, those who attack Hegel's "idealism" might do well to ponder the "realism" of these claims. In short, if all this has been the case in Christian civilization, in which the universal will of God and the particular will of the individual are in principle reconciled, how much more difficult must it be in Islamic civilization, where all true law is said to be strictly from God, and where the fundamental obligation of humans is to submit to the divine will? In the Ottoman Empire, not even the Sultan could make law; that role was reserved for God alone. Since one can only interpret or apply divine law in Islam, how can a democracy be developed (or worse, imposed) in Islamic countries, one that is modeled on Western political institutions and in which the people as a whole *make* law and "govern themselves" in the usual sense of the phrase? For this, as hundreds of millions of Muslims apparently grasp, is an alien form of politics. It is even, in the view of some, an explicitly *Christian* form of politics. And those who say this may well have a point. When all is said and done, and all our qualifications or objections to the claim have been spoken, perhaps what we especially stand to learn from them in the present crisis is the fact that our religious values and our political institutions are, like theirs, inextricably linked.

25. Ill-informed attempts in the past by contemporary Western theologians to comment on economic issues is a good example of the problem, not least because so much of Western Christianity seems merely to be the civil religion of the very liberalism that is questioned.

If this is true, the Western world today is largely oblivious to it, and herein we have the root of a further difficulty, which is bound to be the source of what a good Hegelian might call "the labor and pain of the negative" in our own historical epoch and context. For we have arrived at a paradoxical situation in which we deny the claim of God on political life, yet we do so (if Hegel is to be believed) on the basis of a peculiar development of religious principle itself. In effect — if not in actual principle — we deny the direct claim of God on politics precisely on account of a certain historical development of God's claim on all human existence. After all, most of us would likely concur with the view that our societies are profoundly secular rather than sacred in character, and we could not imagine them otherwise. For example, the constitutional separation of church and state in the United States of America, and the more widely held principles of freedom of religion and conscience, would no doubt be massively endorsed by Christians in the Western world, affirmed by members of the religious right and left alike — whether for the purpose of freedom *of* religion or freedom *from* it. That tensions, contradictions, and outright incoherencies arise between religion and politics in the modern democratic West is scarcely surprising.

We have already investigated the kind of fundamental confusion that can arise from the above in this study: the fact that certain forms of the Christian religion, on the one hand, and movements in contemporary political and social liberalism that ostensibly *reject* the influence of religion, on the other, are in truth intimately related. Indeed, one could go so far as to claim flatly that they have come to be indistinguishable in some cases. In the thinking of a Christian figure such as John Shelby Spong, for instance, the liberating thrust of liberalism and the (totally reconfigured) Christian doctrine of salvation really come to be one and the same: the role of the church should be to advocate for that individual liberation and the achievement of authentic selfhood that is precisely the goal of the liberal political polity. However, what is entirely missing from Spong's argument is any critical awareness of the inadequacy of a theology that places such emphasis on the dignity of the individual without grasping precisely why the individual should be accorded such theological and moral status in the first place.

One of those to whom Spong might devote rather more attention in this regard is a thinker who developed a similar, though more consistent, argument: Thomas J. J. Altizer, one of the dominant figures in the "death of God" movement of the 1960s. In *The Gospel of Christian Atheism,* where he draws largely on nineteenth-century philosophical sources, Altizer concludes that the Christian doctrine of incarnation provides theological ground for one great conclusion: a thoroughgoing this-worldliness in theology. Altizer claims that since God empties himself and assumes human nature in the Christian faith, its inner truth and final deliverance is that it is human nature that we should value supremely.[26] Indeed, for Christians — if they are to be merely self-consistent — humanity itself is the location of all that we call divine. In other words, the substance of Christian faith is a strict humanism, a humanism that represents the full expression of the inner logic of the Christian religion, and that demands its full and unconditional surrender.

At this point, we should scarcely need to say, we have come a long way from the view that Western democratic institutions are independent of religion.[27] On the contrary, we are much closer to explaining the widespread quasi-religious fervor with which secularism is commonly advanced! As I argued in chapter 1, what is especially problematic about the result from a theological standpoint is the insistence that we require nothing other than that we be fulfilled and complete, and that our human dignity be immediate. On the other hand, the Christian theological insistence is that our true dignity is in the final analysis the result of God's original purpose in creation, and of his restorative work of grace, by which our humanity is first of all made the dwelling place of the Son of God, and then made whole through the gift of the Spirit of adoption, so that we become children of God in him. What we should see as the result of the divine initiative alone is, instead, *presupposed* as a purely anthropocentric starting point, and it is assumed in the political and religious culture alike, as opposed to being confessed in faith as the product of the Christian doctrines of creation and salvation.

Theologically considered, such an assumption can only lead to distortion, particularly once the conditions that make it possible have been forgotten. Our problem is not simply what is sometimes said, that, amid our affirmation of the fundamental dignity of individual human nature, we have posited "rights" without "responsibilities." The real problem is that, where the rights of the individual themselves become the basis of all moral and political practice, all else — including those religious principles that led to their

26. Thomas J. J. Altizer, *The Gospel of Christian Atheism* (London: Collins, 1967), pp. 62-69.

27. The idea that modern secular economic and political liberalism developed as a corruption of Christian orthodoxy is one of the seminal arguments of John Milbank, *Theology and Social Theory: Beyond Secular Reason,* 2nd ed. (Oxford: Blackwell, 2005).

formulation and recognition — must yield to their claim. Theologically speaking, this makes superfluous the true condition of the possibility of individual dignity, the creative purpose of God, and the love of God in Jesus Christ. Indeed, the love of God itself is then readily reinterpreted to become an expression of the all-competent individual will, under the impoverished banner of "freedom of religion." Everything is resignified — or better, reduced — to this one new signification.

Inclusiveness and the Liberal Polity

The temptation has always been for the church to assume the values of the prevailing culture, and to claim for them divine warrant and command. It is relatively easy for us to identify this failing in history, for instance, in the Eusebian polity that treated Constantine and his successors as savior figures, or in the Nazification of the Protestant churches of Germany under Hitler. But the failing also lies closer to home. It can be seen, for example, in the obvious tendency of American evangelicalism to identify God's purposes with those of America, or alternatively, on the theological left, in the corresponding error that identifies Christian commitment with the neo-liberal ideal of social inclusion.[28]

The trouble with inclusiveness has been explored recently by the Irish-American Methodist William J. Abraham, who complains that the cost of ecclesiastical commitment to the ideal has been that "a virulent form of moralism" has been encouraged, and that this moralism has "poisoned the church."[29] While not everything that has been done in the name of inclu-

---

28. As I noted in the preface to this book, the British political and economic theorist John Gray has argued that it is precisely because economic globalization has made the central goals of older forms of social democracy unattainable that the political left has moved on (e.g., as in the case of Tony Blair's "New Labour"), seeking electoral advantage by promoting the goal of social inclusion as opposed to the redistribution of wealth. In other words, what redistributive policies such as full employment were to the traditional left, the idea of inclusiveness is to the neo-liberalism embraced by the left during the past two decades. Gray, "Inclusion: A Radical Critique," in Peter Askonas and Angus Stewart, eds., *Social Inclusion: Possibilities and Tensions* (New York: St. Martin's, 2000), pp. 19-36.

29. William J. Abraham, "Inclusivism, Idolatry and the Survival of the (Fittest) Faithful," in Mark Husbands and Daniel J. Treier, eds., *The Community of the Word* (Downers Grove, IL: InterVarsity Press; Leicester, UK: Apollos, 2005), p. 138.

siveness is a bad thing, what is increasingly apparent is that the outcome of inclusiveness as an all-embracing principle is profoundly distorting of the basic structures of Christian theology itself. It is even questionable whether inclusivism is finally conceptually coherent, since its effect is to incite a binary rejection of any alternative vision — and of those who espouse it. The movement, despite the stated goal of inclusiveness, turns out to be actually incompatible with that end: for example, as they have repeatedly discovered at a cost in recent years, conservative Catholics and evangelicals are certainly not among those who are "included" by the committed. Instead, the goal of the committed is to *exclude* from positions of influence, by any means at their disposal, those they deem to be illiberal, since they would impact adversely on the inclusivist agenda. Thus inclusiveness is in the final analysis self-contradictory and unsustainable. In an amusing and insightful polemic, Abraham pleads the case for a theologically informed "sanctified cynicism" in the face of the very considerable power wielded by the (unquestioned) dogma of inclusiveness, and a return to the gospel, which alone should be the content of the church's faith and witness (p. 140).

Abstracting from Abraham's view, one might say that a paradoxical idealism stands at the very heart of the neo-liberal ideal of inclusiveness. On the one hand, the social goal expressed in inclusion is one of belonging: everyone should have access to those activities and services that are central to a society — or, to use the contemporary shorthand, all have equal rights. As far as it goes, this is certainly laudable and good. Yet, one of the conditions of the possibility of a liberal society is found in the *erosion* of community and of communal identity amidst a pervasive individualism. Mediated largely through the mass culture, its impact is to submerge local cultural identities, including religious identity, and correlatively to loosen traditional social bonds.

The ideal of inclusiveness, once adopted, merges neatly with the mass culture, and when it is used bluntly, can even serve as an instrument of the erosion of communal ties. Its message is one of the dignity of the individual, but of an individual who must be abstracted from all the social relationships in which he or she stands, precisely so that individuals should matter supremely. The breakdown of the family is an obvious example of the resulting problem: equally from an economic standpoint, each individual is merely a consumer, while from the political standpoint, and for the sake of this same principle, each person in society must stand in the same relationship to everyone else.[30] There can be no discrimination, but by the same token, there can be no recognition of "rights" belonging to anything other than individuals: the institutions of family and religion, for instance, can have no rights, and in the strict sense no fundamental status in law. They exist only insofar as individuals have rights to them.

Individuals defined in this way are to be included, and for the sake of this goal, inclusivists present as a moral good all rejection of older patterns of social behavior, belief, kinship, and sexual role (i.e., all traditional identity). In contemporary liberalism, it is only radical individuals who, freed from such alien constraints, find the path to personal wholeness. Whether any genuine political community can be brought into existence from such sources is highly debatable, as our experiences of contemporary culture — and especially of contemporary geopolitical turmoil — abundantly reveal. Those most formed by it today are the youth, who are also the least likely to vote or to participate in cultural and political institutions (after all, institutions do not matter), while, geopolitically speaking, secular liberalism is today an imperious global force in conflict with what stands against it.

However, in the church (as Bonhoeffer once put it), community is properly to be seen as something established in Christ and through Christ, who brings us into communion with God the Father in the power of the Holy Spirit. While it is true that contemporary understandings of individual rights and the associated ideal of social inclusion might from time to time be useful as a tool to flesh out what this properly theological concept of community might entail, such things can never finally serve as proxies for the faith of the Christian community itself.[31] Whether the wider society could

---

30. There is an uncomfortable and telling parallel here with totalitarian politics, in which there is a similar affirmation of individual equality, only in this case not by way of securing the supreme status of the particular individual but the supreme status of the social "totality." For the sake of the latter, every individual in a totalitarian politics must stand in the same relationship to everyone else. Both liberalism and totalitarianism are philosophies of freedom, for the sake of which everything else must be made to bow the knee and relinquish any real claim on human life. That the barbarities of totalitarianism exceed those of liberalism should not blind us to the very real evils inflicted by a liberalism cut loose from its moral and spiritual foundations: we can clearly see its limits in the abortion rate, in soaring criminality, and in family and social breakdown.

31. As in the liberal political order, so also in theology: the core claim amounts to a self-destructive assertion that in Christianity there are no theological claims that really matter, since these are of merely subsidiary importance. What is of true importance is not

accept its witness or not, the church, by beginning here, can at least discover that it has its own ways of affirming human dignity, ways that are quite distinct from those of contemporary secular culture, and concerning which the culture badly needs to hear.

These are deep waters, and we cannot indulge in a lengthy immersion in them at this final stage of our study. Nevertheless, we must broach the question, because, among the issues that would most help the church to live more faithfully today, a more profound grasp of its relationship to the dominant political and social order and a corresponding measure both of responsibility for it and of critical distance from it loom extremely large. The absence of such critical understanding is not only harmful for the church but ultimately does disservice to the world. In fact, unless the witness of the church to the world has a properly theological basis, the church has no witness in the true sense to give. Rather than transforming the world, it is transformed by it, providing in its ministry and witness merely what Karl Marx pejoratively said of it: the spiritual confirmation of *what the world already is.*

Here we have abundant cause for an encounter with the Hegelian "labor and pain" of negation that I have mentioned above, and that must indeed accompany religious and political transformation alike on a cultural level. Many Western Christians, for instance, have so fallen into line with the world that, despite what they preach and teach about "justice issues" on the theological left or the authority of the Bible on the theological right, they are ultimately incapable of engaging in any genuine critique of the political world in which they live. To put the same point another way, the problem is that the exploitative aspects of liberal economics, the omnipresence of por-

---

what we say and do with respect to God, but with respect to the persons with whom we deal, and our practices with them. In contemporary parlance, "justice is orthodoxy." The trouble with this assertion is that the question "Whose justice?" is just as acute as the question "What orthodoxy?" For "justice," as contemporary Islam, among multiple other sources, is telling us, means absolutely nothing apart from an already assumed framework within which — or in terms of which — moral meaning is accorded to human life and to the varied relationships in which people stand. Much of the self-evidence that attaches to the "justice is orthodoxy" slogan in the minds of Christian activists (and rather too many Christian leaders) derives from the uncritical readiness with which ideas about the primacy of the human individual have been embraced, for the sake of which all else must be rejected as oppressive. The latter tends to be treated, in practice if not in explicit theory, as a kind of *peccatum originale,* and includes much of the content of the Christian theological tradition, as we have seen from a range of writers cited earlier in this book.

nography, and the obsession with self that is so characteristic of Western culture exist on the basis of precisely the same political and social values that underwrite the idea of justice commonly advanced, on the one hand, and the cherished principles of freedom of conscience and of religion, on the other. These are so firmly embraced that it would require upheaval on a massive scale to effect a modification of the ideals at stake. The question we might venture at this point is not whether jeopardizing one form of freedom is jeopardizing the other, but whether a church whose teaching and existence rest on the same principle as does the existence of rapacious economic exploitation, pornography, and crass individualism can be said to be *theologically* free in any meaningful sense at all. Surely it exists in bondage instead, in a Babylon that will never be abandoned unless it is first recognized as an alien land.

Does the kind of upheaval that could transform this situation appear likely in future? This question requires a prophetic prescience and a prophetic voice that is commonly lacking among the church's leaders.[32] For the church, however, there are reasons for hoping for some such development and discovery. After all, the values of the gospel, when they are encountered afresh, proclaimed, and believed, are such as to shatter the idols of every age. There is in this sense much to be done by way of helping the church to live more faithfully, and reminding the church that its belief, its witness, and its work do not run along lines laid down by the world. Among the most surprising possibilities opened up by this approach to the problem of the church's existence in the modern world is a new opportunity for mission.

Mission: Church and World

Christianity is a "missionary religion," and though the idea has become an unwelcome one in the context of much contemporary culture, it remains true that the doctrine of the church is intimately tied to that concept. One

---

32. Such a struggle — and with it, such prescience and vision — will also be needed if the West is ever to come to terms with militant Islam, which will certainly not be defeated by Western military power. In the end, there must be dialogue between the cultures and an understanding on the part of the West of the religio-political concerns of hundreds of millions of Muslims globally. If this understanding is not developed from the standpoint of the Christian religion, it will likely not be developed at all; nor, indeed, will it be taken seriously by Muslims as something that runs deep enough to trust.

major strand of support for the idea is found in the New Testament itself, the documents of which are a product of the early Christian mission. In the synoptic Gospels, Jesus already sends out the twelve apostles before his death, granting them a special share in his authority and a ministry of teaching and healing (Mark 3:13-19; Matt. 10:1-42; Luke 6:12-16; 9:1-6). This ministry is then continued beyond the resurrection, but universalized so that the mission is to "all nations" (Matt. 28:19-20) rather than only to "the lost sheep of the house of Israel" (Matt. 10:6). The scope of the mission is foreshadowed in the simplicity of a text such as Mark 1:17: "Follow me and I will make you fish for people."

In the New Testament, indeed, the mission of the church is closely connected with the pivotal event of the resurrection of Jesus.[33] It is in the Gospel of John that the link between the resurrection and the mission is clearest, for that is where Jesus' central appearance to his disciples, following his rising from the dead, brings both the bestowal of the Spirit and the ultimate commissioning for the missionary expansion that followed: "As the Father has sent me, so I send you" (John 20:21). This statement picks up on themes scattered elsewhere in John's Gospel (e.g., John 17:1-3, 18, 23); and particularly when it is coupled with the teaching of Paul, it helps us understand what the character of the resurrection appearances might have been. The emphasis falls less on epiphany than on commissioning, or, to put the real point more precisely, it falls on *sharing Christ's mission*. The implication of all of this would be that where there is little appreciation of the importance of the Christian mission, there is a limited grasp of the resurrection faith. Therefore, whatever the cultural difficulties implicit in embracing mission as central to the doctrine of the church, the theological theme can scarcely be avoided.

Much of this biblical insight is also present in the doctrine of the Trinity, according to which, through the sending of the Son into the world, and

---

33. The doctrine of the resurrection is often treated, and too often understood, as concerned purely with the question of God's vindication of Jesus, or alternatively, as God's confirmation that Jesus was indeed the one he sent and the one through whom he will judge the nations. Even the New Testament can at times adopt this way of thinking: for example, Paul's sermon in Acts 17: "[H]e has fixed a day on which he will have the world judged in righteousness by a man whom he has appointed, and of this he has given assurance to all by raising him from the dead" (v. 31). However, the resurrection is much more often linked in the New Testament with the missionary expansion of the church. For example, Paul himself relates his apostleship repeatedly to the resurrection of Jesus (e.g., Rom. 1:4-5; Gal. 1:1, 12).

through the gift of the Spirit, the Father shows himself to be open to the creation, inviting it into his life. The work of the Son and the Spirit, the "two hands of the Father" (Irenaeus), reveals that God takes a "hands-on" approach to the world, an approach that is directed to our becoming "participants of the divine nature" (2 Pet. 1:4). This theme has had an impact on recent missiological thought: it appears in the concept of the *missio Dei* movement, which was developed in the context of the ecumenical work of the International Missionary Council in the mid-twentieth century, before that body was integrated into the World Council of Churches in 1961. According to one of the documents issued in connection with its 1952 conference in Willingen, Germany:

> The mission is not only obedience to a word of the Lord, it is not only the commitment to the gathering of the congregation; it is participation in the sending of the Son, in the *missio Dei*, with the inclusive aim of establishing the lordship of Christ over the whole redeemed creation. The missionary movement of which we are a part has its source in the Triune God Himself.[34]

According to this (rather Barthian) view, mission is not simply something that the church does, as it were, among its several other tasks and duties. Nor would it be strictly accurate as a matter of theological principle to say that the task of mission belongs to the church. Rather, since the mission is fundamentally God's, and since the church merely participates in it, the church belongs to the *missio Dei* rather than the *missio* to the church. Therefore, mission precedes the church and is utterly fundamental: it is effectively the womb from which the church is called into being. Or, to put it another way, it is only by virtue of the church's participation in the divine mission that it actually comes into existence. In this strictly theological sense, then, mission is nothing less than the source and content of all ecclesiology.

The roots of the theology of mission are thus to be found in the depths of who and what God is. God is the one who reaches out to the world through his Word and Spirit, giving birth to the people of God through the ages. Just as the election of Abraham was intended to be a blessing to all the world (Gen. 12:3), and as the election of his descendants was intended, ac-

---

34. Report of the fifth International Missionary Council conference, July 1952, in Norman Goodall, ed., *Missions Under the Cross* (London: Edinburgh House Press, 1953), p. 189.

cording to the "missionary high point" of the Old Testament, to reveal justice and to be a light to the nations (Isa. 42:1-7; 49:1-7), so it is with the
church.[35] It exists not for its own sake, as if its proper goal were its own
maintenance or aggrandizement; rather, it exists only as it is given a share in
the greater mission from which it derives its being. It lives for the sake of the
world, which does not yet know justice and light and the gospel of the love
of God. Like Jesus himself, the church is sent not to be served but to serve.
Unfortunately, it has often gotten this the wrong way around.

The centrality of mission for the existence of the Christian church is a
matter of historical record as well as theological theory. One noted historian
of Christian missions, Andrew F. Walls, in an essay entitled "Culture and Coherence in Christian History," speaks of six "ages" of Christian missionary
expansion, epochs that have successively tended to shape the church in ways
that are utterly fundamental. We are most readily familiar with what Walls
terms the "fifth age" of this expansion, the age of an "expanding Europe," in
the age of colonialism and of the mass emigration of European peoples to
other continents; as a result, by the beginning of the twentieth century, peoples of European origin dominated most of the earth in one way or another,
including in the spread of their religion.[36]

What is of particular interest in Walls's account is that it shows how
wrong it is to understand the missionary endeavor of the Christian church
exclusively in terms of the particular pattern of the "fifth age." The "third
age" of mission, for example, came out of the fall of Rome and of the Western empire to the northern tribes of western Europe, and from the subsequent rise of the Arabs as a major military power, overwhelming the eastern
provinces of the empire where the oldest and arguably the strongest areas of
Christian influence had traditionally been located (pp. 19-20). There fol-

---

35. Johannes Blauw, *The Missionary Nature of the Church* (London: Lutterworth
Press, 1962), pp. 31-32.

36. Andrew F. Walls, "Culture and Coherence in Christian History," in Walls, *The
Missionary Movement in Christian History* (Edinburgh: T&T Clark; Maryknoll, NY:
Orbis Books, 1996), pp. 21-22. Walls presents these six ages in broad terms as follows: the
gentile mission of the New Testament era; the development of Hellenistic-Roman Christianity; the Christianity of the Latin West during the "Dark Ages"; the development of
individualism from the high medieval period down to early modern times (with a piety
markedly different from that of older "barbarian" Europe); the era of the expanding
West; and the current period of cross-cultural transmission of Christianity in the context of globalization.

lowed "centuries of erosion and attrition," with Christianity being saved from oblivion only by a missionary endeavor that took place amidst the dawn of the "barbarian" age of the church. The chief instrument of this mission was the establishment of the disciplined institutions of Latin monasticism: these were clearly suited to the task of fostering a Christian civilization among the warlike northern tribes.[37]

It has been suggested that there is a parallel between our situation in the modern West and that of the church and its missionaries during the "third age" of the church. Alisdair MacIntyre's final paragraph in *After Virtue* famously speaks to this (though qualifying it by noting that such historical parallels can be made less than illuminating if pressed too far):

> A crucial turning point in . . . earlier history occurred when men and women of good will turned aside from shoring up the Roman imperium and ceased to identify the continuation of civility and morality with [its] maintenance. . . . What they set themselves to achieve instead — often not recognizing what they were doing — was the construction of new forms of community within which the moral life could be sustained so that both morality and civility might survive the coming ages of barbarism and darkness. If my account of our moral condition is correct, we ought also to conclude that for some time now we too have reached that turning point. What matters at this stage is the construction of local forms of community within which civility and the intellectual and moral life can be sustained through the new dark ages which are already upon us. And if the tradition of the virtues was able

---

37. The monastic ideal was indeed of special importance during Europe's Dark Ages, for the monasteries were virtually the only centers of learning available. We read with bewilderment in the monastic *Rule of St. Benedict* (c. 480–c. 550) of how newcomers who wished to join the monastic life were obliged to stand knocking on the monastery door for several days, enduring insults and missiles from the brothers within, before at length being admitted (Benedict, *The Rule of Saint Benedict*, ed. and trans. Justin McCann [Westminster, MD: Newman Press, 1952], p. 58). The requirement becomes much more comprehensible, however, when we set the desire of the would-be monk and the perception of civilization and learning within the monastery over against the prevailing squalor and violence outside the monastery. It is for this reason that the monasteries made such an incalculable contribution to Christian civilization at this time: they served as centers for the study of medicine, agriculture, language, and of general learning almost as much as they served as centers for the study of Scripture, for the development of the spiritual life, and for evangelism.

to survive the horrors of the last dark ages, we are not entirely without grounds for hope. This time however the barbarians are not waiting beyond the frontiers; they have already been governing us for quite some time. And it is our lack of consciousness that constitutes part of our predicament. We are waiting not for a Godot, but for another — doubtless very different — St. Benedict. (*After Virtue*, p. 263)

MacIntyre's rhetorical call for another Benedict has actually been followed by a significant stirring of interest in new forms of monasticism, but it is clearly too early to speak with any authority of a major revival — or to predict the course of religious life in the next decades.[38] Only time will tell. In any case, I would like to suggest that Walls's "second age" of missionary expansion holds at least as much promise for us, and if we seek historical parallels to give inspiration to the Christian mission in our own time, this one might do as well: the evangelization of the Hellenistic-Roman world.

According to the New Testament (Acts 11:20), the Jewish national "Messiah" began to be proclaimed as "Lord" to the Greeks starting in Antioch. The historical details are impossible to reconstruct precisely, because even what we know of the early origins of Christianity is hotly disputed, and because there is much that will never be known. But it is at least clear that fundamental changes in the character of the Christian church followed as it entered its "second age" and left behind the earliest stage of Jewish Christianity. Whereas the earliest Christians carefully followed a succession of biblical rituals — keeping the Sabbath, circumcising their boys, and no doubt continuing to offer ritual sacrifice at the Jerusalem temple — the emerging gentile church in the Hellenistic-Roman world was concerned more with questions of right belief and with ecclesiastical organization than with obscure Jewish ("barbarian") practices. In fact, the new gentile church almost universally abandoned those practices. As Walls points out, two particular features of the "second age" of the church stand out: first, the remarkably successful and sustained attempt the early church made to reconcile the best in the intellectual traditions of Hellenism with the new faith, culminating not only in the work of philosopher-theologians such as Gregory of Nyssa (c. 330–c. 395) and Augustine of Hippo (354-430) but also in the great ecclesiastical councils of the fourth and fifth centuries; and second, the organization of the life of

---

38. Cf. Jason Byassee, "The New Monasticism: Alternative Christian Communities," *Christian Century*, 18 October 2005, pp. 38-47.

the church that emerged, based largely on prevailing patterns in Roman legal and administrative practice (pp. 18-19).

The Christian mission in the new context of this "second age" was no longer conducted by itinerant Jewish evangelists; rather, it became nothing less than the Christianization of the Hellenistic-Roman world, a goal that was finally achieved by both intellectual and political means. On the one side, the theologians of the church developed brilliant systems of ideas, synthesizing what was best in Hellenism with biblical faith. On the other, the conversion of Constantine (Roman emperor, 312-337) in the early years of the fourth century led, over a period of some seven decades, to the religious supremacy of Christianity in the empire, finally secured by successive pieces of legislation under the emperor Theodosius I (Roman emperor, 379-395).

It was under Theodosius that the ideal of the "Christian empire" was established, so that, for example, heresy became a crime under the law. It was also at this time that the church assumed the full trappings of imperial religion (taxation revenues, military chaplaincies, and so forth). It is hardly surprising to find that the church was increasingly divided into the traditional territorial and administrative units of dioceses and provinces, which were based on imperial administrative divisions. In this setting the clergy constituted a "celestial militia" that was parallel to the "secular militia" of the imperial civil service, complete with a ladder of offices by which an aspiring candidate might rise through the ranks.

The net result of all this was what we call classical Christian orthodoxy: a single system of belief, authoritatively defined, locating itself within a single and total tradition of thought, under the jurisdiction of a highly organized religious institution, complete with a hierarchical priesthood, and enjoying the support of the state and expecting as a matter of course judicial backing for its beliefs and practices. The church came to operate as if such expectations were entirely normative, in the sense that the church should not have to exist in any other way in a rightly ordered world. We may shudder, but the truth is that it is difficult to see how else a genuinely Hellenistic-Roman church could have been constructed. Although many would go so far as to say that the church was hopelessly corrupted by "imperial" expectations throughout its history (e.g., the later doctrine of the pope as "king of kings" is surely derivative of these developments), the reality is that, as Walls puts it, "Hellenistic-Roman civilization offered a total system of thought, and expected general conformity to its norms" (p. 19).

This is what orthodoxy in the classical period attempted to deliver: a total system of thought, with the ecclesiastical and political apparatus to support it and thus also the means to impose it. It is no accident that bishops who had faced imperial persecution in the third century were regularly using precisely the same imperial power by the end of the fourth century, though admittedly with less violence, that once had persecuted their predecessors. They were using it, instead, to serve the cause of the church's continuing "war" against heresy, schism, and paganism. It had long been their goal to achieve just such a position in the world.

I scarcely need to point out that, in terms of historical parallels, there is much here that would be neither possible nor desirable for the church to emulate in our own day. But that is not the point. Instead, the purpose is to indicate that it is possible to conceive of a missiology that is directed as much to the public order as it is to *individuals,* whose personal faith and welfare dominates as the "end" of doing mission in much contemporary missiology. Of course, there is such a thing as personal faith and well-being, and it is true that people can and do need to find them; but what the history of Christian mission also reveals is that it is possible to conceive of the church's witness as being to the world in a much more comprehensive sense. In short, the Christian mission can involve a public theology, which an individual might be carried along by but which is not directed primarily to the solitary self.

This suggests that what is necessary in a contemporary missiology for the church in the West is something akin to the achievement of figures such as Gregory of Nyssa and Augustine: an *evangelistic* attempt to engage with the outlook of an entire civilization. The need is not for some attempt to relate the new religion to the best that can be found in the civilization of paganism, but to relate the old religion once more to the civilization to which it gave rise, and to call that civilization back to its roots. Such a witness can be found in some places; unfortunately, however, Christian witness in this matter is uneven and divided. Perhaps we can see the best example of such an approach to the mission of the church in the work and witness of Pope John Paul II, whose criticisms of the modern world as resting on a "culture of death," for example, went extraordinarily deep — and still do — striking as they do at the heart of the perverse understanding of freedom that is so characteristic of contemporary secular culture.[39] Yet, at the same time, John

---

39. John Paul II, Encyclical *Evangelium Vitae,* 25 March 1995, p. 12 and passim. One must also acknowledge that this witness was flawed (and whose is not?) by John Paul II's

Paul II was capable of seeing and teaching that some of what one finds in contemporary secular culture can be seen not only as consistent with the insights of Christian faith but as actually stemming from it. Good examples are his teaching on the dignity of human labor, on democracy, and on political renewal grounded in a Christian moral vision, which became so important in Eastern Europe in the years surrounding the revolutions of 1989.[40] One does not have to agree with every sentence John Paul II uttered on these or any other subjects to grasp his witness to the world, that it was immensely effective, and that the call to turn to the gospel that emerged from this overtly *public* witness was a particular hallmark of his ministry. We would do well to learn from it.

The Renewal of the Church

I began this study in a kind of despair about the "suicide of liberal Christianity," on the one hand, and the related problem of the unwillingness of much contemporary theology to engage with the church as a properly *doctrinal* problem, on the other.[41] In response to the problem, I have sought to recall the fundamental structures of the doctrine of the church in order to hold forth the possibility of a rerooting of the church itself — and our thinking about it — in its true sources. After all, the real question in ecclesiology is not why there should be this or that kind of church, or this or that ecclesial praxis, but why there should be *any church* at all. If we assume that we already know the answer to this latter question, or that it can come to us without theological labor from sources external to the gospel, then we can be sure that we have misunderstood the real ecclesiological question.

It may be that in the modern world the church can take its place alongside other voluntary organizations in civil society and can meet a variety of human needs; but this does not in any way qualify it as adequate to the vast

---

often reactionary response to certain movements within Roman Catholicism itself (e.g., his consistent denial of laicization to civilly married priests, or to priests wishing to marry), which many believed contradicted the message he sought to bring to the world.

40. Among the best examples are John Paul II, Encyclicals *Laborem Exercens*, 5 November 1981; *Sollicitudo Rei Socialis*, 25 July 1988; and *Centesimus Annus*, 1 May 1991.

41. The phrase is the apt subtitle of Thomas C. Reeves, *The Empty Church* (New York: The Free Press, 1996).

implications of biblical talk of the church, nor can it begin to comprehend what is contained in the creedal marks of the church: "one, holy, catholic, and apostolic." To grapple seriously with these requires a different intellectual step altogether. Without roots that reach into God's gracious purposes, it is not at all theologically obvious that the church is really something theologically necessary, or something that could not be abandoned and replaced by any number of alternative religious or voluntary organizations. Therefore, it is only when the most basic ecclesiological question of all has been properly answered that there can be any genuinely theological approach to the secondary ecclesiological question of praxis. The obsession with the latter question in contemporary theological circles is a symptom of the problem we face rather than its cure.

Given the fact that present levels of decline in the West suggest that many of the churches are unlikely to survive in recognizable form beyond the present century, the question of why there should be any church at all has to be taken very seriously indeed. The question is not merely one of theory, but is one with an immediate existential reference: Why should these churches continue to exist? One of the more fundamental submissions that I wish to make in this book is that, in truth, much of what calls itself the church has been so evacuated of theological substance across the range of wider theological questions that bear directly on the church as a doctrine of the faith, that it has no real answer to give to this challenge. Wherever we look, classical Protestant Christianity, in particular, has become a curiosity, an "option" taken by increasingly tiny minorities. In the United States, for instance, there are many millions more Mormons than there are in the vast majority of the individual American "mainline" churches — in fact, millions more than in several of them combined. Though the fiction that all is well continues, the catastrophic decline that is underway suggests something very different.

The appeal to the secular outlook of late modernity as the basis for an ecclesiology simply will not do. Nor does the church, to be "relevant," need to be made to serve this or that contemporary cause. Indeed, when not only the church but the gospel itself is assimilated to the demands of modern political liberalism, it becomes strangely irrelevant, since the liberal state can scarcely be said to require such a prop. Of course, though the theologically — and especially the philosophically — naïve may preach it, the hungry sheep look up, remain unfed, and have decided in the hundreds of millions that they can find the same thing (and it *is* the same thing) in more convincing forms from the other available consumerist alternatives that equally serve the end of individual flourishing: popular culture, environmental activism, uninhibited sex, the fulfillment of career ambition, politics, or even crass materialism.

The time has come, then, for taking a long and hard look at the basis of the doctrine of the church. Only when a contemporary ecclesiology takes this difficult step will it become, as Nicholas Healy puts it in the line of thought with which we began this study, a tool for helping the church to live more faithfully. For the church is fundamentally a mystery of Christian faith: before all else, it is something biblical and creedal, something that "we believe," and only as such is the empirical or sociological or even pastoral existence and function of the church also something of theological interest.

The requisite reorientation of ecclesiastical self-understanding, especially among church leaders, is elemental. The church exists not because of pastoral care, financial campaigns, membership programs, or family and cultural loyalties, however important those may be at points along the way. Rather, it exists as the *church of God* solely because of the decision of God to summon it into existence: it is born from God's primal decision that issues in the incarnation of the Son and in the sending and the indwelling of the Holy Spirit, so that it comes into being not only as people of God, but also in one action of God the Father, Son, and Holy Spirit as the body of Christ and the temple of the Spirit. Apart from these, there is, in the strictest possible sense, absolutely no basis for either an ecclesiology as a doctrine of the church or any adequate theological reason for the continuing existence of the church as a human reality. This is what we need to learn afresh, and it is here that we need to begin anew in ecclesiology.

However, after this chastening come the possibilities that arise from Christian faith in God. "I believe in the Holy Spirit, the holy catholic church, the communion of saints, the forgiveness of sins. . . ." In these words, Christians have for centuries confessed their faith, according to which the church is a mystery of salvation rather than a purely human invention or convention. At this point, I must say with gratitude, even the human institution of Christian theology and its conventions must yield, and I must sound the warning that, however bad our theological situation might be, it is not a theology that will cure it. This would be to replace the Word and work of God with human words and works. It would be better to say that the renewal of our thinking about the church will come only when God's labor with us is done. For the church is the product of a divine initiative of grace, and it is that not only in its origins but all along the way, so that there is never a point at which we can say that the church is not in some sense "the house where God lives."

"I believe in the church." In this confession of Christian faith there are, ultimately, grounds for hope. The church is what it is not because of some program, system of thought, or pattern of practice. It is what it is, in the final analysis, because God graciously chooses to deal with us as sinful creatures. As a result, the church is more than a hollow shell in which humans think theological thoughts, dream religious and moral dreams, and do good deeds. Hence neither the existence nor the renewal of the church is strictly *our* task; this is just as well, because on account of our half-formed thinking, our sloth, and our disobedience, the church in itself is bound to be a disappointment. God is able to renew the church, but this is entirely despite the fact of its limitations and sinfulness, despite its wrong-headedness and outright lies at times, rather than because of any inherent holiness or wisdom it possesses. Therefore, the renewal of the church does not even depend on an ecclesiology; in the end, even the theologian who labors to say as much must fall silent, give thanks, and pray.

What is absolutely required here is neither a theology nor a strategy but what was earlier called "God's lightning," the free action of God that strikes unexpectedly, in ways that surpass what we can ask and in the end is totally independent of our answers or our imaginings. For the renewal of the church takes place as God reaches out in power, truth, and love by his Word and Spirit, so that God himself comes to us — God, the unutterable one who transcends all our theological systems and stratagems alike, the one who judges all things and who makes all things new. The renewal of the church, though a goal toward which we can surely work and concerning which we can think, is ultimately something for which we must pray and wait. This is what I intend when I speak of the church as "the house where God lives," that is, affirming what is sufficient for our needs in this age and in all ages, and affirming what is finally the one great theme of ecclesiology as a question of Christian *doctrine*.

Bibliography

Abbott, Walter M., et al., eds. *The Documents of Vatican II: Introductions and Commentaries by Catholic Bishops and Experts; Responses by Protestant and Orthodox Scholars.* Translated by Joseph Gallagher et al. New York: The America Press, 1966.

Achtemeier, Paul J. *1 Peter: A Commentary on First Peter.* Minneapolis: Fortress Press, 1996.

Ainslie, J. L. *The Doctrines of Ministerial Order in the Reformed Churches of the Sixteenth and Seventeenth Centuries.* Edinburgh: T&T Clark, 1940.

Altizer, Thomas J. J. *The Gospel of Christian Atheism.* London: Collins, 1967.

Ambrose of Milan. *The Letters of S. Ambrose.* English translation. Oxford: James Parker and Co., 1881.

————. *Theological and Dogmatic Works.* Edited and translated by Roy Defarri. Washington, DC: Catholic University of America Press, 1963.

Anglican Communion News Service. "Archbishop of Canterbury expresses sadness at New Westminster decision," 29 May 2003. ACNS 3454: http://www.anglicancommunion.org/acns/articles/34/50/acns3454.html (accessed 25 September 2007).

————. "Church of Nigeria cuts ties with the Diocese of New Westminster," 2 June 2003. ACNS 3455: http://www.anglicancommunion.org/acns/articles/34/50/acns3455.html (accessed 25 September 2007).

————. "Rite of Blessing authorized in Diocese of New Westminster," 29 May 2003. ACNS 3453: http://www.anglicancommunion.org/acns/articles/34/50/acns3453.html (accessed 25 September 2007).

Anselm of Canterbury. *Proslogium.* In *St. Anselm: Basic Writings,* pp. 47-80. Translated by S. N. Deane. 2nd ed. La Salle, IL: Open Court Publishing Company, 1962.

Aquinas, Thomas. *Summa Theologiae*. Edited and translated by T. Gilby et al. 61 vols. London: Blackfriars, in conjunction with Eyre & Spottiswoode, 1964-1981.

Aristotle. *The Basic Works of Aristotle*. Edited by Richard McKeon and translated by E. M. Edghill et al. New York: Random House, 1941.

Askonas, Peter, and Angus Stewart, eds. *Social Inclusion: Possibilities and Tensions*. Houndmills, UK: Macmillan Press; New York: St. Martin's Press, 2000.

Augustine of Hippo. *Concerning the City of God Against the Pagans*. Translated by Henry Bettenson. Harmondsworth, UK: Penguin Books, 1972.

————. *Four Anti-Pelagian Writings: On Nature and Grace, On the Proceedings of Pelagius, On the Predestination of the Saints, and On the Gift of Perseverance*. Translated by John A. Mourant and William J. Collinge. Washington, DC: Catholic University of America Press, 1992.

————. *Letters 1-99*. Edited by John E. Rotelle. Translated by Roland Teske. New York: New City Press, 2001.

————. *Tractates on the Gospel of John 11–27*. Translated by John Rettig. Washington, DC: Catholic University of America Press, 1988.

————. *Tractates on the Gospel of John 55–111*. Translated by John W. Rettig. Washington, DC: Catholic University of America Press, 1994.

Avineri, Schlomo. *Hegel's Theory of the Modern State*. Cambridge, UK: Cambridge University Press, 1972.

Avis, Paul. *Ecumenical Theology and the Elusiveness of Doctrine*. London: SPCK, 1986.

Bacon, Francis. *The Advancement of Learning and New Atlantis*. Edited by Arthur Johnson. Oxford: Clarendon Press, 1974.

Bacon, Roger. *Science et Sagesse chez Hughes de Saint-Victor*. Paris: P. Lethielleux, 1957.

Badcock, Gary D. "Divine Freedom in Hegel." *Irish Theological Quarterly* 61 (1995): 265-71.

————. *Light of Truth and Fire of Love: A Theology of the Holy Spirit*. Grand Rapids and Cambridge: Wm. B. Eerdmans Publishing Company, 1997.

Baillie, D. M. *God Was in Christ: An Essay on Incarnation and Atonement*. London: Faber & Faber, 1948.

Baillie, John. *A Reasoned Faith: Collected Addresses*. London: Oxford University Press, 1963.

Bakhtin, Mikhail. *Problems of Dostoyevsky's Poetics*. Edited and translated by Caryl Emerson. Minneapolis: University of Minnesota Press, 1984.

Balthasar, Hans Urs von. *Church and World*. Translated by A. V. Littledale and Alexander Dru. Montreal: Palm Publishers, 1967.

————. *Mysterium Paschale: The Mystery of Easter*. Translated by Aidan Nichols. Edinburgh: T&T Clark, 1990.

————. *The Office of Peter and the Structure of the Church*. Translated by Andrée Emery. San Francisco: Ignatius Press, 1986.

————. *Theo-Drama: Theological Dramatic Theory*. Translated by Graham Harrison. 5 vols. San Francisco: Ignatius Press, 1988-1998.

————. *Truth is Symphonic: Aspects of Christian Pluralism*. Translated by Graham Harrison. San Francisco: Ignatius Press, 1987.

Barrois, G. A. "Temples." In *The Interpreter's Dictionary of the Bible: An Illustrated Encyclopedia Identifying and Explaining*, Vol. 4: 560-68. Edited by G. A. Buttrick et al. New York and Nashville: Abingdon, 1962.

Barth, Karl. *Church Dogmatics*. Vols. I/1-IV/4. Edited by G. W. Bromiley and T. F. Torrance. Translated by G. W. Bromiley et al. Edinburgh: T&T Clark, 1936-1969; 2nd ed. of I/1, 1975.

————. *Die Kirchliche Dogmatik*. Band I/1-IV/4. Zürich: Theologische Verlag, 1932-1968.

————. *Protestant Theology in the Nineteenth Century: Its Background and History*. Translated by Brian Cozens and John Bowden. London: SCM Press, 1972.

————. *The Word of God and the Word of Man*. Translated by Douglas Horton. London: Hodder & Stoughton, 1935.

Barth, Markus. *The People of God*. Sheffield: JSOT Press, 1983.

Bauckham, Richard. *Bible and Mission: Christian Witness in a Postmodern World*. Grand Rapids: Baker Academic; Carlisle, UK: Paternoster, 2003.

Bauer, Walter. *Orthodoxy and Heresy in Earliest Christianity*. Edited by Robert Kraft and Gerhard Krodel. Translated by members of the Philadelphia Seminar on Christian Origins. 2nd ed. Philadelphia: Fortress Press, 1971.

Baylor, M. G., ed. and trans. *The Radical Reformation*. Cambridge, UK: Cambridge University Press, 1991.

Benedict. *The Rule of Saint Benedict, in Latin and English*. Edited and translated by Justin McCann. Westminster, MD: Newman Press, 1952.

Benko, Stephen. *The Meaning of Sanctorum Communio*. London: SCM Press, 1964.

Berkouwer, G. C. *The Church*. Translated by James E. Davison. Grand Rapids: Eerdmans, 1976.

————. *Divine Election*. Translated by Hugo Bekker. Grand Rapids: Eerdmans, 1960.

Bernard of Clairvaux. *Sancti Bernardi Opera*. Edited by J. LeClerq and H. Rochais. 8 vols. Rome: Editiones Cistercienses, 1968.

Best, Ernest. *One Body in Christ: A Study in the Relationship of the Church to Christ in the Epistles of the Apostle Paul*. London: SPCK, 1955.

Bethge, Eberhard. *Dietrich Bonhoeffer: Man of Vision, Man of Courage*. Translated by Eric Mosbacher et al. London: Collins; New York: Harper and Row, 1970.

Blamires, Harry. *The Will and the Way: A Study of Divine Providence and Vocation*. London: SPCK, 1957.

Blauw, Johannes. *The Missionary Nature of the Church: A Survey of the Biblical Theology of Mission.* Guildford and London: Lutterworth Press, 1962.

Bohlin, T. *Die Theologie des Pelagius und ihre Genesis.* Lundequist: Harrassowitz, 1957.

Bonaventure. *Bonaventure: The Soul's Journey Into God, The Tree of Life, The Life of St. Francis.* Translated by Ewert Cousins. New York: Paulist Press, 1978.

Bonhoeffer, Dietrich. *Dietrich Bonhoeffer's Works.* 9 vols. Edited by Wayne Whitson Floyd, Jr. Translated by Daniel W. Bloesch et al. Minneapolis: Fortress Press, 1996-.

———. *No Rusty Swords: Letters, Lectures, and Notes, 1928-1936,* from the *Collected Works of Dietrich Bonhoeffer.* Edited and translated by John Bowden. London: William Collins Sons, 1970.

———. *Sanctorum Communio: A Dogmatic Inquiry into the Sociology of the Church.* Translated by R. Gregor Smith. London: Collins, 1963.

Bornkamm, G. "Das Bekenntnis im Hebräerbrief." In Bornkamm, *Gesammelte Aufsätze,* vol. 2, *Studien zu Antike und Urchristentum,* pp. 188-203. München: Kaiser, 1959.

Braaten, Carl E. *The Apostolic Imperative: The Nature and Aim of the Church's Mission and Ministry.* Minneapolis: Augsburg Publishing House, 1985.

———. *The Flaming Center: A Theology of the Christian Mission.* Philadelphia: Fortress Press, 1977.

Braaten, Carl E., and Robert W. Jenson. *Reclaiming the Bible for the Church.* Grand Rapids: Eerdmans, 1995.

Brom, Luco J. van den. *Divine Presence in the World: A Critical Analysis of the Notion of Divine Omnipresence.* Kampen: Kok Pharos Publishing House, 1993.

Brown, Callum. *The Death of Christian Britain: Understanding Secularisation 1800-2000.* London and New York: Routledge, 2001.

Brown, Peter. *Augustine of Hippo: A Biography.* London and Boston: Faber & Faber, 1967.

Brown, Raymond E. *The Gospel According to John.* 2 vols. New York: Doubleday, 1966-1970.

Brunner, Emil. *The Divine Imperative.* Translated by Olive Wyon. London: Lutterworth Press, 1937.

———. *Truth as Encounter.* Translated by David Cairns et al. 2nd ed. Philadelphia: Westminster Press, 1964.

Bulley, Colin. *The Priesthood of Some Believers: Developments from the General to the Special Priesthood in the Christian Literature of the First Three Centuries.* Carlisle, UK: Paternoster, 2000.

Bultmann, Rudolf. *Theology of the New Testament.* Translated by Kendrick Grebel. 2 vols. London: SCM Press, 1952-1955.

Burkhard, John J. *Apostolicity Then and Now: An Ecumenical Church in a Postmodern World.* Collegeville, MN: Liturgical Press, 2004.

Calvin, John. *Institutes of the Christian Religion.* 2 vols. Edited by John T. McNeill. Translated by Ford Lewis Battles. Philadelphia: Westminster Press, 1960.

————. *The Epistle of Paul the Apostle to the Hebrews and The First and Second Epistles of St Peter.* Edited by David W. Torrance and Thomas F. Torrance. Translated by William B. Johnson. Edinburgh: St. Andrew Press, 1963.

Carruthers, William. *The Shorter Catechism of the Westminster Assembly of Divines.* London: Publication Office of the Presbyterian Church of England, 1897.

Chalmers, Thomas. *The Christian and Civic Economy of Large Towns.* 3 vols. London: Routledge/Thoemmes Press, 1995.

Christ, Carol. "Feminist theology as post-traditional theology." In *The Cambridge Companion to Feminist Theology,* pp. 79-96. Edited by Susan Frank Parsons. Cambridge, UK: Cambridge University Press, 2002.

Christie, Nancy, and Michael Gauvreau. *A Full-Orbed Christianity: The Protestant Churches and Social Welfare in Canada 1900-1940.* Montreal and Kingston: McGill-Queen's University Press, 1996.

Clark, Desmond. "Descartes' Philosophy of Science and the Scientific Revolution." In *The Cambridge Companion to Descartes,* pp. 258-85. Edited by John Cottingham. Cambridge, UK: Cambridge University Press, 1992.

Clayton, Philip. *God and Contemporary Science.* Grand Rapids: Eerdmans, 1998.

Clements, R. E. *God and Temple.* Oxford: Basil Blackwell, 1965.

Colish, Marcia L. *Peter Lombard.* 2 vols. Leiden: Brill, 1994.

Collins, Raymond F. *First Corinthians.* Collegeville, MN: Liturgical Press, 1999.

Comby, Jean. *How to Understand the History of Christian Mission.* Translated by John Bowden. London: SCM Press, 1996.

Confessing Church. *The Barmen Theological Declaration.* Translated by Douglas S. Bax. In Eberhard Jüngel, *Christ, Justice and Peace,* pp. xxi-xxix. Edited and translated by D. Bruce Hamill and Alan J. Torrance. Edinburgh: T&T Clark, 1992.

Congar, Yves. *Fifty Years of Catholic Theology: Conversations with Yves Congar.* Edited by Bernard Lauret. Translated by John Bowden. London: SCM Press, 1988.

————. *I Believe in the Holy Spirit.* Translated by David Smith. 3 vols. London: Geoffrey Chapman, 1983.

————. *The Mystery of the Temple, or, The Manner of God's Presence to His Creatures from Genesis to the Apocalypse.* Translated by Reginald F. Trevett. London: Burns & Oates, 1962.

————. *The Word and the Spirit.* Translated by David Smith. London: Geoffrey Chapman, 1986.

Costello, J. E. *John Macmurray: A Biography.* Edinburgh: Floris Books, 2002.

Cousins, Ewert. "Spirituality in Today's World." In *Religion in Today's World: The Religious Situation of the World from 1945 to the Present Day,* pp. 306-34. Edited by Frank Whaling. Edinburgh: T&T Clark, 1987.

Crouzel, Henri. *Origen.* Translated by A. S. Worrall. Edinburgh: T&T Clark, 1989.

Cuming, G. J., ed. *The Mission of the Church and the Propagation of the Faith: Papers Read at the Seventh Summer Meeting and the Eighth Winter Meeting of the Ecclesiastical History Society.* Cambridge, UK: Cambridge University Press, 1970.

D'Costa, Gavin, ed. *Christian Uniqueness Reconsidered: The Myth of a Pluralistic Theology of Religions.* Maryknoll, NY: Orbis Books, 1990.

Daniélou, Jean. *The Presence of God: A Translation of Le Signe du Temple.* Translated by Walter Roberts. London: A. R. Mowbray, 1958.

Dante Alighieri. *The Divine Comedy.* Translated by Dorothy L. Sayers and Barbara Reynolds. 3 vols. Harmondsworth, UK: Penguin Books, 1949-1962.

De Letter, P. "The Soul of the Mystical Body." *Sciences Ecclésiastiques* 14 (1962): 213-34.

De Lubac, Henri. *Catholicism: A Study of Dogma in Relation to the Corporate Destiny of Mankind.* Translated by Lancelot C. Sheppard. London: Burns & Oates, 1950; San Francisco: Ignatius Press, 1988.

———. *The Christian Faith: An Essay on the Structure of the Apostles' Creed.* Translated by Richard Arnandez. San Francisco: Ignatius Press, 1986.

———. *The Splendor of the Church.* London: Sheed and Ward, 1956.

De Vidas, Elijah. *The Beginning of Wisdom.* Translated by Lawrence Fine. In *Safed Spirituality: Rules of Mystical Piety, The Beginning of Wisdom.* Edited by Lawrence Fine. New York: Paulist Press, 1984.

Degrijse, Omer. *Going Forth: Missionary Consciousness in Third World Catholic Churches.* Maryknoll, NY: Orbis Books, 1984.

Doull, James. "Faith and Enlightenment." *Dionysus* 10 (1986): 129-35.

———. "The Logic of Theology Since Hegel." *Dionysus* 7 (1983): 12-136.

Doyle, Dennis M. *Communion Ecclesiology: Visions and Versions.* Maryknoll, NY: Orbis Books, 2000.

Dulles, Avery. *Models of the Church.* London: The Catholic Book Club, 1976.

———. *The Catholicity of the Church.* Oxford: Clarendon Press, 1985.

Dunn, James D. G. *The Partings of the Ways: Between Christianity and Judaism and their Significance for the Character of Christianity.* London: SCM Press; Philadelphia: Trinity Press International, 1991.

Evans, G. R. *The Church and the Churches: Toward an Ecumenical Ecclesiology.* Cambridge, UK: Cambridge University Press, 1994.

Evans, Robert F. *Pelagius: Inquiries and Reappraisals.* London: Adam and Charles Black, 1968.

Farrelly, M. John. *Predestination, Grace and Free Will.* London: Burns & Oates, 1964.

Fergusson, David. *Community, Liberalism and Christian Ethics.* Cambridge, UK: Cambridge University Press, 1998.

Filoramo, Giovani. *A History of Gnosticism.* Translated by Anthony Alcock. London: Basil Blackwell, 1991.

Florovsky, Georges. *Bible, Church, Tradition: An Eastern Orthodox View.* Belmont, MA: Nordland Publishing Company, 1972.

Frend, W. H. C. *The Donatist Church: A Movement of Protest in Roman North Africa.* 3rd ed. Oxford: Clarendon Press, 1985.

Goppelt, Leonard. *A Commentary on 1 Peter.* Edited by Ferdinand Hahn. Translated by John E. Alsup. Grand Rapids: Wm. B. Eerdmans Publishing Company, 1993.

Gray, John. "Inclusion: A Radical Critique." In *Social Inclusion: Possibilities and Tensions,* pp. 19-36. Edited by Peter Askonas and Angus Stewart. Houndmills, UK: Macmillan Press; New York: St. Martin's Press, Inc., 2000.

Green, Barbara. *Mikhail Bakhtin and Biblical Scholarship: An Introduction.* Atlanta: Society of Biblical Literature, 2000.

Greer, Rowan A. *Theodore of Mopsuestia: Exegete and Theologian.* Westminster, MD: Faith Press, 1961.

Gregory of Nyssa. "An Address on Religious Instruction." In *Christology of the Later Fathers,* pp. 268-325. Edited by E. R. Hardy. London: SCM Press, 1954.

————. *The Life of Moses.* Translated by A. J. Malherbe and E. Fergusson. New York: Paulist Press, 1978.

Grillmeier, Aloys. *Christ in Christian Tradition.* Translated by John Bowden et al. 4 part-vols. London and Oxford: Mowbrays, 1965-1996.

Grillmeier, Aloys, and Heinrich Bacht. *Das Konzil von Chalkedon: Geschichte und Gegenwart.* 3 vols. Würzburg: Echter-Verlag, 1951-1954.

Haendler, G. *Luther on Ministerial Office and Congregational Function.* Translated by Ruth C. Gritsch. Edited by Eric W. Gritsch. Philadelphia: Fortress Press, 1981.

Hahn, Ferdinand. *Mission in the New Testament.* Translated by Frank Clarke. London: SCM Press, 1965.

Hall, Douglas John. *The Stewardship of Life in the Kingdom of Death.* Rev. ed. Grand Rapids: Eerdmans, 1988.

Hamblin, William J., and David Rolph Seely. *Solomon's Temple: Myth and History.* New York: Thames & Hudson, 2007.

Hamer, Jerome. *The Church is a Communion.* Translated by Ronald Matthews. New York: Sheed and Ward, 1964.

Hanson, A. T. *Church, Sacraments and Ministry.* London and Oxford: Mowbrays, 1975.

Hanson, R. P. C. *The Search for the Christian Doctrine of God: The Arian Controversy 318-81.* Edinburgh: T&T Clark, 1988.

Hanson, A. T., and R. P. C. Hanson. *The Identity of the Church: A Guide to Recognizing the Contemporary Church.* London: SCM Press, 1987.

Haran, Menahem. *Temples and Temple-Service in Ancient Israel: An Inquiry into the Character of Cult Phenomena and the Historical Setting of the Priestly School.* Oxford: Clarendon Press, 1978.

Harrington, Daniel J. *God's People in Christ: New Testament Perspectives on the Church and Judaism.* Philadelphia: Fortress Press, 1980.

Hastings, Adrian, ed. *A World History of Christianity.* Grand Rapids: Eerdmans, 1999.

———. "Temple, William." In *Oxford Dictionary of National Biography,* vol. 54, p. 93. Edited by H. G. C. Matthew and Brian Harrison. Oxford: Oxford University Press, 1996.

———. *Mission and Ministry.* London and Sydney: Sheed and Ward, 1971.

Hauerwas, Stanley. *A Community of Character: Towards a Constructive Christian Social Ethic.* Notre Dame, IN: University of Notre Dame Press, 1981.

———. *After Christendom? How the Church is to Behave if Freedom, Justice, and a Christian Nation are Bad Ideas.* Nashville: Abingdon, 1991.

———. *In Good Company: The Church as Polis.* Notre Dame, IN: University of Notre Dame Press, 1995.

———. *The Peaceable Kingdom: A Primer in Christian Ethics.* Notre Dame, IN: University of Notre Dame Press, 1983.

Healy, Nicholas M. *Church, World and the Christian Life: Practical-Prophetic Ecclesiology.* Cambridge, UK: Cambridge University Press, 2000.

Hegel, G. W. F. *Elements of the Philosophy of Right.* Translated by H. B. Nisbet. Cambridge, UK: Cambridge University Press, 1991.

———. *Philosophy of Right.* Translated by T. M. Knox. Oxford: Oxford University Press, 1967.

———. *The Philosophy of History.* Translated by J. B. Sibree. New York: Dover Publications, 1956.

———. *Werke.* Edited by Eva Moldenhauer and Karl Markus Michel. 21 vols. Frankfurt am Main: Suhrkamp, 1969-1979.

Heim, S. Mark. *Salvations: Truth and Difference in Religion.* Maryknoll, NY: Orbis Books, 1995.

Henderson, G. D., ed. *The Scots Confession 1560.* Edinburgh: Church of Scotland Committee on Publication, 1937.

Henderson, John B. *The Construction of Orthodoxy and Heresy: Neo-Confucian, Islamic, Jewish, and Early Christian Patterns.* Albany: State University of New York Press, 1998.

Heron, Alasdair I. C. *Table and Tradition: Towards an Ecumenical Understanding of the Eucharist.* Edinburgh: Hansel Press, 1983.

Hick, John. *An Interpretation of Religion: Human Responses to the Transcendent.* Basingstoke, UK: MacMillon Press, 1989.

Hill, Harvey. *The Politics of Modernism: Alfred Loisy and the Scientific Study of Religion.* Washington, DC: Catholic University of America Press, 2002.

Hobbes, Thomas. *Leviathan.* Edited by Michael Oakeshott. New York: Collier Books, 1962.

Holquist, Michael. *Dialogism: Bakhtin and His World.* London and New York: Routledge, 1990.

Homan, Michael M. "The Tabernacle and the Temple in Ancient Israel." *Religion Compass* 1 (2007): 38-49.

Hugh of St. Victor. *On the Sacraments of the Christian Faith.* Translated by Roy J. Deferrai. Cambridge, MA: Mediaeval Academy of America, 1951.

Husbands, Mark, and Daniel J. Treier, eds. *The Community of the Word: Towards an Evangelical Ecclesiology.* Downers Grove, IL: InterVarsity Press; Leicester, UK: Apollos, 2005.

Hütter, Reinhard. "The Church." In *Knowing the Triune God: The Work of the Spirit in the Practices of the Church,* pp. 23-48. Edited by James J. Buckley and David S. Yeago. Grand Rapids: Eerdmans, 2001.

————. *Suffering Divine Things: Theology as Church Practice.* Translated by Doug Stott. Grand Rapids: Eerdmans, 2000.

Illingworth, J. R. *Divine Immanence: An Essay on the Spiritual Significance of Matter.* London: Macmillan and Co., 1898.

Ingham, Michael. "Sex and Christianity: Re-thinking the Relationship." http://www.anglican.ca/faith/ethics/wmc/ingham.html (accessed 25 September 2007).

Jaspers, Karl. *The Origin and Goal of History.* Translated by Michael Bullock. New Haven, CT: Yale University Press, 1989.

Jenson, Robert W. "The church and the sacraments." In *The Cambridge Companion to Christian Doctrine,* pp. 207-25. Edited by Colin Gunton. Cambridge, UK: Cambridge University Press, 1997.

————. *Systematic Theology.* 2 vols. Oxford: Oxford University Press, 1997-1999.

Jeremias, Joachim. *New Testament Theology.* Translated by John Bowden. London: SCM Press, 1971.

Jocz, Jacob. *A Theology of Election: Israel and the Church.* London: SPCK, 1958.

John Paul II. Encyclical *Centesimus Annus. Acta Apostolicae Sedis* 83 (1 May 1991): 793-867.

————. Encyclical *Evangelium Vitae. Acta Apostolicae Sedis* 87 (25 March 1995): 401-522.

————. Encyclical *Laborem Exercens. Acta Apostolicae Sedis* 73 (5 November 1981): 577-647.

————. Encyclical *Solicitudo Rei Socialis*. *Acta Apostolicae Sedis* 80 (25 July 1988): 513-86.

————. Encyclical *Ut Unum Sint*. *Acta Apostolicae Sedis* 87 (25 May 1995): 921-82.

Jüngel, Eberhard. *Christ, Justice and Peace: Toward a Theology of the State in Dialogue with the Barmen Declaration*. Edited and translated by D. Bruce Hamill and Alan J. Torrance. Edinburgh: T&T Clark, 1992.

————. *God as the Mystery of the World: On the Foundation of the Theology of the Crucified One in the Dispute Between Theism and Atheism*. Translated by Darrell L. Guder. Edinburgh: T&T Clark, 1983.

Kärkkäinen, Veli-Matti. *An Introduction to Ecclesiology: Ecumenical, Historical and Global Perspectives*. Downer's Grove, IL: InterVarsity Press, 2002.

Käsemann, Ernst. *Leib und Leib Christi: Eine Untersuchung zur Paulinischen Begrifflichkeit*. Tübingen: Mohr, 1933.

Kasper, Walter. *Theology and Church*. Translated by Margaret Kohl. London: SCM Press, 1989.

Kee, Howard Clark, and Lynn H. Cohick, eds. *Evolution of the Synagogue: Problems and Progress*. Harrisburg, PA: Trinity Press International, 1999.

Kelly, J. N. D. *A Commentary on the Epistles of Peter and of Jude*. London: Adam and Charles Black, 1969.

————. *Early Christian Creeds*. 3rd ed. Harlow and New York: Longmans, 1972.

Kelly, Robert A. "The Suffering of the Church: A Study of Luther's *Theologia Crucis*." *Concordia Theological Quarterly* 50 (1986): 3-17.

Kent, John. *William Temple*. Cambridge, UK: Cambridge University Press, 1992.

Kerr, Alan R. *The Temple of Jesus' Body: The Temple Theme in the Gospel of John*. New York: Sheffield Academic Press, 2002.

Kerr, Fergus. "French Theology: Yves Congar and Henri de Lubac." In *The Modern Theologians*, pp. 105-17. Edited by David F. Ford. 2nd ed. Oxford: Blackwell, 1997.

Kingdon, Robert. "Calvin and the Government of Geneva." In *Calvinus ecclesiae Genevensis custos*, pp. 49-67. Edited by Wilhelm Neuser. New York: Peter Lang, 1984.

Kirk, J. Andrew, and Kevin J. Vanhoozer. *To Stake a Claim: Mission and the Western Crisis of Knowledge*. Maryknoll, NY: Orbis Books, 1999.

Kirkpatrick, Frank G. *Community: A Trinity of Models*. Washington, DC: Georgetown University Press, 1986.

Kittel, Gerhard, et al., eds. *Theological Dictionary of the New Testament*. Translated by G. W. Bromiley. 10 vols. Grand Rapids: Eerdmans, 1964-1976.

Knitter, Paul F. *No Other Name? A Critical Survey of Christian Attitudes Toward the World Religions*. Maryknoll, NY: Orbis Books, 1985.

Koonz, Claudia. *Mothers in the Fatherland: Women, the Family and Nazi Politics*. London: Cape, 1987.

Küng, Hans. *Infallible? An Inquiry.* Translated by Edward Quinn. Garden City, NY: Doubleday, 1971.

————. *The Church — Maintained in Truth? A Theological Meditation.* Translated by E. Quinn. New York: Seabury Press, 1980.

————. *The Incarnation of God: An Introduction to Hegel's Theological Thought as Prolegomena to a Future Christology.* Translated by J. R. Stephenson. Edinburgh: T&T Clark, 1987.

Lambeth Commission on Communion. *The Windsor Report.* London: The Anglican Communion Office, 2004.

Lampe, Geoffrey. *God as Spirit.* London: SCM Press, 1977.

Lash, Nicholas. *Believing Three Ways in One God: A Reading of the Apostles' Creed.* Notre Dame, IN: University of Notre Dame Press, 1993.

Le Guillou, Marie-Joseph. "Church." In *Sacramentum Mundi,* vol. I, pp. 313-16. Edited by Karl Rahner et al. London: Burns & Oates; New York: Herder and Herder, 1968.

LeCler, Joseph. *Toleration and the Reformation.* 2 vols. Translated by T. L. Westow. New York: Association Press; London: Longmans, 1960.

Lee, Philip J. *Against the Protestant Gnostics.* Oxford and New York: Oxford University Press, 1987.

Leith, John H., ed. *Creeds of the Churches: A Reader in Christian Doctrine from the Bible to the Present.* Rev. ed. Richmond, VA: John Knox Press, 1973.

Lerner, Gerda. *The Creation of Patriarchy.* Oxford and New York: Oxford University Press, 1986.

Lewis, Alan E. *Between Cross and Resurrection: A Theology of Holy Saturday.* Grand Rapids: Eerdmans, 2001.

Limouris, Gennadios, ed. *Church, Kingdom, World: The Church as Mystery and Prophetic Sign.* Faith and Order Paper No. 130. Geneva: World Council of Churches, 1986.

Loades, Ann, ed. *Feminist Theology: A Reader.* Louisville: Westminster John Knox, 1990.

Lochman, Jan M. *The Faith We Confess: An Ecumenical Dogmatics.* Edinburgh: T&T Clark, 1985.

Loisy, Alfred. *The Gospel and the Church.* Translated by Newman Smyth. New York: Charles Scribner's Sons, 1912. Originally published as *l'Évangile et l'Église* (Paris: Picard, 1902).

Long, D. Stephen. "Radical orthodoxy." In *The Cambridge Companion to Postmodern Theology,* pp. 126-45. Edited by Kevin J. Vanhoozer. Cambridge, UK: Cambridge University Press, 2003.

Lord Herbert of Cherbury, Edward. *De Veritate.* Translated by Meyrick H. Carré. Bristol, UK: J. W. Arrowsmith, 1937.

Lossky, Vladimir. *The Mystical Theology of the Eastern Church.* Translated by members of the Fellowship of St. Alban and St. Sergius. Cambridge, UK: James Clarke & Co., 1957.

Luther, Martin. *Luther's Works*. Edited and translated by Jaroslav Pelikan, Helmut T. Lehmann, et al. 55 vols. Philadelphia: Fortress Press, 1959-1986.

MacGregor, Geddes. *Corpus Christi: The Nature of the Church According to the Reformed Tradition*. London: Macmillan, 1959.

MacIntyre, Alisdair. *After Virtue: A Study in Moral Theory*. Notre Dame, IN: University of Notre Dame Press, 1981.

MacKinnon, D. M. *The Church of God*. Westminster: Dacre Press, 1940.

Mackintosh, H. R. *The Doctrine of the Person of Jesus Christ*. 2nd ed. Edinburgh: T&T Clark, 1913.

Macmurray, John. *Persons in Relation: Being the Gifford Lectures Delivered in the University of Glasgow in 1954*. London: Faber & Faber, 1961.

———. *The Structure of Religious Experience*. London: Faber & Faber, 1936.

Macquarrie, John. *Jesus Christ in Modern Thought*. London: SCM Press; Philadelphia: Trinity Press International, 1990.

Maeder, Michael. *Church as People: A Study of Election*. Collegeville, MN: St. John's University Press, 1968.

Mangina, Joseph L. *Karl Barth: Theologian of Christian Witness*. Aldershot, UK: Ashgate, 2004.

Marshall, Bruce D. "Christ and the cultures: the Jewish people and Christian theology." In *The Cambridge Companion to Christian Doctrine*, pp. 81-100. Edited by Colin Gunton. Cambridge, UK: Cambridge University Press, 1997.

Martos, Joseph. *Doors to the Sacred: An Historical Introduction to Sacraments in the Catholic Church*. New York: Doubleday, 1981.

Marty, Martin E. *The Public Church: Mainline-Evangelical-Catholic*. New York: Crossroad, 1981.

Martyn, J. Louis. *Galatians: A New Translation with Introduction and Commentary*. New York: Doubleday, 1997.

Marx, Karl. *Critique of Hegel's 'Philosophy of Right'*. Translated by A. Jolin and J. O'Malley. Cambridge, UK: Cambridge University Press, 1970.

McCullough, W. S. *The History and Literature of the Palestinian Jews from Cyrus to Herod: 550 B.C. to 4 B.C.* Toronto: University of Toronto Press, 1975.

McDonnell, Kilian. *John Calvin, the Church, and the Eucharist*. Princeton, NJ: Princeton University Press, 1967.

McFague, Sallie. *Models of God: Theology for an Ecological, Nuclear Age*. Philadelphia: Fortress Press, 1987.

McGrath, Alister. *A Scientific Theology*. 3 vols. Edinburgh: T&T Clark; Grand Rapids: Eerdmans, 2001-2003.

McIntyre, John. *Theology After the Storm: Reflections on the Upheavals in Modern*

Theology and Culture. Edited by Gary D. Badcock. Grand Rapids: Eerdmans, 1997.

McKelway, Alexander J., and E. David Willis, eds. *The Context of Contemporary Theology: Essays in Honor of Paul Lehmann.* Atlanta: John Knox Press, 1974.

McLelland, Joseph C. *The Visible Words of God: An Exposition of the Sacramental Theology of Peter Martyr Vermigli, A.D. 1500-1562.* Edinburgh and London: Oliver and Boyd, 1957.

McManners, John, ed. *The Oxford Illustrated History of Christianity.* Oxford and New York: Oxford University Press, 1990.

McNeill, John T. *The History and Character of Calvinism.* New York: Oxford University Press, 1954.

McPartlan, Paul. *Sacrament of Salvation: An Introduction to Eucharistic Ecclesiology.* Edinburgh: T&T Clark, 1995.

————. *The Eucharist Makes the Church: Henri de Lubac and John Zizioulas in Dialogue.* Edinburgh: T&T Clark, 1993.

McWilliam, Joanne. "Pelagius, Pelagianism." In *Encyclopedia of Early Christianity,* vol. 2, pp. 887-90. Edited by Everett Fergusson. 2nd ed. New York and London: Garland Publishing, 1997.

Mersch, Emile. *The Theology of the Mystical Body.* Translated by Cyril Vollert. St. Louis and London: B. Herder Book Co., 1952.

————. *The Whole Christ: The Historical Development of the Doctrine of the Mystical Body in Scripture and Tradition.* Translated by John R. Kelly. London: Dennis Dobson, 1939.

Migne, J.-P. *Patrologia Cursus Completus: Series Latina.* 217 vols. Paris, 1878-1890.

Migne, J.-P. *Patrologia Latina: the full flat database.* 221 vols. Ann Arbor, Mich.: ProQuest Information and Learning Company, 1996.

Milbank, John. "The Gospel of Affinity." In *The Strange New World of the Gospel: Re-Evangelizing in the Postmodern World,* pp. 1-20. Edited by Carl E. Braaten and Robert W. Jenson. Grand Rapids: Eerdmans, 2002.

————. *The Word Made Strange: Theology, Language, Culture.* Oxford: Blackwell, 1997.

————. *Theology and Social Theory: Beyond Secular Reason.* 2nd ed. Oxford: Blackwell, 2005.

Milbank, John, and Catherine Pickstock. *Truth in Aquinas.* London and New York: Routledge, 2001.

Minear, Paul S. *Images of the Church in the New Testament.* Philadelphia: Westminster Press, 1960.

Moore, R. I. *The Origins of European Dissent.* New York: St. Martin's Press, 1977.

Mühlen, Heribert. *A Charismatic Theology: Initiation in the Spirit.* Translated by Edward Quinn and Thomas Linton. London: Burns & Oates; New York: Paulist Press, 1978.

————. *Der Heilige Geist als Person: In der Trinität, bei der Inkarnation und im Gnadenbund: Ich-Du-Wir.* Münster: Achendorff, 1966.

————. *L'Esprit dans L'Église.* Translated by A. Liefooghe, M. Massart, and R. Virrion. 2 vols. Paris: Les Éditions du Cerf, 1969.

————. *Morgen Wird Einheit Sein: Das kommende Konzil aller Christen: Zeil der getrennten Kirchen.* Paderborn: Ferdinand Schöningh, 1974.

————. *Una Mystica Persona: Die Kirche als das Mysterium der Identität des Heiligen Geistes in Christus und den Christen: Eine Person in Vielen Personen.* 2nd ed. Paderborn: Ferdinand Schöningh, 1967.

Neill, Stephen. *A History of Christian Missions.* 2nd ed. Revised by Owen Chadwick. London: Penguin Books, 1986.

Neuner, J., and J. Dupuis, eds. *The Christian Faith in the Doctrinal Documents of the Catholic Church.* Rev. ed. New York: Alba House, 1982.

Newbigen, Lesslie. *The Open Secret: Sketches for a Missionary Theology.* Grand Rapids: Eerdmans, 1978.

Newman, John Henry. *Conscience, Consensus, and the Development of Doctrine.* Edited by James Gaffney. New York: Doubleday, 1992.

Nicholas of Cusa. *Nicholas of Cusa on Learned Ignorance: A Translation of De Docta Ignorantia.* Edited and translated by Jasper Hopkins. Minneapolis: Banning, 1985.

Nichols, Aidan. *Holy Order: The Apostolic Ministry from the New Testament to the Second Vatican Council.* Dublin: Veritas, 1990.

————. *Theology in the Russian Diaspora: Church, Fathers, Eucharist in Nikolai Afanasev (1893-1966).* Cambridge, UK: Cambridge University Press, 1990.

Norman, Edward. *Christianity and the World Order.* Oxford: Oxford University Press, 1972.

Norris, R. A. *Manhood and Christ: A Study in the Christology of Theodore of Mopsuestia.* Oxford: Clarendon Press, 1963.

O'Donovan, Oliver. *The Desire of the Nations: Rediscovering the Roots of Political Theology.* Cambridge, UK: Cambridge University Press, 1996.

————. *The Ways of Judgment: The Bampton Lectures, 2003.* Grand Rapids and Cambridge: Eerdmans, 2005.

O'Donovan, Oliver, and Joan Lockwood O'Donovan. *Bonds of Imperfection: Christian Politics, Past and Present.* Grand Rapids and Cambridge: Eerdmans, 2004.

O'Meara, Thomas F. *Theology of Ministry.* New York: Paulist Press, 1999.

Origen. *Contra Celsum.* Translated by Henry Chadwick. Cambridge, UK: Cambridge University Press, 1953.

————. *On First Principles: Being Koetschau's Text of De Principiis.* Translated and edited by G. W. Butterworth. New York: Harper & Row, 1966.

————. *Traité des Principes.* Edited by Henri Crouzel and Manilo Simonetti. 5 vols. Paris: Cerf, 1978-1984.

Owen, John. *The Works of John Owen*. Edited by W. H. Goold. 16 vols. London: The Banner of Truth Trust, 1965.

Pannenberg, Wolfhart. *Systematic Theology*. 3 vols. Translated by Geoffrey W. Bromiley. Grand Rapids: Eerdmans; Edinburgh: T&T Clark, 1991-1998.

Parsons, Susan Frank. "Feminist theology as dogmatic theology." In *The Cambridge Companion to Feminist Theology*, pp. 114-34. Edited by Susan Frank Parsons. Cambridge, UK: Cambridge University Press, 2002.

Pelikan, Jaroslav. *The Christian Tradition*. 5 vols. Chicago and London: The University of Chicago Press, 1971-1989.

Peter Lombard. *Sententiae in IV Libris Distinctae*. 2 vols. Edited by Ignatius Brady. 3rd ed. Rome: Collegii S. Bonaventurae ad Claras Aquas, 1971-1981.

Phythian-Adams, W. J. *The People and the Presence*. London: Oxford University Press, 1942.

Preston, Geoffrey. *Faces of the Church: Meditations on a Mystery and Its Images*. Edinburgh: T&T Clark; Grand Rapids: Eerdmans, 1997.

Puttick, Helen. "Working Women Sick of Super Mothers." *The Glasgow Herald*, 13 June 2004.

Quick, Oliver. *The Christian Sacraments*. London: Nisbet, 1928.

Radner, Ephraim. *The End of the Church: A Pneumatology of Christian Division in the West*. Grand Rapids and Cambridge: Eerdmans, 1998.

Rahner, Karl. *Theological Investigations*. Translated by Cornelius Ernst et al. 20 vols. London: Darton, Longman & Todd, 1961-1984.

Rattenbury, J. E. *The Eucharistic Hymns of John and Charles Wesley*. London: Epworth Press, 1948.

Ratzinger, Joseph. *Das Neue Volk Gottes: Entwürfe zur Ekklesiologie*. Düsseldorf: Patmos, 1969.

—————. *Principles of Catholic Theology: Building Stones for a Fundamental Theology*. Translated by Mary F. McCarthy. San Francisco: Ignatius Press, 1987.

Reeves, Thomas C. *The Empty Church: The Suicide of Liberal Christianity*. New York: The Free Press, 1996.

Reynolds, Blair. *Towards a Process Pneumatology*. Selinsgrove, PA: Susquehanna University Press, and London and Toronto: Associated University Presses, 1990.

Reynolds, Noel B., and W. Cole Durham, Jr., eds. *Religious Liberty in Western Thought*. Atlanta: Scholars Press, 1996.

Ritmeyer, Leen. *The Quest: Revealing the Temple Mount in Jerusalem*. Jerusalem: Carta, 2006.

Robinson, John A. T. *Honest to God*. London: SCM Press, 1963.

—————. *The Body: A Study in Pauline Theology*. London: SCM Press, 1952.

—————. *The New Reformation?* London: SCM Press, 1965.

Rosato, Philip J. *The Spirit as Lord: The Pneumatology of Karl Barth*. Edinburgh: T&T Clark, 1981.

Ross, Andrew C. *A Vision Betrayed: The Jesuits in Japan and China, 1542-1742.* Edinburgh: Edinburgh University Press, 1994.

Rowley, H. H. *The Biblical Doctrine of Election.* London: Lutterworth Press, 1950.

Royo, Antonio, and Jordan Auymann. *The Theology of Christian Perfection.* Dubuque, IA: The Priory Press, 1962.

Russell, Letty M. *Church in the Round: Feminist Interpretation of the Church.* Louisville: Westminster John Knox, 1993.

Sacks, Jonathan. "Credo." *The Times,* 3 November 2001.

Saeed, Abdullah, and Hassan Saeed. *Freedom of Religion, Apostasy and Islam.* Aldershot, UK, and Burlington, VT: Ashgate, 2002.

Sanders, E. P. *Jesus and Judaism.* Philadelphia: Fortress Press, 1985.

———. *Judaism: Practice and Belief 63 BCE — 66 CE.* London: SCM Press; Philadelphia: Trinity Press International, 1992.

Sanneh, Lamin. "The horizontal and the vertical in mission: An African perspective." *International Bulletin of Missionary Research* 7 (1983): 165-71.

Schaff, Philip, ed. *The Creeds of the Evangelical Protestant Churches.* London: Hodder and Stoughton, 1877.

Scherer, James A. *Gospel, Church, and Kingdom: Comparative Studies in World Mission Theology.* Minneapolis: Augsburg Publishing House, 1987.

Schillebeeckx, Eduard. *The Church With a Human Face: A New and Expanded Theology of Ministry.* Translated by John Bowden. London: SCM Press, 1985.

———. *The Eucharist.* Translated by N. D. Smith. London: Sheed and Ward, 1968.

Schleiermacher, Friedrich. *On Religion: Speeches to Its Cultured Despisers.* Translated by Richard Crouter. Cambridge, UK: Cambridge University Press, 1988.

Schmemann, Alexander. *Church, World, Mission: Reflections on Orthodoxy in the West.* Crestwood, NY: St. Vladimir's Seminary Press, 1979.

Schweitzer, Albert. *The Mysticism of Paul the Apostle.* Translated by W. Montgomery. London: A. & C. Black, 1931.

Schweizer, Eduard. *Church Order in the New Testament.* London: SCM Press, 1961.

———. *The Church as the Body of Christ.* London: SPCK, 1965.

Sozomen's Ecclesiastical History. English translation. London: Samuel Bagster and Sons, 1846.

Spong, John Shelby. *Why Christianity Must Change or Die: A Bishop Speaks to Believers in Exile.* San Francisco: Harper, 1998.

Stevenson, J., and W. H. Frend, eds. *Creeds, Councils and Controversies: Documents Illustrating the History of the Church AD 337-461.* London: SPCK, 1989.

Stewart, Ray A. *Rabbinic Theology: An Introductory Study.* Edinburgh and London: Oliver and Boyd, 1961.

Stinespring, W. F. "Temple, Jerusalem." In *The Interpreter's Dictionary of the Bible,* vol. 4, pp. 534-60. Edited by G. A. Buttrick et al. New York and Nashville: Abingdon, 1962.

Sykes, Stephen. *The Identity of Christianity: Theologians and the Essence of Christianity from Schleiermacher to Barth.* Philadelphia: Fortress Press, 1984.

Tamburello, Dennis. *Union with Christ: John Calvin and the Mysticism of St. Bernard.* Louisville: Westminster John Knox, 1994.

Tanner, Norman P., ed. *Decrees of the Ecumenical Councils.* 2 vols. London: Sheed & Ward; Washington, DC: Georgetown University Press, 1990.

Taylor, John V. *A Matter of Life and Death.* London: SCM Press, 1986.

Temple, William. *Christ in His Church: A Charge Delivered by the Right Rev. William, Lord Bishop of Manchester, at His Primary Visitation, 1924.* London: Macmillan, 1925.

———. *Christianity and Social Order.* London: SCM Press, 1942.

Thiessen, Gerd, and Annette Merz. *The Historical Jesus: A Comprehensive Guide.* Translated by John Bowden. Minneapolis: Fortress Press, 1998.

Todorov, Tzvetan. *Mikhail Bakhtin: The Dialogical Imperative.* Translated by Wlad Godzich. Minneapolis: University of Minneapolis Press, 1984.

Toland, John. *Christianity Not Mysterious.* Edited by Philip McGuinness et al. Dublin: The Lilliput Press, 1997.

Torrance, T. F. *Royal Priesthood: A Theology of Ordained Ministry.* 2nd ed. Edinburgh: T&T Clark, 1993.

Van Den Eynde, D., and G. A. Zinn. "Hugh of St. Victor." In *New Catholic Encyclopedia,* vol. 7, pp. 156-59. Edited by Berard L. Marthaler et al. 2nd ed. San Francisco: McGraw-Hill, 1967-1996.

Vanhoozer, Kevin J. *The Drama of Doctrine: A Canonical-Linguistic Approach to Christian Theology.* Louisville: Westminster John Knox, 2005.

Verkuyl, Johannes. *Contemporary Missiology: An Introduction.* Edited and translated by Dale Cooper. Grand Rapids: Eerdmans, 1978.

Vicedom, Georg F. *The Mission of God: An Introduction to the Theology of Mission.* Translated by Gilbert A. Thiele and Dennis Hilgendorf. St. Louis: Concordia Publishing House, 1965.

Visser 'T Hooft, W. A. *The Renewal of the Church.* London: SCM Press, 1956.

Vogel, Heinrich. *Das Nicaenische Glaubens bekenntnis: Eine Doxologie.* Berlin and Stuttgart: Lettner, 1963.

Volf, Miroslav. *After Our Likeness: The Church as the Image of the Trinity.* Grand Rapids: Eerdmans, 1998.

Walls, Andrew F. *The Missionary Movement in Christian History: Studies in the Transmission of Faith.* Maryknoll, NY: Orbis Books; Edinburgh: T&T Clark, 1996.

Watt, W. Montgomery. "The Muslim Tradition in Today's World." In *Religion in Today's World,* pp. 230-49. Edited by Frank Whaling. Edinburgh: T&T Clark, 1987.

Wesley, John. *The Works of John Wesley.* Edited by Albert Outler et al. 24 vols. Nashville: Abingdon Press, 1984-2003.

West, Angela. *Deadly Innocence: Feminism and the Mythology of Sin.* London and New York: Cassell, 1995.

Westminster Assembly. *The Confession of Faith.* Edinburgh and London: William Blackwood & Sons, 1959.

Whaling, Frank, ed. *John and Charles Wesley.* New York: Paulist Press, 1981.

Whitehead, A. N. *Process and Reality: An Essay in Cosmology.* New York: The Humanities Press, 1929.

Williams, Colin W. *The Church.* London: Lutterworth Press, 1969.

Williams, Rowan, ed. *The Making of Orthodoxy: Essays in Honour of Henry Chadwick.* Cambridge, UK: Cambridge University Press, 1989.

Willis, G. G. *St. Augustine and the Donatist Controversy.* London: SPCK, 1952.

World Council of Churches. *Baptism, Eucharist and Ministry.* Geneva: World Council of Churches, 1982.

Wyschogrod, Michael. *The Body of Faith: Judaism as Corporeal Election.* New York: Seabury Press, 1983.

Yorke, G. *The Church as the Body of Christ in the Pauline Corpus: A Re-examination.* Lanham, MD: University Press of America, 1991.

Young, Frances. *Biblical Exegesis and the Formation of Christian Culture.* Cambridge, UK: Cambridge University Press, 1997.

———. *From Nicaea to Chalcedon: A Guide to the Literature and Its Background.* Philadelphia: Fortress Press, 1983.

Zizioulas, John. *Being as Communion: Studies in Personhood and the Church.* Crestwood, NY: St Vladimir's Seminary Press, 1993.

Index of Names and Subjects

Index of Scripture References